What the critics said about t
Alfred Glossbrenner's *Complete* ....
Computer Communications:

"For intelligence and thoroughness, no one else comes close."
—*The Whole Earth Software Review*

"The first truly complete book on 'connecting your computer to the word.'"
—*Esquire*

"Essential . . ."
—*Forbes*

"Still considered by many insiders to be the best.'
—U.P.I.

"Definitive . . . worth every cent."
—*John Dvorak, InfoWorld*

"One of the best and most complete sources of information. There have probably been more words written about this book than any other serious book in the personal computer field."
—*Personal Computing*

"If any book can be described as 'the bible' on telecomputing, this is it.'
—*Link-Up*

Praise for Alfred Glossbrenner's other books,
Alfred Glossbrenner's Master Guide to Free Software
for IBMs and Compatible Computers . . .

"Excellent . . ."

—U.P.I.

"An essential purchase . . ."

—*Booklist*

"One of the all-time best books . . ."

—Brit Hume in *The Washington Post*

"Glossbrenner is absolutely the best guide through this foreign territory . . . . He writes with authority, clarity, grace and wit."

—*Chicago Tribune*

"The *Master Guide*, like Mr. Glossbrenner's previous books . . . is an excellent reference for anyone with a PC and a modem. It is full of wise and thrifty advice for experienced as well as novice computer users."

—Peter H. Lewis in *The New York Times*

"It is hard to go wrong with the *Master Guide*. . . . The book is filled with valuable computer tips and information about how to get free software."

—*Seattle Daily Journal of Commerce*

THE
COMPLETE HANDBOOK
OF
PERSONAL COMPUTER
COMMUNICATIONS

THE
COMPLETE HANDBOOK
OF
PERSONAL COMPUTER
COMMUNICATIONS

— All-New Third Edition —

Alfred
Glossbrenner

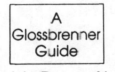

A
Glossbrenner
Guide

St. Martin's Press   New York

The author has made every effort to check information such as shipping charges, addresses, telephone numbers, and availability of updated products, but cautions the reader that these are subject to change. Readers should verify costs and product descriptions with sources before ordering.

THE COMPLETE HANDBOOK OF PERSONAL COMPUTER COMMUNICATIONS THIRD EDITION. Copyright © 1990 by Alfred Glossbrenner. All rights reserved. Printed in the United States of America. No part of this book may be used or reproduced in any manner whatsoever without written permission except in the case of brief quotations embodied in critical articles or reviews. For information, address St. Martin's Press, 175 Fifth Avenue, New York, N.Y. 10010.

Editor: Jared Kieling

Library of Congress Cataloging-in-Publication Data

Glossbrenner, Alfred.
    The complete handbook of personal computer communications / Alfred Glossbrenner—All new, 3rd ed.
        p.   cm.
    Rev. ed. of: Going online. c1984.
    Includes index.
    ISBN 0-312-03311-7 (hbk)   ISBN 0-312-03312-5 (pbk)
    1. On-line data processing. 2. Computer networks.
I. Glossbrenner, Alfred. Going online. II. Title.
QA76.55.G56 1989
004.6'16—dc20   89-34838
                                                                                  CIP

Books are available in quantity for promotional or premium use. Write to Director of Special Sales, St. Martin's Press, 175 Fifth Avenue, New York, NY 10010, for information on discounts and terms, or call toll-free (800) 221-7945. In New York, call (212) 674-5151.

First Edition

10 9 8 7 6 5 4 3 2 1

Contents

PART II • Online Utilities

PART III · Information Services

PART IV • Communication

PART V · Applications

xii . . . *Contents*

Foreword

The French have a saying: "The more things change, the more they stay the same." It's as true of personal computer communications as it is of anything else. Readers of previous editions of this book will find many familiar names within these pages, but they will find that the services they represent have changed and grown. In some cases, the growth has been spectacular. In others, it has been steady and measured, as winning features are expanded and refined, while unpopular ones are allowed to pass from the scene. In every case, however, you will find more activity, more excitement, and more possibilities than ever before.

If you're new to the online world, we can only say one thing: You have an incredible treat in store. By the time you finish this book you will be able to sit at your computer and:

- Communicate with anyone—day or night—regardless of where they are in the world.

- Find any fact on any subject you can imagine—and many subjects that may never have occurred to you.

- Locate an expert in any field and contact him or her electronically to seek advice, help, or merely to say hello.

- Send and receive messages to and from any telex, TWX, or fax machine on the planet.

- Buy and sell stocks, bonds, and other securities—get an instant fix on the current value of your portfolio—and pay all of your bills. About the only thing you can't do from your keyboard is get a cash advance.

• Earn a college degree—or earn your regular paycheck—without ever leaving home.

• Instantly scan listings and descriptions of over a quarter of a million products for the one model at the one price that meets your needs.

• Save hundreds—even thousands—of dollars on software by tapping vast online treasure houses of commercial quality public-domain and shareware programs, all of it ready for instant delivery to your machine day or night.

And this barely scratches the surface of what you can do—once you hook your computer to the phone lines and go online with the world. We haven't mentioned the people you'll meet, each with a different interest and unique personality, or the globe-girdling networks of people who can help you solve any computer problem or answer any question you may have about your machine. We haven't talked about computer-mediated conferencing or real-time CB-like chat with people all over the continent. Or online photo exchanges or community-based services that offer everything from museum and movie schedules to real-estate listings and access to the county registry of deeds. Nor have we said anything about the thousands of free, publicly available bulletin board systems and their unique contributions.

If you're one of the tens of millions of people who own a personal computer—or one of the tens of millions more who are thinking of buying one—this book could change your life. We'll give you everything you need to get off to a great start. But equally important, we'll give you the tools you need to achieve your personal online goals.

In 1982 we christened this area of personal computing "the electronic universe." And like our own physical universe, it is constantly spinning, changing, and expanding. No single book can encompass it all, and no printed product of any kind can ever be absolutely up to date.

We have dealt with the first problem by producing two companion volumes. *How to Look It Up Online* (St. Martin's Press, New York) explores in detail the industrial-strength databases and information resources now available to everyone and how to tap them most effectively. The second book, *Alfred Glossbrenner's Master Guide to FREE Software for IBMs and Compatible Computers* (St. Martin's Press, New York) devotes hundreds of pages to the various online sources of public-domain and shareware software and the techniques for winkling out of them just the program you need. Though it is IBM-specific, and we would not recommend buying it if you don't own a compatible machine, the information it contains about online software libraries applies to every computer user. You may thus want to see if your local library has a copy for you to borrow.

The book you're holding, however, is designed to provide the big picture. The survey course. The whole enchilada. As for keeping it up to date, the only practical solution is to rewrite it every couple of years or so. Publishing schedules won't admit greater frequency. If there is sufficient interest, a newsletter—either online or in print—is a possibility. The author would welcome comments and suggestions (see the back of the book for contact information). In the meantime, we can only urge you to use the resources and access points we have provided.

For example, though no longer free, the telephone company's directory assistance service will give you the current phone number should you find that any of those listed here have changed. And since they're making you pay for it, have no compunction about asking for the mailing address as well. Many people don't know it, but there is a directory assistance service for toll-free numbers as well. Simply dial 1 (800) 555–1212.

Finally, it is the goal of this book to make it possible for you to tap into the power and possibilities of the electronic universe as easily and inexpensively as possible. We have tried to emphasize money-saving tricks and tips throughout. We have also arranged a variety of special deals and discounts. These are presented at the very back of the book as a series of special offers that can save you literally hundreds of dollars on subscription fees and connect-time costs. You probably won't want to use them all—only an online addict or equally crazy computer author would subscribe to every system—but they can certainly ease your transition into this exciting new world.

Now, with the preliminaries out of the way, let the adventure begin.

—Alfred Glossbrenner
"Kabeyun"
Yardley, Pennsylvania

Part I

—GOING ONLINE
WITH THE WORLD—

...1...

The Electronic Universe:
Introduction and Overview

Virtually every personal computer available today has the ability to take its owner online. You need only add a plug-in circuit board, a cable, a device called a "modem," and some software. Later on we'll tell you how to buy these components and explain how to get the software for free. But in many cases you may not need any additional equipment at all, since a growing number of computer manufacturers have begun to build communications circuitry and even modems into their machines.

Nor do you need to know anything about programming. You can forget about BASIC and all the other computer languages. Some institutions should be sued for educational malpractice because they foist the idea on the American public that computer literacy equals computer programming. In point of fact, all you really need to know is how to turn your computer on and get it to load a program.

Points to Remember

This chapter presents an overview of the book's various sections and explains what you can expect to find in each. But before we get started, there are a few preliminary points you should be aware of regarding the assumptions we have made, the conventions that have been followed, and other somewhat dull but essential information.

• The book assumes that you are familiar with your own equipment. It probably goes without saying, but different computers accomplish the same things in different ways. Fortunately, telecommunications is a reasonably standardized area, and all communicating computers can generate the same basic signals. But the actual keystrokes required by each machine may differ. Since it would be impossible to note all the variations, you may have to consult your manuals to find out how your particular system and software do things.

• At various times, we will mention printers in the text. But you should know that while they are very convenient, printers have nothing to do with going online.

• The term "carriage return" refers to the action caused by hitting your <Enter> key, and is often abbreviated as CR in the communcations industry. This is a holdover from the days when the "carriage" was the mechanism that held the printing element on a typewriter-like communications device. The carriage return key caused the mechanism to return to its original position at the far left margin.

• The term "Control-C" means hold down the key marked <Ctrl> and hit <C> or <c>. All other control characters are generated the same way.

• Whether you are entering a control character or a command to an online system, it usually doesn't matter whether you use upper or lower case. To make commands stand out, we have used capital letters in this book, but you don't have to. It goes without saying that if a command sequence comes at the end of a sentence ending with a period, don't enter the period when you use the command. Don't enter quotation marks unless specifically told to do so. And by all means remember that most systems will not act on a command until you hit <Enter>.

• When we say "key in" we mean "type the command or instruction as shown and hit your <Enter> key."

• Finally, throughout the text, you'll find numerous "Online Tips" set off in boxes. These contain suggestions, ideas, and other information that is relevant, but not necessarily vital, to the issue at hand. Some are also addressed to the more experienced user and thus make no attempt to explain everything in detail. If you are new to this field, some of this information may not make much sense the first time you read it. Don't let that slow you down. Whenever you find an "Online Tip" that you don't understand, simply skip it and go back later after you've had a little more experience.

Essence and the Beginning

The electronic universe exists because all computers can talk to each other. The size, cost, and power of the machines involved are irrelevant in this context. Communicating computers no larger than this book can be used to control minicomputers the size of an executive's desk or multimillion-dollar mainframes that occupy entire rooms. And they can do it from any distance using ordinary telephone lines.

That is the essence of the electronic universe. But it is the endless variations on this theme that make things so interesting. During 1981 and 1982, when the first edition of this book was being written, there were 600 databases offered by 93 online services, according to the authoritative Cuadra/Elsevier *Directory of Online Databases*. At this writing, some eight years later, there are 4024 databases offered by 586 online systems.

In addition, there are today more than 14,000 free computer bulletin board systems (BBS), each of which is a mini-online service consisting of someone's personal computer using special software and hardware that lets it automatically answer the phone. There are information/communication utility services; computerized conferencing systems; electronic mail, telex, TWX, and fax systems; online shopping services; community information systems; telephone company "gateway" services; systems run by gigantic companies and systems offered by entrepreneurs; and much more besides. Clearly, the field is alive with activity.

Which may be good for its general health and well-being, but not so good for a new user trying to get a handle on it all. So let's first make clear exactly what we're dealing with. Today's online information industry evolved from the "remote data processing" (RDP) services that began in the 1960s as a low-cost alternative to buying or leasing a mainframe computer. In those pre-microchip years, few businesses could afford to have their own on-site mainframe. Yet they needed the power such machines could provide. RDP provided the answer. New companies sprang up with the sole purpose of acquiring and maintaining one or more large computers—and selling computer time to firms unable to afford machines of their own. This is called "time-sharing," and it has nothing to do with Colorado ski lodges or Las Vegas condominiums.

The point is that for a mainframe in Columbus to service a customer in Cleveland, some form of electronic communication had to take place. Using a relatively inexpensive terminal—basically just a keyboard and a screen—the customer had to be able to send payroll, billing, accounts payable, and other information to the mainframe for processing, and there had to be a way to get the computer's output back.

This certainly wasn't the start of computer communications. But there can be no doubt that the needs of the RDP firms and their customers stimulated enormous growth and refinement in the techniques and technology of the field.

The result was a *delivery mechanism*—a well-developed system of computers, specialized software, standards and protocols, electronic packet-switching networks, and other components capable of reliably transmitting information from one computer to another.

Once the delivery mechanism was in place, it was only a matter of time before individuals and companies began to find ways to use it for something other than the transmission of the day's banking transactions to a remote mainframe computer. The only obstacle to further expansion was the cost of the equipment needed to use the delivery mechanism. The price simply prohibited widespread usage.

The development of affordable microcomputers changed everything. The electronic information industry took off, and it has been tooling along adding features, systems, and services ever since.

A Handle on the Universe

The best way to get a handle on all of the various options at your disposal is to realize that everything in the online world falls into one of four categories: information, communication, services, and special-interest groups or clubs. Of these, information and communication are the two major categories. Services and special-interest groups are really just combinations of the other two, as we'll see later. For now, however, if you keep this four-part matrix in mind you'll have a much easier time figuring out where everything fits.

This book is laid out along similar lines. The chapters in Part I are designed to map the territory and get you suited up with everything you'll need to join the expedition. Chapter 3, Getting Technical, explains such arcane subjects as error checking file-transfer protocols, crossover cables, RS-232 pinouts, and the like. You will probably want to refer to it more than once, but if you're a new user, give it a miss the first time through.

Part II begins with a description of the "essential online utility," the one type of service virtually everyone will want to subscribe to. Online utilities offer a blend of information, communication, services, and special-interest group features. As you can see from the book's table of contents, there are seven leading systems to consider. The chapters in Part II will give you a feeling for each of them, and hopefully help you find the utility or utilities that are right for you.

The last chapter in Part II considers the ferment in the firmament caused by the North American invasion of the French Minitel system, the advent of the IBM/Sears Prodigy system, the gateway services being tested by the Regional Bell Operating Companies (RBOCs; pronounced "are-box"), Canadian Bell's new Alex system, and other developments sure to affect all online communicators in the future.

In Part III, the focus shifts to pure commercial-grade information. The online services profiled here, starting with Knight-Ridder's DIALOG and ending with Mead Data Central's Lexis/Nexis system, are the ones used by researchers, librarians, and other information professionals. These industrial-strength systems are among the best in the world. Though most are not priced for casual use, they are open to everyone, and they can pay big dividends to those who know how to use them. With these systems, even the tiniest company can achieve a nearly equal footing with a Fortune-100 behemoth, and a college student can knock a professor's socks or stockings off. The section begins with an introductory chapter designed to quickly bring you up to speed in this field.

The many communications options open to you are discussed in Part IV. Here we'll look at facilities for sending and receiving electronic mail, computerized conferencing, arranging for hand-delivered hard copy of your electronic messages to those lacking a computer, and how to send and receive messages from the more than 1.8 million telex and TWX machines around the world. We will also look at computer-to-facsimile machine options, fax boards, and the option of receiving fax messages on your computer as well as sending them.

The chapters in Part V discuss the many exciting ways you can apply personal computer communications to your daily work and personal life. The first chapters look at that staff of modern life—money. We'll show you how you can pay all of your bills—even the local paperboy—with electronic banking. Then we'll look at how you can (hopefully) make your money grow through online stock trading. For a PC user, brokerage firms never close. You can enter buy and sell orders round the clock, every day of the week. Next we'll show you how to spend money—wisely—through online shopping. Among other things, we'll look at a service that lets you electronically search a database of over 250,000 products for the item with the exact features you want. The service also guarantees you the lowest available price on every item, should you wish to key in your order.

The next chapter in Part V looks at the growing phenomenon of telecommuting—going online to go to work. According to some authorities, millions of people already work at home one or more days a week, communicating with their offices via modem and personal computer. And speaking of work, anyone interested in improving his or her prospects for a better job will want to look into online education. In Chapter 28, we'll show you how to do everything from taking a single course to earning a bachelor's, masters, or doctoral degree from fully accredited colleges through your computer.

Next, we'll look at free computer bulletin board systems and show you how to plug into this fascinating world. Then we'll look at "the international connection" and tell you what to do to access U.S.-based systems from abroad. With a portable computer and a telephone, you need never be out of touch, regardless of where you are on the globe. Part V concludes with a discussion of how to go online from literally anywhere using packet radio and cellular telephones. And the book concludes with appendices containing access points and contacts for additional information, an ASCII table for your convenience, and a clutch of special discounts that can make it easier than ever to get started online.

It may be that you'll want to read straight through the book. On the other hand, you may find it more useful to read just those sections that interest you at a particular time, skipping around among the chapters as your interests dictate. If you're a brand-new user, however, we do have some specific suggestions.

Start with Chapter 2 to make sure you're familiar with the fundamentals of the field. Save Chapter 3 for later, unless you're inately curious about the technical side of things, and make Chapter 4 your next stop. Chapter 4 describes the concept of an online utility and tells you what you can expect from these unique services. As mentioned earlier, nearly everyone—doctor, dentist, lawyer, or candlestick maker—will want to subscribe to at least one online utility service. Next, browse through the other chapters in Part II to see if there is a particular system that is likely to fill your needs.

After that, you're on your own, though you will probably want to read the overview chapters at the beginning of Parts III and IV before reading the chapters that follow them. Now, following a brief interlude for those who are already equipped to go online, it's on to a look at the fundamentals.

––––––––––––––––––––––––– **Special Section** –––––––––––––––––––––––––

Online in an Instant—for FREE!

If your personal computer is already equipped for communications, and you have a modem and the proper software, you don't have to wait to go online. As long as you have a general idea of how to operate your equipment, you can do it right now for free. As explained elsewhere in this book, in most cases you will be able to dial a local phone number to connect with the various online systems in the electronic universe. The local number is part of a network that uses a technique called "packet switching" to route your call to its destination.

Virtually all commercial systems are accessible via one or more packet-switching networks. The two leaders in the field are U.S. Sprint's (GTE and Sprint) Telenet and McDonnell Douglas Tymnet. Many Canadian users first connect with Datapac, which then gates them through to one of these two American-based systems. Most people don't know it, but these networks will provide you with free online information—if you know what commands to enter. Both can be used to search for the network phone numbers operating in a particular area. Similar information is available on Canadian cities via Datapac.

This service can be especially valuable if you plan to be taking a computer with you on a trip. But it can also save you money. Many commercial systems offer a similar feature that provides the identical information. The difference is that on a commercial system you must pay for it.

Though the specific commands you must enter are different for each network, the steps you should follow are essentially the same. First, call the toll-free customer service number we've provided and ask for the network number nearest your location. Since some network numbers can handle only certain speeds, tell the customer service representative whether you will be communicating at 300, 1200, or 2400 bits per second or "baud." Then dial the phone and follow the steps outlined below. If you have any problems using these free information services, contact customer service for the latest instructions.

Telenet

Telenet
U.S. Sprint, Inc.
12490 Sunrise Valley Drive
Reston, VA 22096

Free data line: (800) 424–9494
Customer service: (800) 336–0437
In Virginia: (800) 572–0408

Note that you can call the free data line shown above from anywhere in the continental United States. Set your system to seven data bits, even parity, and one stop bit, and hit three carriage returns once you are connected. Then follow the instructions given below. Alternatively,

Going Online with the World

you can phone customer service and request the number of your local Telenet node.

When you dial Telenet, and see that your modem has locked onto the tone the node sends, hit your <Enter> key twice to let Telenet sense and match itself to your communications settings. The network herald announcing that you are using Telenet will then appear. Key in D1 when prompted for your terminal identifier. (This is the identifier that applies to virtually every personal computer.) When the "at" sign (@) appears, key in MAIL. Then type PHONES when prompted for a user name and PHONES *again* for your password. (The password PHONES will not show on your screen.)

The term "TCO" mentioned in the listings you will then see stands for "Telenet Central Office." As with a phone company's central office (those windowless block houses you see in some parts of the country), this is a switching station and network node. Just think of it as your local Telenet phone number. Telenet also provides service in over 50 countries. For information on accessing this part of its service, key in INTL/ASSOCIATES at the "User Name?" prompt. Then enter INTL at the "Password?" prompt.

Online Tip: If you live outside the United States, follow the local access procedures established by your PTT to connect to 311020200141 (Telenet's address). This will generate the @ prompt and you can then proceed as described above to obtain international information.

Datapac via Telenet

Call your local PTT authority for your local node number.
For a booklet called the "Datapac Directory," contact:

> Datapac Support Centre
> Telecom Canada
> Room 1890, 160 Elgin Street
> Ottawa, Ontario K1G 3J4
> (613) 567–8374

There is also plenty of information available on the Canadian Datapac network. For information (in English) about Datapac public dial-up telephone numbers and locations, enter the following network address at the Datapac prompt sign: C 03020 92100086. This number works from the United States as well, so you may want to give it a try when using Telenet. Here's part of what you can expect to see if you dial Telenet and enter the above number at the @ prompt.

```
@C 03020 92100086
3020 92100086 CONNECTED

WELCOME to the Datapac Information System.

EFFECTIVE FEBRUARY 7 1989 THE FOLLOWING CITIES OFFER AUTO 0-1200 SPEED
PUBLIC DIAL PORTS FOR OUR DATAPAC 3101 SERVICE
ONTARIO
                    COLLINGWOOD    PEMBROKE
                    RENFREW        SIMCOE
                    BOLTON         FORT ERIE
                    HUNTSVILLE     MARKHAM
                    NEWMARKET      ST-THOMAS
QUEBEC
        ALMA        CHATEAUGUAY    RIVIERE DU LOUP
        STE-AGATHE  ST-BRUNO       ST-EUSTACHE
Page 1 of 1
    1   DESCRIPTION.OF.DATAPAC.FAMILY.OF.SERVICES/LAST UP: 89-02-23
    2   DATAPAC.RATES/LAST UPDATED: 89 01 10
    3   DATAPAC.3101.PUBLIC.DIAL.PORTS.ALL.SPEEDS/LAST UP: 89 02 17
    4   DATAPAC.3305.PUBLIC.DIAL.PORTS/LAST UPDATED: 89 02 10
    5   DATAPAC.DOCUMENTATION/LAST UPDATED: 88-03-15
                            (etc.)

Help —brief command list    BYE —logoff Datapac Directory
DIS:
```

Tymnet

Tymnet, Inc.
2710 Orchard Parkway
San Jose, CA 95134
(408) 942–5254
Worldwide customer service: (800) 336–0149

If you sign on to Tymnet at 1200 bps, you will get a line of garbage characters like this x||x|x on your screen. Hit your <A> key at any time. But do not hit <Enter>. Tymnet will sense your communications settings from that, and you will see the network's "please log in:" prompt. At this point, key in INFORMATION and hit <Enter>. You will then be welcomed to Tymnet's Information Service and be presented with a menu of choices.

Online Tip: On July 31, 1989, McDonnell Douglas Corporation announced that it had "reached a preliminary agreement to sell its Network Systems Business which includes the Tymnet public data network, to British Telecom for $355 million." At this writing the acquisition is conditional, pending regulatory clearances.

More than likely the sale will have no affect on online communicators. However, it may be that some of the addresses and customer service numbers given here will change.

...2...

Fundamentals: Everything You Need to Go Online with the World

Going online these days is much easier than in years past. Though there have been some improvements, the technology hasn't really changed all that much since the mid-1970s. But people are much more familiar with the hardware and the basic concept. *The New York Times*, for example, no longer bothers to define the word "modem" when it appears in a general interest story. And articles about personal computer communications have begun to appear frequently in noncomputer magazines.

In addition, prices have dropped tremendously while availability has risen. One can now buy modems, cables, and software almost anywhere—and save literally hundreds of dollars over the prices of only a few years ago.

As a result, the equipment you need to go online can be summed up in just a few words. We will do just that in a moment in the form of a quick-start guide later in this chapter. Then, for those who need more information, we will discuss those components in more detail. Those who want to get started right away can leave after the quick-start guide. But everyone needs the overview of the online process that follows.

An Overview of the Process

Regardless of what you plan to do once you get there, and regardless of the kind of system you plan to call, the fundamental goal of going online is always the same: You want to establish a connection that will transport the characters and commands you type at your keyboard to a distant computer—and transport that computer's responses back to your screen. A variety of systems and components are needed to achieve this goal.

The process can best be explained by following a bit of electronic information as it travels from your keyboard into your system, and out into the telephone stream. The various components of a personal computer—the keyboard, disk drives, printer, memory, video hardware, and so on—communicate with each other by transmitting electronic impulses that for the purposes of this discussion we can think of as jelly beans. When you press your <R> key, for example, your keyboard sends a hail of colored jelly beans hurtling into the system to tell it that you want it to display the letter R on the screen. Your system responds correctly because it recognizes the particular pattern of colored beans the keyboard has selected as representing the letter R.

The jelly beans, of course, are "bits" (*binary* di*gits*) of computer information. And there are only two colors, red and blue. There are no pinks, powder blues, purples, or other shades. There is red and blue and only red and blue. For convenience, programmers and other binary bean counters symbolize these two colors on paper as 1s and 0s. They could just as easily use exclamation points and dollar signs or some other pair of symbols. As long as each symbol is unique and as long as there are two and only two of them, the actual symbols used do not matter.

As surprising as it may seem, the simple concept of two symbols is at the very core of personal and every other kind of computing, and we will be encountering it again and again in computer communications. For example, in reality, the bits on a floppy disk are symbolized by areas of the disk track that are either magnetized or not magnetized. The disk drive heads see these areas as a pattern that they use to generate a matching series of electronic pulses that flow into the computer. The drive heads, in other words, make a copy of the pattern on the disk by translating its elements into voltage pulses. The pulses are of either a "high" voltage ("on") or a "low" voltage ("off"), with nothing in between.

The UART and the Modem: Necessary Conversions

The disk drive batches these pulses together into units of eight bits each. And when the keyboard communicates with the system unit, *it* sends eight bits as well for each key. For its part, whether it is talking to the printer or the video display, the system sends eight bits for each character as well.

As you may know, each of these eight-bit units is called a "byte" (pronounced "bite"). And when they flow into and out of a computer, they travel along eight wires in a parallel formation. If you like, you can think of them as combinations of eight red and blue jelly beans rolling down eight parallel chutes, or down eight parallel wires in a ribbon cable, should you happen to see such a cable coming out of your computer.

As long as the jelly bean bits stay within the confines of the computer system, everything is fine. Where you begin to run into difficulties is when you want to make the bits flow *outside* of the system—and into the telephone network.

In the first place, everything inside the computer is set up for the bits to roll along in parallel formation. That takes eight wires at least. But most phone hookups have only two wires, and even special leased lines have only four. In the second place, things are pretty quiet inside the computer, electrically speaking. So each bit can be the electrical equivalent of a whisper and still be heard. In the big wide world of telecommunications, however, there is a lot of electronic noise and electrical resistance that would make your average computer bit inaudible.

The solution is to perform a conversion. Two conversions, in fact. First, the natural parallel paths of computer bits must be changed from eight-all-at-once to one-at-a-time. This is called a conversion from parallel to "serial" data communications. Second, each bit has got to be changed into a more rugged form suitable for telephone transmission. Since phone systems were designed to handle sound, that's what the bits must be changed into.

There is a piece of equipment to handle each conversion. The first conversion is done by a microchip called a UART (pronounced "you-art"). This stands for universal asynchronous receiver-transmitter. UARTs are the central element of components that are variously called "comm," "asynch" (pronounced "a-sink") or "serial" cards, "RS-232 interfaces," or "communications ports." These chips are responsible for getting each eight-bit unit lined up, adding two bits of what for now we can think of as packing material, and sending the entire ten-bit package out the door.

Fortunately, you rarely need to worry about UARTs or even be aware that they are there. What you *do* need with most PCs is a plug-in circuit board that includes "communications" as one of its features. Either that, or you need a computer with a built-in serial interface. One way or another, the UART will be in there someplace.

The second conversion, the one from electrical signals into sound, is performed by a modem. This term is a compression of the words *mod*ulator/*dem*odulator, and it refers to the device that changes outgoing computer signals into sound and incoming sound into computer signals. As noted, phone lines are designed for sound, not computer voltage levels. So the red or blue jelly bean bits must be transformed into two and only two different sounds.

You can think of them as a high-pitched tone and a low-pitched tone, if you like. Though of course in reality things are more complex. You don't need to know about all that, but it is helpful to know that modems deal in two sets of paired tones of frequencies. One pair of tones is for outgoing and one pair is for incoming information. These two sets are referred to as the modem's "originate" and "answer" modes. For communications to take place one modem must be set to originate and the other must be set to answer. Thus, regardless of who calls whom, if you want to establish a connection with a friend or colleague, one of you will have to be set to "answer," and the other to "originate."

By convention, the system you call is referred to as the "host system" regardless of its size or function. It could actually be a computer identical to your own. In almost every case, if you are calling a remote host, your modem should be set to "originate." Again by convention, the modems attached to any system designed to receive incoming calls will be set to "answer." As we'll see in a moment, modems can also operate at different speeds, commonly called "baud rates." And these, too, must match for communications to take place.

Cables and Plugs

Modems are usually connected to the computer by a cable that is plugged into the "RS-232 interface" on the card containing the UART. This is pronounced "R-S-two-thirty-two," and it stands for recommended standard number 232. Its official name is RS-232, revision C, a designation you will find on some communications products as RS-232-C. The standard was developed by the Electronic Industries Association (EIA), the Bell System, and the computer and modem industries, and it is nearly universally endorsed. It specifies that an RS-232 interface consists of 25 pins or sockets, and it describes how each pin should be wired, what signals it will carry, and so forth.

The actual hardware is called a DB-25 connector (the plug looks like an elongated D), but you can think of it as your computer's back door, for it is through this portal that your system's bits come and go. A second cable leads from the modem to the telephone jack. Thus, the modem stands between the computer and the telephone system, modulating and demodulating sound and computer signals.

Online Tip: The computer industry has a long tradition of doing things for its own convenience and leaving consumers to fend for themselves. Thus, to celebrate the 25th anniversary of its creation of the RS-232 standard, the Electronics Industries Association in 1987 upgraded it to revision D and changed its name. The official name is now EIA-232D. The change was made to satisfy another organization, the American National Standards Institute (ANSI), which requires that the initials of a standard's creator be part of its approved name. With three vowels in a row, "eee-eye-a two-thirty-two dee" does not exactly roll trippingly off the tongue, and it does tend to put one in mind of a farmer named MacDonald. But neither organization allowed this fact or any potential for con-sumer confusion to stand in its way. Traditions must be upheld, after all.

Public Data Networks and Packet Switching

All of this sounds great, doesn't it? Imagine being able to call any communicating computer anywhere in the world and use it as if you were sitting at its very own keyboard. Imagine the size of your phone bill when all of these long distance charges are added up each month— calls to California, calls to Washington, D.C., calls to Great Britain or France. Obviously, if one had to pay regular long-distance rates for per-sonal computer communications, the only systems most of us would call would be the bulletin board systems in our own neighborhoods.

Fortunately, although most systems can be reached by direct dial, there's usually no need to make your connection that way, thanks to the public data networks (PDNs). The PDNs use a technology called "packet switching" that is specifically designed to allow one computer to talk to another and to do so inexpensively. As long as both locations are within the continental United States, for example, the cost of using a PDN has historically been as low as $2 an hour (a little over three cents a minute) during nonbusiness, evening hours.

The two leading public data networks in the United States are Tele-net, owned by U.S. Sprint Communications Corporation, which in turn is owned by GTE and United Telecommunications; and Tymnet, owned by the McDonnell Douglas Corporation. In Canada, the leading network is Datapac, owned and operated by Telecom Canada. Other companies, like CompuServe and General Electric, operate networks as well, but all work in essentially the same way.

You don't need to know a great deal about the PDNs, but it's important to have a broad familiarity with them. (For information on some of their "secret" commands, see Chapter 3.) You will be using a PDN virtually every time you connect with a major commercial system—and you may be able to use one for BBSs in selected cities as well. And you will almost certainly be using them for international calls.

Data Packets and the Virtual Circuit

A packet-switching network consists of hundreds of computers and thousands of modems. The computers and modems are scattered all over the country and connected to each other by high-speed (up to 56,000 bits per second, or 56 Kbps) data lines. Each location on the network is called a "node," and if you live near a medium to large city, the chances are there is at least one node within your local calling area.

When you and your computer dial one of these local nodes, one of the modems at that location will answer the phone and you will immediately hear a high-pitched tone, often followed by a gravelly noise, through your modem's speaker. Your modem will sense these sounds and establish a connection with the node modem at your chosen speed. As soon as that has happened, the noise will stop. Next, you will probably see the word CONNECT on your screen. This comes from the modem to tell you that everything is ready for you to begin your session.

At this point you and your computer will be in direct contact with the node computer, and after keying in some preliminary information, you will be free to tell the network node which commercial system you wish to talk to. The node computer will then patch you through to your target system using the most efficient network route available at the time. In the target system's computer room—let's say it's Palo Alto, California, where DIALOG's massive array of computers are located—the phone will ring and one of DIALOG's modems will answer to complete the connection.

The word "efficient" is the key here, since the efficiencies made possible by packet-switching technology are one of the main reasons using a PDN is cheaper than placing a conventional long-distance call. When you make a voice call, an actual physical circuit must be established between your phone and the person you are calling. This requires lots of switches and a lot of wires leading to a lot of different places. But the result is a circuit that's as real and complete as any you ever assembled in seventh-grade science class. And of course the circuit must remain in existence for the duration of your call, tying up all of the physical resources involved in making the connection.

Computer-to-computer calls are different. Because they communicate digitally—using the 1s and 0s or "jelly beans" we've spoken of before—their transmissions can easily be chopped up into discrete units or packets. Like the counterman at a hardware store pulling lengths of rope off a spool and cutting them to a uniform size, the node computer cuts your computer's data stream into uniformly sized packets of bits. It then stamps them with the address of your target system and a packet sequence number, and sends them on their way.

PDN follow an international recommended standard called X.25 (pronounced "X dot twenty-five"). The standard specifies, for example, that a PDN packet always contain 128 bits. Padding characters are used to round out the packet when necessary to bring it up to that level. When a packet comes into the node computer from a remote system, the computer strips off any irrelevant bits, checks the packet's address, and channels it to the correct caller. This is why a network node computer is often referred to as a "packet assembler/disassembler" or PAD.

A single PAD may have many incoming lines but only two or three high-speed lines connecting it to the network. However, since each packet is unique, the packets from several callers can be interleaved. What's more, they can be shot out into the network in different directions as the PAD strives for maximum efficiency in the face of ever-changing network load conditions and traffic patterns. Other node computers at various locations in the network receive the packets, check their address, and relay them to another node or to the host system itself. Thanks to the address and sequence number, however, the packets are received by the correct host in the correct order, regardless of the route each packet took to reach its destination.

The result is what's called a "virtual circuit." In most cases, when you use a packet-switching network, the connection between you and a host system appears to be identical to the connection that would exist were you to dial the remote system directly, even though an unbroken, continuous physical connection between you never actually exists.

The Impact of the PDNs

So what effect does this have on you? The first and most important effect is that a PDN's ability to interleave packets from several callers on the same line, and its ability to constantly reconfigure connections in response to varying load factors, makes for very efficient use of the equipment. Greater efficiency means lower costs which mean lower prices.

Second, it helps explain at least some of the delays that can occur on a PDN during peak times of the day. It explains other points as well. Sometimes, for example, you may call your local node and the local node computer will tell you that no outgoing lines are available. You may also find that occasionally all incoming lines are in use, resulting in a conventional busy signal when you call. The solutions are the same in both cases: Keep trying, wait a while and try again, or simply call a different node. There is also the potential effect of a PDN when you are transferring files using an error-checking protocol like XMODEM, but we'll consider that in the next chapter.

ASCII Text and Machine Language

Now that you've got the entire online connection in mind and can see the data bits traveling from your machine to your modem to the telephone system and eventually to a host computer, it's time for the tough questions. To wit, how is it that Macintoshes, Apples, IBMs, Amigas, Commodore 64s and 128s, and every other personal computer, can talk to each other? They can't run each other's programs or even read each other's disks.

The answer is the American Standard Code for Information Interchange or ASCII (pronounced "as-key"). The idea underlying this code is simplicity itself. Computers communicate in numbers, so if you want machines of all makes and models to be able to exchange information, you just assign a number to each letter of the alphabet and make sure that all manufacturers agree on those assignments. As it happens, the ASCII code set is the creation of the American National Standards Institute (ANSI; pronounced "an-see"), a nonprofit organization made up of representatives from nearly all corners of the computer world. Its main role is to create and maintain a wide range of voluntary standards.

There is an ASCII code for each lowercase letter of the alphabet, each uppercase letter, the numbers from 0 through 9, and most standard punctuation marks. There is also a code for a blank space, one for a carriage return, and one to cause the paper in a printer or the text on your screen to move up one line (line feed). There are several other codes as well that need not concern us here.

We said before that computers communicate in eight-bit units called "bytes." Without getting into the binary numbering system at this point, take it on faith that it is possible to represent any decimal number from 0 through 255 using different eight-bean combinations of red and blue jelly beans. Each byte, then, is a number. And since we know that each number represents a character in the ASCII code set, one byte equals one character.

Because the ASCII code is used to represent text, the term ASCII has become synonomous with "text." An ASCII file, in other words, is a text file and contains nothing that cannot be displayed on the screen. ASCII files can be exchanged and viewed at will among all brands of computers.

Binary or Machine-Language Files

Not so with "machine-language" files. Machine language is also made up of eight-bit bytes, but any correspondence between those bytes and readable characters is purely coincidental. Machine language is the language of the microprocessor chip that sits at the heart of each computer. The chip can't deal with anything else, so before it can do anything at all, everything that goes into it must be converted into the only language it can understand.

That means that before the chip can run a program, the program must be machine-language form. But since most people don't write or program in machine language, human-readable information must be converted. This is typically done in one of two ways. It is either done each and every time a program is run, as with interpreted BASIC programs. This is why you must first load the BASIC interpreter before you can run a BASIC (".BAS") program. Or the conversion is performed once and the translation is recorded on disk as a machine-language file.

Compiler and assembler programs are responsible for performing this one-time conversion. They produce program files that can be loaded and run as is. In the IBM world, for example, such files end with either .COM or .EXE, and to run them you need only key in the filename to the left of the period. Machine language files can be transmitted from one machine to another using one of the error-checking protocols discussed in the next chapter. But you can't run an IBM program on a Mac or a Mac program on a Commodore.

Spreadsheet, Word Processing, and Other Files

There is one final point to make on this subject. We've spoken of ASCII text files and we've spoken of machine-language program files. A third type of file is one that mixes the two. A Lotus or Excel spreadsheet file, for example, contains all of the text you keyed in when you created it. But it also contains machine-language characters that cannot be displayed on the screen. These machine-language codes are put into the file by the program that created it for its own use. Files of this sort must be treated as if they were program files.

Similarly, many word-processing programs insert machine codes into a file to symbolize things like a soft hyphen. Soft hyphens come and go as text is adjusted to fit between the margins. A hard hyphen, in contrast, is one you enter yourself, and the program will not remove it. Both look the same on the screen, so how can the program tell the difference? By tagging the soft hyphen with an invisible machine code. You don't see these codes and may not until this moment have realized that they're there. But they are in the file, and if you transmit that file to someone else, it may come out looking like a pig's breakfast on his or her screen.

Online Tip: Not all word-processing programs insert machine codes in their files. If you're an IBM user, you can find out by getting to the DOS prompt and keying in TYPE filename.ext, where filename.ext is the name of a file created by your word-processing program. If no funny looking characters appear, then the file is clean.

These days, programs that do insert machine codes usually give you an option to remove them from a file before communicating it. There are also various free utility programs, available from user groups and other sources, for combing out machine-language characters. Check your word-processing-program manual first, then consult with your favorite computer guru for suggestions and advice.

Signing On to a System

As you would expect, all commercial systems require you to open an account before they will grant you access. Usually you need only contact the company that runs the host system and request a subscription form, though some systems also sell starter kits through computer stores and other outlets. Some systems, notably those specializing in information, operate by direct billing. But in most cases you will be asked for a credit card number and your mailing address. You will then be given an account number or ID and a password. Both will be necessary to sign on.

Once you sign on and are into the system, you will probably see a welcoming message, a series of short announcements, and either a greeting or "top" menu or a naked command prompt. There is no standardization in this area, though in most cases these days there will be some kind of menu. From the top menu you will be able to wend your way through subsidiary menus until you reach the feature you want. In many cases, there will be a way to turn off the menus and operate solely by commands after you have gained some experience.

There is no standardization in the way commercial systems charge you, either. Generally, there will be a basic connect-time charge, billed to the nearest minute or fraction of a second. This may or may not include "communications charges" to cover your use of Telenet or Tymnet. On some systems you will find that certain features carry connect-time surcharges over and above the basic rate. On others, especially information systems, every database has a different price.

Some systems, like Quantum Link and Prodigy, charge a flat monthly rate for unlimited basic service, though some of their most interesting features carry surcharges that bring the costs up to about where they would be on most other systems. Prodigy and Quantum Link, incidently, are "videotex" (no final *t*) systems. That means they put a heavy emphasis on graphics. An airline schedule might appear with the image of a plane on the screen, or stock quotes might appear next to images of corporate logos. In contrast to traditional ASCII-based systems, you need special software to use a real videotex system. We say "real videotex" because while Prodigy and Quantum fit the traditional definition, some people have begun to apply the term to all online systems.

Quick-Start Guide to Going Online

How to Choose a Modem

Years ago it was necessary to purchase either a separate communications "adaptor" card for a computer or a combination card offering additional memory, a clock/calender, and other features in addition to a communications RS-232 port. That's still the case today with an Apple-II-compatible computer, where the "comm card" of choice is the Super Serial Card, or with most IBM/XT and IBM/AT style machines. But increasingly, manufacturers are including communications ports as standard equipment.

Modems are a different story. Laptops and portable machines may include built-in modems, but in most other cases the choice will be up to you. Which is just as well, because there are lots of models, features, and capabilities to choose from. On the other hand, over-choice can make things very complicated for a new user.

Accordingly, if you will accept our advice, here is what most new online communicators should get: A Hayes-compatible, external (that is, a separate, free-standing box) 2400 bit-per-second modem. At this writing, units meeting those criteria are available for as little as $119. Units operating at 1200 bps sell for about $50 less. But in our opinion, the higher speed is worth the extra cost. Since not every online system currently offers a 2400 bps option, you won't be able to use this speed all the time. (All 2400 bps units can operate at 300 and 1200 as well.) But it can be awfully nice to have, particularly if you plan to download software, graphic image files, and other large files from systems like GEnie and CompuServe or from bulletin boards.

You will certainly want to shop around for the best prices, and if you have special needs, examine the various features of competing units carefully. However, from long personal experience we can recommend both a specific manufacturer and supplier. The manufacturer is Elec & Eltek (USA) Corporation's E + E Data Comm unit, makers of the Avatex line of modems.

We have absolutely no connection with this company or with Megatronics, the leading supplier of Avatex modems. We have simply found both to offer superb value and performance over the years. But you don't have to take our word for it. See the winter 1987–1988 edition of *MacGuide Magazine* (page 157A) for a review that earned a MacGuide rating of 95 out of 100. Or look at the December "best buys" issues of *Computer Shopper* for the past several years, where Avatex and Megatronics have consistently been voted number one by the magazine's readers. Your best bet is to send for the information and then make up your own mind. Contact E + E Data Comm for product information and Megatronics for current prices:

E + E Data Comm   Megatronics, Inc.
1230 Oakmead Parkway, Suite 310   P.O. Box 3660
Sunnyvale, CA 94086   Logan, UT 84321
(408) 732–1181   (800) 232–6342
Telex: 887740 (HKECCSNTA)   (800) 752–2642, in Utah

How to Choose a Communications Program

An external modem can be used with any brand of personal computer. But communications software is machine-specific. With so many machines and so many top-quality "comm programs" out there it is simply impossible to recommend specific commercial packages. Unless you have some special need, these days it is hard to go too far wrong whichever program you buy.

We will discuss major comm program features and what they will mean to you later. What we'd like to do here is to suggest that you may not have to *buy* a comm program at all. Or at least, you may not have to pay commercial prices for commercial quality communications software. In most cases, you can get everything you want—and much more besides—in a public domain or "shareware" package.

Space constraints prohibit a full discussion, but the quick explanation is this. Creating a top-quality computer program requires only two things—a computer and a talented programmer. You don't need a plant, a factory, or capital equipment. Advertising and marketing such a program is another matter. Following the conventional route requires a lot of money. But thanks to computer bulletin boards, online utility systems, mail-order houses, and most important of all, computer user groups, a programmer can eliminate those expenses as well.

The key is shareware—or software on the honor system. Shareware programs are available free of charge to all who want them. At most, you'll have to pay a few dollars to cover the cost of the disk and postage and handling, but not a penny for the software itself. If you like and use the program, you are asked to register it by sending the programmer a small fee (usually $25 to $50). In return, you usually receive a bound and printed manual to accompany the manual included on the disk, free telephone support, and notification of improvements and updates. Some programmers don't even ask for a registration fee. They either place their work in the public domain or permit all who want to to use it free of charge.

Not all public domain (PD) and shareware software is of commercial quality, of course. With literally tens of thousands of programs available for every brand of machine, how could it be otherwise? But there are a number of outstanding examples that can go toe-to-toe with the best commercial products. Comm programs like Red Ryder for the Macintosh or ProComm for IBMs and compatibles are often reviewed with commercial products in computer magazines and consistently earn high ratings.

How to Get Free Software

To take full advantage of shareware you need to know two things: which specific program to get and where to get it. Your first step should be to ask your computer-using friends for their suggestions. If you know someone who is a real computer enthusiast, the chances are he or she belongs to one or more computer user groups (clubs) in your area. You might also contact nearby computer stores and ask them if they can give you the name of someone to contact about user groups for your machine. Since computer stores are in the business of selling software, you might want to simply say that you have heard user groups can be an invaluable resource to any computer owner (which they are) and would like to get in touch with one in your city.

When you make contact with a user group, ask to speak with the software librarian. This person is in the best position to both guide your choices and supply you with the software. In some cases, you may be able to simply bring a blank disk to a user group meeting and make your copy right there. Or you may be able to buy the disk for a few dollars.

Mail-order sources also make this software available for a small fee. And, once you have a comm program, you will also be able to download software from online sources, either for free from a local BBS or for a few cents or dollars in connect time on a commercial system. (It all depends on how big the program is and how long it takes to transmit.)

ProComm for IBMs and Compatibles

If you have an IBM or compatible computer, you will fall in love with ProComm 2.4.3, the shareware communications program from Datastorm Technologies. Used by many Fortune-500 companies, thanks to Datastorm's vigorous site-licensing activities, it is, in our opinion, even better than ProComm PLUS, the company's latest offering. The program is widely available from the various sources cited above, but if you like, we will be happy to send you a copy from our Glossbrenner's Choice collection. Please see the back of this book for ordering details.

Red Ryder for the Macintosh

Written by Scott Watson and published by his organization, the Free-Soft Company, Red Ryder is the shareware program of choice in the Macintosh world. Copies are available from many sources, but one mail-order house we can recommend is Educomp Computer Services. The cost is $6.99, plus $4 per order for shipping and handling. To order or request a free catalog, contact:

> Educomp Computer Services
> 531 Stevens Avenue, Suite B
> Solana Beach, CA 92075
> (619) 259-0255

Apple II Models, Apple CP/M, and Compatibles

Although the PD and shareware libraries for most computers contain dozens of communications programs, for some reason this is not the case in the Apple II world. A full-featured program called T.I.C. ("Talk Is Cheap") used to be available as shareware. But since its author decided to go commercial, it is impossible to find a PD Apple program that will work with something other than the Hayes Micromodem (a popular card-mounted modem) at a speed of 300 bits per second. One of the best of these Micromodem programs, however, is the Hayes Terminal Program disk, from the Washington Apple Pi (WAP) users group in Washington, D.C. The cost is $5 for members, $8 for nonmembers, plus $1 for postage in both cases.

"The Pi," as it is often called, publishes a monthly magazine that normally runs about 76 Macintosh desktop-published, typeset pages, and it is truly impressive. Membership is $32 for the first year and $25 a year thereafter. You will also find ProDOS programs and Apple CP/M programs in the WAP library. If you're interested in one of these 300-bps comm programs, or if you simply need more information on WAP, write to this address:

DISKATERIA
Washington Apple Pi, Ltd.
7910 Woodmont Avenue, Suite 910
Bethesda, MD 20814
(301) 654–8060

Commodore and Amiga

The place to contact if you are a Commodore user (64, 128, Amiga, and so on) is the Toronto PET Users Group (TPUG). This is the largest Commodore group in the world, and it has huge public domain libraries for all Commodore machines. Prices vary with the disk format, but you can usually expect to pay about $10 apiece, postage included. The group publishes *TPUG* magazine ten times a year, and it's an excellent source of Commodore information. Membership fees vary with your location. If you don't live in the Toronto area, the cost is $25 for U.S. and Canadian members. If you live overseas, the cost is $35 (surface mail) or $45 (airmail). For more information contact:

TPUG, Inc.
5334 Young Street
P.O. Box 116
Don Mills, ON
Canada M2N GN2
(416) 733–2933

Modems and Comm Programs: In More Detail

If you are a new user, here is what we suggest you do at this point. First, turn to the chapters in Part II, beginning with CompuServe and running through Quantum Link, and contact the various online systems to request free information. Second, pursue getting your modem and communications software. Once you have these things started, come back here and read about modem and (especially) comm program features and what they will mean to you. This way, when your modem, program, and literature arrive, you'll already be up to speed and prepared to go online.

As noted at the beginning of this chapter, none of the material that follows is required reading. But you will find it helpful, even if you're a novice user.

The Importance of Hayes Compatibility

All of us owe a debt of gratitude to Hayes Microcomputer Products of Norcross, Georgia. Because of the quality and popularity of its products, Hayes has become the IBM of modem manufacturers. The Hayes Smartmodem has set the de facto standard that of necessity nearly everyone obeys.

Hayes was among the first manufacturers to produce an "intelligent" modem. The company did it by including a Z-8 microprocessor (a relative of the Z-80 chip of CP/M fame) on the modem's circuit board. This microprocessor is really a small computer and like the rest of the breed, it can be programmed to perform useful work, like automatically dialing the telephone for you or answering it when it rings.

The programming language Hayes developed to make this possible has become known as the "Hayes AT command set." The AT is short for "ATTENTION, modem, prepare to meet your next command." Thus when you are connected to a Hayes-compatible modem and you enter ATDT 1–800–555–1212 at your keyboard, the modem knows that you want to dial the phone (D) using Touch-Tone (T), and it knows to dial the digits you have included. As soon as you hit your <Enter> key, the command will be sent to the modem and dialing will commence.

There are many other commands as well, though you'll probably never use most of them. The key thing is to get a modem that responds to the Hayes command set, for it makes life so much simpler. For example, most communications programs let you prepare and record a menu/list of frequently called numbers. Once this has been created, dialing a number is as simple as choosing a menu item. Most communications programs are set by default to send the corresponding phone numbers to the modem using the Hayes command set. Though you can change things around to match any modem, if you have a Hayes-compatible modem, this will be one less thing you'll have to worry about.

As for buying an external, stand-alone modem, we have never found the arguments made by promoters of the internal, board-mounted units to be convincing. Chief among these is the notion that putting a modem inside a computer frees up space on your desktop. Since it is a simple matter to place a telephone set on top of an external modem box— indeed, many were designed with this in mind—it is difficult to see how the net available space on a desktop is affected either way. In addition, an external modem does not take up a slot inside your computer, does not add heat to your system, and can be used with any brand or model of computer. An internal modem has no front panel lights to let you know at a glance whether it's working properly or not. There is also the fact that most internal modem boards do not give you an RS-232 interface, which means you will not be able to cable your laptop and desktop machines together to dump files from one to the other. (See Chapter 3 for more information on this technique.)

Baud Rates, Bits per Second, and Speed Considerations

Next, there's the matter of speed. Traditionally, data communications speed have been measured in units called "bauds," named after J.M.E. Baudot, the inventor of the Baudot telegraph code. This is why you will read of 300-baud, 1200-baud, and 2400-baud modems.

Technology has outstripped terminology, however. For in reality, only 300 baud is an accurate term. A "1200-baud" modem actually communicates at 600 baud. Things get more complex from there. The misuse of the term was understandable and natural back when 300 baud was the standard speed and modems capable of four times that speed (1200 "baud") were being introduced. But with the advent of 2400 and even 9600-"baud" units, the inaccuracy is no longer acceptable.

The proper term is "bits per second" or bps, and that is what we will use from now on. As long as two systems are in agreement, computer communications can take place at virtually any speed. But the most widely agreed upon levels in the personal computer world are 110, 300, 1200, 2400, 4800, 9600, and 19,200 bits per second, with most activity centering around 300, 1200, and 2400 bps.

Modem technology has advanced steadily over the years. When we began communicating, the only way to make a connection was with an acoustic coupler. This device mated a microphone to the earpiece and a small speaker to the mouthpiece of a telephone handset and operated at 300 baud. (You can still purchase 300/1200-bps acoustic couplers from stores like Radio Shack for about $60, and they may still be useful when communicating from a pay phone.) Direct-connect modems were next, followed by intelligent modems like the Hayes 300-baud Smartmodem. The price on 1200-bps units then began to fall, tracing the path now being followed by 2400-bps units.

What's next—4800 bps units selling for $125? Probably not. The industry appears to have leaped past that speed in favor of 9600 bits per second. Such units sell for around $1500 each—and you need two of them, one for each end of the connection. At this writing there is no widely agreed upon standard for 9600-bps communications. Each manufacturer does it differently, which is why you need two identical units.

The key point through all this is that the phone system has not changed. Certainly fiber-optic cables and other improvements have been added, but copper wires are still in the loop for almost every connection, and they represent a major roadblock to ever-increasing data speeds.

Think of it this way. At 2400 bits per second, you are transmitting twice as many bits in each second as you are at 1200, and eight times as many as at 300. If twice as many bits are going to fit into the same second of time, then each bit must be "smaller." Which is to say, each bit must occupy a smaller fraction of a second. The faster you go, the finer the bits. And from this perspective copper wire represents a coarse and rocky road.

Unless you have a truly awful phone connection, you should have few problems at 1200 bps. But at 2400 bps, a blast of static or electrical noise can cause major problems. After all, the same duration of static at 2400 bps wipes out twice as many bits as at 1200. At 2400 bits per second, in other words, we are apparently pushing the limit of what the public switched telephone network (PSTN) can handle. (Several protocols have been developed to cope with this problem, including MNP,X.PC, and V.42. Please see Chapter 3 for details.)

Then again, new techniques keep coming along that make formerly unthinkable data rates a reality. One of the ways 9600-bps units get around PSTN limitations, for example, is to operate in half-duplex mode, like a CB radio. This allows each unit to use the entire available bandwidth when sending, instead of sharing it with its partner as full-duplex modems do.

Online Tip: At a transmission rate of 300 bps, the voltage associated with a single bit exists for 3.33 milliseconds. Thus, if the receiving system notices that the 0 bit voltage has been coming through for 6.66 milliseconds, it knows that it has received not one, but two 0 bits. The same principle applies, of course, to the voltage (or sound or other analogous signal) associated with a 1 bit. If you want to send information at a rate of 1200 bps, the information is going out four times faster, so each bit time must be much shorter. And it is. At 1200 bps, the voltage associated with a single bit exists only one fourth as long as at 300 bps. The actual figure is 3.33 milliseconds divided by four, or 833 *micro*seconds.

Here are the bit times for the most common bps rates used by personal computers:

Bit Times

1200 bps	833	microseconds
600 bps	1667	microseconds
300 bps	3.33	milliseconds
150 bps	6.67	milliseconds
110 bps	9.09	milliseconds

There are other points to consider as well. You can't read text at 2400 bps. It simply scrolls by too fast. At this writing, not every online system and not even every PDN node supports 2400 bps. (You may have to call a special number.) Some online systems charge more for a 2400-bps connection, reasoning that the higher your speed, the more information you're going to "take" from them, and therefore the more you should pay. Finally, a great deal of online activity involves reading, writing, and capturing short pieces of text from the host system. A 2400-bps connection probably won't be of much use to you there.

On the other hand, if you will be downloading large text files, programs, or other material into your system, or exchanging large quantities of data with an associate or branch office, then a good phone connection and a 2400-bps modem can be a real boon. For example, here is a comparison of the time required to transmit one page of single-spaced text. That's 55 lines of 65 characters each, or approximately 3600 characters. For technical reasons, one character requires 10 bits to transmit.

Rate (bps)	Transmission time (1 page)
300	2 minutes
1200	30 seconds
2400	7.5 seconds

If prices were still at the $400 to $700 level, as they were until a short time ago, we would have no hesitation about recommending against buying a 2400-bps unit in most cases. But at $120 or less, it's pretty hard to pass up. And from our perspective, it does look as though 2400 bps will replace 1200 as speed of choice, just as 1200 replaced 300 some years ago.

Online Tip: One of the advantages of a monopoly is its power to set standards almost by fiat. AT&T did that in the modem field with the Bell 103 standard for 300-baud communications, and 212A for full-duplex 1200-bps modems. But divestiture occurred just as 2400-bps technology momentum was building, so although there was a Bell standard, the company no longer had the clout to impose it.

Instead American modem manufacturers adopted the V.22 *bis* standard recommended by the International Telephone and Telegraph Consultative Committee. This organization is part of the International Telecommunications Union, which in turn is part of the United Nations. It is normally referred to as CCITT, the abbreviation of its French name.

The European standard for 1200-bps communications is V.22. The French word *bis* can be translated as "again" or as "the same

Online Tip (cont.)

but slightly different." All U.S.-made modems follow the V.22 bis standard for their 2400-bps communications. But some can also handle the CCITT V.22 standard as well as Bell 212A for 1200-bps communications. Most do not include circuitry for V.21, the CCITT 300-baud standard.

When operating in auto answer mode, most American modems will try for a connection using V.22 bis, and then fall back to 212A if the connection cannot be established. If you want them to fall back to V.22 instead, you may have to issue a special setup command.

Online Tip: As a matter of interest, the CCITT maintains a number of study groups charged with the responsibility of developing recommendations. Study Group XVII works on standards for sending data over regular telephone lines and publishes recommendations that begin with a V. Study Group VII works on standards for public data networks and packet switchers and publishes recommendations beginning with an X. For example, X.25 ("X-dot-twenty-five") defines the standards and protocols used by Telenet, Tymnet, and other packet switchers.

CCITT recommendations are published in books denoted by color (*The Green Book, The Orange Book*, and so on). For more information, you might contact the United Nations bookstore:

> UN Bookstore
> United Nations Assembly Building
> New York, NY 10017
> (212) 754-7680
> (212) 754-1234

You can also contact the ITU, the organization of which the CCITT is a part:

> International Telecommunications Union
> General Secretariat—Sales Section
> Place des Nations
> CH-1211 Geneva 20
> Switzerland
> Phone: (022) 99 51 11
> Telex: 421 000

Additional Modem Features

There's an acronym in the communications business: POTS. It stands for "Plain Old Telephone Service." Nothing fancy. No state-of-the-art technology and features. Just a reassuring, dependable dial tone when you pick up the phone. In considering the lists of features available from the latest modems, one wishes for an equivalent acronym—POM or "Plain Old Modem"—since in point of fact, that's all most people need. If you're an MIS or DP manager, obviously you have special requirements and will find all the extra features meaningful. But if you're a new online communicator, you'll merely find them confusing.

Most modems today have "feature-itis." In fact, with their microprocessor CPUs, nonvolatile random access memory, dynamic RAM, and elaborate built-in programs, modems have become significant small computers in their own right. As a consequence, they now have the ability to take over functions normally performed by communications software progams. Some modems, for example, can store pages of telephone numbers. Others can be controlled and customized down to the last millisecond. And all of them can be programmed with a special set of commands.

This is perfectly fine. But if you've got a good, full-featured communications program that you like and know how to use, why would you want to also learn how to program your modem to do many of the same things? It doesn't make sense, particularly since virtually all communications programs are both good and feature-filled today. In fact, as we'll see, many of them have feature-itis as well.

In our opinion, as long as you get a Hayes-compatible modem, you can forget about everything else. Take it from an old hand, you're never going to need to know how to initiate the digital loop-back test your modem offers. Something goes wrong, you call customer service and ask them what to do. Life is too short and there are too many other things to do online to spend a lot of time getting there.

For the record, there are a number of features about which a word of explanation would not come amiss. If you need an exhaustive roundup, see *PC Magazine* or *InfoWorld*, both of which run at least one such feature piece each year. Now, here are the points and terms you might want to know about.

- *Full-duplex/half-duplex.* These terms refer to sending and receiving information at the same time (full-duplex) or sending and switching over to receive and back again (half-duplex). The best way to think of half-duplex is to think of CB or other radio transmissions where one party says "over" when he or she is finished speaking and takes the thumb off the "send" button.

- *Auto-dial.* All Hayes-compatible modems can automatically dial the telephone. And you can tell them to use either tones (ATDT) or rotary pulse (ATDP) when doing so.

- *Manual dial.* When you want to communicate with a friend, you'll probably dial the phone manually and have a brief chat before you begin communicating. One of you must then issue a command to set the modem to answer (ATA), while the other sets the modem to originate (ATO). The two modems will then lock onto each other and you will be able to continue your conversation by typing at the keyboard or initiate a file transfer. Some modems have an answer/originate front panel switch as well.

- *Adaptive dialing or "DTMF" (dual tone multiple frequency).* This refers to a modem's ability to automatically change from tone to pulse-dialing or vice versa, depending on the system it happens to be talking to at the time. This is likely to be especially useful to PBX users whose business phones are connected to a phone company central office that has yet to implement Touch-Tone. Your modem might tone-dial 9 for an outside line, then pulse-dial your local MCI access number, then switch back to tone-dialing to dial your target number via the MCI system—automatically. Modems with this feature typically try tone-dialing first and, if there is no response, repeat the number using rotary pulse.

- *Dial-tone sensitivity.* Another feature likely to be of interest to PBX-using businesspeople. No need to worry about building pauses into your dialing command string. The modem can dial 9 to get out and then wait until it "hears" the dial tone of an outside line before starting to dial the next number.

- *Built-in speaker.* Important for monitoring the progress of a call. You can actually hear the call being dialed and the answering modem tone. After the connection has been made, the speaker cuts out and you hear nothing. Most modems let you adjust the volume of the speaker, either with a dial or with a command.

- *LED status-indicator lights.* Found on most external modems. Tell you what's going on when you are online (or trying to get there), and help you identify the probable cause of communications problems. You can actually see data going out, for example, by the blinking of the SD (send data) light. If that light does not blink when you hit a key, then you know that there is a problem somewhere between your system and the modem (probably a loose connection).

- *"Busy" tone detect.* Some modems can sense whether the number you are calling is busy or not and issue some kind of response—such as an on-screen message—if it is. This makes it possible for your software to respond by trying the next entry in a list of phone numbers. Modems without this feature simply remain in their "dialing" state until you switch them off or tell them to do something else.

- *Auto-answer.* Enables the unit to answer the phone and issue a modem tone just like a packet-switching node. Found in all Hayes-compatible modems. Useful if you want to access your desktop system while on the road or set up your own BBS. You'll need the proper software in either case.

- *Password security.* Some modems when in auto-answer mode can be set to demand a password from a caller before giving him or her access to your computer system. Crucial question: How many different passwords can the modem store? This function can also be performed by your host software.

- *Answerback strings.* Another security feature. The unit can be programmed to automatically send out a WRU ("who are you?") query to the caller. The caller responds with an answerback string. The modem matches the string against its stored list of authorized callers and grants or denies access to your system. In originate mode, the modem can be programmed to issue an answerback in response to a WRU.

- *Call-back protection.* The modem stores a list of passwords and phone numbers associated with each. You call the modem and enter your password. It then hangs up and calls you back using the phone number in its memory. For top security, the host modem should use one line for receiving calls and a second line for callbacks.

- *Built-in error correction.* A very new feature that may or may not become standard in 2400-bps units. Most activity centers around the MNP (Microcom Networking Protocol) built into modems sold by Microcom Company and its licensees. Both sender and receiver must use such a modem for the protocol to take effect. (See Chapter 3 for more details.)

Get a Phone and Power Surge Protector

We cannot leave the subject of communications hardware without saying that every online communicator ought to have a surge protector to insulate a computer—not only the power line but the phone line as well. The wizard speaks from experience here—the experience of having a distant lightening bolt burn out a board because the killer surge got into the machine through the phone line when both computer and modem were turned off.

Most of the so-called surge-protection devices on the market are junk. The three crucial specifications to look for are:

1. A "first stage peak clamping voltage" of 200 volts, plus or minus five percent. This is the voltage at which the unit responds. The lower the figure, the better.
2. A response time of five picoseconds. A picosecond is a *trillionth* of a second, or 1000 times faster than a nanosecond or billionth of a second. The faster the response, the better.
3. Identical protection for both the electrical *and* the phone line.

Hard disk users who live in an area prone to frequent electrical brownouts, should also consider a unit offering "voltage dropout" protection. Such units should automatically shut everything off if the power falls to 80 volts, plus or minus five percent. The read/write head of a hard disk floats on a cushion of air created by the spinning hard disk platter. If the voltage drops and the disk spins more slowly, that cushion can disappear. The head can then plow into the platter, causing a great deal of heartache for all concerned.

Two of the leading manufacturers of really good surge suppressors are Dynatech and Panamax. Both offer a variety of power and phone protection units that meet the above specifications. Models and prices differ with the number of electrical receptacles. We've quoted list prices here, but most units are routinely discounted.

Dynatech's DSLP model has a single power receptacle and lists for $75, while the firm's DS4LP has four receptacles and lists for $110. At this writing, neither unit includes brownout protection, though that feature is being considered. For brownout protection, but no phone line, the firm offers its four-outlet Surge Sentry DSD at $120. You could thus get the DSD for your computer and peripherals and the DSLP for your phone line and modem. All Dynatech units come with a ten-year warranty, and a one-year damaged equipment replacement plan. The company will replace any electrical equipment damaged due to the failure of the power line surge protection circuitry in its units up to a maximum of $5000.

Panamax offers a similar line. The company's TeleMAX 1 has a single power receptacle and lists for $89. The TeleMAX 4 has four outlets and lists for $129. The SuperMAX has four outlets and includes brownout protection. It lists for $149. Like the Dynatech units above, each plugs into the wall with a six-foot cord. Panamax products carry a five-year warranty.

Here is where to send for more information and the names of the dealers in your area carrying Dynatech or Panamax products:

Dynatech Computer Power, Inc.
5800 Butler Lane
Scotts Valley, CA 95066
(800) 638–9098
(408) 438–5760

Panamax
150 Mitchell Blvd.
San Rafael, CA 94903
(800) 472–5555
(800) 472–6262, in California
(800) 443–2391, from Canada
(415) 499–3900

Communications Software: An Explanation

As we said earlier, you can't go far wrong with most communications programs today. If you have special needs—like the need to emulate a rare type of terminal or use some file-transfer protocol that is not widely supported—then you will have to exercise extra care in picking a program. But most people will find that today's communications programs give them everything they need—plus a great deal that they don't need and will never use. In fact, communications programs accumulate features the way a snowball picks up sticks, twigs, and bits of gravel as it rolls down a hill. We can offer no statistical support for the notion, but byte for byte, comm programs probably offer more features than any other type of software.

This may be because at its base, the communications function is about the simplest of all computer activities. After all, what's really involved? You've got to initialize a communications port and tell the system to send keystrokes out the door while displaying incoming characters on the screen. That's it. IBM users can do roughly the same thing with two DOS commands (MODE and CTTY). Thus it may be that software houses feel compelled to pile on features to increase the perceived value of their products.

But don't let that confuse you. There are really only a few essential comm program features. The rest, while they may be nice to have, are mainly smoke and glitter. It is the essential features that will occupy us here. We'll tell you what they are, what they do, and what they can mean to you when you go online. This will not only make you more comfortable when you take the plunge—because you'll understand what's happening—it will also help you make short work of your comm program manual. We'll track the features with the communications process presented at the beginning of this chapter.

Online Tip: If you will be talking to a corporate mainframe, you may need to emulate one of its native terminals. All PC-to-mainframe communcation is based on the concept of fooling the mainframe into thinking it is talking to one of its own dumb terminals (A dumb terminal is nothing more than a display and a keyboard.) But PCs have the ability to extend the illusion even further. Many programs include an option that will let your machine emulate specific terminal models, like DEC's VT-52 or VT-100 boxes or IBM's 3101 series, or terminals made by Wyse, Televideo, Heath/Zenith, and others.

Often, when terminal emulation is selected, the communications session becomes page-oriented. That means that the mainframe will send you a page of information at a time and you will be able to move around the screen as you might with a word processor. Different colors may be used to highlight certain areas of the page/screen as well. The only real problem is the keyboard. Under terminal emulation a PC can generate most of the codes the mainframe needs, but the keys needed to do so will obviously be in a different place than they are with a real terminal.

If you want to tap your company's mainframe from home, contact the firm's MIS or microcomputer manager for help and suggestions. He or she will probably know which software package you should buy for your personal computer for greatest ease of operation. In fact, you may be able to get the person to set everything up for you.

Setup and Settings: 7/E/1 and 8/N/1

The cardinal rule of online communications is that everything must match. Thus before you can communicate with anybody, there are six primary settings to be concerned with. Fortunately, most of the time you can set them once and forget about them.

The first setting is speed. If a system does not support 2400 bps, there is no point in trying to make a connection at that speed. If it does support 2400, there may be a special node you must call to make the connection since at this writing not all PDN nodes support 300/1200/2400.

Items two, three, and four are the number of data bits, the parity sense, and the number of stop bits. Remember the packing material we spoke of earlier as the UART was getting the jelly beans lined up to go out the door? Well, here's where it comes into play.

In the ASCII code set only seven bits are required to symbolize the numbers from 0 through 127—more than enough to cover all of the text and control characters. But computers have an eighth bit to work with, and because of the way the binary numbering system operates, this give them the ability to represent an additional 128 code numbers (128 through 255). Trouble is, there is no agreement on what those extra "high" codes will represent, and every computer manufacturer has treated them differently.

Therefore, the lowest common denominator that lets you talk to all systems regardless of make or model, is seven data bits, since at this setting only standard ASCII text will be sent and received. In reality, most host systems will accept seven or eight, but to be sure of filtering out any unintentional high codes, you should almost always set your system at seven when calling a commercial online system.

So what happens to the eighth bit? Since it is always there, the powers that be have decided to put it to work as an error-checking mechanism. This is what parity sense is all about. Visualize your seven data bits lined up single file ready to go out the door. Some are 1s and some are 0s. Now add up all of the 1s. Let's say the sum is an odd number. If you're set to even parity, you make the eighth bit a 1 to turn the eight-bit total into an even number. If you're set to odd parity, you make the eighth bit a 0 to leave the sum unchanged.

The reason this works as an error-checking mechanism is that both you and your correspondent are set to the same parity sense. Let's call it even. If the remote system expects each eight-bit unit to add up to an even number, but a unit comes in that is odd, the sytem knows that something has happened to one of the bits along the way. It has been transformed from a 0 to a 1 or vice versa, throwing off the oddness or evenness of the total.

Whether that system takes any action based on this discovery is another matter. Most systems don't do anything at all. In addition, parity checking is not really all that effective, since if two bits are changed by a crackle of electrical noise, the oddness or evenness of the unit may remain unaffected.

Finally, there's the stop bit. The package that goes out the door to represent a single ASCII character actually consists of 10 bits. First, there's the start bit (always a 0). This tells the receiving system that a new character is about to begin. Next there are the seven data bits and a parity bit—or eight data bits. Finally, there is a stop bit (always a 1) to tell the receiver "That's all, folks." (The ten-bit package makes it easy to translate speed in bits per second into characters per second. Just divide the bps by 10. A speed of 1200 bps is 120 characters per second or cps, 2400 is 240 cps, and so on.)

The most common settings in the online world are 7/E/1 and 8/N/1. Translated, this is seven data bits and even parity and one stop bit, or eight data bits and no parity and one stop bit. (Obviously if both systems are set to interpret all eight bits as data, there is no bit to use for parity.) The only time you might ever use two stop bits is when talking directly to a 110-bps Teletype machine. The extra stop bit gives the machine's printhead the extra time it needs.

Duplex and Line Feeds

The last of the six settings concern full or half-duplex and whether or not you want to add a line feed to each carriage return. The duplex setting determines where the characters that appear on your screen come from. When operating in full-duplex, the host system echoes back the characters you send. (Which is why the really correct term is "echoplex," though no one uses it.) That means that the R you just typed first went out of your computer and traveled to the host system, which echoed it back to your computer. Your computer then put it on the screen. It happened so quickly that you probably thought the character went from your keyboard straight to the screen. That's what full-duplex means.

If a host system does not echo characters—if it operates at half-duplex—then, if you are set for full-duplex, nothing you type will appear on the screen. (General Electric's GEnie is the only system discussed in this book that likes to operate at half-duplex.) What to do? The answer is to toggle on your local echo. That means, issue a software command that tells the program to send the characters you type to both the remote system *and* to the screen.

But suppose you've got the opposite problem. Suppose you've got too many of each character on the screen, like tthhiiss. If that happens, the host system is obviously echoing characters and your system is obviously putting characters on the screen as well. Solution: Toggle off your local echo and return to full-duplex.

A line feed, as noted earlier, is an ASCII control character that tells a printer to advance the paper one line or a computer to scroll the screen up one line. A carriage return is an ASCII control character that tells the print head on a printer or the cursor on a computer to return to the far left margin. If you have a carriage return without a line feed, then each line of text will print on top of the preceding line.

Almost every system, yours included, puts a carriage return character at the end of each line. The question is, who is responsible for adding the line feeds—you or the host? In addition, there are two opportunities to add line feeds—to the text you're sending and to text coming into your machine.

This is actually less complicated than it appears. In almost every case, you shouldn't add line feeds at all. Mainframe host systems like to get text with carriage returns alone, and they will add line feeds to the text they send you. Should you ever see text on your screen that is double or triple spaced, however, it's a sure bet that your software is adding its own line feeds. Solve the problem by toggling off that feature.

To recap, then, here are the comm program settings you will use most of the time:

• 300, 1200, or 2400 bps, depending on your modem and the host system's capabilities.

• Seven data bits, even parity, and one stop bit, *or* eight data bits no parity, and one stop bit.

• Full-duplex (FDX), except when using the GEnie system.

• No line feed on carriage return, either for incoming or outgoing text.

Dialing Directories, Macros, and Scripts

Most comm programs will let you specify the above settings as your chosen defaults. They will record the settings in a file on disk and use them each time you load the program. Most also give you the option of recording frequently dialed phone numbers in a dialing or phone directory. Some dialing directories can accommodate hundreds of numbers. There will usually be one line for each and you will be able to specify the name of the system, its phone number, and the comm settings you want the program to use with it. The software will handle all the modem commands; all you need to worry about is the phone number.

To dial a number in the directory, you simply mouse down to it and click or key in its item number and hit <Enter>. Should the target number be busy, you may be able to tell your program to wait a specified period of time before automatically redialing. You will probably be able to control how many attempts the program makes as well, and more than likely you will be able to hand the program a list and tell it to dial each number in sequence until it gets an answer.

Communications programs frequently support keyboard macros and script files. You might use a keyboard macro to issue your account number and password to an online system. That way, instead of keying all of those characters in each time, you could hit a single key. Script files are actually little (and sometimes not so little) programs written in your software's command language. Scripts are text files and you would normally prepare them with your word processor.

Depending on the program, scripts can be quite elaborate and quite powerful. For example, you could create one that might automatically sign on to two or three different systems at some preset time of day. It might then pick up any electronic mail that was waiting for you and transmit any letters you wanted to send, sign off, and hang up the phone. All while you slept. Sample scripts may come with the program, but you will almost certainly find many more in the SIG data libraries found on online utility systems. In fact some commercial and shareware vendors operate SIGs of their own with all kinds of goodies for you to download.

Capture Buffer and Up and Downloading

Speaking of which—there are three ways to preserve the information coming into your system before it scrolls off the screen. The least desirable way is to toggle on your printer. All comm programs include a command for this, but printers slow things down terribly. It is much better to use the second option, which is to capture incoming information to disk. To do this, you key in a command to "open your capture buffer." The program will then ask you for the filename you would like it to use for recording incoming information. When you've chosen a name, the capture feature will be operational and everything that appears on the screen will be recorded on disk.

The word "buffer" refers to a portion of memory used as a temporary holding tank. As information comes in, it is first placed in the buffer, and as the buffer fills, the program dumps it to disk. We suggest that you use this feature to "log" all online sessions, at least in the beginning. After all, what's to lose? You can always erase the log file if nothing worth saving came in. If there is something you want to save, you can edit the file with your word processor once you are offline. The one thing to remember is to close the capture buffer (turn off your capture feature) before you exit the program. If you don't, there's a chance that the last bit of information that came in will not be recorded.

The third technique for recording incoming information is called "downloading." Think of it as loading information into your system sent down from the host on high. When you use the capture buffer technique, you are in effect downloading information, but the term also refers to the transfer of entire files—without displaying them on the screen. "Uploading" works the same way, but in the opposite direction.

The key point is that a file transfer of this sort is a computer-to-computer transaction. Once your system and the host have entered file-transfer mode, the only thing you will see on your screen is a report on how things are progressing. You can terminate the process at any time, but you won't be able to do anything else until it's over.

You can upload and download any kind of file, text or otherwise. But you must use this technique if you want to transfer programs or files containing machine language. And since even the slightest error in transmission can render a machine-language program useless, you must use an "error-checking file transfer protocol." And, as with everything else in communications, the protocols used by sender and receiver must match.

We're going to explain protocols in the next chapter, but if you like, you can handle it "cookbook" fashion. Check your comm program documentation to see what protocols are available. Then look for a match on the system you want to call. Follow the online system's instructions for selecting the file you want to download and the protocol you want to use, and follow your own program's instructions on the same topics, and you'll be fine.

Conclusion

School's out. At this point, you should have your modem and software in hand and have a pretty good idea of how to enter the electronic universe. The signpost on that chapter up ahead says "Getting Technical," but as you know we suggest you skip it for now. Instead, warp your way around it to reach the online utilities on the other side. You may want to look at other kinds of systems as well, but you will almost certainly want to start the adventure with a subscription to one of these multifaceted systems.

Online Tip: One final tip for this chapter. If you will be using a phone line with the phone company's "call waiting" feature, disable it before you go online. Should you fail to do this and receive a call while you are connected to a remote system, the call waiting signal may knock you offline. To disable call waiting, key in *70 or dial 1170 on a rotary phone before you place each modem call. See the front pages of your phone book under Tone*Block for more information.

...3...

Getting Technical: Null Modems, Error-Checking Protocols, and Other Telecommunications Arcana

F rom at least one perspective the phrase "nontechnical telecommunications" is an oxymoron—a pairing of words that is a contradiction in terms, like an iron butterfly, a lead zeppelin, or a courageous politician. There are so many applications, each with its own jargon, standards, and variations, that one could easily submerge into the field, never to surface again.

Thankfully, this is not a trip we have to take. There are people for that, trained specialists who thrive on intricacy and minute detail. There are trade journals, newsletters, and very thin, very expensive technical books by the yard that explore every electronic nook, taking it apart and putting it back together again. There are lots of resources, many of them available online through systems like BRS, DIALOG, and NewsNet, for those with special needs.

Here, in contrast, we will focus on two primary goals. First, since so many people now have both a laptop computer and a desktop system, each of which uses a different disk format, we'll look at the hardware you need to move files from one system to the other. Second, since many readers will want to download free software programs from BBSs and online utility systems, while still others will want to transfer spreadsheets and other machine-language files, we will tell you what you need to know about error-checking protocols. Along the way, we'll cover some other minor, but useful, points as well. We'll start with ASCII control codes.

Control Characters and Codes

As discussed in the previous chapter, the ASCII code set runs from 0 to 127. These are the "low codes" that everyone agrees on. "High codes"—from 128 through 255—are often used by computer manufacturers to represent various graphics characters, and there is no standardization in this area. If you think about it, even if you include the shifted versions of all the keys on your keyboard, you find that you can only generate about 100 characters. So how can you generate the remaining 28 ASCII low codes, and more importantly, why would you want to?

The answer lies with the "control" or <Ctrl> key (or your machine's equivalent). The <Ctrl> key acts exactly like the <Shift> key in giving you the ability to generate characters that are not on your keyboard. If you hold your <Ctrl> key down and hit <A>, you generate an ASCII 1. Do the same thing with your <Z> key, and you generate an ASCII 26. ASCII control codes, in other words, track with the alphabet.

Most communications programs treat control codes the same way they treat any other ASCII character. They pass them straight through to the host computer. The host may or may not respond, but some control codes do have widely accepted meanings. With many systems, for example, a Control-C acts as a BREAK signal. Other systems may respond to a Control-P. Either way, the host will stop whatever it is doing and return you to some kind of prompt.

Online Tip: A true BREAK signal is not an ASCII code. It is a sustained high signal—also called a space or a logical 0—lasting between 200 and 600 milliseconds. Some online systems specify the duration of the BREAK signal to which they will respond. And comm communications programs let you control how long your BREAK signal will be.

There are other commonly accepted meanings as well. A Control-F is an ACK ("acknowledge") signal, while a Control-U is a NAK ("negative acknowledge"). We'll run into these again when we look at file transfer protocols. Control-G is the signal to sound a system's "bell," though personal computer users will hear a beep should a Control-G come in. A Control-I is a tab character. Some word processors and other software insert this code instead of, say, five blank spaces. (A space is an ASCII 32.) Should you ever receive such a file, you may want to use a utility program to expand the tab characters to a certain number of spaces; you may be able to set your comm program to do it for you as the file is received.

A Control-Q is technically called Device Control 1, but most people refer to it as an X-ON. Its mate is a Control-S (X-OFF). We'll have more to say on these two codes in a minute. Control-M is a carriage return; Control-J, a line feed; and Control-L, a form feed to cause printers to advance to the top of the next page or to clear your video screen. Many programs use a Control-Z to signify the end of a file.

Online Tip: If you are an IBM or compatible user, you can generate any control code by holding down your <Alt> key and keying in the code's ASCII number on your numeric keypad. As an experiment, key in COPY CON:BEL at your DOS prompt and hit <Enter>. Then key in several <Alt><7> combinations. This will show up as a carat sign followed by a capital G. Close the file by hitting <F6> and <Enter>. Then key in TYPE BEL and hit <Enter>. You should hear a beep tone for each of the Control-Gs you put into the file.

Translation Tables

Before we leave the ASCII code set, we should say a word about the translation tables you will find built into many communications programs. Most people never need concern themselves with this feature. But if you are dealing with two incompatible computers, or a machine that has special requirements, translation tables may hold the answer.

Normally, there are two tables—one for outgoing text and one for incoming. In many cases, you can fiddle with every code on each table if you like. If you want to turn an exclamation point (ASCII 33) into a special graphics character on the receiving system, say an ASCII 149, you need only locate 33 on the outgoing table and replace it with 149. As long as that table is in effect, your 33s will be translated into 149s as they are sent out the door. Incoming translation tables work the same way, but in reverse. Thus if your company's mainframe needs to see a character that your keyboard can't normally generate, you can simply translate a little-used character that you *can* generate.

A Matter of Protocol

Now let's turn to the fine art of protocol file transfer. A file-transfer protocol is an agreement. An agreement between two communicating systems that they will respond to the same control codes or commands in the same way, and that they will follow a certain specified procedure when transferring a file. At the bottom of the scale is the stop-start, X-ON/X-OFF flow control protocol. At the top are highly sophisticated multilevel protocols like MNP, X.PC, LAPM, and V.42. In between are the protocols like XMODEM, YMODEM, and Kermit, that you will probably use most often. All have one thing in common—each is intended to make sure that information gets from point A to point B in a controlled and orderly fashion. After all, if one cannot reliably move information between two points, there is no point in having a connection in the first place.

Simple X-ON/X-OFF Flow Control

Question: How can a mainframe computer thousands of miles away know that your personal computer is busy writing to disk at the moment and thus unprepared to deal with the next page of text? Answer: Your personal computer can send a code to the remote host saying, "Caught short here, boss. Hold it up a minute, will you?" If your system didn't do this, it is a virtual certainty that some of the lines of text you are receiving would not make it. The bits might come in the comm port, but they would vanish, replaced by the next wave, because your machine was too busy to do anything with them. When your system is again ready to receive, it can send a code indicating as much to the host and the transfer can continue where it left off.

For obvious reasons, this protocol is called "flow control." The two codes used are an X-ON (Control-Q) and an X-OFF (Control-S). The X is communications shorthand for "transfer" as an X-fer. Remote hosts, PDNs, and comm programs implement flow control automatically. However, should you ever get into a situation where transmission seems to have stopped, you might try sending a Control-Q to get it started again. Sometimes one of these signals will be sent inadvertently, and that may be the cause of your problem. In addition, if you need to read the text you are being sent while you are online and find it scrolling by too quickly, you can usually send a Control-S to stop it and a Control-Q to get it started again.

The XMODEM Family of Protocols

Flow control is fine for text files, but when you're downloading a machine-language program, nothing short of 100 percent accuracy will do. One or two bits out of place may or may not render a program completely useless, but such errors certainly create a potential for unpredictable results, which amounts to the same thing. This is why error-checking file-transfer protocols were developed.

The most famous of these is XMODEM. Like most microcomputer protocols, XMODEM operates by dividing the target file up into uniform-sized chunks called blocks. The blocks are 128 bytes long, and each is assigned a number. As the first block leaves the sender's system, the ASCII values of each byte (0 through 255) are noted. When the last byte in that block has been sent, the values of all of those ASCII codes are added up, and that sum is sent down the line. That sum has a special meaning to the receiver because it too is adding up the ASCII values of the bytes in the first block and calculating a sum.

If the transmission has been flawless, the two sums must match. If they do, the receiver "ACK"s the block (sends the ASCII code for "acknowledge"). That is the sender's signal to send the next block. If the sums do *not* match, the receiver "NAK"s the block and the sender sends it again. The total of the ASCII values is called a "checksum," for obvious reasons. The checksum actually occupies only one byte, produced by dividing the actual checksum by 255, but you don't have to worry about that. The important thing is the overall process.

What we have just described is the essence of the original (checksum) version of a protocol created by Ward Christensen in August 1977. Ward Christensen is without question a seminal figure in personal computing, yet with characteristic modesty, he refers to XMODEM as "a quick hack" produced to fill the immediate need of transferring files from a bulletin board he and fellow Chicagoan Randy Suess had created to other personal computers. But its simplicity, its high accuracy rate, and its public domain status have made it the most widely used protocol in the microcomputer world.

Online Tip: If you have trouble effecting XMODEM transfers using Datapac, you might try this solution uploaded to CompuServe by one Canadian user:

> For those of us in Canada who access U.S.-based information services via Datapac and would like to upload or download with the XMODEM protocol, here are the commands that Datapac requires for proper transmission via XMODEM:

```
Control-P
PROF 1 <ENTER>
SET 126:004,003:000,004:004,001:000 <ENTER>
<ENTER>
GOODBYE <ENTER>
```

> Note that the spaces after PROF and SET are mandatory! That's all it takes. Happy downloading!
>
> JLG (Joe Gagnon)

XMODEM CRC-16

You may sometimes hear XMODEM referred to as the MODEM7 protocol, after the communications program that made it famous. MODEM7 is used mostly by CP/M systems. It can operate in batch mode, which lets you tell it to send a list of files instead having to specify each file in sequence. TELINK, a protocol designed by Tom Jennings, is similar to MODEM7, but it includes the file size and creation date as well as the filename when it gets started. TELINK is found most frequently on BBSs running Mr. Jennings's Fido BBS program.

Of much greater importance these days is the version of XMODEM called XMODEM CRC-16 or just XMODEM CRC. The checksum technique of XMODEM/MODEM7 will detect about 95 percent of all potential transmission errors for XMODEM's 128-byte blocks. However, different techniques can boost that percentage still further. Consequently, in later versions of XMODEM, programmers in the community of users added a "cyclic redundancy check" or "CRC-16" capability to the protocol, raising its error-detection accuracy to between 99.969 and 99.9984 percent. The CRC-16 technique is backed by some heavy-duty math, but its essence is based on the fact that if an integer is divided by a prime number, the remainder is always unique.

To summarize, then, XMODEM is a block-oriented, half-duplex protocol. It sends a block, waits for a response, and sends another block. It can support two types of error checking, the simple checksum of the original and the even more accurate CRC-16 method. Generally, commercial systems and BBSs support either checksum only or both checksum and CRC-16. We know of none that support only CRC-16. Some will give you a choice of methods before you begin to download. Others will let your communications software call the tune and base their response on how your program requests the first block of data.

If your comm program supports only the checksum approach, it will automatically send a NAK to request the first (and every other) block. However, if your software supports both techniques, it will probably try for a CRC-16 transfer first. To signal that intent, it will send a capital C (ASCII 67) when requesting the first block instead of a NAK. Should the sending system fail to respond appropriately, your program may automatically fall back to the checksum method, issue a NAK, and proceed with the transfer.

XMODEM-1K and "Relaxed" XMODEM

You may also encounter "XMODEM-1K" and "relaxed XMODEM." Designed by Chuck Forsberg, XMODEM-1K lets two systems agree to increase the normal 128-byte XMODEM block size to 1K for faster throughput. "Relaxed" XMODEM was designed by John Friel, author of the IBM shareware program Qmodem. This protocol differs from conventional XMODEM implementations in that it is about ten times more tolerant of the delays introduced by PDNs and by busy mainframe hosts like those of CompuServe. Conventional XMODEM is designed to send a signal, wait a specified time for a response, send the signal again if no response is forthcoming, and so on. The protocol calls for the machine to cycle through this sequence a certain number of times and then abort the transfer.

The problem is that the load factor on the mainframe host at the time of the up- or download, and the processing caused by the packet-switching networks, can introduce unpredictable delays. If it takes the host too long to respond to your system, signals can get confused and misinterpreted, which can create a mell of a hess. Relaxed XMODEM loosens the normal timing requirements and increases your chance of a successful transfer.

The Forsberg YMODEM Protocol

YMODEM is a major enhancement to the XMODEM protocol designed and implemented by Chuck Forsberg. In addition to an optional batch mode that allows you to send a list of files instead of having to specify each one in turn, YMODEM lets you use one-kilobyte blocks (1024 bytes) instead of the 128-byte blocks used by XMODEM. YMODEM is thus an example of software keeping up with hardware. Christensen used 128-byte blocks in his protocol because computer memory at the time was both limited and expensive. (In 1978 a machine with a 32K of RAM and a 70K-floppy disk sold for $2315, and you had to add your own monitor and keyboard!)

With the more capacious machines of today the 1K blocks of YMODEM are easy to handle. And if the telephone connection is good, they result in faster transfers. But when a poor connection exists, YMODEM may take longer since it must retransmit more data each time an error is detected in a block. Mr. Forsberg certainly deserves the title of communications wizard. Working from his houseboat on Sauvie Island Road in Portland, Oregon, he has produced the enormously powerful (and technical) YAM communications program. The initials stand for Yet Another Modem [program] and they are the source of the name YMODEM. The trademarked term True YMODEM means that the protocol implements all YMODEM features, including the batch file send/receive feature. (Some YMODEM implementations do not include this feature.)

Forsberg's ZMODEM

. Chuck Forsberg was commissioned by Telenet to develop a protocol that could be used on a wide variety of systems operating in a wide variety of environments (modems, timesharing systems, satellite relays, wide-area packet-switched networks, and so on). The result was the public domain ZMODEM protocol. There is much to be said about ZMODEM, but here we will simply note two of its most important features. One feature is its use of a 32-bit CRC for even greater accuracy, and the other is the fact that ZMODEM sends data continuously until the receiver interrupts to request the retransmission of garbled data. To put it another way, ZMODEM uses the entire file as its "window," a term and technique we will look at next.

WXMODEM: Windowed XMODEM

There is also a protocol called WXMODEM ("windowed XMODEM"). Under the conventional XMODEM protocol, the sending system cannot put a block into the pipeline until it hears back from the receiving system that the block it just sent was okay. If that block was not okay, XMODEM immediately tries to send it again. Under WXMODEM, the sending system can send up to four blocks without getting an acknowledgment from the receiver. In communications terms, it thus has a "window" of four blocks.

Imagine that the sender has just transmitted the fourth of 16 blocks and has just heard back that the third block was garbled. In that case, under WXMODEM, the sender would back up to the block containing the error and begin sending again. That is, it would back up, resend the third block, followed by the fourth block (which it has already sent), and so on. This is not a terribly elegant technique, but it is significantly faster than regular XMODEM. A file requiring six minutes to transmit under XMODEM, can be transmitted in as little as four minutes under WXMODEM. Useful whenever a packet-switching network is part of the connection, WXMODEM is the preferred protocol of the People/Link system. The protocol was designed by Peter Boswell (People/Link user name: TOPPER).

The Kermit Protocol

In Love with a Big Green Frog

The XMODEM family of protocols has certainly had a good run. But in micro-to-mainframe communications at least, it seems likely that XMODEM will eventually be replaced by a protocol called Kermit. Kermit was developed at Columbia University's Center for Computing Activities, and the name is used with the permission of Henson Associates (HA!), creators of the famous green amphibian. Though not in the public domain—Columbia University holds the copyright and tries to maintain the definitive set of Kermit implementations—the protocol may be incorporated into software free of charge.

Kermit is already used widely, but like XMODEM before it, it has continued to evolve. The main purpose of the original or so-called Classic Kermit was to overcome the difficulties involved in transferring files between fundamentally incompatible systems. Some older mainframe computers can handle only seven-bit characters, for example. Others go crazy if they receive anything resembling a control code byte, even if those bytes are part of a file that is being transferred.

Classic and Super Kermit

Classic Kermit, like XMODEM, operates in a half-duplex, send-and-wait mode. It sends a packet, waits for an acknowledgment, and then either sends the next packet or re-sends the former packet if it turns out to have been received in error. A newer version, informally known as "Super Kermit," includes all of the features of its predecessor, plus "sliding windows." This means in effect that Kermit can pitch and catch at the same time. And that makes for a continuous, full-duplex transfer instead of the send-and-wait, half-duplex approach used by Classic Kermit and XMODEM.

Unless otherwise specified, you can assume that all references to Kermit from this point on refer to the sliding-window version. It is the sliding window that gives Kermit its speed, and the concept is not difficult to understand.

You can start with the fact that Kermit uses the same ideas employed by Telenet and Tymnet to divide a file into discrete packets. Each packet is stamped with a sequence number, the number of characters the packet contains, and possibly some other information. A checksum or CRC is then calculated and tacked onto the packet. Each packet is thus a self-contained unit, and as with Telenet and Tymnet, the order in which packets are sent doesn't really matter. The receiver has only to open the packet, read the sequence number, and slot the packet into its correct position in memory to reassemble the file.

The size of the packets is flexible and in most implementations can vary between 0 and 94 bytes. The size actually used in any given transfer is agreed upon by the two systems as part of their initial handshaking. Once the handshaking is over, each system sets up a "table," which you might visualize as a bank of pigeonholes of the sort you would find in an antique desk. There may be as few as one or as many as 31 pigeon-holes in each table, depending on what the two systems agree upon.

When a transfer begins, the sending system loads up its table with packets, one per pigeonhole, and starts pitching them to the receiver. At the same time, it also starts listening to catch the receiver's response concerning the checksum or CRC of each packet. That's the full-duplex aspect of the protocol. The sender can pitch as many as 31 packets without receiving an acknowledgment of any sort. That's its "window."

Sliding the Window

Now, suppose that the sender has just transmitted packet number 7 when the first responses begin to come in: Packet number 1's okay? Good. Oops, a problem with number 2 but number 3's fine? Okay, here's the rest of packet number 7. And now here's a retransmission of packet number 2. Now on to number 8.

This sounds a little daft, but you get the idea. Kermit's tables allow it to send and resend packets continuously in whatever sequence is required. When the oldest packet in a table—the packet in slot 1—is acknowledged to have been successfully received, the sender "rotates the table" or "slides the window." This means it moves the packet currently in slot 2 into slot 1, while the packet in slot 3 is moved into slot 2, and so on. Since each packet has its own sequence number, the sending system always knows where to find it, regardless of the number of the slot in the table it currently occupies.

Sliding the window leaves an empty slot at the top of the table, which the system fills with the next sequential packet in the file. The process continues until the entire file has been transmitted and the two systems have agreed that the transfer is complete.

This is only a brief sketch of how Kermit's sliding window feature works. Kermit has many other interesting features, including a batch mode command and a "server" option, but they need not concern us here. For our purposes, the most important point is that Kermit's sliding window approach makes for speedy file transfers—up to 50 percent faster than XMODEM in many cases.

The development of sliding windows within Kermit was funded by The Source and implemented by Capital PC User Group members Larry Jordan and Jan van der Eijk. At this writing, three of our five systems (CompuServe, Delphi, and BIX) support Kermit. But the protocol is so well suited to micro-to-mainframe, packet-switched communications that others may offer it in the future.

FreeTip: For more detailed information on Kermit, you might want to send for the book cited below. Written by Frank da Cruz, one of the protocol's developers, it is the definitive text at this writing:

> *Kermit: A File Transfer Protocol*
> by Frank da Cruz
> Digital Press, 1987
> (379 pages, $25)

You can order through your local bookseller or contact Digital Press directly by dialing (800) 343–8321 between 8:00 A.M. and 4:00 P.M. Eastern time. Visa and MasterCard phone orders are accepted. You can also order by modem by logging on to DEC's innovative Electronic Store by dialing (800) 332–3366. (To take full advantage of this system's on-screen graphics, set your software for VT-100 terminal emulation if possible.) Of course, you may also send your order by paper mail:

> Digital Press—Order Processing
> Digital Equipment Corporation
> 12 A Esquire Road
> Billerica, MA 01862

MNP, X.PC, V.42., and LAPM

It's hard to pinpoint the date, but at some time in the recent past a change began to take place in personal computer communications. The change has not been felt by most users and probably won't be felt for many years to come. But there is no doubt that something's happening.

PC communications at the technical level are evolving beyond the comparatively simple asynchronous links and block-oriented file-transfer protocols of the past. At least two engines are driving the change. The first is the demand for ever-faster communications speeds and the need to cope with the limitations of a phone system designed to carry voice and not data signals. The second is the proliferation of many different personal computers, minicomputers, mainframes, and other equipment, and the need for all of them to be able to talk to each other. The computer communications industry's response at this writing has been a series of protocols designed to meet these challenges.

We will not discuss these protocols in detail here. Instead, we will give you enough information to have some idea of who the major players are and of the issues involved. The two main competitors in this area are Tymnet with its X.PC ("X dot PC") protocol, and Microcom with its MNP (Microcom Networking Protocol). Although they have many other features, both are designed to reduce the error rate when using 2400-bps modems over common telephone lines.

MNP can be implemented in software, but authorities generally agree it is most effective when incorporated in a modem as a firmware ROM (read only memory) chip. The full implementation includes some six classes of service, the throughput increasing with each level. One of the protocol's outstanding features is its ability to negotiate the class of service that will be used for a given session. Thus if your modem can handle everything up to MNP class-5 service, but the modem you are communicating with only goes up to class 3, the two modems will do some initial handshaking when they connect to agree to operate at class 3.

The two modems, in other words, talk to each other to determine their highest common denominator. If both are able to use MNP's data-compression techniques, for example, those techniques will be used (which can result in an effective throughput of 48,000 bits per second or higher with a 2400-bps modem). But if one of the two does not support data compression, the next best technique will be used. And so on.

One of the most outstanding features of X.PC is its multitasking ability. This means that you can use X.PC to conduct several simultaneous online sessions. Tymnet has placed X.PC in the public domain, and it is usually implemented in software, so there is no need to buy a new modem as might be the case with MNP. (Microcom licenses its protocol for a fee.)

Both protocols offer error correction during interactive sessions. That means that error correction is in effect from the moment you log on to an online system until you sign off, whether or not you download any files. If the protocol is implemented in the modem, however, it does not include any file-transfer functions. Thus, even with an error-correcting modem, you will need to use one of the file-transfer protocols discussed above.

This double protection naturally introduces delays, what with both the modems and you and the host system exchanging CRC checks. At this writing, there are at least two personal computer software protocols you can use to improve the situation. One is Chuck Forsberg's YMODEM-G (and YMODEM-G Batch) and the other is John Friel's I-MODEM.

Both are "streaming protocols" specifically designed for use with error-correcting modems. They provide no error correction of their own (and thus do not introduce additional delays). Instead, they provide a mechanism to tell your system to take a file, cut it up into packets, and keep sending the packets to the modem until told to stop; or to accept incoming packets and write them properly to disk. The only problem is that both you and your correspondent must have compatible error-correcting modems and compatible streaming protocols, and at this writing, you're not likely to find a commercial online system that offers either.

In the future, it is possible that both X.PC and MNP will go away. Some authorities have referred to them as a flash in the pan. The protocol that will take their place is the CCITT recommendation V.42 for an international standard for modem error detection and correction. According to industry sources, the working group committee responsible for writing the recommendation was divided between MNP supporters and supporters of the Link Access Protocol M (LAPM). (Like X.PC, LAPM is designed to work closely with the widely accepted X.25 protocol that packet-switching networks use.) A compromise was reached under which LAPM specifications formed the body of the V.42 document, but under which an "annex" document was incorporated that essentially followed MNP. By designating this section as an annex instead of an appendix, the committee made MNP part of the standard.

The net-net for PC users is that the situation regarding new protocols is still very much in flux. All of us want standards, and most of us don't care about the minutia as long as everyone uses the same standard. It seems clear that a standard will indeed emerge, but it seems equally clear that it will be several years before it has an effect—if any—on most PC users. In the meantime, current file-transfer protocols are easily equal to the task on all but the worst post-divestiture phone lines.

Online Tip: For more information on X.PC and MNP, contact Tymnet and Microcom at the addresses shown below. Both companies will be happy to tell you which modems, communications programs, and PDNs support their protocols.

Tymnet
P.O. Box 49019
San Jose, CA 95161-9019
(800) 872-7654

Microcom, Inc.
1400A Providence Highway
Norwood, MA 02062
(617) 762–4982

How to Connect Two Computers

Now let's look at how to cable two machines together to dump files back and forth. It's a topic that has special interest today among the growing legions of laptop owners. Laptop computers typically use 3½-inch disks, while most desktop machines still use 5½-inch floppies. So how can you get those memos and reports you wrote while waiting in the Sea-Tac Airport into your desktop machine once you return to your office in Atlanta?

One solution is to spend anywhere from $60 to $130 on a special cable and software package designed just for this purpose. Another solution is to spend $250 or more on a 3½-inch external drive for your system. IBM–XT and compatible computers can handle up to four floppy drives (3¼, 5½, or a mixture of the two, it doesn't matter), two of which can be connected via the DB37 port at the back end of the disk controller card. DOS 3.2 or higher is required to support 3½-inch drives on PC-compatible machines. Or you can spend $7.95 at Radio Shack for a "null modem" adaptor plug (Catalog Number 26-1496) that will accomplish the same thing as the other two options.

It is the null modem approach we will focus on here. Clearly, however, if you frequently need to exchange files between your laptop and desktop systems, you really ought to get an external 3½-inch drive. One company we've had good luck dealing with over the years is Princeton Computer Products in Monmouth Junction, New Jersey. You can call (800) 223–0306 for a free catalog. You may also be able to find a similarly good source closer to home.

To connect two computers, both must be equipped with an RS-232 port. There are other kinds of serial ports, but most people have an RS-232. If your laptop doesn't have such a port, you will either have to add one or use the laptop's built-in modem to call your desktop system and exchange files over the phone. These ports are set up to think that they will be talking to a modem. Thus if you use a cable that is wired straight through, you'll set up a situation where the ports on both machines are trying to talk to each other instead of the modems they were expecting.

A null modem adaptor or null modem cable is not wired straight through. Some of the wires have been crossed-over so that both machines think they are talking to a modem. To use the adaptor, remove the RS-232 cable from your external modem and plug it into the adaptor, and then plug the adaptor into your laptop machine. If the genders don't match, you can get a male/male or female/female gender changer plug from Radio Shack for $7.95. (Be sure to check before you go out to buy your null modem adaptor.)

With the null modem in place, transferring files is a simple matter of loading a communications program on each machine and uploading or downloading, depending on your point of view. And, since there is no modem or phone system to slow things down, you can set your communications speed for the maximum that your UART can handle. In most cases, you can communicate at 9600 bits per second, though you may be able to run at 19,200 bps or higher in some cases. Note that your communications program must support these higher speeds if you are to use them.

Three final notes before we delve into the technicalities. First, there is no reason why two completely incompatible computers cannot be connected, as long as they each have a serial port and communications software and you have the proper cable. Second, you may find that a null modem cable is more convenient to use than an adaptor plug. Computer stores can make these up for you in any length you specify, though you can get a ready made five-foot cable from Black Box and other mail-order suppliers for $18. (Fifty feet is the theoretical limit for connections of this sort.) Third, if you frequently cable different machines and devices together, consider getting a universal RS-232 cable adaptor with a male and a female DB25 connector on each end. These too are available ($29) from Black Box, P.O. Box 12800, Pittsburgh, PA 15241. Call (412) 746–5530 for a catalog.

How to Build a Null Modem Cable

If you're reasonably dexterous, you can build your own null modem cable, often without touching a soldering iron, thanks to crimpable pins, sockets, and shells. All it takes is the hardware and the right connections. Before plunging in, take a look at Figure 3.1 for a quick overview of the pin assignments on an RS-232 interface.

A first look at the RS-232C standard can be rather dismaying—until you realize that of the 25 pins, personal computer owners need only be concerned with six or seven (and possibly only three) when preparing for direct connection. Here are the main pins you may have to deal with:

2. Transmit data (TD)
3. Receive data (RD)
4. Request to send (RTS)

5. Clear to send (CTS)
6. Data set ready (DSR)
7. Signal ground (SGND)
8. Carrier detect (CD)
20. Data terminal ready (DTR)

Of these, the ones responsible for sending (pin 2) and receiving (pin 3) data are the most important. Most of the other signals are typically used for the handshaking dialogue between your computer and your modem to make sure that everything is ready before any data are transmitted.

The two pins that must be crossed-over in every case are pins 2 and 3. Each computer's data-sending pin in one plug must be connected to the data-receiving pin in the other plug. You will also need to make sure there is a wire running between each plug's pin 7, since this line carries the signal ground that both systems use as a comparison or reference point when determining the state of the other lines. These three connections may be all you need. And they are what you should try first.

Assuming your connections and plugs aren't lose, if this arrangement does not work, do not despair. The communications software you are running is probably responsible. Some comm programs make the computer generate a continuous "Request to Send" signal. The software won't let the computer send data until it receives a "Clear to Send" from the "modem."

The problem is solved by connecting the "Request to Send" pin from one machine to the "Clear to Send" pin on the other. A signal is a signal. Electrically they are identical. What matters to the computer is the pin it receives a signal on.

This is the second thing to try, and it should work in most cases. But each system is different, and you may have to fiddle with some of the other pins. If you are having difficulty, try to obtain or find in your manuals a listing of the "pin out" (the list of what signals are on which pins) for the machines. You might also consult the technical sections (if any) of your communications software manual. Finally, in addition to the crossover wiring already described, you may want to try one or more of the following connections:

System A		*System B*
Pin 6	to	Pin 20
and/or		
pin 8		

System A   System B

Pin 20   to   Pin 6
                        and/or
                        pin 8

——————— **Figure 3.1. The RS-232C: Pins with a Purpose** ———————

1. Protective ground
2. Transmit data
3. Receive data
4. Request to send
5. Clear to send
6. Data set ready
7. Signal ground (circuit common)
8. Carrier detect
9. (Reserved for testing)
10. (Reserved for testing)
11. Not assigned
12. Secondary carrier on

13. Secondary clear to send
14. Secondary transmit data
15. Transmission signal timing
16. Secondary received data
17. Receiver signal timing
18. Not assigned
19. Secondary request to send
20. Data terminal ready
21. Signal quality detector
22. Ring indicator
23. Data rate selector
24. Transmission signal timing
25. Not assigned

Online Tip: If you really get involved in RS-232 hardware, communications problem solving, testing, and the like, one of the best sources for the equipment you'll need is B&B Electronics in Ottawa, Illinois. The company designs, builds, and sells high-quality plugs, breakout boxes, data generators, line boosters, and related devices at very reasonable prices. We have found their technical staff's knowledge of the RS-232 and other interfaces to be unsurpassed. For a free catalog, contact:

B&B Electronics
1500 Boyce Memorial Drive
P.O. Box 1008
Ottawa, IL 61350
(815) 434–0846

"Secret" Telenet or Tymnet Commands

Though it isn't actually a secret, there are special commands you can send to Telenet and Tymnet to alter your communications environment. Each company publishes a free booklet describing them, so you have only to contact their customer service staffs at the addresses given in the previous chapter.

Normally, there will never be a need to issue any of these commands. But every now and then a special situation may arise when it can be helpful to know about them. If you're having difficulty, though, look to your own software first. For example, if the host system doesn't seem to be receiving all of the characters you send, see if your comm program will let you add a delay of several milliseconds after each line it transmits or even after each character. This is called an "upload throttle." Second, if the host system has a customer service number, take the easy way out and give them a call. If they can't solve it, Telenet or Tymnet customer service may be able to help. Third, some users report that uploading large amounts of text directly from disk on Telenet works best if you put the network into half-duplex and enable its X-ON/X-OFF flow control.

Telenet

Telenet is unique in that it has two modes: Network Command Mode and Data Transfer Mode. When you first access Telenet and see the "at" sign (@), you are in the Telenet Network Command Mode. You enter C for "connect," followed by the address number of the host you want to access, and Telenet does the rest. At that point it switches to its completely transparent Data Transfer Mode.

To alert Telenet that you want to give it a command, you must first escape from the Data Transfer Mode into the Network Command Mode. Then you must enter your command. Whenever you are using Telenet, even if you are connected to The Source or some other system, you can escape to Network Command Mode by hitting the following sequence of keys: <Enter> <@> <Enter>. This will cause the Telenet @ sign to appear on your screen, indicating that the network is awaiting your instructions.

To put Telenet into half-duplex, key in HALF and hit <Enter>. You will then be back in touch with the system you escaped from a moment ago. Execute your upload, then escape again to Network Command Mode. Since the network is in half-duplex, it will not echo what you type next to your screen. But key in FULL and hit <Enter> to return it to full-duplex.

If the system you are talking to does not support X-ON/X-OFF flow control, you can get Telenet to do it for you. At the @ prompt, key in ENAB FLOW to activate this feature and DISAB FLOW (the network's default setting) to turn it off.

Telenet also has certain buffers that can be used to smooth out the data flow. These were created for customers who transmit large amounts of data stored on computer tape from one machine to another, but you can use them as well. At the Network Command Level key in either DTAPE or TAPE to activate the Telenet upload buffer. Since file uploading is more reliable at half-duplex, the system will automatically go to that setting when either of these commands is entered. To return to Data Transfer Mode, send a BREAK signal when your upload is complete. Telenet accepts no substitutes for BREAK.

Tymnet

When you connect with Tymnet at a speed other than 300 bps, you are likely to get a line of garbage characters on your screen, depending on the particular node you are accessing. This is because Tymnet has no way of knowing what speed you are using until you send it a character. So simply hit your <A> key to tell Tymnet both what speed you are using and to identify your terminal type. Don't hit <Enter> after the <A>.

At that point, Tymnet sends a line containing the number of the node followed by the number of your port on the node. The next line will read "please log in:". Tymnet does things differently than Telenet and it is at this point that you must enter any network control commands, not after you have keyed in the target system's name. The commands of greatest interest here are:

• Control-H—Puts Tymnet into half-duplex mode

• Control-R—"Receive" data control. Enables X-ON/X-OFF flow control. The network will respond to your computer's X-ON/X-OFF signals. This is the command to use if your computer is having trouble capturing and recording all the incoming data. You might use it when downloading information from the Dow Jones News/Retrieval Service or some other system that does not support flow control on its own.

• Control-X—"Transmit" data control. Allows Tymnet to stop and start the flow of data going from your machine and into the network using X-ON and X-OFF. This prevents data loss in case the network is having difficulty keeping up with your data flow.

- Control-I—Interactive data session request. Asks the network to use the shortest circuit path to your destination equipment. Enables faster response time for some interactive sessions.

- Control-V—Volume bandwidth request. Asks the network to increase the bandwidth in the circuit to your destination to enable faster file transfers.

Do not use Control-X or Control-R with a binary file transfer, since these settings can cause a file-transfer session to hang (stop for no apparent reason). Do not use Control-I for anything but an interactive session. Do not use Control-V for anything but file transfers. If you mix the two, you may "significantly lower overall throughput," according to Tymnet.

Online Tip: Canadian users, if you want to put Datapac into half-duplex, enter a Control-P to get to the network's command level. Then key in SET 2:0 to initiate half-duplex. To return to full-duplex, enter Control-P again and key in SET 2:1.

Part II

—ONLINE UTILITIES—

...4...

Overview: The Essential
Online Utility

I f you're like most people, the online utility services are *the* place to
begin your online electronic adventure. There are other alternatives, of course, notably local bulletin board systems (BBSs).
BBSs are wonderful inventions that are filled with possibilities, and
we'll have a lot more to say about them later in this book. But while
"the boards" are free and while you can almost certainly reach one or
more in your area with a local phone call, BBSs can be confusing to the
uninitiated. It often seems that each has its own customized set of commands and features, and since most boards are run by and for computer
hobbyists, their features and content tend to reflect technical interests.
In addition, most BBSs have only one incoming phone line, which means
you may get a lot of frustrating busy signals when you try to call.

The online utility services, on the other hand, are generally aimed at
nontechnical users. As we'll see later, though, they offer vast stores of
technical information for those who want it. Utilities are available round
the clock and for all intents and purposes have an unlimited capacity to
handle multiple users. Most have been designed for easy interaction,
with menus, prompts, and instantly available help information. For
power users, most also offer a command mode to bypass the menus and
go directly to the feature you want.

As for features and services, the keyword here is "multifaceted." It is
probably not accurate to say that the utility services try to be all things
to all people. They don't. But at the same time, the range of information, communications facilities, and services they make available is so
vast that truly, if you have a computer and are interested in going
online, you are guaranteed to find something that will intrigue you. By
pulling these features and literally hundreds of thousands of people to-

gether under the same electronic roof, online utilities can both enhance your life and expand your consciousness. Or they can simply deliver the news. How you use the options the systems make available is totally up to you.

What Is an "Online Utility?"

At this point we should say a word about the word "utility." "Online utility" is derived from the term "information utility," the name by which these kinds of services were originally known. There's a constant struggle in the online world to come up with terms that are both accurate and descriptive but also understandable to the public as a whole. "Information utility" was coined by The Source, the original full-featured service of this type. The idea was that just as people used public utility companies for water, gas, electric, and telephone services in their homes, they would use The Source for home information services.

Unfortunately, the public's appetite for information and its willingness to pay for same has always been overrated by the online industry. So the *information* utility concept eventually fell by the wayside. It was never completely accurate in any case, since all so-called information utilities offered significant communications services as well. Indeed, it is the communications services that have proved to be the most popular offerings.

Online Tip: On June 29, 1989, CompuServe, Inc. announced that it had purchased Source Telecomputing Corporation for an undisclosed sum. Source subscribers were mailed CompuServe IDs and passwords and given a $20 usage credit. The Source itself ceased operation on August 1, 1989.

We have done our best to find and remove references to The Source in this book. But The Source was such a seminal institution that, as with the industry as a whole, it was woven into the book's fabric. The news came so close to press time that we may not have found all the threads.

The Source was more than just another online system. It was the system that started it all. It made the mistakes and experienced the successes that paved the way for those who followed. Above all, it contributed a *vision* of what an online utility could and should be. The industry is probably stronger for its passing, but The Source will still be missed. *Ave atque vale.*

The idea of a home-based service isn't valid any longer either. Readers of this book who have only recently acquired a machine may not remember, but not too long ago "home computers" were all the rage. You don't hear that term anymore, and with the exception of the services offered by Quantum Computer Company (which will be considered later), no online company wants to be limited to the "home" market. They tend to see themselves instead as services for executives, managers, professionals, and others with discretionary income to spend, who may use the service at home but may also use it at the office.

So for want of a better term, we will refer to all of these multifaceted services as "online utilities." After all, they are certainly online, and like conventional utilities, they are certainly useful.

The Six Leading Online Utilities

In this part of the book we will look at the six leading online utilities. There *are* other nationally available commercial services, and the movement to establish regional or city-based services appears to be gathering steam at last. There are profession-specific services like AMA/Net (American Medical Association) and ABA/Net (American Bar Association) as well. (See Appendix A: Resources for more information on how to locate online systems and databases.) But most people, whether they're on one of these other systems or not, will want to subscribe to one or more online utilities because, frankly, this is where the action is.

At this writing, the six leading online utilities are CompuServe, GEnie, Delphi, BIX, People/Link, and the machine-specific services offered by Quantum Computer Corporation. The Quantum services, including Q-Link for Commodore users, AppleLink for users of Apple II models, and PC-Link for users of IBM and compatible computers, offer many of the same features found on the other six systems. However, they package, present, and price them in a different way. With Quantum, the emphasis is on four-color "videotex"-style graphics and flat-rate pricing. We'll explain all of this later. For now, we need only note that the information given below may or may not apply to the Quantum systems.

The Essential Online Utility

Over the past decade many companies have tried many things in an attempt to hit the hot button of the online public. There have been more failures than successes. But through it all a more or less standard array of features and services has evolved. It is this configuration that we call "the essential online utility." It consists of those features you can expect to find on all systems of this sort. Features like electronic mail, real-time CB-like chat, special-interest groups (clubs), airline schedules, online shopping, and the ubiquitous Grolier's *Academic American Encyclopedia*.

In this chapter we will present and discuss those standard features and the brand name products you will find on many systems. In the chapters that follow, we will focus on the unique aspects, special features, significant variations, and Best Bets for each of the seven leading online utilities. The goal is to as nearly as possible give you the flavor and feeling of each individual system to aid you in finding the one or ones that are right for you.

Three words of advice apply throughout:

1. The online world is dynamic. Features and services come and go. Prices, subscription policies, connect-time rates, system commands, menus, and everything else is subject to change.
2. Call customer service! The only way to have the latest information is to get it straight from the horse's mouth. Most online services make this easy by supplying toll-free customer service numbers. We've highlighted these numbers at the beginning of each chapter. Use them. That's what they're there for.
3. All online utility services have information packets they would love to send you free of charge. Since it doesn't cost you anything and since each of these packets can include far more information than we have room to give you here, it only makes good sense to send for them. In fact, we'll go a step further—send for them right *now*. That way when you're ready to choose a service you will already have all the information you need.

As discussed in an earlier chapter, online services physically consist of what we can simply call a mainframe computer with lots of attached hard disk drives, magnetic tape readers, and racks of modems and other equipment connected to lots of incoming phone lines and public data networks (PDNs) like Telenet and Tymnet.

Online Tip: In reality, the host system may consist of several processors or free-standing mainframe systems that have been cabled together. An online utility may store all of its electronic mail features on one of these systems, all interactive games on another, and news and financial information on a third. As a user, none of this really matters to you, except that you may occasionally see a prompt reading "Please wait" or something similar after requesting a particular feature. The reason for this is that the feature you have asked for is housed on a different system and a few seconds are required to patch you through.

Access

You may be able to access utility services in many ways—by dialing them direct and paying long-distance charges, by dialing an 800 number and paying a per-minute surcharge, or by dialing your local Telenet or Tymnet number. Systems lilke CompuServe and General Electric's GEnie are available via packet-switching networks of their own as well. This is the cheapest way to access CompuServe and, in fact, the only way you can reach GEnie. (But the General Electric Information Systems network GEnie uses reaches more than 90 percent of the free world, so finding a local node should not be a problem in most cases.)

Subscriptions and Sign-On

All of the six services considered in this part of the book operate on a subscription basis. Signing up is usually a simple matter of paying an initial fee and telling the company which credit card to use for billing. Two Quantum Link services are the only systems requiring a monthly commitment. Quantum's Commodore and PC services charge a flat monthly fee of $9.95 for unlimited nonprime time usage. In both cases, you can cancel your subscription at any time.

As part of your subscription, you may receive a certain amount of storage space on the system. The storage space may go by different names, but it is basically your personal filing area. You might use it to store electronic mail distribution lists, electronic news clippings, or form letters or other materials you need to send to others on a regular basis.

You will also receive a user ID number and a secret password. Both will be required to sign on. In most cases you can change your password to whatever you want after you log on for the first time. Most utilities also send out a printed manual and possibly a quick-reference command card, and most have some kind of monthly publication that is sent free to all subscribers.

The publication could be a high-quality four-page newsletter or it might be a full-blown four-color magazine. The purpose of these publications is to keep you informed about new features and other developments on the system, to foster a sense of community among subscribers, and—most important of all—to encourage online usage.

Online Tip: In 1988 GEnie began an experimental program with U.S. West to offer "976" access in Denver. Under this program, Denver residents could call 976-GEIS and log on instantly, without first establishing an account on the system. The cost was a flat $15 per hour (25 cents a minute) and was billed to the caller's phone bill. GEis users had complete access to the GEnie system, including normally surcharged features. Given the entrepreneural drive that now characterizes many Regional Bell Operating Companies (RBOCs), you may want to check to see if similar programs are offered in your area, either for GEnie or one of the other services. This would give you a chance to try such a service right now.

Signing on usually involves connecting with Telenet or Tymnet and, after you've gotten them all squared away by sending two carriage returns (<Enter>) to Telnet and specifying D1 as your terminal type or simply hitting an <A> for Tymnet, you will have to tell them the address of your target system. On Telenet the normal procedure is to key in something like C 30128 at the "at sign" prompt (@). The C stands for "connect." The first three digits are the host computer's telephone area code and the last two are its number. With Tymnet, one normally responds to the "please log in:" prompt with the name of the target system. Like "Delphi," for example.

Once you're in, you'll be prompted for your user ID and password. For increased security—in case someone is looking over your shoulder—the password will not be displayed as you key it in. If you make a mistake in your typing, the system may give you another chance. Or it may terminate the connection, in which case you'll have to redial.

Online Tip: As mentioned in Chapter 2, even the most basic communications programs these days have the ability to execute "scripts." A script is in effect a little program you write using the commands supplied by your comm software to handle chores like logging you onto a host system. Some scripts can be so sophisticated that they can call a system at some specified time, download your mail, upload letters you have written, and sign off, all without human intervention.

Eventually you will want to have scripts for all of the systems you use most often. Be aware, however, that the script files on your disk will contain not only your system IDs but your passwords as well. Accordingly, you may want to keep your script files on a separate, removable disk, or take other appropriate steps to prevent unauthorized use of your passwords.

Navigation: Menus and Commands

With the exception of the Quantum Link systems, all online utilities communicate in plain ASCII text. As the lowest common denominator of the online world, ASCII text can be received and displayed by all makes and models of personal computers.

The first thing you see in most cases will be the system's greeting menu. This menu may also be referred to as the "main" or "top" menu. Each item on a greeting menu leads to a subsidiary menu, and each item on that menu leads to yet another menu, and so on. Novice users can thus operate most systems with a single finger, alternately hitting the number key for the desired menu item and the <Enter> key to activate the choice. In some cases, the first text you see at sign-on will be a series of bulletins or even a complete menu designed to notify you of "what's new on the system." In most cases if you just hit <Enter>, the main menu will then appear. Most systems will also automatically notify you at sign-on if you have electronic mail waiting. For examples of typical greeting menus, please turn to the system profile chapters that follow.

Menus are fine for new users, and even for experienced users they offer a safety railing one can always grab hold of in a pinch. More than likely, however, after you have had some online experience you will find that the menus get in your way. Fortunately, most systems will also respond to specific, rifle-shot commands.

Thus if you are at CompuServe's main menu and you want to visit the Apple clubs, you can key in GO MAUG to get to the Micronetworked Apple User Groups feature. Or GO IBMCOM to get to the IBM Communications forum. With commands, there is no need to wend your way through a series of menus to get where you want to go.

With the exception of Quantum, all systems offer this feature, but they implement it in slightly different ways. On GEnie and CompuServe, for example, you can key in a command from any menu prompt. The command may take the form of a mnemonic (GO MAIL) or it may involve specifying a particular "page" of the system (M 616—"move to page 616"). On BIX, in contrast, you must leave the menu system and go into Command Mode where you will see a simple colon prompt (:). You can almost always return to the menu system by keying in MENU at a command prompt.

> **Online Tip:** All of these techniques will be explained in the manual
> you receive with your subscription. However, we should take this
> opportunity to suggest that you look for a particular command-
> related feature. Look for the command or menu option that will
> generate an alphabetized list of all available commands on the sys-
> tem. Go to that area of the system, open your communications
> program's capture buffer, and download the list. Close the buffer
> and write the information to disk. Then sign off and print it out.
> This will give you your own, up-to-date, quick-reference command
> card.

Connect-Time Costs and Surcharges

From the moment the system accepts your password, the connect-
time meter will be running with your accumulated session charges being
billed to your credit card. (Quantum's Commodore and PC systems supply unlimited basic service for a flat monthly subscription fee.)

Connect-time rates vary all over the lot. But generally, two factors
are involved—time of day and speed of communication. In most cases,
connect-time rates are lower at night and on the weekends (nonprime
time) than during business hours (prime time). This may be due to the
pricing policy of the service, or it may be due to the fact that Telenet
and Tymnet also have prime and nonprime rates. Some services may
charge you more to communicate at 2400 bits per second (bps) than at
300 or 1200. Others, like Delphi, charge the same regardless of speed.
Services may quote their rate by the hour or by the minute. For ease of
comparison, both hourly and per-minute rates are given in the chapters
that follow.

Most utilities offer surcharged services that are billed at a higher
rate. These include some information products, certain enhanced news
products, and other special features. Surcharges are fine in principle.
They make such features available for those who want them without
forcing you to pay higher connect-time rates to subsidize features you
may never use. In considering a given online utility, however, it can be
important to ask yourself whether the features you think you will use
most often carry a surcharge or not. If they do, it may be worth shopping around for the lowest-cost alternative or option. The surcharges
for the identical feature may differ among systems, or the features may
carry an extra charge on one system but be included in basic service on
another.

At the other end of the spectrum, many systems offer special deals
and discounts for those willing to commit to paying a certain flat fee

each month. These may apply to the entire system, as with the Delphi Advantage plan. Or they may be limited to interactive chat features like those on CompuServe's CB Simulator. Contact customer service in each case for the latest details.

Customization: Having It Your Way

Most utilities allow you to customize your interaction with the system by specifying default settings or creating a personal profile. How many characters do you want the system to send you before it starts a new line, for example? Which of the many error-checking protocols would you like the system to automatically use when transmitting a file? Would you like to be automatically taken to a particular feature each time you sign on? How about setting up your own customized main menu? And so on.

Not all systems offer the same degree of control, but it can be important to be aware that options like these are available. If you are using a laptop computer, for example, you may want to tell the system to send you 40 characters per line instead of the 80 characters you prefer when using your desktop system. In most cases you will be given the option of making a particular default profile "permanent" (until you decide to change it again) or "temporary" (for this session only).

If you are a new user and a new computer owner, you probably shouldn't dip into this area of a system until you've had some experience. However, the one thing you may want to do is get the system to send you text without pausing. In most cases, this means setting your default screen size to 0 lines. If you don't do this, the chances are that the system will prompt you to hit <Enter> every 25 lines or so whenever it is displaying text.

Systems make 25 lines their default screen size to allow you to read text without having it quickly scroll off into space. But in our opinion, it is foolish to spend much time reading text online. It is much more cost-effective to issue the command your own software requires to open a capture buffer and record incoming information on disk, sign off, close the capture buffer, and print out and read the text at your leisure, with no connect-time meter ticking in the background. A system that pauses every 25 lines and prompts you to hit <Enter> for more frustrates this approach. Besides, it inserts a lot of prompts into the text that you may have to remove later.

If you're a new online communicator, we suggest using the system for a while, pauses and all. But when they begin to annoy you, check the beginning of each of the utility profile chapters that follow for the appropriate technique for eliminating pauses on your system. If you have any questions, as always, call customer service.

Online Tip: Most services support the X-ON/X-OFF flow-control protocol discussed in Chapter 3. (An X is the traditional abbreviation for "transfer" as in "X-fer.") That means that if you send them a Control-S (hold down your <Ctrl> key and hit <S>), they will see that signal as an X-OFF and stop transmitting. To get a display going again, send a Control-Q (X-ON).

Depending on your computer and available software, you could turn these commands into one-key macros. But it may be more convenient to use a comm program with a "scroll recall" feature. This feature lets you redisplay text that has scrolled off the screen, in case there is something you missed or need to read right away. Check your comm program manual—you may have this feature and not be aware of it.

Personally, we use and would not go online without a program called FANSI Console. This is a shareware program for IBMs and compatibles that turns <Scroll Lock> into a one-button scroll recall key. FANSI loads in at boot-up and is always available, regardless of the program you are running. FANSI is distributed by virtually all public domain and shareware sources. It is also available on Glossbrenner's Choice Disks Core 1 and Core 2. (Please see the back of this book for more information.) In our opinion, it is the single most important shareware program an IBM or compatible user can have.

Scram Commands and File-Transfer Protocols

It is also important to know how to stop a system from merrily scrolling unwanted text up your screen, or how to break out of a feature you don't want to be in. All systems have what we have called a "scram command" designed to let you stop such a scroll or other activity in its tracks. Often a BREAK signal or a Control-C will do the trick, but it is worth checking before you sign on. It is also worth checking the exit or sign-off command. How can you get out of a system quickly and stop that connect-time meter from running? In most cases, keying in BYE or OFF at any menu prompt will get you out quick, though not always. In the profile chapters that follow, we have called out the scram and sign-off commands each system requires.

Finally, there is the matter of file-transfer protocols. As you know from Chapter 2, if you want to download (transfer to your system), a spreadsheet, a machine-language program, or anything other than plain ASCII text, you will have to use a file-transfer protocol. Virtually all online utilities offer the XMODEM protocol, though it should usually be your choice of last resort. XMODEM was not designed for mainframe-to-micro hookups and, depending on its implementation, can cause problems when a packet-switching network connection is involved. General Electric's GEnie is the one exception since it implements XMODEM in a way that insures high-speed transfers.

If you have a choice, and if your own software supports it, pick the protocol that has the system's "most favored" status. On CompuServe, this is either the CompuServe Quick B or B protocol. On GEnie, either XMODEM-1K or YMODEM is the one to choose. (IBM-compatible owners using ProComm 2.4.3 should opt for XMODEM-1K on GEnie, but YMODEM on ProComm. See the DATASTORM/ProComm Round-Table on GEnie for the explanation.) On People/Link, the most favored protocol is WXMODEM. On Delphi you can do just about anything you want.

What's On the System?

Online utilities offer literally hundreds of features. There are so many features, in fact, that even experienced users can have trouble keeping them all straight. Part of the problem is that even today, some ten years since the first utility went live, most online executives don't really know what people want. That's understandable since they're trying to hit a moving, ever-changing target. But it leads to a shotgun approach in terms of services and features that can be very confusing to new online communicators.

Fortunately, there are at least two things you can do to make sense of it all. The first is to issue a command to download the system's complete index of services and features. This will give you a comprehensive, up-to-date overview of the entire system. The relevant commands or techniques for each system are highlighted in the profile chapters that follow.

The second thing you can do is realize that all online utility offerings can be classified under one of four categories: Information, Communications, Services, and SIGs (special-interest groups or clubs). These four categories provide an excellent matrix for getting a handle on any online utility, and you can use them as a roadmap to find your way around and identify the features that are most important to you.

Interestingly, when you begin to look at things from that perspective, you will discover that the online utilities are fundamentally the same in many areas. Each has its own personality, to be sure. And each has certain unique features important enough to cause you to choose it over its rivals. But all of them offer the same basic features, whether it's a function like electronic mail or a brand-name feature like the *Official Airline Guide* or Grolier's *Academic American Encyclopedia.*

This is the approach we will take in the sections that follow. We will look at the kinds of things you can expect to find in each of these four major categories on all utility systems. Since it is impossible to cover every feature on every system, the brand-name features cited below were chosen based on the frequency with which they show up on multiple utility services. Please bear in mind that while some are available on all systems, at this writing, some can be found only on one or two.

Information-Related Features

News, Weather, and Sports

All online utilities offer news features, and they love to highlight them in their promotional literature. But if you stop and think about it for a moment, with daily newspapers, round-the-clock news radio stations, and Turner Broadcasting's Cable News Network and Headline News operations so readily available, does it really make sense to pay to read news stories and headlines online? In most cases, the answer can only be "no."

We suspect that the reason all utilities offer news is that it is relatively easy to plug a newswire into an online service. After all, the newswires already exist and are already in electronic form. So it's not like building a feature from scratch. In addition, everyone has heard of the Associated Press, UPI, or *USA Today,* so when you tell them that this is one of the features your online utility offers, they immediately have a clear idea of at least part of what you offer. And if one utility offers news, all others must follow suit to appear competitive.

In reality, online news can be extraordinarily valuable. But not if you are limited to viewing a list of current headlines and choosing the corresponding wire service story you wish to read. On the other hand, if you can electronically search a database of past news and pull up every story pretaining to your subject of interest, you will have a very powerful tool. Unfortunately, at this writing, one can do this only on industrial-strength systems like DIALOG.

The utilities take a different tack to adding value. On some systems, you can create your own, customized electronic clipping service for news items. This means you can specify a series of keywords (such as Macintosh, Sculley, and hypercard) as your search profile. The utility mainframe will then automatically scan each incoming news story for those keywords. Whenever it finds a match, it will put a copy of the story in your online mail box or personal filing area.

This too can be a powerful tool—in the information business it is called "SDI" for "selective dissemination of information"—but some caveats apply. First, creating a successful search profile requires more than a little thought. You must try to think of the most unique word or phrase that would almost certainly appear in every story on your subject of interest. Otherwise, you'll end up receiving lots of irrelevant stories. Second, most utilities offering this feature charge extra for it. You will want to make sure you know exactly what costs are involved before plunging in.

Now, let's look at the major brand-name news and information features you can expect to find on most online utility services.

Accu-Weather. Regional, national, and international weather conditions. Detailed three-day forecasts for major metropolitan areas and three-day temperature and condition forecasts for over 100 major U.S. cities and 45 cities internationally.

AP Videotex. National and international news stories filed daily by Associated Press reporters. Features are edited to fit a 40-character line, the lowest common denominator for a so-called videotex service. Coverage includes business, sports, and weather as well. Approximately 250 news stories each day.

Bylines. From United Features Syndicate. Includes about 60 newspaper feature columns. Coverage includes astrology, politics, sports, health and beauty, "Miss Manners," "Jack Anderson," and more. Updated daily.

Kyodo News Service. Domestic and international news items and feature stories (in English) related to Japan. Economic and political news, lifestyle, Pacific Rim countries, and more. Updated daily.

Newsgrid. Specially edited stories and headlines drawn from the following newswire services: Agence France Presse, Associated Press, Deutsche Presse-Agentur, United Press International, Kyodo News Service, PR Newswire, Bridge Market Data, U.S. Securities and Exchange Commission, and Xinhua (New China) News Agency. National and international news, economic and corporate stories, stock market information, sports, and standing stories. Updated continuously throughout the day.

UPI News. Items from United Press International. Coverage includes international, U.S. general, regional, and state news; feature stories, regular columns, stock market reports, and more. Updated continuously.

USA Today Decisionlines. Categorized stories and information drawn from *USA Today* and over 200 other sources, including *The Boston Globe*, *The New York Times*, *The Philadelphia Inquirer*, news services, newsletters, and trade magazines. Information is presented as summaries in certain business and industry areas (such as banking, insurance, real estate, and energy). Decisionlines is updated daily.

Washington Post. Complete stories selected from the current edition of *The Washington Post*. Emphasis is on the federal government, especially congress, the administration, business and finance, science and technology, the courts, politics, and world and national events. Editorials and commentary are also included. Anywhere from 40 to 80 new stories each day.

Business News and Investment Information
The Business Wire. Complete press releases from over 9000 companies, institutions, and other organizations. Coverage includes new product announcements, legal actions, financial information and personnel changes, and corporate announcements deemed of general interest. Updated throughout the day.

McGraw-Hill News. Breaking news stories from McGraw-Hill correspondents all over the world. Follow-up stories prepared by McGraw-Hill News editors, drawing on the expertise of over 800 specialists, reporters, and editors in the McGraw-Hill organization (Standard & Poor's, *Business Week*, Data Resources Inc., and many more). Coverage includes mergers and acquisitions and other corporate developments, stock prices, major contract awards, leading economic indicators, business-related political and legal developments, regulatory decisions, and more. Updated every 15 minutes for a total of about 200 stories a day.

DISCLOSURE II. Corporate financials on over 12,000 publicly owned companies. Information is from the reports companies must file with the Securities and Exchange Commission. Reports include 10K, 20F, 10Q, 8K, proxy statements, annual reports, and name, address, and state of incorporation. There is much, much more as well, but since the implementation of DISCLOSURE II can vary, you may want to check the coverage available on your chosen system.

S & P MarketScope. Descriptive and financial information on over 4700 companies, including reports and analyses of the stock and bond markets and financial news.

Stock Quotes. All online utilities offer stock quotes. Usually, by agreement with the various exchanges, quote information is delayed 15 minutes. Current quotes may be available as a surcharged service. Also, since some services charge by the quote, while others levy no fee at all, you may want to investigate competing services carefully. Also, on most services you can also get commodity, precious metals, options, and virtually every other kind of quote, though you may have to ask where to find them.

TrendVest. Investment ratings for over 1600 common stocks, plus aggregate indicators for the stock, bond, and gold markets. Each rating constitutes a single number ($+42$, -178, and so on) based on market values, market price momentum, and other factors. High positive ratings indicate investment opportunities; low negative ratings indicate the issue should be viewed as an, er, "source of funds." Updated twice weekly.

ValueLine. Over 400,000 annual and quarterly time series covering over 200 variables (including financial histories, projections, earnings estimates, quarterly results, and risk measures), plus trading volume figures for approximately 1700 major industrial, transportation, utility, retail, bank, insurance, and savings and loan companies. And more.

Vestor. A database system based on proprietary software designed to evaluate stocks, options, commodities, and indexes. Covers data on more than 6000 securities that can be retrieved by up to 15 criteria. Allows you to produce short and long-term projections on how your securities portfolio will perform compared to the market in general. Updated daily and weekly.

Travel and Leisure
A–Z Travel Service. Corresponds to the *ABC Worldwide Hotel Guides*. Contains information on over 25,000 hotels worldwide (approximately 15,000 of which are in the United States). Includes address, phone, rates, credit cards accepted, room features (such as air condi-

tioner, telephone, doorman), services available (restaurants, baybsitters, language translators, and so on), recreational facilities (golf course, pool), and more. Updated with approximately 6000 revised records. You can search by price range, facilities, hotel name, and many other criteria.

Cineman. Over 4000 movie reviews written for syndication by film critic Jay A. Brown. Reviews consist of 60 to 90-word summaries, a list of principal stars, and a rating (great, good, fair, boring, or poor). Also, coming attractions for movies about to be released. The same reviews are published in more than 60 newspapers worldwide.

Eaasy Sabre. That's not a misspelling—the two a's stand for American Airlines, the producer of this database. Based on the Commercial Sabre product long available to professional travel agents, Eaasy Sabre is a searchable database of domestic and international flight schedules and fares for over 650 airlines. You can reserve flights on more than 300 carriers, order tickets, arrange and confirm hotel reservations, reserve rental cars, and check your bonus miles status if you belong to the American Airlines AAdvantage program.

Hollywood Hotline. Motion pictures, television, music, and home entertainment—Eliot Stein's Hollywood Hotline covers it all. Including programming, production, deals and contracts, new scripts, celebrities, and reviews. Plus summaries of major movies prior to release, ratings of the top ten in movies, television shows, record albums, videocassettes, and daily summaries of 14 soap operas. Plus book reviews of new best sellers.

Magazines. People who sell magazine advertising space tend to wax eloquent about the special relationship readers have with their product. Some print magazines have carried this a step further by extending the relationship into the online world. It's a good concept, though understandably it is currently limited to computer publications. On CompuServe one can tap into PCMAGNET (*PC Magazine*) or *Dr. Dobbs* to download programs that appeared in print and offer feedback to the editors and columnists. On Delphi there is *Rainbow* magazine and C*SIX, the *Computer Shopper* Information Exchange.

Official Airline Guide (OAG). Flight schedules and fares for over 750 North American and international airlines. Information includes origin and destination airports, fares, airline, type of plane, flight number, services provided, departure and arrival times, trip duration, number of stops. Also contains information from the *OAG Travel Planner Hotel & Motel RedBook* covering over 21,000 hotels, motels, and resorts in North America. Airline reservations can be made and confirmed online.

Reference
Grolier's Academic American Encyclopedia. Available on almost every system, this database includes the contents (sans pictures) of the 20-volume *Academic American Encyclopedia*. Over 34,000 articles on almost every subject, including tables, fact boxes, bibliographies, and cross-references. Updated four times a year. Grolier's isn't going to cause anyone at the *Encyclopedia Britannica* to lose much sleep, but it will give the publishers of other medium-duty encyclopedias aimed at school kids insomnia. Widely available and easy to use, it's the perfect way to whip together a school report Sunday night when you've spent the weekend playing. Pricing policies vary with the system—on Compu-Serve, for example, you must have a special Grolier's subscription to use this feature—so be sure to check.

Online Manuals and Supplementary Documentation. On some systems, the best way to learn about a feature is to open your capture buffer and simply type in HELP. Often this yields either information that is more current than you will find in your manual or information that never made it into the manual in the first place. Some systems—notably GEnie, BIX, and People/Link—even make their manuals available for downloading online.

Peterson's College Guides. Current information on over 3200 colleges and universities in the United States and Canada. Includes the college name, size, and location; its enrollment and admissions data; graduation requirements; athletics and the availability of athletic scholarships; special programs; career services; costs; and housing and financial aid availability. Corresponds to the *Peterson's Annual Guides to Undergraduate Study* series. You can locate schools on almost any criterion and keep adding specifications to narrow the set to a manageable number of institutions meeting your criteria.

Communications Features

Electronic Mail
All online utilities—and what's more, online services of every sort—let you send and receive messages from fellow subscribers. The technique is simple. You go into the mail area, type in your letter, tell the

system you're finished, and it prompts you for an address. The address is always the account or ID number of your correspondent, though many systems let you create an address book containing names and account numbers of frequent correspondents. This eliminates the need to key in a string of ID number digits each time. Once you have set up your address book, you can tell a system to send a letter to Bob or Betty, and it will know what to do.

When Bob or Betty next signs on, more than likely the system will send out a line reading "You have electronic mail waiting" before displaying its main menu. Your correspondent will then be free to go about his or her business or go to the mail feature and read your letter.

The letter will be displayed on Bob or Betty's screen as a text file, which your correspondent can capture to disk if desired. Most systems will also let the recipient of a letter file it in a personal storage area, forward it to another subscriber, or do something else with it.

Online Tip: Most systems will let you key in an immediate reply to a letter after it has been displayed. Often this is the best way to handle a reply, since the alternative is to download your mail, print it out, read your letters, and compose replies offline, and then sign on and send each of them. That may be the most cost-effective method, but it is also the most time consuming.

When a reply must be longer than a quick note or when you need to think carefully about what you want to say, sign off the system and use your word-processing program to prepare the text. Then sign back on and transmit the file to the mail system. You won't need to use a file-transfer protocol since you're dealing with pure text.

Under no circumstances should any human being be subjected to learning how to use a mainframe system's line-at-a-time editing program. Online utility manuals tend to go on at great length explaining how to use these dinosaurs, probably because they got most of the text from the company that made their host computers. Forget it. Use the word-processing program you have come to know and love and compose your text offline. Then sign on and transmit it. The mainframe will never know the difference.

You can almost always send courtesy copies of an electronic letter to one or more people, and you may be able to send your letter "return receipt requested." This means that the host system will take note of when your correspondent reads your letter and send a short report of that fact to your own mailbox. There may or may not be an extra charge for this service. And you may be able to store a list of names or account IDs on the system for use as a mailing or distribution list.

Fax, Telex, and other Transmission Options

Electronic mail has always suffered from at least two limitations. First, sending an instantly available message does no good at all if your correspondent doesn't check the mailbox on a regular basis. (For a small fee, MCI Mail will actually telephone a recipient to tell him or her your letter is waiting, but we'll discuss that in another chapter.)

The second limitation is the fact that you can only correspond with people who subscribe to the same system you do. Gradually we are moving toward the day when all e-mail systems will be interconnected, thanks to the X.400 and X.500 United-Nations-sponsored protocols. At this writing, for example, CompuServe and MCI Mail users can exchange messages, though you must know the correct subscriber ID in each case. But right now, that's about it.

Most online utilities do offer additional options, however. On GEnie you can send your message as a Western Union Mailgram, for example. Or you can send it to your correspondent's telex or TWX machine anywhere in the world. You can also receive replies sent from telex and TWX equipment to your electronic mailbox, but you will want to contact customer service in each case for specific addressing details.

Most important of all for many people, you can now send your letter to any Group III facsimile machine from most online utility systems. All you need to know here is the phone number of the target fax machine. Once you tell the system to send your letter, it will keep trying a certain number of times until it gets through. There are extra charges for all of these special services, so it can pay you to compare prices.

File-Transfer Options

On most systems it is also possible to exchange files with other users. Obviously one way to exchange a text file is to send it as an e-mail message. But if 100-percent accuracy is vital, as with your company's price list or a list of addresses and phone numbers, you may wish to use an error-checking transfer protocol. If the file is a binary program or contains machine-language characters (as with a spreadsheet), you *must* use a transfer protocol.

Some utility systems now allow you to upload a binary file to their e-mail systems and send it as an electronic letter. Your recipient, of course, must download it using a protocol as well. Another alternative is to upload the file to your personal storage space on the system, lower its protection level, and give your recipient permission to go into your space and download it.

Online Tip: The utilities are far ahead of dedicated electronic mail services in file-transfer options. At this writing, the only way to exchange machine-language files on MCI Mail is for both people to be using either Lotus Express or Lotus Desktop as their communications programs. Either that, or an expensive program supporting the MNP protocol. The lesson is that if you expect to regularly transfer files, stick with an online utility. At least for the present.

Pictures and Graphics

As we have emphasized throughout this chapter, online utilities display information exclusively in plain ASCII text (except Quantum Link, as noted previously). So you would think there would be no way to transfer graphic images from one user to another. In reality, there are several.

The most obvious is to prepare a graphic image with a drawing or paint program and upload it as a binary file. As long as your recipient has a program capable of displaying your program's image files, he or she will be able to see exactly what you created. If your recipient does not have such a program, the file will be useless.

Suppose, on the other hand, that you and all of your correspondents have the same graphics display program. Suppose that it is designed only to display files in an agreed-upon format. And suppose it is available for free. That, in effect, is how most online users these days exchange graphic information. The files may be .RLE (run-length encoded) or .GIF (graphics interchange format). Free display programs are available for both. It is even possible for Macintosh and IBM users to display each other's graphics files (albeit with the help of a free translation program).

The best place to get appropriate information for your brand of computer is the Graphics Support Forum on CompuServe. (Key in GO GRAPHICS.) CompuServe, in fact, has always been the site of the most graphics/communications-related activity among the utilities. CB simulator users, for example, can send their photographs to Compu-Serve, where they will be scanned and stored as a file in the CB Forum for anyone to download. (People/Link has a similar feature.) The Hollywood Hotline feature on CompuServe offers pictures of movie stars for downloading. And the infamous FBI's Ten Most Wanted list feature can give you graphic images of criminals, tattoos and all.

CB Simulators: Real-time Conferencing and Chat

Most systems now offer a "CB simulator" feature for real-time, multi-person conversations online. CompuServe originated the feature years ago at a time when everyone and his "good buddy" neighbor were buying citizen band radios. That fad has past, but the name for this feature has stuck, and it's really rather descriptive of what you will encounter online. The feature proved to be so popular and profitable that it is now available nearly everywhere. In fact, the People/Link system was created primarily to offer CB facilities at a lower cost than competing systems.

Briefly, when you opt for CB, you will be asked to key in the handle by which you would like to be known for the current session. No one will know your real name (unless you tell them), but they will be able to see your user ID. Accordingly, under no circumstances should you ever key in your password, even if some official-sounding notice appears on the screen requesting you to do so. No online system ever asks users to key in their passwords at any time other than sign-on. Ever. If you see such a message, rest assured some joker is trying to rip you off.

When you've selected your handle, you will be asked to choose the band (A, B, C, and so on) and channel (1 to 40) you wish to enter. To help you make a choice, most systems will show you how many people are currently tuned to each channel.

Tuning into a well-populated channel can be like entering a noisy room. Lines of text will immediately begin appearing on your screen, each one beginning with a person's identifying handle, followed by whatever it is he or she has just said. Multiple, overlaid conversations are the norm, and it can take a little getting used to all the chatter. But it can be well worth your effort.

Our advice is to simply plunge right in. The system you are using may automatically announce the fact that you have joined the group. But whether it does or not, it is considered polite to key in a greeting like "Hi, all!" or "What's happening," or something else to personally acknowledge the fact that you have entered the room. CBers who simply sit in the background and watch are called "lurkers" and are generally frowned upon.

More than likely some or all of the people there will fire off a quick word of welcome. They may then return to their conversations or invite you to say where you're calling from or otherwise start to chat. Usually you'll want to watch the conversation for a bit to gauge its drift and then add a comment should the spirit move you. If nothing interests you on one channel, you can easily tune to another. Indeed, on some systems you can opt to monitor two or three channels while actually participating on another.

CB simulator features typically offer a battery of special commands. If the noise on a channel is interfering with your conversation, you and your friends can opt for a private conversation. You can even opt to scramble it so that it will be completely private. If you want to concentrate on just a few users you can do so, or you can squelch the transmissions of one or more users. If you want to see the handles of everyone using the CB simulator and the channels to which they are tuned, you can do that as well.

CB is a wonderful place to meet people and to engage in true mind-to-mind communication, free of the prejudice of looks, sex, race, and the other impediments that prevent real communication in the real world. Remember, no one can see you or hear you. They know you only through the words you type at your keyboard. Not surprisingly, perhaps, many a deep and lasting friendship has taken root on CB. And on most systems, an entire electronic society has grown up around CB and its "regulars." You can view and use it as a feature, but if you like, it can become an entire world.

Online Tip: Several weddings have resulted from CB friendships. And in more than one case, the wedding ceremony was held online. The minister was in one state, the parents in two other states, and the happy couple in a fourth. Guests attended from all over the country. And when the ceremony was over, everyone threw rice by hitting their hyphen keys: - - - - -.

Other Communications Features

Most systems also have a "feedback" feature that lets you send a message, question, complaint, or whatever directly to customer service. In most cases a representative will reply by e-mail in a day or so. There may also be a member directory to use in locating people with similar interests or needed expertise. Listings in such directories are usually voluntary, so the fact that you don't find a particular person there doesn't mean he or she isn't on the system. To enter your own listing, you normally key in your first name (and your last name if you like) and several subjects of interest. Other subscribers will then be able to search the directory for a name, account number, or specified interest and message you by e-mail. Some systems, like Delphi, have a command to tell you who is currently logged onto the system. Then, using a different command, you can send them an instant request to chat.

Finally, most systems have a classified ad or bulletin board section. The advantage here is that you can search for items or topics of interest. The disadvantage is that the search language most utilities make available isn't very powerful. Often you must specify a keyword exactly, without using wildcards, for example. This problem is exacerbated by the fact that most people who post ads tend not to be very careful about the keywords they tack on. If you search on the keyword "Apple," you may get notices dealing with everything from commercial software to printer ribbons to user groups to bulletin board systems, for example.

Service-Related Features

"Services" is the category under which one can place everything a system offers that isn't clearly centered on either communications or information. Admittedly, it is a fine line, for obviously a service involves both communication and information. The difference is that most service features take the information you communicate to them and do something with it. Some program or party other than you and your fellow subscribers is involved.

Shopping Services

For example, most systems offer some kind of shopping and travel services. Online shopping features fall into two distinct categories of their own. On the one hand, there are small "boutiques" offering limited selections of products, and on the other there are services offering a huge searchable database of products. In our opinion, only the latter are worth serious consideration. But online boutiques are in fashion right now, so we must say a word or two about them as well.

Like so many things among the online utilities, the boutique concept started with CompuServe. Some years ago CompuServe, in conjunction with L. M. Berry & Company, developed The Electronic Mall. CompuServe now owns the operation, lock, stock, and escalator and reports a high level of success. Other systems now have malls of their own, though none is as extensive as CompuServe's.

Briefly, each store in an online mall consists of a list of selected items and their descriptions. There is also, of course, a checkout counter where you make your final purchase decisions. The cachet is in the merchants one can buy from in this way. The list includes Bloomingdales, Brooks Brothers, a gourmet coffee shop, a shop selling fruit direct from Florida, videotape and record stores, flower shops, and other purveyors of generally upscale merchandise. The problem is that you can't order just anything in the real-life store. You can usually send for a free mail-order catalog, but as far as online ordering is concerned, you are usually limited to just a few items. Nor, in most cases, are you going to save any money by shopping online in this way. So frankly, what's the point?

We'll take a glossy, four-color catalog, an 800 number, and a credit card any day.

Comp-u-Store, the leading database-style shopping service, is something else again. Available on almost every system, the Comp-u-Store database contains over 250,000 products and their descriptions. You can thus search for, say, the VCR that has all of the features that are most important to you and compare brands and prices. And when you buy from Comp-u-Store, the company guarantees you the lowest possible price. If you see a product advertised for less within 30 days of your purchase, the company will refund the difference. Comp-u-Store, in short, uses online computer technology to add convenience and value, and we'll have more to say about it in Chapter 26.

Another shopping feature worthy of special mention is the Boston Computer Exchange (BCE), currently available on both Delphi and CompuServe. This service specializes in matching buyers and sellers of used computer equipment. Buyer and seller negotiate their own price and BCE takes its commission from the seller. BCE uses the technology to let you scan a constantly changing database of equipment for the machine and price range you want. If you find one or more listings of interest, you can tell the service what you want and it will put you in touch with the seller.

Travel Services

In general, online travel-related services appear to have undergone a contraction in recent years. Perhaps planning a trip loses something without color brochures (and now, videotapes). In any case, the Official Airline Guide and Eaasy Sabre services discussed previously certainly qualify as travel services. As noted, once you have chosen your flight(s), you can book your ticket online.

In the future, travel agencies may once again operate online features as they did in the past. For now, your main choice is American Express Advance, a feature for American Express cardmembers that is available on several systems. Here you can shop for and reserve American Express vacation packages and other products. You can also check the current status of your account.

Games

Two main types of games are available from the online utilities. There are single-player games, like Adventure, Chess, or trivia, which you play against the computer. And there are multiplayer games that you play with and against people all over the country. Some systems try to spice up single-player games by operating contests in which scores are kept and matched against other players. But in general, there is little point to paying hard-earned connect-time dollars to play a game you can play for free offline on your own system. The public domain and share-ware collections for all brands of computers are filled with games, and all of them are available for the price of a disk and postage. Ask some-one at your favorite computer store for the names of computer user groups in your area. Join the group and ask the software librarian which game disks he or she recommends.

Multiplayer games, in contrast, can be a true online adventure. In fact, they can be addictive. Imagine entering a Star-Trek-like universe as the captain of an escort vessel and spotting an enemy ship in your sector. The captain of that ship could be physically located anywhere in the country. You don't know his or her name or level of experience. All you know is that right now the ship is locked in on you and is preparing to launch photon torpedos. What do you do?

Now imagine a universe filled with ships, captains, and crews of every description, each with a different configuration of powers, cruis-ing ranges, and good or bad intentions. Alliances are a natural, and more than one wolf pack has been formed to meet regularly online and take on all comers. In the clubhouse afterwards, there's time to chat via the CB facility and exchange lies about your prowess.

The only caveat—aside from "Keep your head down"—is that you *will* have to use your imagination. You'll be dealing with text characters on a screen whose movements you can view only in sequential snap-shots. And, of course, you'll have to learn the game—or games, for there are several of them.

Account-Related Services

Finally, all online utilities have account-related services. These are the options you use to change your password, customize your user pro-file, check your current or past bills, get a summary of the system's connect-time and surcharge rates, locate telephone access numbers, and get online help, command summaries, and an index of features. Two services at this writing—Delphi and CompuServe—also offer guided tours designed to introduce new users to the system.

Special-Interest Groups (SIGs)

Online special-interest groups or "SIGs" may well be the single most unique and significant feature in the entire electronic universe. You don't have to send your mail electronically, and you don't have to do your shopping online. You can get your news from many other sources, and if you need information, you can go to a library. The online option adds convenience and power to all of these activities, but it is not your only alternative.

Not so with special-interest groups. There is no other way to bring thousands—yea, tens of thousands—of people together to exchange information, solve each other's problems, discuss matters of common interest, and trade computer files and programs. And we're not talking about just people living in the United States or North America. Most online special-interest groups have members located all over the world.

Special-interest groups synergistically combine the various communication and information features we've already discussed into a whole that is easily greater than the sum of its parts. Each exists as a free-standing feature on a system. Or to put it another way, if you think of entering an online utility as comparable to strolling through the ivy-covered iron gates of a college campus—one with many separate buildings, each dedicated to a particular function—the SIGs can be found on fraternity or sorority row.

Entering a SIG is thus like entering a clubhouse. You'll find that each clubhouse has a bulletin board for posting and exchanging messages, one or more meeting rooms for all-night bull sessions or lectures from special guests, plus a library packed with interesting files and vast numbers of public domain and shareware programs. Unlike a college fraternity, sorority, or eating club, SIGs are devoted to one particular interest. There are thus SIGs for people interested in organic gardening, photography and videotaping, science fiction, CB, Christian ethics, telecommuting and working from home, art, music, rock 'n roll, genealogy, law, medicine, scuba, entrepreneuring, and many, many other subjects. Not surprisingly, there are SIGs for virtually every make and model of personal computer, and there are SIGs for users of specific commercial and shareware programs (Ashton-Tate, Lotus, Red Ryder, Qmodem, and so on).

CompuServe originated the SIG concept years ago. On that system these features are now officially called "forums," though "SIG" is still widely used. Delphi follows the tradition by referring to their online groups as SIGs. GEnie uses the term "RoundTables" or "RTs." People/Link calls such groups "clubs," and BIX uses the word "conferences." We'll refer to all such groups as SIGs unless otherwise indicated.

As with the best fraternity houses, all SIGs have a manager. This is the person whose job it is to make sure everything runs smoothly. Different systems have different official titles (such as "forum administrator" or "club chairman"), but almost everyone refers to SIG managers as "sysops" (pronounced "sis-op"). That's short for "system operator," and it is derived directly from the BBS world.

Running a good SIG takes a lot of time and effort, and all sysops on commercial systems are compensated for their labors. Generally they receive between two to fifteen percent of the connect-time dollars you spend using the SIGs they run. Since the online system does not charge you any more for using a SIG than for your other activities, and since compensation acts as an incentive to the sysop and his or her assistants to run a vigorous, interesting operation, this policy works out well for everyone. Indeed, some sysops earn five and six-figure incomes from their activities.

Online Tip: If being a sysop on a commercial system sounds intriguing, you should know that all of these systems are looking for people with good ideas for SIGs. You can't go into it half-heartedly, and if your main goal is the free connect time sysops receive, you might as well forget it. On the other hand, if you look at it as a business and are willing to make the large commitment of time and energy required to run a first-class SIG, it can be a very worthwhile and profitable enterprise.

You should be aware, however, that the contractual arrangements offered by each online system differ widely. On some systems, for example, you may find that you don't own the SIG or any of its files. (In other words, the SIG can continue without you should you wish to terminate your relationship.) Other systems see their role as similar to that of a landlord renting space to a retail store. Should you want to leave when the lease is up, you take everything with you and the space becomes vacant.

Clearly, as in any business deal, it pays to survey the field and the various offerings and get some professional advice before making a commitment. You can start by contacting *all* of the systems and requesting copies of their system operator/SIG contracts.

How to Use a SIG

When you access a SIG feature for the first time, you will be shown some information describing the organization, its purpose and focus, and inviting you to join. By all means do so. Joining involves merely keying in your first and last name and hitting <Enter>. There is no cost or continuing obligation, but in most cases, you will not be allowed to download any files until you become a member.

Once you're in, you'll find that most SIGs use the same floorplan. The features of this floorplan include a public message exchange that makes it possible for you to ask a question ("Does anyone know how to connect a PS/2 Model 30 to a Diablo printer?") that can be read and responded to by all SIG members. There may also be a bulletin board for members to post for sale, wanted, and other notices. There is usually a keyword-searchable membership directory to help you locate people with similar interests. There may also be some kind of CB-like conferencing facility to let you converse in real time with other SIG members or attend online lectures and question-and-answer sessions with industry notables.

Each online system does things in a slightly different way. For example, as previously discussed, most systems as a whole have a large real-time conferencing facility called the "CB simulator." But each SIG will have its own real-time conferencing area for use by SIG members and guests. The same commands apply in both cases.

SIGs may also have their own public and private message exchange that is quite separate from the system's main electronic mail facility. Message boards tend to keep their messages classified by topic. (You cannot leave a message on most boards until you tell the system which of the available topics to file it under.) This means that in addition to searching the entire message base, you can also opt to search or read just those messages on a particular topic.

Following the Thread

One key point regarding SIG messages is the concept of "threads." Each message is automatically given a number by the system. And each time you read a given message, you are free to key in a reply, which is also given a number. Thus, if someone asks a question like "Can anyone suggest some good hypercard stacks for me to use on my Mac SE?" his or her message may be given the number 100. People will read and respond to that message at various times. But since many messages on different topics may be placed on the board in the meantime, the responses to message 100 may have numbers like 147, 206, 332, and so on.

This is where the thread concept comes in. If you are interested in stackware for your Mac, you might search the message base on the keyword "stacks" and be shown message 100. After reading the message, you will be given the option of reading the next message meeting your search criterion (it could be message 101 or message 189, there is no way to know). Or, you will be told that there are replies to message 100 and be given the option to read them. In other words, you will be able to follow the thread of a given message—in this case, to see what other members of the SIG have recommended to the person who sent message 100—if you like. That's all there is to it.

Two final notes on SIG message boards. First, most have a limited capacity. Once that capacity is reached, each new message causes the oldest message to "scroll off the board." In a really active SIG a board can turn over completely every three or four days, even with a capacity of thousands of messages. Once a message has scrolled off the board, it is lost forever. Unless the sysop has taken steps to preserve it. And that is the second point. Sometimes a series of messages is so informative, useful, or entertaining that the SIG sysop will put the entire thread into a file and store it in the library for all to download. Library files are permanent, until the sysop decides to remove them.

SIG Libraries Are the Treasure Rooms

All SIGs on all systems have file libraries. Libraries can contain everything from message board threads and transcripts of real-time conferences to articles excerpted from user group magazines. They may also contain musical compositions or transcriptions, user-created graphic images, machine-language programs (with or without BASIC, C, Pascal, or assembler source code), and enough small utility programs, games, and full-featured applications packages to keep you busy for years.

The techniques for tapping these treasure houses on each online utility system are detailed in *Alfred Glossbrenner's Master Guide to FREE Software for IBMs and Compatible Computers* (St. Martin's Press, New York). Each system does things a little differently, but once you know how to tap one SIG on a given system, you automatically know how to tap every other SIG on that system. The brand of computer you use makes no difference.

Briefly, all SIG files have four parts: the filename, a tacked-on list of keywords, a paragraph of description, and the file itself. The person who uploads the file is responsible for supplying each of these components. Most SIG libraries have a "browse" function that lets you specify a keyword and read the descriptions of matching files.

Better still, most computer SIG sysops regularly prepare a single master file giving the name of every file in the library, its size in kilobytes, and a one-sentence description. These are the files to look for. Download them, sign off, then use your word-processing program's "search" function or some other program to locate interesting files. Make a note of the names and library locations of these files. Then sign back on and read their associated one-paragraph descriptions. Then, and only then, make your decision on whether or not to download the file.

Most SIGs have files describing how to use their libraries, where to find the master list file, and how to handle files that have been compressed to reduce transmission time. The names of these files may appear on the greeting screen each time you enter a SIG, or they may be part of the new member announcement. If no such information is given, or if you need further assistance, don't hesitate to send a message to the sysop.

We should also say a word about so-called "virus" programs. Certainly such things exist, but the popular press has grossly exaggerated the threat. Even so, it is worth knowing that no one can download a file someone else has uploaded to a SIG until it has been reviewed and approved by the sysop. And by contract, most sysops must vet every file before making it available for downloading. If they were to let something slip through, there is a very good chance that they would lose their SIG franchise and the income it produces. So they have an incentive to be extra vigilant.

Conclusion

This, then, is the essential online utility. In the chapters that follow we'll see how utility concept has been applied by seven different systems. Then we'll take a look at what the future may hold in Chapter 12. We're going to spend quite a bit of time on CompuServe, for not only does it have hundreds of thousands more subscribers (at this writing) than anyone else, it also offers more features. There is probably no direct correlation between those two facts. CompuServe was one of the originators of the business and so was in a position to try many different things. Most of the systems that have come into being since deliberately concentrate on just those features CompuServe has proven are the most successful.

...5...

CompuServe

CompuServe Information Service, Inc.
5000 Arlington Centre Boulevard
Columbus, OH 43220
(617) 457–8600

CUSTOMER SERVICE
(800) 848–8990

In Ohio and outside the
continental United
States:
(617) 457–8650

Customer Service Hours
(Eastern standard time)

Mon.–Fri.: 8:00 A.M.–midnight
Weekends: 2:00 P.M.–midnight

Initial Subscription:

There are lots of ways to subscribe to CompuServe, and each of them includes a certain amount of free time on the system. Modems and commercially sold communications programs, for example, often include CompuServe IntroPaks as a special promotion. An IntroPak is a 45-page descriptive brochure that includes a sealed envelope with an account number and initial password good for perhaps $15 worth of free connect time.

You might also purchase the Radio Shack Universal Sign-Up Kit (product number 26-2224; $19.95). Available from your local Radio Shack store, this includes subscriptions to both CompuServe and the Dow Jones News/Retrieval Service, plus an hour of free time on each system. The main system manual, *The CompuServe User's*

Guide, is not included, but you can order it once you are online for a total postage-paid cost of $12.95. (Note that CompuServe also publishes a variety of supplemental manuals that discuss specific features in great detail—like financial features, the CB Simulator, or various online games. Contact customer service or key in GO ORDER for the latest list.)

The best deal may be the CompuServe Subscription Kit. This package includes the user's guide, an account number, and password good for $25 of free time. Available in computer stores at a list price of $39.95, you can also order it at a discount from mail-order firms. At this writing, for example, the PC Connection (800–243–8088) in Marlow, New Hampshire sells CompuServe Subscription Kits for $24 plus $2 for shipping and handling.

CompuServe charges a membership support fee of $1.50 per month. The fee is waived for the first three months of a new membership.

See the special discount offer at the end of this book for a money-saving offer.

Access:

Telenet, Tymnet, the CompuServe Network, and direct dial. Contact CompuServe for more information concerning access via Computer Sciences Corporation (International Access Network) and LATA networks.

For detailed instructions on accessing CompuServe from virtually any country, key in GO INTERNATIONAL. This feature is likely to be most useful to U.S. subscribers planning a trip abroad. However, if you do not live in North America and are interested in subscribing, you might write to customer service and request a printout of the online access information for your country.

Rates:

CompuServe has two primary rates: one for 300 bps and one for 1200 or 2400-bps communications. These rates are the same, regardless of the time of day. The cost of using CompuServe's own packet-switching network remains the same as well (30¢ an hour). What changes are the rates charged by Telenet and Tymnet, the "via others" in the table that follows.

Connect time is billed in one-minute increments, with a minimum of one minute per session. Connect-time rates do not include communications network surcharges or product surcharges such as those discussed below. Several features are available free of charge (no connect-time cost), including billing information, the network access phone list, the personal profile area, "What's New," the system's index, Membership Feedback, the Practice Forum, online ordering, and the CompuServe Tour.

Service between the hours of 5:00 A.M. and 8:00 A.M. weekdays is on an as-available basis.

CompuServe Connect Rates

Prime Time
(Mon.–Fri.: 8:00 A.M.–7:00 P.M.)

Speed (bps)	CompuServe connect time (per hour)	Packet-switching network charges (per hour)	TOTAL (per hour)	TOTAL (per minute)
300	$6.00	30¢ via CompuServe	$6.30	11¢
		$12 via others	$18.00	30¢
1200/	$12.50	30¢ via CompuServe	$12.85	22¢
2400		$12 via others	$22.50	41¢

Nonprime Time
(Mon.–Fri.: 7:00 P.M.–8:00 A.M., and all day weekends and holidays

Speed (bps)	CompuServe connect time (per hour)	Packet-switching network charges (per hour)	TOTAL (per hour)	TOTAL (per minute)
300	$6.00	30¢ via CompuServe	$6.25	11¢
		$2 via others	$8.00	14¢
1200/	$12.50	30¢ via CompuServe	$12.80	22¢
2400		$2 via others	$14.50	25¢

Surcharges and Extras:

CompuServe has always taken a cafeteria-style approach to pricing. Everyone pays the same low connect rate, but separately priced extras are available for those who want them. Investment and demographic reports, commodities quotes, current and historical stock quotes, and other information, for example, is sold by the piece. A single commodity quote may cost a nickel, while an ACORN Target Marketing Report may be as much as $100.

Alternatively, some features may carry connect-time surcharges. For example, PaperChase, a menu-driven feature that lets you search the MEDLINE database operated by the National Library of Medicine, costs an additional $24 per hour during prime time and $10 per hour more during evening time. The AP Sports Wire carries a $15 per hour surcharge, regardless of the time of day. And so on.

It is important not to get the wrong impression, however. Surcharges are the exception. Most of what you do on CompuServe is billed at the regular rate. By making additional features available at an additional cost, CompuServe does not force you to subsidize or otherwise pay for features you yourself may never use.

One can join the CB Club (GO CBCLUB) and elect to pay a flat fee of $70 a month for unlimited nonprime-time usage of the CB Simulator. A reduced rate plan is also available. In return for paying either $25 or $100 a month, you can sign on at any time of day and pay either $4 an hour or $1 an hour for unlimited usage. Normal network communications charges apply at all times. At this writing 2400-bps service is not included.

For a complete summary of current costs, surcharges, and optional extras, key in GO RATES at any menu prompt on the system.

Personal Defaults:

Key in GO TERMINAL and select the item on the resulting menu that reads "View or Change Current Terminal Parameters." This produces a list of items you may change. To eliminate pauses when using most sections of CompuServe, set your "screen size" to 0 lines. In most cases, all of the other settings will be fine (terminal type, other; form feeds, simulated; and so on). However, unless you are using one of CompuServe's own VIDTEX communication software packages, you should probably turn the "inquiry for VIDTEX" setting off, since it can save time by eliminating the inquiry each time you sign on.

From the same TERMINAL/OPTIONS menu, choose "Setting your Logon Actions" and opt to have the system notify you if you have electronic mail waiting whenever you sign on.

Scram Command: Control-C or BREAK

Sign-Off Command: OFF

Protocols: CompuServe B and Quick B, XMODEM, and Kermit

Special Notes:

In addition to its standard service, CompuServe also offers what it calls its "Executive Option." Benefits include a ten-percent dis-

count on all CompuServe documentation and products, additional
free storage space on the system, access to certain special (largely
financial) features, and access to the system's Executive News
Service electronic clipping feature. There are other benefits as
well.

Two costs are involved. There is an initial one-time sign-up fee
of $5 if you sign up when you first activate your subscription. If
you want to switch later, the cost will be $10. The second cost is a
minimum usage requirement of $10 a month. (CompuServe's $1.50
per month subscription fee counts toward that minimum.) At 22¢ a
minute, that's about 45 minutes of connect time a month or about
11 minutes a week. Since most people easily spend that much time
on the system in the normal course of things, the Executive Option
is worth strong consideration, even if you're not an executive.

CompuServe sells communications software specifically designed
for use with the system (GO ORDER). The programs are reasonably priced ($40 to $60) and versions are available for most brands
of computers. Macintosh users should be sure to look at the
CompuServe Navigator.

These programs generally represent a good value, but in our
opinion it is worth holding off until you see how you will be using
the system. The built-in graphics display capabilities these programs offer are available for free in Data Library 3 (graphics en-
coders/decoders) Graphics Support SIG (GO GRAPHICS), and
IBM users at least may prefer the special SIG accessing features
of AutoSIG (free) or TAPCIS (shareware) to those offered by
CompuServe's Professional Connection program.

System Overview:
New subscribers might consider keying in GO TOUR. This leads
to a series of menus offering explanations of most major Compu-
Serve features. You can get off the bus any time you like, or enter
a command to actually begin using one of the features being discussed. Communications costs apply, but there is no connect-time
cost for taking the Tour.

A more comprehensive technique is to simply download the system's index by GO-ing IND and opting to view the complete list of
system features and topics and the quick command words you can
use to reach them. While you're there, we suggest using the IN-
DEX search feature and specifying the keyword FORUM. (Connect-time charges are suspended while you are using the INDEX
feature.) This will produce a list of every SIG currently on the

system. Even experienced users will probably want to take these two steps every six months or so. The velocity of change is that high.

────── **Figure 5.1. Typical CompuServe Greeting Menus** ──────

When you sign onto CompuServe you will see either the system's TOP menu or the "What's New" menu. "What's New" changes every Thursday and appears the next three times you sign on. After that, the TOP menu appears until "What's New" changes again.

```
CompuServe Information Service
  hh:mm EST Sunday dd-mmm-yy
        (Executive Option)
Last access: hh:mm dd-mmm-yy

      Copyright (C) 19--
    CompuServe Incorporated
      All Rights Reserved

CompuServe              TOP
  1 Subscriber Assistance
  2 Find a Topic
  3 Communications/Bulletin Bds.
  4 News/Weather/Sports
  5 Travel
  6 The Electronic MALL/Shopping
  7 Money Matters/Markets
  8 Entertainment/Games
  9 Home/Health/Education
 10 Reference
 11 Computers/Technology
 12 Business/Other Interests



                    — * —


What's New This Week            NEW
  1 Disclosure II Improves Appearance/Simplifies Surcharges
  2 IBM/Special Needs Forum Debuts Online
  3 Ticker Retrieval Adds S&P Online, Price/Volume Graph
  4 Receive Free Credit for Recommending a Member
  5 Portfolio Redesigned to Access Current Market Quotes
  6 Official Airline Guides Has New Recreation Guide
  7 Save $20 on IQuest TRW Business Credit Profiles
  8 New Access Number in California
  9 Online Today Daily Edition
 10 Uploads: New Forum Files
 11 Forum Conference Schedules
Enter Choice!
```

Capsule Summary

Long a subsidiary of H&R Block, the CompuServe Information Service has grown by accretion, starting small, with a limited number of offerings, and adding features and improvements in response to the needs and demands of its users. Although the company officially eschews the abbreviation due to a conflict with the Congressional Information Service database, most online users refer to CompuServe as "CIS," pronounced, "see-eye-ess."

Based in Columbus, Ohio, CompuServe began as a remote data processing time-sharing service in 1972, and that is still a substantial part of the firm's business. Indeed, while its consumer services are much better known, business users still account for more than half of the firm's revenue. Some 1300 companies, supported by a field staff in 31 U.S. cities, currently use CompuServe's packet-switching network and services.

For a fee, businesses and governmental organizations are offered telephone access to the company's Digital Equipment Corporation (DEC) and Systems Concepts SC-25 mainframes to run their payrolls, handle their accounting, and do everything else that a mainframe computer can do. Time-sharing saves individual clients the expense of buying and maintaining their own machines and gives them access to special CompuServe software and decision support features.

The trouble with running a time-sharing service is that once the workday rush is over, your large, expensive machines typically have a lot of idle capacity. Their circuits are warm, and they're still gobbling electricity. But they aren't earning any income. It's not an unusual problem, but in August of 1979, CompuServe came up with an unusual solution. The firm began to make its computers available to hobbyists and other individuals with computing expertise. Most of these folks built their own machines, either from a kit or from parts they acquired and assembled on their own. Thus for a very modest hardware investment, an individual could sign on to CompuServe during the idle evening and weekend hours and "play" with millions of dollars worth of mainframe computing power.

The system was called "MicroNET." For a one-time charge of $9.00 and a cost of $5.00 per hour, an individual not only received 128K bytes of personal storage space on the system, but could write and run programs in X-BASIC, Fortran, Pascal, Macro-10, APL, and other computer languages, run a variety of standard CompuServe programs, and communicate with other users through a rudimentary form of electronic mail.

The idea caught on, and soon CompuServe began to add such features as stock quotes, news and weather information, and magazine articles. These additional features evolved into what the firm used to call the "Videotex" (no *t*) or "Display" portion of its product. In 1980, a separate CompuServe Information Division was created within the company to develop and market the service, now available around the clock.

With the remote data processing business to serve as a cushion, the information division was able to grow with the market. Unlike The Source and other early competitors, CompuServe has never had to gamble on its ability to *create* a market to survive. Consequently, it was able to offer extremely attractive rates without requiring subscribers to commit themselves to a minimum monthly charge. Nor did it require a large initial subscription fee. Indeed, to this day CompuServe virtually gives away the "razors" (subscriptions) in hopes of making its money on the "blades" (connect time).

By any measurement, this has proved to be a winning formula. On March 16, 1989, CompuServe announced the signing of its 500,000th member. (The individual was showered with gifts from the merchants in CompuServe's Electronic Mall and given $100 in free connect time.) Most competing services can boast only a fraction of that number. And although exact figures are not available, there is every indication that the CompuServe Information Service is quite profitable, something that cannot be said about most consumer-oriented online services.

PPNs and Other Strange Terms

CompuServe is much easier to use today and its documentation is much slicker and more complete than the smeary mainframe line-printer-produced pages of the old days. But as a new user, you may still occasionally encounter vestiges of the system's computerist past.

For example, you may be downloading a message from someone and read about a person's "PPN." This is DEC-speak for "Project, Programer Number," and it simply refers to your CompuServe account number (for example, 70000,1234). Similarly, if you are using the CB Simulator or some of the multiplayer games, you will encounter the term "job number." This is more mainframe computerese for a person's electronic address while they are using those features. (In CB, for example, when you want to talk privately to a specific individual person, you address your request to the individual's "job number.")

_____ BEST BETS _____

Information

The Computer Library

If you're interested in computers of any kind, key in GO COMPLIB to reach The Computer Library. This is an easy-to-use, menu-driven version of The Computer Database Plus, a product of Ziff-Davis's Information Access Company (IAC) subsidiary that is available on major-league information systems like DIALOG and BRS. This feature allows you to search through back issues of some 130 computer-related publications, including *PC Magazine, BYTE, Mac User, Lotus, A+, Computer Shopper,* and many technical trade publications and journals. Hardware and software reviews, how-to pieces, and just about anything else that appeared in these magazines can be located in an instant.

At this writing, the Computer Library carries a surcharge of 40¢ per minute in connect time and $1 for each abstract (article summary) you read and $1.50 for each full text article you choose to view. For more information on this database, or a complete list of the publications it covers, contact Information Access Company, 362 Lakeside Drive, Foster City, CA 94404; (800) 227–8431.

PC Magazine and *Consumer Reports* Online

If you are an IBM or compatible user, you will also want to look at PCMAGNET, a feature operated by *PC Magazine* to facilitate reader feedback, information exchange, and the downloading of the free programs that appear in nearly every issue of that publication. And speaking of magazines, nearly everyone will want to consult *Consumer Reports* online (GO CONSUMER) at one time or another. Here you will be able to search for product reviews and recommendations published in the magazine during the last two years. Each report you download costs $2, but as long-time readers know, a single *Consumer Reports* article can save you hundreds of times that amount.

The Doctor Is In: PaperChase

If medicine interests you, or if you simply want to know more about virtually any medical matter under the sun, check into PaperChase. Developed by Boston's Beth Israel Hospital for the U.S. Department of Health and Human Services's National Library of Medicine (MEDLARS), PaperChase puts a user-friendly menu-driven front end

on the huge MEDLARS database. There is a surcharge for using Paper-
Chase, but the CompuServe gateway is still one of the cheapest ways of
tapping MEDLARS, as well as the most friendly.

Online Tip: As noted, both The Computer Library and Paper-
Chase are industrial-quality databases that have been equipped
with user-friendly front ends. Sort of full-strength information
with a human face. For access to an even greater universe of the
information industry's finest, key in GO IQUEST. This will take
you to the CompuServe version of the EasyNet system discussed
elsewhere in this book. EasyNet/IQUEST gives you access to
over 750 of the world's leading databases wrapped in a user-
friendly menu system. (Advanced users may specify native command mode if they like.) With these databases at your beck and
call, you can find out literally anything you want to know.

Financial Information to Rival DJN/R

CompuServe provides financial and investment information, of
course. These days, who doesn't? What most people don't know, however, is that CompuServe's offerings in these areas are so extensive
that they rival those available on the Dow Jones News/Retrieval Service (DJN/R). Not only that—you may find that CompuServe gives you
the identical information at a far lower price. Unfortunately, in the past
CompuServe has not done a very good job of telling people how to use
these features, a situation we tried to remedy in *Alfred Glossbrenner's
Master Guide to CompuServe* (Prentice-Hall Brady Books, 1987). That
book carries our highest recommendation. Naturally.

Electronic News Clipping

Finally, you should also consider the Executive News Service. The
problem with most online news services is that they are little more than
newswires that have been plugged into an online system. Cheap, easy,
and obvious, this kind of lash-up actually subtracts, instead of adds,
value. In return for paying around 25¢ a minute in connect time, you are
given the high honor and privilege of reading the identical headlines and
newstories you can get for free on television and almost for free in most
newspapers.

CompuServe's Executive News Service (GO ENS) is different. ENS
does not merely offer you a menu of the current headlines with an option to read the relevant stories. It also lets you create a filter of key-

words, concepts, and phrases and shunt relevant stories into one or more personal clipping folders *as they come in.*

The service operates round the clock, often electronically examining as many as 4000 stories a day on your behalf. Sources include the Associated Press national newswire, Reuters Financial Report, McGraw-Hill News, *The Washington Post,* and OTC NewsAlert. ENS is normally available only to Executive Option subscribers, though CompuServe occasionally runs monthly specials during which all subscribers can give it a whirl. ENS carries a $15 per hour connect-time surcharge at this writing.

You can tell the system to monitor any and all sources, and powerful commands are available to make your search profile(s) quite precise. You will want to spend a little time experimenting with those commands. But you would also do well to spend a little time offline getting your brain into search mode, particularly if you have never looked for keywords in a database before.

Remember, specifying APPLE and MACINTOSH will not only net you all stories about that brand of computer, but also all stories dealing with the Macintosh apple crop. You would thus probably want to add COMPUTER* (use the * to allow for plurals) to your search profile to increase your chances of getting only the information you really want. It doesn't take long to get the knack of online searching, but it does require some thought and some experimentation.

Communications

CompuServe offers a particularly rich selection of communications options, but at this writing, its many mail-related features aren't always easy to find. We'll look at those features in a moment. But first, a brief summary of non-mail-related communications features may be of interest.

BULLET and the CB Simulator

CompuServe's National Bulletin Board System (GO BULLET) is one feature you can safely skip. Though it has been made easier to use than in years past, to these eyes this feature is moribund and more than a little pathetic. On one recent foray there were a total of only 1100 for sale, wanted, and notice bulletins combined. This on a system boasting nearly half a million subscribers.

On the other hand, at some point every CompuServe subscriber should at least try the CB Simulator (GO CB). This feature connects you to a special "multiplayer host" computer capable of supporting and connecting many users simultaneously. There are two CB "bands" (A and B), each with 36 to 40 "channels" to carry on real-time conversations with people all over the continent or world.

There is something fascinating about conversing purely through words, with no visual or aural signals to enhance or hinder communication. And it's exciting to realize that in such a world you can be anybody you want to be. But ultimately, those who get the most out of CB are those who join the community of CompuServe CB users. That's easy to do (start by joining the CB Forum), but not if you are pretending to be anything other than yourself.

Electronic Mail with Many Options

In years past CompuServe had one of the worst mail systems in the entire electronic universe. Today it has one of the best. As with any electronic mail system, there are two major steps to the process: getting your message into the system and telling the system how and to whom you would like it delivered. CompuServe easily handles both binary files and ASCII text files. So if you want to, you can use EasyPlex to send a program, a spreadsheet file, or a graphic image file to your correspondent. To do so, you will have to upload it to CompuServe using one of the four or five available error-checking protocols.

You can also use a protocol to upload a text file. Normally this isn't necessary for text files, and it is certainly not the best way to handle your daily correspondence. But if it is crucial that a document arrive absolutely error-free, it is well worth the extra time and bother. In fact, we know of at least one magazine editor who insists that columnists and contributors use a protocol upload to send him their articles. The gentleman lives in an area served by noisy phone lines and simply got tired of garbled text.

Online Tip: The current size limit of EasyPlex files is 50K, whether text or binary. If you need to transmit a larger file to a correspondent, key in GO ACCESS to reach the public file-exchange area. Upload your file, make it invisible when prompted for your choices, and then send an EasyPlex message to your correspondent containing the file's name. Only someone who knows the correct filename can download an invisible file from ACCESS. Your file will be available for downloading by your correspondent within 24 hours of the time you uploaded it. Files can also be SUBmitted to ACCESS from your Personal Filing Area. (See your CompuServe manual for details.)

Online Tip: Here's a trick that can save you a lot of time and make transmitting your outgoing letters more convenient. Assuming your correspondent is not plagued with poor-quality phone lines, choose the COMPOSE option from the EasyPlex menu. Wait for the "Enter text" prompt, then do a non-protocol ASCII text upload from your computer to CompuServe. The system will think you are keying in the characters by hand, but it will accept them gladly. And CompuServe's default stop–start (X-ON/XOFF) flow control will prevent it from taking more than it can handle at one time. Just make sure your own software supports X-ON/XOFF and that this feature is enabled. (See Chapter 3 for details.) When the upload is over, key in /EX by hand to tell the system that you have finished entering text.

Once you have gotten a text file into the system, CompuServe will prompt you for its destination and the subject tag you wish it to carry. The system automatically adds "FROM:" information that includes your name, ID number, date, and time.

Most of the time you will probably be sending mail to another Compu-Serve subscriber, and thus will simply key in his or her ID number at the prompt. However, as noted, there *are* other options. The best way to get an overview of these options is to simply key in HELP at the EasyPlex menu prompt. This will generate a list of help topics, including telex, fax, and MCI Mail. Open your capture buffer and key in the topic of interest at the next prompt. The relevant help text will tell you exactly what to do to use these options, what they cost, and so on.

Briefly, you can send your EasyPlex text message to any telex or TWX machine anywhere in the world. You can send it to any Group 3 fax machine anywhere in the world. And you can send it to any MCI Mail subscriber as well. As explained in the online help text, you can also receive telex, TWX, and MCI Mail messages through your Compu-Serve account. Full instructions are given online for determining what each of these options will cost.

Services and SIGs

Many of CompuServe's online service options are considered separately in the applications-specific chapters later in this book. We should note here, however, that CompuServe created and operates the premier online shopping service, the Electronic Mall. This feature lets you review and order selected products from such leading merchants as

Bloomingdales, Brooks Brothers, Crabtree & Evelyn, Godiva Chocolates, and many more.

Home banking services are also available on the system, and there are at least two online stock trading services (Max Ule and Quick & Reilly). Both the Official Airline Guide and American Airline's Eaasy Sabre services are available. So too are a variety of domestic and international hotel and city guides to help you do your travel planning from your keyboard.

As for special-interest groups (SIGs), well, CompuServe invented the form. Or "forum," which is the term the company likes to use instead of SIGs. Over the years, most of the activity on the system has shifted into the SIGs. Indeed, in our opinion, the SIGs have become the very center of CompuServe.

The SIGs as Philosopher's Stone

We have no hard facts to support the notion, but it may be that by offering subscribers a vast array of features and letting them vote with their connect-time dollars on those they like best, CompuServe has discovered the secret to creating a successful consumer-oriented online service. It is a secret many companies have lost scores of millions of dollars trying to find over the past decade. But CompuServe appears to have it now.

Forums on CompuServe are used to meet people, find answers to questions, make business and professional contacts, discuss issues related to the forum's focus, and distribute information, graphic images, musical compositions, and public-domain and shareware software. Hardware and software companies use the forums to deliver customer support, answer questions, and alert users to their latest and greatest products.

Most forums hold regularly scheduled real-time online conferences using the same system software that makes the CB Simulator possible. These typically take place weeknights at 9:00 or 10:00 P.M. (eastern time) or on Sunday evening. Sometimes celebrity guests like Apple's John Sculley, Steve Wozniak, or even the occasional computer book author will be invited to appear. (When special guests are scheduled, the sysops will announce the fact in the forum bulletin that greets you as you enter.)

AutoSIG and TAPCIS

Though we would not recommend them for the casual SIG visitor, if you are an IBM user you should at least be aware of the existence of AutoSIG (ATO) and TAPCIS. These two programs are specifically designed to automate your interactions with CompuServe, particularly with CompuServe SIGs. They allow you to prepare messages and issue instructions while you are offline, and then sign on and have the software handle everything at the highest possible speed. The goal, of course, is to save on connect time. In fact, both programs have the ability to keep a monthly log of your online charges.

AutoSIG is a free program and is available in Data Library 1 of the IBM Communications forum (GO IBMCOM). TAPCIS is shareware. The registration fee is $79, which is completely refundable for 90 days if for any reason you wish to return the product. TAPCIS is available for downloading in the TAPCIS Forum (GO TAPCIS). AutoSIG and TAPCIS are also available from Glossbrenner's Choice (CommPack 6 and CommPack 7), as are the utilities needed to view RLE or GIF graphics on an IBM-compatible system. (See the back of this book for ordering details.)

SIGs on the System

There are so many SIGs, and each of them is so interesting, that it would be impossible to discuss them all. In addition, like everything else on CompuServe, SIGs do change. However it is crucial for brand-new online communicators to have some idea of what all the shouting's about. Accordingly, we have included here (Figure 5.2) the list of SIGs on CompuServe at this writing. It is a long list. But we urge you to examine it carefully, for it is certain that everyone will find something of interest here. As previously noted, you can download your own current SIG list by keying in GO IND and telling the system you want to search on the keyword FORUM.

———————— **Figure 5.2. SIGs on the System** ————————

Here is the complete list of forums or SIGs available on CompuServe at this writing. Given are both the forum name and the quick word you should "GO" to in order to reach it. Forums with the names of software publishers (Ashton-Tate, Autodesk, Nantucket, and so on) offer information, answers, and customer support. Forums bearing the names of computer brands usually have no connection with a company but serve as meeting places for users of those types of computers.

Forum Name	*Quick Word*
ADCIS Forum	ADCIS
AEJMC Forum	AEJMC
AI EXPERT Forum	AIE-100
ALDUS Forum	ALDUS

Forum Name	*Quick Word*
Adobe Forum	ADOBE
Amiga Arts Forum	AMIGAARTS
Amiga Tech Forum	AMIGATECH
Amiga Vendor Forum	AMIGAVENDOR
Apple Developers Forum	APPDEV
Apple Hyper Forum	APPHYP
Apple II & III Forum	APPLE
Apple Vendor A Forum	APVENA
Apple Vendor B Forum	APVENB
Apple Vendor Forum	APPVEN
Aquaria/Fish Forum	FISHNET
Ashton-Tate Forum	ASHFORUM
Ask3Com Forum	ASKFORUM
Astronomy Forum	ASTROFORUM
Atari 8-Bit Forum	ATARI8
Atari ST Arts Forum	ATARIARTS
Atari ST Productivity Forum	ATARIPRO
Atari Vendor Forum	ATARIVEN
Autodesk Software Forum	AUTODESK
Aviation Forum (AVSIG)	AVSIG
Bacchus Wine Forum	WINEFORUM
Borland Applications Forum	BORAPP
Borland International	BORLAND
Borland Programming Forum A	BPROGA
Borland Programming Forum B	BPROGB
Broadcast Professionals Forum	BPFORUM
CADKEY Forum	CADKEY
CB Forum	CBFORUM
CDROM Forum	CDROM
CP/M (CPM) Users Group	CPMFORUM
Cancer Forum	CANCER
Color Computer Forum	COCO
Comic Book Forum	COMIC
Commodore Arts and Games Forum	CBMART
Commodore Communications Forum	CBMCOM
Commodore Programming Forum	CBMPRG
Commodore Service Forum	CBMSER
Computer Club Forum	CLUB
Computer Consultant's Forum	CONSULT
Computer Language Magazine	CLM
Computer Training Forum	DPTRAIN

Forum Name	*Quick Word*
Consumer Electronics Forum	CEFORUM
Cooks Online Forum	COOKS
CrossTalk Forum	XTALK
DEC PC Forum	DECPC
DEC Users Network	DECUNET
Digital Research Forum	DRFORUM
Disabilities Forum	DISABILITIES
Dr. Dobb's Journal Forum	DDJFORUM
Educational Research Forum	EDRESEARCH
Educators Forum	EDFORUM
Epson Forum	EPSON
Financial Forums	FINFORUM
Florida Forum	FLORIDA
Foreign Language Forum	FLEFO
Forth Forum/Creative Solutions	FORTH
Forums	FORUMS
Game Vendors Forum	GAMVEN
Gamers Forum	GAMERS
Gaming Connection	GAMECO
Genealogy Forum	ROOTS
Good Earth Forum	GOODEARTH
Graphics Forum	GRAPHICS
Hardware Forums	HARDWARE
Health Forum	GOODHEALTH
Hewlett Packard Forum	HP
IBM Applications Forum	IBMAPP
IBM Communications Forum	IBMCOM
IBM Hardware Forum	IBMHW
IBM Junior Forum	IBMJR
IBM New Users Forum	IBMNEW
IBM Programming Forum	IBMPRO
IBM Special Needs Forum	IBMSPEC
IBM Systems/Utilities Forum	IBMSYS
IBM Users Network	IBMNET
Int'l Entrepreneurs' Network	USEN
Investors Forum	INVFORUM
Javelin User's Forum	JAVELIN
Journalism Forum	JFORUM
LDOS/TRSDOS6 Users Group	LDOS
LOGO Forum	LOGOFORUM
Legal Forum	LAWSIG

Forum Name	*Quick Word*
Literary Forum	LITFORUM
Living Videotext Forum	LVTFORUM
Lotus Integrated Prod. Forum	LTS-1042
Lotus Stand-Alone Prod. Forum	LTS-1608
MAUG(tm)	MAUG
MEDSIG	MEDSIG
MSC MIDI/Music Forum	MIDI
MUSUS Forum	MUSUS
Mac Arts and Entertain. Forum	MACFUN
Mac Personal Prod. Forum	MACPRO
Macintosh Business Forum	MACBIZ
MicroPro Forum	MICROPRO
Microsoft Applications Forum	MSAPP
Microsoft Connection	MSOFT
Microsoft Systems Forum	MSSYS
Military Veterans Services	VETERAN
Model Aviation Forum	MODELNET
Monogram Software	MONOGRAM
Motor Sports Forum	RACING
Multi-Player Games Forum	MPGAMES
NAIC Investor Education Forum	NAIC
Nantucket Forum	NANFORUM
National Issues & People Forum	ISSUES
National Issues Forum	ISSUESFORUM
Novell Forum ($)	NOVFORUM
Novell User Forum	NOVUSER
OS9 Forum	OS9
Outdoor Forum	OUTDOORFORUM
PC MagNet	PCMAGNET
PC Vendor Support Forum	PCVEN
PDP-11 Forum	PDP11
PR and Marketing Forum	PRSIG
Photogrphy Forum	PHOTOFORUM
Play-By-Mail Games Forum	PBMGAMES
Programmers Forum	PROGFORUM
Religion Forum	RELIGION
RockNet	ROCK
Role-Playing Games Forum	RPGAMES
Safetynet Forum	SAFETY
Sailing Forum	SAILING
Science Fiction Forum	SCI-FI

Forum Name	*Quick Word*
Science/Math Education Forum	SCIENCE
Scuba Forum	DIVING
Software Publishing Forum	SPCFORUM
Space Education Forum	SPACEED
Sports Forum	FANS
Students' Forum	STUFO
TANGENT Forum	TANGENT
TAPCIS Forum	TAPCIS
Tandy Model 100 Forum	M100SIG
Tandy Professional Forum	TRS80PRO
Texas Instruments Forum	TIFORUM
Texas Instruments News	TINEWS
Travel SIG	TRAVSIG
UNIX Forum	UNIXFORUM
VAX Forum	VAXFORUM
WITSIG	WITSIG
WordPerfect Support Grp Forum	WPSG
Working-From-Home Forum	WORK
Zenith Users Forum	ZENITH

Conclusion

In the second edition of this book the chapter on CompuServe was subtitled "The Place to Start." That advice is more applicable today than ever. We have no desire to play favorites, but as a former President once said, "Facts are stubborn things." And the fact is that CompuServe today is quite simply the premier online utility. More than that, with literally hundreds of thousands of subscribers, the system has reached a critical mass.

The IBM SIGs alone have more than 20,000 members—which means your chances of encountering someone who can answer your questions or help you find the hardware or software you're looking for are much greater than on smaller systems. With so many people contributing and with such a large audience, it also means that the best and latest public domain and shareware programs appear on CompuServe first. Finally, it means that if you are in business and want to correspond with a customer or client, the chances are very good that he or she will already have a CompuServe account. That makes things a lot easier for all concerned.

In short, we can say with complete confidence that *everyone* will find something of interest on CompuServe. And given the company's subscription policies, it is difficult to see how you can lose. If after exploring the system with the free time that comes with your subscription you find that it is not to your liking, you never need sign on again. The most you'll be in for is the $25 or so you paid for your subscription, if that. There is no continuing obligation.

CompuServe doesn't have everything its own way, of course. In fact, it has some very serious competition in the form of GEnie, a system sponsored by, of all things, a maker of lamps, light bulbs, and one or two other things—General Electric. And it is GEnie that we will turn to in the next chapter.

...6...

GEnie

GEnie
GE Information Services, Dept. 02B
401 North Washington Street
Rockville, MD 20850
(301) 340–4000

CUSTOMER SERVICE
(800) 638–9636
Includes Alaska,
Canada, and Hawaii

Customer Service Hours
(Eastern standard time)

Mon.–Fri.: 9:00 A.M.–midnight
Weekends and holidays: noon–8:00 P.M.

Initial Subscription:
"GEnie" stands for the General Electric Network for Information Exchange. There is a one-time sign-up charge of $29.95. There are no monthly minimums. This includes an attractively printed 200-page spiral-bound manual, a subscription to the GEnie *LiveWire* magazine, and a $10 usage credit.

See the special discount offer at the end of this book for a money-saving offer.

All subscriptions are initiated electronically. Set your system for 300 or 1200 bps, and since GEnie prefers to operate at half-duplex, enable your local echo when you call. U.S. callers should dial (800) 638–8369. In Canada, the data numbers to dial are as follows:

Toronto (416) 858–1230
Montreal (514) 333–1117

Calgary (403) 232–6121
Vancouver (604) 437–7313

When the connection has been established, hit three or more capital Hs (HHH) and <Enter>. The U#= ("user number") prompt will then appear. Key in the user number and ID given under "Special Deal" at the back of this book and hit <Enter>. You will then be welcomed to the online sign-up procedure.

Have your Visa, American Express, Discover, or MasterCard, ready. You will also be asked for your home and work phone numbers and your mother's maiden name. And you will be asked to key in an electronic mail address "handle" of your choosing. The limit is 12 alphanumeric characters (K.CARLETON is the example given online). It's worth thinking carefully about your electronic mail name, since changing it later incurs an administrative charge ($10). According to GEnie, "The very next business day, your GEnie representative will call you with your new GEnie User ID#. . . . In a few days you will receive your GEnie information kit." The kit contains your manual (if you have ordered one), a pocket reference guide booklet, and other materials.

Access:

The only way to access GEnie is through the network operated by its parent, GE Information Services. There are some 650 nodes in the United States, plus the Canadian nodes cited above. Additional cities may be added in the future. Started in 1964, the GE Information Services network now reaches 90 percent of the free world. That makes GEnie particularly attractive to non-U.S. users since it keeps communications costs to a minimum. Note that if you cannot toggle on a local echo (so you can see the characters you type when you're in half-duplex), send the system a Control-R during sign on. This must be done after the U#= prompt appears but before keying in your user ID and password. Do not press <Enter> after the Control-R.

Rates:

GEnie has both prime and a nonprime-time rates, both of which are very competitive. The U.S. rates shown below *include* Alaska, Hawaii, and Puerto Rico. Alaska and Hawaii are considered Pacific time and Puerto Rico is considered eastern. A surcharge (at all hours) of $2 per hour applies to nodes in a few low-density cities, and some GEnie features carry additional charges if you use them. All connect-time charges are billed in one-second increments. Key in RATES at any menu prompt to get the latest information.

GEnie Connect Rates

Prime Time
(Mon.–Fri.: 8:00 A.M.–6:00 P.M.)

Speed *(bps)*	*TOTAL* *(per hour)*	*TOTAL* *(per minute)*
300/1200/2400	$18.00	30¢

Nonprime Time
(Mon.–Fri.: 6:00 P.M.–8:00 A.M.,
and all day weekends and holidays)

Speed *(bps)*	*TOTAL* *(per hour)*	*TOTAL* *(per minute)*
300	$5.00	9¢
1200	$6.00	10¢
2400	$10.00	17¢

Surcharges and Extras:
  Some financial service products carry a surcharge of $5 an hour. Others, like GEnie Quotes and VESTOR, carry nonprime-time surcharges of $10 an hour and prime-time surcharges of $35 an hour.
  The "KnowledgeBase" portion of the Microsoft RoundTable carries a $5 per hour surcharge at all times. This is a searchable database of documents concerning Microsoft products, updated daily. The QuickNews clipping services requires a commitment of $25 a month, but the NewsGrid clipping service is free.
  Uploads to GEnie RoundTables are free during nonprime time. And there is a CB Club: $50 a month for unlimited nonprime-time usage of the CB Simulator. Network surcharges still apply. CB Clubers may communicate at 300, 1200, or 2400 bps.

Personal Defaults:
  Choose the "About GEnie . . ." option from the TOP menu, and from the subsidiary menu that will then appear, select "Password & User Settings." Follow the resulting menus and instructions. Alternatively, you may enter the word SET at any prompt to reach the terminal setup menu directly. To eliminate pauses, set your terminal page length to 0 lines per screen.

Scram Command:
>A true BREAK (250 milliseconds or longer). If your comm program cannot generate a true BREAK, you may select any single ASCII character to serve as your scram command. This is done in the terminal SETUP area described under "Personal Defaults," above.

Sign-Off Command: BYE

Protocols: XMODEM, implemented at the local node for much faster throughput.

Special Notes:
>GEnie supports both 7/E/1 and 8/N/1 comm parameters. It senses your settings through the series of upper or lowercase Hs (three or more separated by a pause of at least one tenth of a second) you send after you connect to the system. If you sign on at 8/N/1, do not be disturbed by any garbage characters that appear next to the U#= prompt. Simply pretend they are not there. At 7/E/1, no garbage characters will appear.

>As noted, the system operates at half-duplex, which means that if you are set for full-duplex you will not see the characters you type. You will thus have to echo characters locally. You may be tempted to set your Hayes-compatible intelligent modem to handle the local echo by sending it (ATF0). Don't do it. XMODEM transfers require a straight shot from host to local system, without interference from a well-intentioned though misguided smart modem. Use your comm program to toggle your local echo on instead.

System Overview:
>Key in INDEX, open your capture buffer, and on the menu that will then appear opt for "Long description in alphabetical order." This produces a lengthy printout that includes the feature name, category, system page number location, GE Mail address, and 200-word description of every feature on the system.

>Other index printout options are available, and you may wish to use them later on to keep up to date. But get this master list first. Once you're offline, you can use an MS-DOS program like Vernon Buerg's famous shareware LIST program to display the file and *search* for keywords of interest. Or simply bring the file into your word-processing program and use its search feature.

———————— **Figure 6.1. GEnie's Greeting or TOP Menu** ————————

This is the menu you will see (or a reasonable facsimile thereof) each time you sign on to GEnie. You can return here from nearly anywhere on the system by keying in TOP.

```
GEnie          TOP              Page   1
        GE Information Services
  1. About GEnie . . .   2. New on GEnie
  3. GE Mail            4. LiveWire CB
  5. Computing          6. Travel
  7. Finance            8. Shopping
  9. News              10. Games
 11. Professional      12. Leisure
 13. Reference         14. Logoff

Enter #, or <H>elp?
```

Capsule Overview

The key to understanding the General Electric Network for Information Exchange (GEnie) can be found in the advertising tagline the company used during its first year and a half of operation: "GEnie—Stay online longer, for less!" That initial 18 months—starting October 21, 1985—proved to be very successful for this pretender to the CompuServe throne, for it saw GEnie reach 63,000 subscribers.

By March 16, 1988, subscribership had topped the 100,000 mark, and the company treated its 100,000th subscriber to an all-expenses-paid family vacation. By the following March, 50,000 more GEnie subscribers were online. At this writing GEnie is closing in on the 200,000 mark, earning it the sobriquet of the world's fastest-growing online utility.

It is easy to see why. GEnie quite simply offers the features that most people want for a lot less. At this writing, you can shop at an electronic mall, send and receive mail, converse with others using a CB-like feature, join and participate in special-interest groups, get the latest news (electronically clipped for you, if you like), and play interactive games on GEnie—all for 45 to 60 percent less than CompuServe's nonprime 300/1200-bps connect-time rate of 22¢ per minute. At 2400 bps, GEnie is 23 percent cheaper than CompuServe.

CompuServe has the edge during prime time, however, at 22¢ versus 30¢ per minute for GEnie. But that edge isn't as great as it used to be, thanks to an aggressive new price structure introduced by GEnie on May 1, 1989. Our point here isn't so much the prices themselves. After all, prices can always change. The point is pricing competition of a vigor the online world has rarely seen. In our opinion, it bodes well for the consumer.

The similarities between the two systems are neither superficial nor accidental. In the first place, like CompuServe, General Electric has for many years operated a remote data processing business (GEIS) that was vastly underused during nonbusiness hours. Since such systems have to be up and running round the clock, offering a consumer-oriented service during nonbusiness hours made as much sense to General Electric as it did to CompuServe.

In the second place, GEnie's general manager, and one of the creative forces behind its design and implementation, is William H. Louden. Mr. Louden has been involved with online information utilities from the beginning. He was the second person to take out a CompuServe subscription back in the 1970s, and by 1980 he was working for the company. Over the next four years Bill Louden was involved in developing and marketing CompuServe's Consumer Information Service and in organizing that system's SIGs. He left CompuServe in 1984 and shortly after that General Electric asked him to design and implement its as-yet-unnamed consumer information service.

Mr. Louden cheerfully acknowledges that in shape and substance GEnie owes a lot to CompuServe. The gentleman clearly knows from long experience which features people want and are eager to use, and that is precisely what GEnie offers.

────────────────── **BEST BETS** ──────────────────

Information

GEnie offers the ubiquitous Grolier's *Academic American Encyclopedia*, Cineman movie reviews, USA Today Decisionlines, and similar information features. There is also a gateway connection to the Dow Jones News/Retrieval Service (DJN/R) for those who already have a subscription to DJN/R. (You can sign up via GEnie if you like.) And there is a RoundTable sponsored by *Computer Shopper* where, among other things, you can search for and download selected articles from that magazine.

GEnie QuickNews and NewsGrid

The most outstanding information-related feature, however, is GEnie QuickNews, followed by its implementation of NewsGrid. QuickNews costs $25 a month. In return, you may specify up to ten keywords or standing stories (explained in a moment) for your personal clipping search profile. Additional items in your profile cost $1 a month each. Stories matching your criteria are immediately routed to your GEnie mailbox for you to read the next time you sign on.

Information sources include all of the NewsGrid newswires listed below, USA Today Decisionlines, Soap Opera Updates (!), and several print and electronic columnists. The full text of each incoming story is scanned for QuickNews, as are the headline and any keywords that have been attached to the piece by NewsGrid editors. The search commands are fairly powerful. You can specify part of a word, for example, like COMPUT* to find COMPUTER, COMPUTERS, COMPUTING, and so on. You can also use AND and NOT logical operators.

A NewsGrid-only clipping service is also available to all GEnie subscribers free of charge. The main differences are that only the headlines of a story are scanned, you must specify exact words (no wildcards or truncation), and all information comes from NewsGrid. NewsGrid is a product of Comtex Scientific Corporation of Stamford, Connecticut (Phone 203–358–0007). The system offers news and financial information, sports, features, and political reporting from the following wire services:

The Associated Press	(United States)
United Press International	(United States)
Agence France Presse	(France)
Deutsche Presse-Agentur	(West Germany)
Kyodo	(Japan)
PR Newswire	(United States)
Xinhua	(Chinese News Agency)
INTEX	(Freight Futures)
Garvin Guybutler	(Federal Funds)
Security Trader's Handbook	(United States)
Panhandle Eastern Pipeline Corporation	(United States)

In addition, there are over 100 standing stories to choose among. These are short, often statistic-filled stories that appear at set times each day or on some other regular schedule. Examples include the American League Standings, Chicago Butter and Egg Selling Rates, U. S. New Home Sales, U. S. Leading Economic Indicators, NBA Box Scores, NHL Roundup, and so on. These stories are referenced by number, so make a point of downloading and printing out the complete list for your GEnie reference file.

Communications and Services

It would be nice to be able to say something positive about GEnie's electronic mail feature, but frankly, it is a remnant of the Dark Ages. There may well be a way to key in an instant reply to a letter you have just read, for example, but if there is we haven't found it. It is possible to send and receive programs and machine-language files with GEnie mail, and there are indications that an e-mail-to-fax feature will be implemented soon.

Meantime, if you want to send a message to someone who is not on the system, you can opt to send a GEnie Quick-Gram letter. The length is limited to 240 lines of no more than 69 characters each. The cost is $2 for the first 40 lines and 75¢ for each additional 40 lines.

GEnie's CB simulator feature is called the LiveWire, and it offers 40 channels and an array of commands quite similar to CompuServe's. There is also the CB-based Real Time Conference (RTC) with as many as 40 meeting rooms. The difference between RTC and CB is that in the former there is a discussion leader who can exercise some control over the proceedings.

GEnie offers a variety of shopping and travel services, including its own electronic mall and both the Official Airline Guide and American Airline's Eaasy Sabre. Of special note, however, are Rohn Engh's PhotoSource International (PSI) and Moment's Notice (MOMENT).

PhotoSource International is a clearinghouse for *information about* the current photo needs of many of the nation's publication editors. It does not handle photos themselves. The editor's name, a description of the desired subject(s), the payment range, and other information is provided in each listing. It is up to you to make the sale. PSI carries a subscription fee, but you can opt to view one of its publications at any time for "one-shot" fees ranging from $6 to $15. Sample issues may be viewed free of charge.

Moment's Notice is a travel club that specializes in notifying members of last-minute, deep-discount travel opportunities. Airlines, cruise ships, and tour operators eager to fill unsold seats as their deadlines approach are the source of these bargains. Membership in Moment's Notice is $45 a year, but you can send for a free catalog online. Unfortunately, at this writing, you cannot search for travel opportunities with this feature, though given the time-sensitive nature of these commodities, making it possible to do so would seem like a logical thing to do in the future.

Special-Interest Groups

SIGs on GEnie are called "RoundTables" or "RTs" for short. As you can see from Figure 6.2, there are quite a few of them, both for hardware and software support, shareware support (ProComm, Qmodem, and Red Ryder, for example), and topics of interest. As with virtually all SIGs, GEnie RTs have a categorized bulletin board for exchanging messages, an array of data libraries for exchanging public-domain and shareware software and files, and a conferencing area.

Most RTs hold regular conferences each week, and many invite special guests. In the IBM RT at least some members are such enthusiastic participants that they actively exchange "faces" for use with the PC Visual COnferencing system (PC-VCO). PC-VCO is a shareware ($35) program written by R. Scott McGinnis that allows users to create up to nine images of themselves (happy, sad, bored, angry, and so on) offline. The images are tagged with their creator's personal CB handle and uploaded as a file.

Fellow conferencers download these files to their own systems and keep them on disk. Once your fellow GEnie users have your "face" on file, that face will pop onto their screens whenever your handle appears during a CB-like conference. For your part, you can control which face is displayed at any time by issuing a particular command. So you can show people that you are bored, angry, or whatever. An IBM color graphics adaptor or equivalent is required to use PC-VCO. The program can be downloaded from the IBM RT or we can send it to you, along with ZOO.EXE and other popular GEnie IBM utilities, on Glossbrenner's Choice CommPack 5.

Almost all GEnie RoundTables have an item on their greeting menus that offers an explanation of the feature, what it covers, its purpose, and so on. Most require you to join the RT before entering, but there is no cost or obligation involved. Some RTs restrict membership to qualified personnel (like the various developers' RTs) and some may be open only to registered customers (such as some of the product support RTs). But most are open to all. And if you are like most GEnie users, you will find that the RTs are one of the best features on the system.

Online Tip: If you use an IBM-compatible computer and you become a regular GEnie user, you may want to consider Aladdin. This is a shareware ($59) communications program that, like TAPCIS and AutoSIG on CompuServe, is designed to completely automate your online sessions. The shareware version, at this writing, has been crippled to make some features unavailable, but it is an

Online Tip (cont.)

> impressive program even so. Registration yields a fully functional
> version. You can download it from the IBM RT or send for Gloss-
> brenner's Choice CommPack 8.

_____ **Figure 6.2. RoundTables (SIGs) on GEnie** _____

Here are the many special interest group RoundTables you will find on
GEnie. The list is current at this writing, of course, but more are certain to be added. For an update, key in INDEX and search on the
keyword ROUNDTABLE. Then search on the keyword RT.

Amiga	Macintosh Developers
Apple II	Medical
Apple II Developers	MichTron
Atari ST	Microsoft
Atari 8-Bit	MUMPS
Borland	National Association of DeskTop
Bulletin Board Systems	Publishers
Commodore	NoChange Software
Computer Shopper	Odesta Corporation's OdestaLink
CP/M	Photography
Data Pacific	Pro/Am
Database	Protree Product Support
Datastorm Technologies, Inc.	QMODEM
(ProComm)	Science Fiction and Fantasy
Enable Product Support	Scuba
FOG	Softronics
FORTH Interest Group	Spaceport
Freesoft (Red Ryder)	SuperMac
Gadgets	Symmetry
Games by Scorpia	Tandy
Genealogy	TeleVision
Generic Software	Texas Instrument
IBM	Traveler's Information
Laptops	Vendix
Legacy Law	WordPerfect
Letraset GDS	Writers' Ink
MACH 2	X-10 Powerhouse
Macintosh	

Conclusion

We said at the beginning of this chapter that the tagline "Stay online longer, for less" was the key to understanding GEnie. But there is even more to that phrase than immediately meets the eye. In order for those words to have any impact at all, a person must *already* appreciate the benefits and pleasures of being online and be interested in paying less for them. On balance, that's a good way to characterize GEnie at this writing.

Certainly GEnie is a fine place to start, and its lower rates reduce the cost of ascending the online learning curve. But GEnie does not offer all the bells and whistles of a full-blown online experience. Instead, it offers what most people find themselves using most often after they've had the opportunity to choose from a rich array of other features. Today it may not be everyone's first system, but it is certainly everyone's second. And given the talent and resources it has to draw upon, that could easily change.

... 7 ...

Delphi

Delphi
General Videotex Corporation
3 Blackstone Street
Cambridge, MA 02139
(617) 491–3393

CUSTOMER SERVICE
(800) 544–4005

In Massachusetts and
outside the continental
United States:
(617) 491–3393

Customer Service Hours
(Eastern standard time)

Mon.–Fri.: 8:30 A.M.–9:00 P.M.
Weekends and holidays: 11:00 A.M.–1:00 P.M.

Initial Subscription:

The cost for a lifetime Delphi membership if $49.95. This includes a copy of *Delphi: The Official Guide* by science-fiction author Michael Banks (512 pages; Brady Books, 1987). This book was written in conjunction with General Videotex Corporation, Delphi's parent, and it serves as the main system manual. It includes a pull-out quick-reference command card and is available in bookstores for $19.95. Also included in the standard subscription are two free evening hours of connect time, a $14.40 value.

See the special discount offer at the back of this book for a money-saving offer.

Access: Tymnet, Telenet, and direct dial

Rates:

Delphi has always had an aggressive rate policy. It was the first utility to offer 2400-bps access, and the first to eliminate the extra charge for using 1200 bps instead of 300. The company has also traditionally offered "Summer Specials" for late-night access during July and August. The Delphi Advantage rates cited below are explained in the Special Notes section.

For an instant summary of current rates, key in USING RATES at the main menu. This will skip past the intervening "Using Delphi" menu (which includes RATES as one of its selections) and take you directly to the "Rates and Prices" section.

Delphi Connect Rates

(Packet-switching costs are *included* in the rates given below.)

Prime ("Office") Time
(Mon.–Fri. 7:00 A.M.–6:00 P.M.)

Speed (bps)	Standard connect time (per hour)	(per minute)	Delphi Advantage rate (per hour)	(per minute)
300/1200/2400	$17.40	29¢	$12.60	21¢

Nonprime ("Home") Time
(Mon.–Fri. 6:00 P.M.–7:00 A.M.,
and all day weekends and holidays)

Speed (bps)	Standard connect time (per hour)	(per minute)	Delphi Advantage rate (per hour)	(per minute)
300/1200/2400	$7.20	12¢	$5.40	9¢

Personal Defaults:

Set by modifying your "Profile." Key in USING SET from the main menu to reach the correct section of the service.

Scram Command:

BREAK signal (300 milliseconds or longer) preferred. A Control-O will also stop output and "fast-forward" you to the end of whatever is being displayed, though there will be a delay due to undisplayed text still in the pipeline. You may want to use Control-O should you take the online tour Delphi offers. The tour guide's name is Max and he resolutely refuses to acknowledge a BREAK.

Sign-Off Command: BYE

Protocols: XMODEM (CRC and checksum), Kermit (classic), WX-MODEM, YMODEM, and YMODEM batch.

Special Notes:
For frequent users, Delphi offers the Delphi Advantage. Under this plan, you pay a one-time fee of $19 and agree to use $24 worth of Delphi connect time per month, charged at the standard Delphi rates. After you have met that requirement, however, the special discounted rates cited in the rate table apply. You must already be a Delphi subscriber to take advantage of this plan. At this writing, it is not available as an initial subscription option.

System Overview:
Delphi offers a complete feature and command index for you to download. Key in USING from the main menu and opt for INDEX on the menu that will then appear. Be sure to open your capture buffer to catch it all, and then print it out once you are offline. You will find it a handy command summary. At this writing, the index is not keyword-searchable.

—— Figure 7.1. Delphi's Main, Using, and Setting Menus ——

Here are three of the menus you will almost certainly encounter during your first sessions on Delphi. Notice that you enter words instead of numbers to indicate menu selections. Although we have used complete words here for clarity, in actual practice you can abbreviate your choices "to uniqueness." Thus "BUS" (or even "B") would be fine if you wanted to choose "Business & Finance" from the Main Menu below.

```
Welcome to DELPHI
Copyright (c) 19--
General Videotex Corporation

MAIN Menu:

            Business & Finance      News-Weather-Sports
            Conference              People on DELPHI
            DELPHI/Regional         Travel
            Entertainment           Workspace
```

Groups and Clubs   Using DELPHI
Library   HELP
Mail   EXIT
Merchants' Row

MAIN>What do you want to do? using

USING-DELPHI Menu:

Advantage Plan   Premium Services
Advice From DELPHI   Rates and Prices
Boston Membership Plan   Review Bills/Invoices
Change Address   Settings (PROFILE)
Credit Policy   Software Changes
Feedback   Telex-Codes
Guided Tour   Terms of Agreement
Index   Update Credit Card
Mail To SERVICE   Usage History
Manuals   What's New On DELPHI
Member Service   Worldwide Access Info
Network Info   HELP
Past Bills/Invoices   EXIT

USING-DELPHI>(Please Select an Item)> settings

SETTINGS Menu:

BUSY-Mode   PROMPT-Mode
DEFAULT-Menu   SET-High-bit
DOWNLOAD-Line-terminators   SLASH-Term-settings
ECHO-Mode   TERMINAL-Type
EDITOR   TIMEOUT
FILE-TRANSFERS   UTILITIES
KERMIT-SETTINGS   WIDTH (Columns)
LENGTH (Lines/page)   XMODEM-SETTINGS
NETWORK-PARAMETERS   HELP
PASSWORD (Change)   EXIT

SETTINGS>What would you like to set?

Capsule Summary

The best way to characterize this system is to say quite simply that Delphi has brought the joy back to going online. All new industries go through a cycle of initial innovation and excitement followed by a shake-out, consolidation, and maturity. And while no one is suggesting that the online utility industry is mature, there can be no doubt that much of the original sense of fun, adventure, and surprise has been replaced by predictability and a certain sense of sameness. Apparently, however, the people at General Videotex haven't gotten the word. For Delphi is as vibrant, creative, and surprising as ever.

Indeed, Delphi has long been the most innovative and flexible of all online utilities. It is the guerrilla fighter of the industry, traveling light, moving fast, and hitting hard with new tactics and creative approaches to serving the growing online public. This way of doing things has both an upside and a downside. It means that while Delphi can be enormously entertaining and fun to use, it is probably not the system for a brand new, nontechnical user to start on. It is reasonably friendly, and of course one can get used to anything. But while customer service is always there to help, the system itself does not coddle new communicators. If you've had some online experience, however, Delphi could just be the system to offer the sense of fun and adventure you've been looking for.

Part of what makes the system unique lies behind the scenes. For example, Delphi is the only system to use the DEC VAXCluster architecture for its hosts. This is a technical distinction, to be sure, but it means that you can move from one feature to another faster than you can on systems whose host computers are wired in a "daisy chain" or rely on front-end processors. As a result, you will not see "Please wait" messages when you key in a command to enter a SIG or use some other feature.

The cluster architecture also makes it easy to expand, and more importantly from Delphi's viewpoint, it makes it easy to implement *local* hosts. Delphi has already begun to implement its "distributed host" approach with franchises in Buenos Aires, Argentina, Kansas City, and Boston. These systems are operated by entrepreneurs in their local cities. When you "gateway" through to them from the main system, you have access to most standard Delphi features but many locally produced features as well. At this writing, no one else has anything even remotely comparable.

A service of General Videotex Corporation (GVC), Delphi went live in February 1983. In 1986, according to the company, Delphi's user base grew at a rate of 288 percent, while revenue grew at a rate of 225 percent. Yet the management team, headed by founder J. Wesley Kussmaul (CEO), Daniel J. Bruns (President), and John Gilbert (Product Manager) remains small and as yet resistant to the bureaucracy that can stifle innovation. In the sections that follow, we'll highlight the kinds of innovations and new approaches that are typical of the Delphi system.

————————————— **BEST BETS** —————————————

Information

Delphi's general information offerings are not exceptional. You'll find news, weather, sports, stock quotes, and financial features. But you will also find a gateway to DIALOG. As noted later in this book, DIALOG gives you access to over 350 databases covering virtually every conceivable field of human knowledge. It is an industrial-strength system with its own command structure and considerably higher rates than Delphi, but you can order DIALOG manuals and get online help through Delphi. More importantly for our purposes here, no other online utility offers you a *direct* link. (You can reach DIALOG through IQUEST on CompuServe, but you must go through IQUEST.)

To take another example, look at the Using Delphi menu in Figure 7.1. There you will see a selection labelled "Worldwide Access Info." When you select this feature you will be able to obtain information on accessing Delphi via Telenet or Tymnet from any country served by these two packet-switching networks. As you know, the identical information is available at the Telenet or Tymnet network prompts when you enter the proper codes. But someone at Delphi had the wit to realize that the information would make a worthwhile and useful feature. Other systems will give you local PDN node phone numbers, but no one else offers the international information found here.

You will also want to look into the "Views on News" feature accessible from the news menu. In addition to serious information, this feature includes the irreverent, on point series called "Articles of Lasting Strangeness" by Bob Fried. Sample titles include "Desk Drawer Stress Disorder," "The Joy of Caulking," "Daylight Savings Time Explained," and "Movies—A Good Reason to Stay Home." There is also The Answer Tree, your opportunity to submit questions on virtually any topic or scan/search the questions others have posted and the Answer Tree's response.

Communications, Services, and SIGs

Mail, Fax, Telex, and More

Delphi's electronic mail system is simply awful. It may rival GEnie's for the title of Worst in Show. When you enter the mail system, for example, to read or send a letter all you will see on your screen is the prompt "MAIL>." That's the kind of prompt that makes someone accustomed to using mainframes and minicomputers feel right at home. Others, unfortunately, will have to work at discovering and mastering the system's many powerful features. Michael Banks's book/manual is a great help, but you might also want to open your capture buffer and key in HELP the first time you see the MAIL> prompt.

The mail system aside, Delphi has been a leader in offering additional communications facilities before (sometimes long before) its competitors. In the past, for example, it was possible to send messages to people on The Source, CompuServe, and other systems. This was years before CompuServe and MCI Mail announced their special "X.400" interconnection. (Delphi did it by collecting the messages sent by its subscribers to other systems and transmitting them by hand each morning at 4:00 A.M.) You can also use Delphi to send and receive telex messages anywhere in the world, to send messages by fax, and engage in CB-like conferencing.

You can find out who is on the system at the moment by going to the conferencing area and keying in WHO. You can then page anyone on the system. This sends a canned invitation to join you for a chat. You can also send a file directly to a fellow member's mailbox by merely entering the filename followed by the person's member name. If you need to have something translated to or from Spanish, French, German, Italian, or Portugese, an interface to a translation service is available.

Services

Delphi offers the standard array of travel and shopping services. It's "electronic mall" is called "Merchant's Row." And while the list of merchants is neither long nor terribly unique, there are at least two menu entries of special interest. The first is The Boston Computer Exchange (BCE), one of the country's leading used computer brokers. BCE has long made its current catalog (equipment for sale and equipment wanted) available for searching on Delphi. (BCE has recently become available on CompuServe as well.) This is a great place to find a deal or simply to get a better idea of what your own equipment is worth on the current market. BCE operates by putting buyer and seller together and taking a commission from the seller.

The second item of note is the selection called "Set Billing Address." This is yet another innovative Delphi feature. Selecting it gives you the chance to key in your name and mailing address—once. From then on, whenever you want to order something from a merchant, you hit a single key and the system repeats your address automatically. (You can make changes, of course.) On most other systems, at this writing, you must type in your address information each and every time you want to place an order.

SIGs: Delphi Groups and Clubs

Special-interest groups on Delphi are called "Groups and Clubs," and the system software that makes them contains enough special features to delight the most jaded of SIG users from other systems. Within each Delphi SIG you will find person-to-person private mail, categorized bulletin and message boards, discussion threads, a member directory, real-time conferencing, databases, and an option for setting your personal defaults while in the SIG. But you will also find a feature for taking a poll on any topic and reviewing the results of past polls. You will find an entry log that you can use to check when a particular member was last in the SIG. And you will find the option of setting up sub-SIGs (SIGs within SIGs) to focus on some especially specific topic or narrow interest.

Shown below is the list of major SIGs currently on Delphi. The focus of most of these groups will be obvious from their names. However, a few require a word of explanation. Close Encounters is an adult, human contact and intimate feelings group. C*SIX is the *Computer Shopper* Information Exchange, a group sponsored by that magazine. Macintosh ICONtact is the main Apple Macintosh SIG, with a sub-SIG for developers. MANIAC is the place for people to exchange and discuss music, graphics, and other creative works (regardless of computer brand). Music City is aimed at professional aspiring musicians. OS9 On-Line focuses on a UNIX-like operating system (OS9) for Tandy Color Computers. ViP deals with all matters concerning videotape, film, and photography.

Here, then, is the current lineup of Delphi SIGs:

Amiga SIG	Micro Art—MANIAC
Atari SIG	Music City
Apple][& ///	OS9 On-Line
Aviation SIG	PC Compatibles/IBM
Business Forum	Portable Place
Close Encounters	Science Fiction SIG
Color Computer	ST-Log
Commodore SIGs	Tandy PC SIG
C*SIX	TI Intl Users Net
GameSig	Theological Network
Hobby Shop	ViP—Video & Photo
Macintosh	Wang Users SIG
ICONtact	Writers Group

Conclusion

As we have emphasized throughout, Delphi continues to maintain its position as the most innovative and creative of online utilities. As such, it gives a user an extraordinary amount of control in some areas. For example, if there is no activity from your keyboard for ten minutes, the system will automatically log you off and stop the meter. That's true for most online systems, but on Delphi, you can set your own "timeout" time.

The parameters you can set for your terminal or your interaction with the Telenet or Tymnet PAD are mind-boggling, though most subscribers need not concern themselves with these matters. Nor need most users concern themselves with customizing the way the system handles XMODEM and Kermit file transfers, though this can be done as well. And at this writing, none of the other systems supports so many of the popular error-checking protocols.

The traditional computer industry tradeoff between power and ease of use applies here as it does everywhere else. While Delphi is genuinely friendly in the way only a smaller system can be—one sometimes gets the feeling that members and management are joined together on an exciting voyage of exploration and discovery—the system has not erected a huge user-friendly superstructure and padded it with cotton wool. Accordingly, while Delphi may not be the system for most people to start on, it is certainly the system many people come to after they have had some experience and instinctively call "home."

...8...

BIX: The *BYTE* Information Exchange

BYTE Information Exchange (BIX)
One Phoenix Mill Lane
Peterborough, NH 03458-9990
(603) 924-9281

CUSTOMER SERVICE
From the continental
United States and
Canada: (800) 227-2983

In New Hampshire and
outside the continental
United States: (603)
924-7681

Customer Service Hours
(Eastern standard time)

Mon.–Fri.: 8:30 A.M.–11:00 P.M.

Subscription and Rates:

BIX now operates on a flat-fee, unlimited usage basis. A one-year subscription is $156, whether you elect to pay it all at once or at a rate of $39 per quarter. A three-month trial subscription is also available for $59. All subscriptions include the BIX system manual and documentation. And all subscriptions may be canceled at any time.

These fees do not cover Tymnet costs. At this writing, using Tymnet during prime time (6:00 A.M. to 7:00 P.M., weekdays costs $8 an hour. The off-peak rate (evenings, weekends, and holidays) is $2 per hour. However, through BIX you can get a special deal on Tymnet access. For $15 per month, you can have unlimited off-peak Tymnet usage at all speeds (300/1200/2400). Call BIX customer service for details.

    That means your total cost for unlimited off-peak usage of BIX via Tymnet can be as low as $28 a month. See the special-discount offer at the back of this book for even more savings.

Access: Tymnet and direct dial.

Personal Defaults:

    Set by modifying your "Profile." Your Profile is a recorded series of commands that are executed automatically each time you sign on, much as the batch file AUTOEXEC.BAT is executed (if it exists) each time you boot up an IBM/MS-DOS computer, or the way Apples run the program HELLO. Choose "Individual Options" from the main menu and "Change your logon profile" from the menu that will then appear. This results in the "Command→" prompt. Enter L for "List," to view current settings, or H for "Help." We recommend keying in C for "Clear" to produce a prompt for a new line (input->). Key in the items shown here:

```
Begin entering your text. When you are finished enter '.<CR>'.

input-> opt verbose
input-> edit verbose
input-> term width 80
input-> term pagelen 0
input-> Q
input-> .
```

Your BIX manual will explain the first two items. The next two, as you can guess, set your terminal width to 80 columns and your page length to 0 to eliminate pauses. The Q tells the system to quit the Options section after this portion of your Profile has been run each time. The period gets you out of input mode. The next thing you see will be "Command->," and here you should key in W to tell the system to write your new profile to disk, then Q to quit Profile editing and return to the main system. Once recorded by the W command, the profile will remain in effect until you decide to change it again.

Scram Command: Control-C or a true BREAK (no more than 350 milliseconds).

Sign-off Command: BYE

Protocols: XMODEM (checksum and CRC), YMODEM, ZMODEM, and Kermit

Special Notes:
BIX supports full-duplex seettings of 7/E/1 and 8/N/1. Do not send a line feed on carriage return.

System Overview:
You can get an overview by following the menus, but the best way (even for novices) is to get into Command Mode. Choose that option from the main menu and you will see the colon prompt (:). At that point, open your capture buffer and key in SHOW ALL. Then sit back and watch as the names of more than 300 conferences scroll by.

Close your capture buffer to write its contents to disk. Then key in BYE to sign off. Print the file listing BIX conference names. Pick out the conferences of interest. Then sign back on and follow the menus to the conferencing system. When the system prompts you for the conference you would like to join, simply consult your printed list. Note that you can return to menu mode from the command level at any time by keying in MENU. And when using the menus the command MM always returns you to the system's top or main menu.

To get an overview of the databases, choose "Listings" from the main menu and when prompted to choose an "area" key in a question mark (?). This will generate a list of all of the subject areas one can enter to look for files.

——————————— **Figure 8.1. Welcome to BIX!** ———————————

Here's what you can expect to see when you log onto BIX for the first time. After you become an experienced user, you can set your personal Profile so that the system comes up on Command Mode instead of presenting a menu. Whether you're an experienced user or not, you can also decide whether you want the system to display the numbers of messages that have been added to the conferences you have joined since the last time you signed on or not. Again, this is done by changing your Profile.

BIX: call connected

Welcome to BIX -- ttyx4b, 1578
= = B Y T E   C O S Y   3.1.9 = =

Welcome to BIX, the BYTE Information Exchange

McGraw-Hill Information Services Co.
Copyright © 1989 by McGraw-Hill Inc.

CoSy Conferencing System, Copyright © 1984 University of Guelph
Need BIX voice help . . .
In the U.S. and Canada call 800-227-2983, in NH and elsewhere
call 603-924-7681 8:30 A.M. to 11:00 P.M. EDT (-4 GMT) weekdays

Name? GLOSSBRENNER
Password:

Last on: DDD MMM NN 15:21:59 YYYY
You have 0 mail messages in your in-basket.
You are a member of 4 conferences.

    BIX Main Menu

1   Electronic Mail
2   Conference Subsystem
3   Listings
4   CBix
5   MicroBytes - Industry News Briefs
6   McGraw-Hill News
7   Subscriber Information
8   Individual Options
9   Quick Download
10 Command Mode (abandon menus)
11 Logoff (bye)

Enter a menu option or ? for help: 1
No unread in-basket messages.

Capsule Overview

As you know by now, BIX stands for "BYTE Information Exchange." Never has an online utility been more aptly named. The exchange of information likely to be of interest to regular readers of McGraw-Hill's *BYTE* magazine is precisely what BIX is all about. As such, BIX isn't really an online utility in the conventional sense. There are no shopping, travel, or multi-option communications features (no fax, telex, or hard-copy mail, for example). There are no interactive games. And while McGraw-Hill News is available (as a surcharged service), BIX is not the place to go for stock quotes, political reports, or crisis-of-the-week information.

BIX *is* the place to go if you are interested in anything—anything at all—dealing with computers, communications, hardware, software, programming, computer languages, microchips, artificial intelligence, operating systems, and technology in general. BIX is a truly amazing resource, and now with a menu system to supplement (at your option) its traditional command mode, BIX is much easier to use. We'll have more to say about how to tap BIX in a moment. But first a bit of background.

BYTE magazine is one of the original publications of the personal computer revolution (first issue: September 1975). BIX was the brainchild of Phil Lemmons, the magazine's longtime editor-in-chief, and from its conception in 1984 through its nationwide implementation in November 1985 to the present day, the system's primary focus has always been computerized conferencing and electronic messaging. BIX is designed to promote free and vigorous interaction among *BYTE* subscribers, editors, contributors, and others who are interested in computer hardware and software, particularly in the technical aspects of these and related subjects. Not incidently, the system spins off copious material for use in the pages of the magazine.

Making the Most of BIX

Although BIX offers more than computerized conferencing—the databases in its LISTINGS areas are stuffed with software and files for you to download—it is easiest to approach BIX from that angle. As we will see in a later chapter, computerized conferencing systems are essentially collections of notes or messages from various users on a variety of subjects. As with all successful computerized conferencing systems, however, there are a lot of messages on a lot of subjects—far too many to simply give each note a number and expect users to deal with the entire list each time they sign on. The challenge that BIX and all such systems face is *organizing* thousands of messages on scores of topics in a logical and convenient way. As noted, BIX offers other features, but at its heart is the "Conferences" area.

At the top of the BIX organization scheme are conference groups. At this writing, there are 15 groups ranging from Artificial Intelligence to Operating Systems to the Macintosh to Vendor Support. Each group contains one or more conferences, and each conference contains one or more topics. This is basically just a filing system to keep related items together and to make information easy to find. Conference titles range from ADA (a programming language named after the world's first programmer, Ada Agusta, Countess of Lovelace) to BASIC to HAM.RADIO to UNIX. There are conferences for every major brand of computer, and often separate conferences for major models.

At the next level are the "topics" covered within each conference. The IBM.PC conference, for example, includes such topics as SOFTWARE, HARDWARE, DRIVES, PROGRAMMING, HINTS, and CLONES. The final level consists of the messages themselves. The actual messages you will want to read are stored and numbered sequentially under the topics. You must select a topic whenever you enter a particular conference. Though, of course, you can easily move from one topic to another.

Thus if you wanted to see what the BIX community of IBM-PC users had to say about interleave factors on hard disk drives, you would first sign on to BIX and follow the menus until you got to a prompt asking you if you want to join a conference and specify its name. Key in IBM.PC. This will take you into that conference, and after some initial announcements and bulletins have appeared, you will be asked to pick a topic from the displayed list. Keying in DRIVES would take you to that topic. The Conference Action Menu shown in Figure 8.2 would then appear.

——————— **Figure 8.2. The BIX Conference Action Menu** ———————

This menu appears in all conferences on the system. Notice that here we have chosen to search the message base for the keyword INTER-LEAVE.

Conference Action Menu

```
 1   Read next message
 2   Read this message again
 3   Read comments to this message
 4   Read original message
 5   Contribute a new message
 6   Comment to this message
 7   Skip to a message
 8   Search messages
 9   Change to a different topic
10   CBix
11   Search BIX subscriber list
12   Show a subscriber's online resume
13   Show members of current conference
14   Show last login time of current conference members
 p   Previous menu
mm   Main menu

Enter a menu option or ? or help: 8
Enter search string or phrase: INTERLEAVE
```

From that menu, you would almost certainly opt to search the messages under the DRIVES topic for a word like "interleave." If the system found that word, or any part of it, in the text of any message under the topic, it would display a list of message numbers and their first lines. You could then opt to read any or all of these messages by specifying their numbers.

Now, that's the way to tap BIX when you are interested in a machine-specific subject or some other subject for which BIX has a conference. But what if you're interested in a more general concept—like government regulation, trade policy, chip dumping, or import quotas, as these things affect many brands of computers? By its nature, BIX attracts experts and others with deep knowledge of their respective fields. But how can you find out what these folks have had to say on a subject, short of joining scores of conferences and searching their message bases individually?

The answer is to take advantage of BIX's power to search the *entire system* all at once. Opt for the Conferencing System from the main menu, then opt to "Search conference index" from the menu that will then appear. You will be prompted for the keyword you wish to search on. The system will blink for just a second and then tell you how many entries it has found. When we searched for "regulation," for example, the system found 63 entries (messages containing that keyword). It then gave us the conference, the topic, and the message number in each case. What's more, it not only searched for "regulation," it also automatically searched for "regulations" and noted those entries separately.

When the entire list has been displayed, you will be returned to the Conference Subsystem Menu. From there, you can quickly "Join a conference by name," and select the target topic and message number to read once you do. (It goes without saying that you will want to have pen and paper at the ready when you run your search since you will want to note the items of interest.)

It may be that you have to be a computerist, researcher, or writer to appreciate this power. At the very least, you have to have some awareness of the tips, tricks, contacts, hands-on hardware and software reviews, discounts, special deals, help information, and technical knowledge that are available through online conferences and SIGs. If you aren't, you will simply have to take it on faith that this is a truly incredible feature.

Other Features in Brief

BIX also offers a four-band CB simulator with 40 channels per band. There is electronic mail, and a method for locating a user and reading his or her resume (providing one is voluntary) online. There is also a feature called MICROBYTES with, among other things, the latest computer-related information from the editors of *BYTE*. The full text of *BYTE* magazine is also online. As is the complete BIX user manual

(JOIN USER.MANUAL). And as mentioned, the LISTINGS area is filled with databases that are filled with programs and files. Clearly, there is much to explore on BIX.

There is one system feature in particular we want to be sure to mention, however. It is called Quick Download and is accessible from the main menu. When you select this feature, you will be given the option of automatically downloading all of your mail messages, the contents of your scratchpad (work space), and/or all new messages that have been added to the conferences you have joined. It is this last option that is unique. You do not need to go into every conference and download new messages. Nor do you need a special high-efficiency message-handling program like TAPCIS or ATO on CompuServe or Aladdin on GEnie. The system does all the work for you, and it can be a real convenience.

One word of caution, however. If you have joined a lot of conferences, you will receive a *lot* of new messages. Consequently, you may want to use the conference menu option to resign from some of them before choosing Quick Download. You can rejoin at any time, of course.

Conclusion

If you like *BYTE*, you'll love BIX, for BIX is nothing if not an extension of the magazine. If you are a new computer owner or a novice online user, you might want to save BIX for later. The system is much easier to use now that it offers menus—hard as it may be to believe, BIX used to greet everyone with nothing but the Command Mode prompt (:)—but it is not likely to win any awards for elegance or visual design. Menu screens overflow with text and options, and until you get into the BIX groove of groups/conferences/topics/messages, the system can be a challenge to figure out.

Ultimately, though, it is a system's content that matters most. If *BYTE* magazine is not your cup of tea, there's probably no point in investigating BIX. But if computers, software, and technical discussions of all kinds are your meat, BIX offers you a veritable banquet of possibilities.

...9...

People/Link (PLINK)

American People/Link
165 N. Canal Street, Suite 950
Chicago, IL 60606
(312) 648–0660

CUSTOMER SERVICE
(800) 524–0100

In Illinois and outside
the continental United
States: (312) 648–0660

Customer Service Hours
(Central time)

Mon.–Fri.: 9:00 A.M.–5:00 P.M.
(Weekend coverage will be available in the future.)

Initial Subscription:
There is an initial subscription of $24.95 See the special discount
offer at the back of this book for a money-saving offer.

Access: Telenet, Tymnet, direct dial, ConnNet, and Mercury (U.K.).

Rates:
Packet-switching costs are *included* in the rates given below. Note
that Tymnet prime time extends until 7:00 P.M. on weekdays.
Telenet prime time ends at 6:00 P.M. on weekdays. Subscribers to
Telenet's PC Pursuit (PCP) can use PCP to access People/Link.
Key in: C PLINK,(PCP ID),(PCP PASSWORD) at the Telenet
"@" prompt. You will need a PLINK subscription, of course.
PC Pursuit (PCP) is used primarily for accessing free public bul-

145

letin board systems and is discussed in more detail elsewhere in this book. For more information right now, dial the PCP modem number (800) 835–3001, hit <Enter> once or twice, and follow the prompts.

In the past People/Link has offered special flat-fee deals providing unlimited connect time during the month. PC Pursuit users, or those using People/Link's local Chicago number, have also been able to pay $50 each and use the system with no further charges. Other discount plans may be available for non-PCP users (see "Special Notes," below). Contact customer service for the latest offers and information.

People/Link Connect Rates

Prime Time
(Mon.–Fri.: 7:01 A.M.–6:00 P.M.)

Speed (bps)	Connect time (per hour)	Connect time (per minute)
300/1200	$7.95	14¢
2400	$9.95	17¢

Non-prime Time
(Mon.–Fri.: 6:01 P.M.–7:00 A.M.;
all day Sat., Sun., and holidays)

Speed (bps)	Connect time (per hour)	Connect time (per minute)
300/1200/2400	$4.50	8¢

Data Transfer Charges
(Charges apply to XMODEM file downloads; uploads are free)

Prime Time: $.18 per 5 kilobytes (or any part thereof)
Non-prime: $.09 per 5 kilobytes (or any part thereof)
Local/PCP: $.04 per 5 kilobytes (or any part thereof)

Calls are billed to the nearest minute, and there is a three-minute minimum per call. Direct dial ("local") calls to People/Link's Chicago nodes and connections made through PC Pursuit (PCP) are $2.70 per hour, regardless of time of day. For a rate summary, key in /BILL or choose "Information" from the main menu and "Rates and Billing" from the menu that will then appear.

Personal Defaults:
> Key in /DEF at the People/Link Top menu and follow the result-
> ing instructions. Note that the maximum page length available is
> 66 lines per page. There is no way to permanently eliminate
> "more" prompts. However, you can key in /NOMORE each time
> you sign on to make the system scroll continuously during the cur-
> rent session. In some sections of the service, you may also have to
> key in /NOPAUSE.

Scram Command: Control-C or BREAK

Sign-Off Command: /OFF

Protocols:
> PLINK will automatically try WXMODEM first. If your system
> indicates that it does not support WXMODEM, PLINK will fall
> back to conventional XMODEM.

Special Notes:
> In the past, People/Link has always offered special discounted
> rates (25 percent off) to members of the Frequent Plinker Club.
> Subscribers using 1200 bps would thus pay either $9.72 or $3.72 an
> hour, depending on time of day. One-time sign up cost is $12.50.
> Monthly dues are $10. You may join at any time. People/Link ad-
> vises that the club is cost-effective for anyone using ten hours a
> month or more.

System Overview:
> The command /DIR will list the names of all People/Link Clubs
> (SIGs) and the handles of the people who run them. Alternatively,
> you can choose "Clubs and Forums" from the main menu, and
> "General Information About Clubs" from the "Club Selection"
> menu that will then appear. This will give you a short description
> of each club, its purpose, goals, subject focus, etc.
>
> For a list of system-wide commands, choose "Information" from
> the main menu and "System Command Lists" from the menu that
> will then appear.

_ **Figure 9.1. The People/Link Greeting and PartyLine Menus** _

As you can see below, People/Link offers clean, easy-to-use menus that
have been thoughtfully designed so that even novice users won't get
stuck or lost. If you can read, you can use PLINK from the moment you

sign on. Experienced users can shut the menus off and operate from command mode. But most slash commands (like /HELP) will work with the menus as well.

CONNECTED TO PEOPLE/LINK!

USER ID: IGNATZ

PASSWORD:

Welcome to PEOPLE/LINK, IGNATZ

Today is Friday, DD MMM YY, HH:MM:SS
Last visit Thursday, DD MMM YY, HH:MM:SS

NEW! DESKTOP PUBLISHING CLUB /GO DEPOT
Congratulations Choclady & Flo /GO PLAY

            PEOPLE/LINK Main Menu

```
1   PartyLine              /PARTY
2   Clubs & Forums         /CLUBS
3   Online Shops           /SHOPS
4   Mail                   /MAIL
5   Travel                 /TRAV
6   User Directory         /UD
7   Bulletin Boards        /BB
8   Information            /GO 411
9   News and Publications  /GO NEWS
```

Enter number, command or /HELP
MAIN MENU> 1

Welcome to PartyLine!

            PARTYLINE FEATURES MENU

```
1    Show PartyLines In Use    /SUM
2    List PartyLine Users      /LIST
3    Join Public Conversation  /LINE
4    Request Private Chat       /CHAT
5    Join Private Conversation  /CODE
6    Change Your Handle (Name)  /NAME
7    Additional PartyLine Features
8    Change Screen Formats
9    Exit PartyLine To MAIN Menu/QUIT
10   PartyLine Information      /HELP
```

Please enter number or command:
PARTY> 7

```
ADDITIONAL PARTYLINE FEATURES MENU

1  Find User Online        /FIND
2  Find Where YOU Are      /WHE
3  Send A Private Message  /MSG
4  Stop Messages To You    /GAG
5  Return To PARTYLINE Menu /TOP
6  Info On These Features  /HELP
7  Info On Other Features

Please enter number or command:
PARTY>
```

Capsule Summary

People/Link or "PLINK" as it is usually called, owes its existence to the popularity of CompuServe's CB Simulator. As is the case with most mainframe and minicomputer systems, CompuServe users have always been able to chat with each other in real time on a one-to-one basis. But when CompuServe introduced its "multiplayer host" several years ago, it became possible for lots of people to gather and hold CB-like conversations. CompuServe used the same facility to let groups of people battle each other in online Star-Trek-like games.

Both features became enormously popular. What wasn't popular was the CompuServe rate structure at the time. Merrill Millman thought he had a better idea. He created People/Link as a low-cost alternative for people who were primarily interested in CompuServe's communications features. People/Link has no information, news, investment, or similar features common to online utilities. At this writing, it does offer the widely available TravelSaver service, but the system's main focus is real-time chat and special interest groups ("Clubs").

On Saturday December 29, 1984 the system went live at the rock bottom nonprime rate of $2.95 an hour for 300 bps. The prime time rate was $8.95, and 1200 bps capability was not added until April of 1985. The rates have changed since then, but the emphasis has remained on people-to-people communications facilities offered at a low cost.

Undoubtedly as a consequence of its low rates and communications orientation, People/Link has not spent a great deal on documentation and other frills. Indeed, the documentation is barely worthy of the name and the system's file downloading facilities are awkward to say the least. At this writing the "manual" is a 14-page pocket guide that amounts to little more than a command summary. Originally, People/Link had no SIGs. When it added them in the form of Clubs, it issued a single page of information that was as limited as the manual it was designed to supplement. A new manual is said to be in the works. Unfortunately, given the irregular publication schedule of the system's paper newsletter, one should probably not look for an early release date.

On the other hand, People/Link is very good at what it is designed to do. And in truth, its menus are so well thought out and helpful that you really can "go bare" and plunge in without reading the instructions. PLINK is fun, and with some 40,000 subscribers, it is a popular system. Plinkers, as subscribers call themselves, hold frequent get-togethers around the country, and more than one real-life romance has blossomed online.

Online Tip: As for the lack of documentation, you should know that Scott Hoffrage has prepared an extensive manual for all Plinkers to download. It can be found in the GAMERS GUILD, the club for inveterate online game players. Key in /GO GAMERS at the main system menu and join the club. From the club menu, enter the library of transfer files. Choose "Select Library Section" and opt for the Book Room. This section of the club library was created specifically to preserve Hoffrage's unofficial PLINK manual. The Club Data Library menu will appear again, and from here you should opt to "List Library Entries" (for the section you have just entered). Be sure to open your capture buffer first.

Among the entries you will see PLINK USERS' MANUAL: PART 1, followed by parts 2 through 4. These are the files you will want to download. Together, they total 215K, though one of the files contains a gargantuan appendix of nothing but Telenet, Tymnet, and ConnNet phone numbers. We suggest that you download each part of the manual, as prompted, using the ASCII option. But when the phone number list starts to appear, send the system a BREAK or Control-C to stop that particular download. Why pay for hundreds of numbers when the one you need can be gotten free of charge from People/Link customer service or one of the packet-switching networks?

_____ **Figure 9.2. PLINK Clubs (Special-Interest Groups)** _____

Shown below are the People/Link clubs offered at this writing. The club name is given in the left column and the name of the chairperson (sysop) is in the right. Some general information is available without entering a club, but the best way to find out what a club is all about is to opt to join it and read the bulletins and opening announcements that will then appear.

```
                    Directory of Public Clubs
          ---------------------------------------------------

          Club                      Chair
          ---------------------------------------------------
          ACE                       ALEX* ACE
          ACOA SELF-HELP            12STEPPER
          AMIGA ZONE                CBM*HARV
          APPLE/LINK                APPLE-LINK
          ATARI ST                  ATARI*TROS
          AUDIOPHILE                J TAMBURO
          BUSINESS WORLD            BW*CHRIS
          CHRISTIAN                 KOINE
          COMMODOR E                CBM*LARRY
          COMPUTER                  COMPUTER
          DEBATE                    MODERATOR
          DEPOT                     JOHN*S
          EDUCATION                 TEACH
          GAMERS GUILD              GAMERUNNER
          *GAY LINK                 LA COP
          GRANDY                    J THURSTON
          IBM                       IBMPC
          INK*LINK                  DAEDALUS
          JEWISH QUARTER            ACTIVIST
          LOVE/LINK                 LOVEBUNNY
          MESSAGE BOARD             PEOPLELINK
          NATURIST                  MIKE C
          OSIN                      PRECISION
          PLAYROOM                  ROSEY DAWN
          SF&F CLUB                 CAPT*VIDEO
          SKORBOARD TRAVEL          SKOR
          TEEN                      MR MIKE
          THEOS                     MIKAEL
```

* = By Request

PLINK CLUBS (SIGs)

As you see from Figure 9.2 PLINK offers a very respectable selection of special-interest groups for you to join. Each PLINK Club has three areas for its members to use. These are the notice boards (bulletins and messages), the data libraries (text and program files to download), and the conference area (real-time chat focusing on the Club's main area of interest).

Notice boards and data libraries are divided into sections, each dealing with a particular interest area. The club chairperson (sysop) is in charge of setting up the sections. How he or she does this depends on how he or she views the way the club will be used. Some clubs have lots of sections, others have very few. Most have a section for information about the club designed to help new members get up to speed fast. As is the case in many online SIGs, the identical section arrangement applies to both the notice boards and the libraries.

Conclusion

As we said, PLINK is a lot of fun. It is specifically designed for non-technical computer users. Meeting people online is always intriguing, and can often lead to romance and long-standing friendships. But while other systems offer similar opportunities, none is so thoroughly oriented to the goal of bringing people together. Plinkers frequently use the system to arrange face-to-face meetings, and major vacation trips are often planned, scheduled, announced, and attended by People/Link users.

...10...

Quantum: Q-Link, AppleLink, and PC-Link

Quantum Computer Services, Inc.

Corporate Headquarters:
8619 Westwood Center Drive
Vienna, VA 22180
(703) 448–8700

West Coast Office:
3 Lagoon Drive, Suite 320
Redwood City, CA 94605
(415) 592–9592

And Now for Something Completely Different . . .

Quantum Computer Services is the quiet company that, until recently, one didn't hear much about. This may have been because Quantum formerly focused exclusively on Commodore computers, specifically the C-64 and C-128, and those machines rarely attract the attention of the press today. Yet while no one was paying much attention, Quantum was quietly snaring 17 percent of the online market, according to LINK Resources (May 1988). (The same report alloted 23 percent to Dow Jones, 35 percent to CompuServe, and 25 percent to everyone else.)

A number of factors were responsible for the company's quiet success, but they can be summarized in a single word: Q-Link. Q-Link (or QuantumLink as it was originally called) is Quantum's online service designed exclusively for C-64 and C-128 users. If you don't have one of these machines, you can't use Q-Link. That's a limitation that on the surface at least, one wouldn't think made any sense. But it does.

For one thing, it enormously simplifies the technical aspects. Since you know from the very start that all of your customers are using essentially identical hardware, you can put some whiz-bang graphics on the

153

screens and make the system truly easy to use. You don't have to limit yourself to the lowest common denominator (ASCII text) or build in the complexity needed to deal with scores of different hardware makes and models.

For another, thanks to demographic studies done by computer manufacturers, you have a pretty good idea of who your prospective customers are, what they want and need, and where and how they use their machines. Instead of trying to please everyone, you're free to focus on just Commodore owners, the vast majority of whom use their machines at home.

Finally, if you're going to concentrate on one maker's brand of computer, it's a natural and logical step to form a mutually beneficial alliance with that manufacturer. The manufacturer can supply input to your system, offering your subscribers the latest information on hardware and software of interest and providing customer support. And you can supply valuable customer feedback to the manufacturer, while your service provides yet another reason for someone to buy the company's machine. Indeed, each of you can help market the other's products.

The sine qua non, of course, is an installed user base large enough to make it all work. At the time it went live, Quantum had an installed base of over 3 million Commodore machines to work with. And work it did. Quantum reports that Q-Link users annually log over a quarter of a million hours on the system.

Other Secrets of Success

Q-Link was so successful that Quantum decided to extend the concept to other computer brands as well. In August 1988 it announced PC-Link, a system jointly developed with Tandy Corporation aimed at all PC/MS-DOS compatible users. The following month it announced Applelink–Personal Edition, a service for users of Apple II models developed with Apple Computer Company. At this writing, a Macintosh version of the service is scheduled to be announced soon.

All three currently available Quantum services have a number of crucial points in common. And that is how we will discuss them. Be aware, however, that there are some differences in features and pricing. As always, contact customer service at the company for more information (see the appropriate 800 number on page 159). For convenience, we will use the term "Quantum" to refer to all three services.

Packaging and Price

The best quick handle on the system is this: Quantum has some unique features, but in general it offers most of the same services every other online utility offers. The difference is in packaging and price. The packaging is both visual and conceptual. Visually the system owes a lot to what used to be called "videotex"—a heavy emphasis on full-screen color graphics and asthetically pleasing displays. For example, on most utilities a single line of stark text informs you that you have chosen, say, the system's news feature. On Q-Link, a full, four-color screen with a face, a line chart, and an image of the space shuttle appear. The information one obtains in both cases may be identical. In fact it may have come from the same source. But on Quantum it is presented in a more visually entertaining way. More like television.

In fact, "television" is the essence of Quantum's *conceptual* packaging. Virtually all online utilities have a conferencing area where subscribers can meet for real-time chats, and on many systems the people who run the special-interest groups will use these facilities to present a guest speaker. The discussion leader will ask the guest questions and at various points other subscribers are invited to join in. Traditionally this activity has been called real-time computer conferencing.

Now, suppose you take the same activity and instead of calling it computer conferencing you call it a "talk show." Specifically, The Max Webbe Show on PC-Link. And suppose you publish a schedule each month of who Max's guests will be each night. Add a soupcon of showbiz glitz, and voila—the dull-sounding computer conference has been transformed into an entertainment event. Yet it is the identical activity.

One Monthly Fee, Unlimited Usage

Quantum is priced like television as well—cable television. For $9.95 a month Q-Link and PC-Link subscribers get unlimited nonprime-time usage of the system. Access is through Tymnet (or Datapac) and communications charges are included in the monthly fee. Nonprime time runs between 6:00 P.M. and 6:00 A.M. AppleLink at this writing is priced at 10 cents a minute with no monthly fee, and both the Apple and the Tandy products are available during prime time at 25 cents and 15 cents per minute, respectively. Q-Link and PC-Link also have "Plus" (surcharged) features. On Q-Link Plus services cost 8 cents a minute, but you get one hour free with your monthly subscription. On PC-Link the Plus surcharge is 10 cents a minute.

Initial Subscriptions

Subscription policies vary. Commodore users who don't find a Q-Link subscription offer bundled with their computers or modems can purchase one for $9.95. For AppleLink, the cost is $35 and it includes the special AppleLink software and two free hours on the system (a $12 value). For users of IBM compatible equipment, the cost is $29.95 for a run-time version of Tandy's DeskMate software and a Quantum subscription. Subscriptions may be included in the full DeskMate package ($100).

Subscribers to all Quantum systems receive a system-specific monthly magazine. The magazine is crucial to the television concept and, not surprisingly, it resembles a combination of *TV Guide* and the magazine you get when you contribute to your local public television station. The Quantum magazine always includes a Calendar of Events (topics to be discussed in conferences, industry luminaries who will be appearing, and so on) that can best be thought of as a guide to "what's on the system tonight."

There are also expanded program highlights, short best-bet style articles singling out specific features, hints, tips, letters, the Top Ten Downloads (the ten most popular downloadable files), and more. A lot more. In fact, *too much* more in our opinion. All of the various issues we looked at were so stuffed with text that they were difficult to read, let alone absorb. Apparently Quantum's editorial philosophy is to pack as many different things into the magazine as possible in hopes that at least something will connect with each reader.

The Quantum communications disk is crucial to the system's operation. It is responsible for creating Quantum's easy-to-use on-screen graphics environment, pop-up menus, help features, and other visual effects. The run-time version of Tandy's DeskMate software that is supplied to PC-Link subscribers lets you edit an entire letter before sending it or preview a file in a pop-up window before deciding to download it. The Quantum "system" graphics for many features are stored on the disk. This means that Quantum's host computers do not have to transmit every bit of every screen to your computer (an extremely time-consuming process). Instead, they can send a simple command instructing your software to "Display screen 4-E," or something similar.

What's On the System?

Low cost and ease of use are probably the most important elements in the Quantum formula, but there are some unique aspects to the content and array of features it offers as well. The most remarkable of these is the close involvement of the various computer manufacturers. Years ago, Tandy and Commodore were among the first vendors to offer online support and direct access to customer service and technical advisors via commercial online systems like CompuServe. But their presence and commitment was never as evident as it is (along with Apple's) on Quantum. You really do get the feeling that you have a direct pipeline to the people who designed and wrote the programs for your computer.

As noted, Quantum has packaged many of the service and information features you will find on other systems into its special interface. But it also has some highly unique offerings. Each version of the Quantum service has various named areas or sections. There is Commodore or Apple or Tandy Headquarters, for example, a place where you will find the latest information on company products, special-interest groups devoted to products and applications, a real-time conferencing area, and a hotline feature to shoot your questions to the company. There is a shopping "mall," a clubhouse, a recreation center, and so on.

Specific Features

For specifics, we can use the offerings currently on PC-Link as an example. Basic PC-Link service includes a Software Buyer's Guide with press releases from various software developers describing new and upcoming products and a catalog one can browse to find packages for particular needs. There is the Reference Desk with Grolier's *Academic American Encyclopedia* and the best-seller list from *Publisher's Weekly;* Dollars and Cents (stock quotes, market summaries, investment advice, and financial news from *USA Today*); and a headline service covering news, weather, and sports. In the Entertainment Guide section you will find soap opera summaries, horoscopes, travel news, movie reviews, Hollywood Hotline, American's Eaasy Sabre travel service, and other vendors.

The Quiz Center offers news and trivia quizzes, the Academic Bowl, and opportunities to win prizes and free Plus connect time. There is an opinion poll section called Our World for user polls and surveys on political, social, and leisure topics. And there is a home shopping area (Comp-u-Store and other merchants), Quantum Customer Service, and Tandy Headquarters.

Unlimited nonprime-time use of all of those features is included in your monthly $9.95 PC-Link subscription. Plus features (surcharged at 10 cents a minute/$6 an hour) include the Financial Center (online stock trading, professional investment advice, management consulting services, news, and a forum called Manager's Network); the Software Library (downloadable public-domain and shareware programs); the Publisher's Connection and Forum (SIGs hosted by software developers like Activision, Broderbund, Sierra On-Line, Electronic Arts, and others); Computer Forums (SIGs); The Community Center (join—or create—SIGs devoted to topics of interest); the Post Office (electronic mail); The Mall (shopping and classified ads); and the People Connection (CB simulator chat).

The services and features offered by Q-Link and AppleLink are similar. Of course, features come and go and change in the online world, so be sure to check with Quantum for current information. Of special interest is the Learning Center feature found on all Quantum services. This feature is a Plus service on Q-Link and PC-Link. It's on AppleLink too at the standard rate.

Real, Live Tutors

Quantum has put a real emphasis on online education. In the Learning Center, courses may include elementary and secondary mathematics, English, science, programming in BASIC, programming in C, astronomy, history of religion, creative writing, and many other subjects. There are programs one can download that offer instruction when you are offline. There are interactive programs and quizzes (multiple choice, fill-in-the-blanks, true/false) you can run while online. And there are real, live human tutors conducting hour-long sessions on various topics. Students are free to correspond with tutors in addition to attending classes. Courses are usually taught by professional educators whose experience runs from elementary through the university level.

Poetic Justice

It may be that by melding videotex-style graphics with the features of an online utility service Quantum has found the winning formula for a home-based computer information service. It's a formula that many much larger companies have lost literally hundreds of millions of dollars looking for. There is also a touch of poetic justice in Quantum's apparent success. Years ago an entrepreneur and idea man named William von Meister had a concept he called an "information utility." He and his partners found the financial backing and designed a system from the ground up. The system would tap into the growing home computer boom and, in addition to an initial subscription fee, would involve a commitment of $10 a month. The system was called The Source.

After leaving The Source, one of the things von Meister did was found a company called Control Video Corporation. Control Video was going to become the MTV of video games by offering Atari owners the chance to play and download games via the phone lines. After spending nearly $20 million in the venture, and ending up with only a few thousand subscribers, Control Video was almost zapped out of existence. But it hung on and with management changes and new financing became Quantum Computer Services.

It is far too early to say whether Quantum will take the lion's share of the home market. Its competition, in the form of IBM/Sears's Prodigy and similar services, is only now gearing up. But Quantum will certainly be a player.

Conclusion

The various Quantum systems can't really be fully described in words or pictures. The on-screen graphics and ease of interaction are an integral part of the system and must be experienced to be fully appreciated. Demonstrations and tutorials are included on all three program disks, but at this writing it is not possible to get a demo-only disk. (It may be in the future.) Your best bet is to contact your computer dealer and see if he or she sells Quantum and would be willing to run a demo in the store.

For more information, or to order a subscription package over the phone (Visa or MasterCard), contact the appropriate number below:

Apple and Commodore
(800) 782–2278

Tandy and IBM-compatible
(800) 458–8532

...11...

Systems to Watch:
Minitel, Prodigy,
CitiNet, and More

Nineteen eighty-six was the year of the Big Crash in consumer online services. On March 21 of that year Viewtron, a home-based videotex system on which Knight-Ridder Newspapers had spent over $55 million, suddenly shut down. This came almost immediately on the heels of the March 7th demise of Gateway, a videotex service created by the Times Mirror Company that cost the company millions of dollars and attracted only 3000 subscribers. "We found that our subscribers only used the service sporadically," said James H. Holly, president of Times Mirror Videotex Services. "Our goal was to have an average revenue of $20 per month per user. We just didn't see anything close to that. People would sign up for the service, try it out a few times, and then just drift off."

To appreciate the deathly silence that followed, you have to realize what glorious expectations these and other companies had at the time. In June of 1983, for example, the consulting and research firm Booz Allen & Hamilton proclaimed that a huge home information systems market was only 24 to 36 months away. The prediction, based on a two-year, $2 million study, affirmed that as early as 1985 a $30-billion market would exist, with consumers willingly paying $32 to $35 a month for the convenience such systems would offer (bill paying, information, home security, games, and so on). The message was clear: "You better get aboard now 'cause the train's leaving the station."

Other wise men and experts added their voices to the din, including communications consultant Gary Arlen, president of Arlen Communications and member of the board of the Videotex Industry Association. Mr. Arlen predicted (*Business Week*, February 27, 1984) that videotex could be a $30-billion industry by the mid-1990s.

160

All the pundits and experts were similarly optimistic. And all of them were wrong. Seriously wrong. As Herbert Brody pointed out in his article "Sorry, Wrong Number" (*High Technology Business,* September 1988), sales in the videotex market totaled a mere $113 million in 1987. The article's leading subhead was "Market-research firms routinely mispredict the course of technology businesses. Why do executives still listen?"

Why indeed? Particularly when, like your local TV weather personality, the same pundits and industry experts are once again predicting sunny skies—without acknowledging for a moment that the last time they said it would be fair it rained cats and dogs. Gradually life has begun creeping back to the burned-out forest of home-based information systems, and major firms are gearing up to give it another try. Clearly some overwhelmingly powerful force must be driving things, else why would anyone risk scores, even hundreds, of millions of dollars on a concept that has eaten nearly everyone else alive.

There is such a force, of course. In fact, there are at least two of them. The reason Knight-Ridder, Times Mirror, *The Washington Post,* and many other newspaper companies were among the first players in this field is that they saw it as a potential threat to their traditional markets. If people were going to be getting their daily ration of printed news on a screen, where would that leave the Wednesday supermarket ads or the Sunday real-estate ads, or a paper's other main financial arteries?

Fortunately for the nation's newspapers, the threat did not materialize. As James Batten of Knight-Ridder said on the Viewtron shutdown, "It is now clear that videotex is not likely to be a threat to either newspaper advertising or readership in the foreseeable future." He added, "It is also clear that the American public is not ready to support a videotex service at a level that would justify the continuing expense [of operating Viewtron]."

The second force driving this end of the business can be stated quite simply: The companies that sell things in this country want to gain access to your home. The pot of gold most of them see at the end of every domestic telephone line or TV cable in the country is so dazzling that it makes it impossible to see the red ink on their balance sheets. Imagine today's home shopping television networks with push-button buying. No need to pick up the phone. No need to pry yourself out of the couch. "You'd like this beaut-i-ful Capadamonte dust collector—at our special sale price of only $49.95? Then just push the "Yes" key on your combination TV clicker and remote terminal. We'll send it right out."

That's the kind of vision that makes marketing executives dab the corners of their mouths. That's what the new home-based videotex services are all about. And that's why companies like IBM and Sears are willing to pony up nearly $600 million to make it a reality. What's more, there have been some notable videotex successes, specifically the Teletel system with its Minitel terminals in France.

In this chapter we will look briefly at the ferment taking place in the online world and offer quick-sketch profiles of some of the systems and online options you will be hearing more about in the future. At this writing, none of them is available nationally, though that is expected to change.

We'll start with Minitel, the name by which the French system is generally known in this country; look in briefly on the Regional Bell Operating Companies (RBOCs) and the gateway services many of them are putting up; tell you what you can expect on Prodigy, the IBM /Sears-created system; and look at CitiNet and Canada's Alex system. The usual caveat about online change applies here to the nth degree, for absolutely nothing is certain about these systems, even—ultimately— their survival.

Parlez-Vous Minitel?

Late in 1983 the French Ministry of Posts and Telecommunications, which operates both the post office and the phone system in that country, began offering telephone subscribers in an area of Paris the option of a computer terminal instead of the annual two-volume Paris telephone book. The idea was that instead of looking in the book for someone's phone number, users would look online. The system started with about 3000 subscribers, and ten years later it had grown to some 3.5 million. The system's features had grown as well, from an initial 15 services (news, stock quotes, catalog shopping, railroad, airline, and movie schedules, and so on) to more than 6000. At this writing, the French spend some 52 million hours a year using the system. Along the way, the French government spent over $1 billion operating the system and *giving away* hundreds of thousands of free terminals, a fact that most U.S. companies somehow always forget to mention when pointing to Minitel as an indication of their future success.

The Minitel box itself is a dumb terminal about the size of a small portable television. It weighs in at about nine pounds, can handle only uppercase letters, displayed in a 25-line by 40 or 80-character format. The built-in modem receives information at 1200 bps but sends at only 75 bps, the thought being that it need only be fast enough to keep up with someone typing on the Chiclet-style keyboard. Reportedly it costs less than $50 to make. Souped-up models, with a color display, memory dialer, speakerphone, and other features (like the ability to transmit at

1200 bps) are also available. There are also Minitel-emulator programs for most major brands of personal computers.

The cost of leasing a terminal ranges from a few dollars a month for a basic model to about $25 a month for a more advanced version. Some Minitel-accessible services are supported by advertising and thus are free. Others cost about 20 cents a minute during prime time and about seven cents a minute during nonprime time. No subscriptions are required, and all charges are billed to your phone bill.

None of this would be terribly significant were it not that Minitel is coming to America. Indeed, it's already here. In January 1988, Houston-based U.S. Videotel announced that it had secured the exclusive distribution rights to the Minitel M1B terminal and detailed its plans to set up a system based on the French model. In May of 1988, France Telecom formed Minitel USA and opened an office in New York.

At about the same time James Monaco, president of Baseline, announced that his firm would lease Minitel terminals to all subscribers who preferred them to a personal computer. Baseline is *the* entertainment industry database and online system, covering the latest TV and movie credits, box office grosses, projects in development, new scripts, and much more. Later that year a Minitel system called Reseau CETI ("CETI Network") went live in Montreal and US West, one of the American Regional Bell Operating Companies, announced an agreement with Minitel USA to jointly explore the application of the French Minitel videotex concept in the United States.

Here are the relevant addresses, should you wish more information:

Minitel USA
1700 Broadway
New York, NY 10019
(212) 307–5005

Information Provider Market
U.S. West Communications
1801 California Street
Denver, CO 80202
(303) 896–2355

Baseline, Inc.
838 Broadway, Fourth Floor
New York, NY 10003
(212) 254–8235

CETI
425 De Maisonneuve W., Suite 1200
Montreal, Quebec H3A 3G5
CANADA
(514) 844–5539

RBOC Gateway Services

The most important aspect of the French system isn't the Minitel terminal itself. It is ease of use: The fact that by flipping a switch one can access literally thousands of online features, with all costs being charged to your phone bill. Every Minitel terminal, for example, has seven dedicated function keys, including, "Next page," "Previous Page," "Hang Up," and "Help." Since all services available through the system operate in exactly the same way, there are no complex commands to learn. Just press the appropriate function key for what you want, whether you are reading *Nouvel Observateur* (a left-leaning monthly magazine) or chatting with your latest love interest. You don't have to set up an account, send in your credit card number and expiration date, or go through any of the other delays common to American systems. If you are a telephone customer and you have a terminal, you can begin using the system's feature immediately.

Needless to say, this idea is more than a little attractive to this nation's phone companies, for in return for providing access and billing services, the French phone company gets a cut of the proceeds. And thanks to Judge Harold Greene's September 1987 and March 1988 rulings regarding the AT&T divestiture agreement, the RBOCs now have the green light to offer such services. RBOCs can provide (and charge for) the links that make Minitel-like systems possible, but they are prohibited from creating and providing any information services, a prohibition that no longer applies to AT & T.

US West, Nynex, Bell Atlantic, PacBell, and especially BellSouth, have been actively exploring what they call "gateway" services. At this writing most such systems are still in the early stage, and still looking for a few good information providers. But the basic outlines are clear.

First, a standard navigational system in which all features respond the same way to the same commands. Second, single-number access to multiple services. This is at the heart of the gateway concept. You won't have to dial Telenet for one system and Tymnet for another. You'll be able to move "effortlessly" from one feature to another, even though those features may be housed on different host systems. Third, telephone company billing. Very important. It's convenient. It eliminates a major headache and expense for information providers. And everyone pays their phone bill or risks having services, er, "discontinued." Hopefully the phone companies will take the opportunity to hire design consultants to make their bills more readable.

There will almost certainly be a low, flat monthly fee—say about $6— for unlimited access to the system. Plus surcharges, of course, for any premium features you choose to use. There also seems to be a consensus that Americans will want "smart" terminals, capable of storing and printing out text, downloading programs, and offering all the other features common to personal computer communications. In any case, it is virtually certain that each of us will be offered subscriptions to RBOC gateway services in the not-too-distant future.

IBM and Sears: The Prodigy Project

In 1984 a number of formidable corporate combines were announced that spelled a full frontal assault on the videotex problem. RCA, J.C. Penny, Bank of America, CBS, and others formed various apparently synergystic alliances to bring videotex into the home. Although things can most assuredly change, at this writing the only combine that is still a major player is Trintex, a three-company joint venture that originally included IBM, Sears, and CBS. CBS dropped out after spending nearly $20 million on the project and facing a reported possible additional investment of $80 million.

The Trintex system, now appearing in selected cities, is called Prodigy. According to literature supplied by the company, Prodigy is aimed at baby boomers in two-income households who are starved for time and frustrated by lack of control over their lives. Also, "home-bound elderly, young people without cars, and people with physical disabilities" who find "many transactions, such as grocery shopping, a formidable task." Plus "the newly retired, college students, single parents, professionals working at home." And apparently, everyone else whose needs can be satisfied by "a service that's delivered through their regular telephone lines" and that has been "designed to become second nature." Like breathing out and breathing in. Or "as familiar as the TV set" and "as easy to use as a microwave or a VCR."

"With its vivid color and compelling graphics, the Prodigy service has a distinctive style and personality that has to be experienced to be fully appreciated."

Current features included in the supplied "summary of 500 services and features" are news, weather, and sports from *USA Today* and other sources; electronic mail; continuously updated stock quotes; online shopping; educational information on science, geography, and other subjects, plus an interactive version of *My Weekly Reader;* stock brokerage services from Donaldson, Lufkin & Jenrette; American Airlines Eaasy Sabre for airline schedules and online reservations; *Consumer Reports;* grocery shopping (in some cities); banking and bill paying; some 30 expert columns covering health, gardening, movies, books, politics, sports, and fashion; and, under "Entertainment," trivia quizzes, contests, humor and interactive fiction, and the interactive game "Where in the World is Carmen Sandiego?"

Prodigy Graphics

It has long been a truism in the videotex industry that the cost of creating and delivering a high-quality service forces companies to charge a price that is far beyond what the mass market is willing to pay. Consequently, as with television and radio, carrying advertising has always seemed like a logical solution. Even some of the ASCII-based online utilities have begun slipping in short, one or two-sentence ads between menu displays. But by and large, advertisers have never been enthusiastic about paying for a simple text-based message. At the very least, most want to be able to use high-quality, full-color graphic illustrations.

Knight-Ridder responded to this need by initially forcing its subscribers to purchase an AT&T Sceptre terminal system ($600) capable of decoding and displaying North American Presentation Level Syntax (NAPLPS, pronounced "nap-lips") graphics. The cost of this system may have had something to do with why people stayed away in droves.

In any case, Prodigy also uses a "screen-frames" format based on NAPLPS, which allows sophisticated text fonts and complex graphics to be displayed on any IBM Color Graphics Adaptor-compatible system. Like the Quantum systems profiled earlier, however, much of the graphic display information is stored on the user's disk. This means that even though Prodigy operates at 1200 bps, it can put a graphics frame on your screen fairly quickly, without having to transmit a bit for each and every pixel (picture element).

Most Prodigy screen frames have a text and graphics area that occupies about two thirds of the available space. Approximately one quarter of the screen is occupied by an advertising box. The remaining space is taken up by a single command line. If you request it, the advertising box can be expanded to a full screen, and some ads can occupy several frames in a series. Significantly, each Prodigy subscriber has a personal profile, provided at sign-up time. (Up to six profiles can be created per household.) You thus receive only those ads that match your specified interests.

Trintex mainframes carefully track your actions on the system and record the files and features you access. They then produce a report regarding customer demographics correlated with feature use and response patterns. As *PC Week* (March 15, 1988) points out, "These reports, and the marketing power they represent, are the true heart of Prodigy as a business concept."

The same article quoted Ross Glatzer, senior vice president of marketing at Trintex, as saying "We can allow ads to achieve certain demographic cuts. Without invading the privacy of our members—which is very important to us—we can provide advertisers with a way to reach a certain number of people with particular characteristics."

At this writing, Prodigy subscription kits sell for $49.95 for the software, or $149.95 for the start-up kit and a special wall-mounted 1200-bps genuine Hayes modem. As long as you have communications software, you can use the modem to access other services as well. At this writing, you must own an IBM-compatible machine, though non-IBM versions of the software are expected in the near future.

Prodigy's monthly subscription fee is $9.95 for unlimited access to most of the features detailed above. According to *Interactivity Report* (April 1988), the Trintex business plan calls for subscribing households to spend 30 minutes per day online with the service. And, according to literature supplied by the company, nationwide coverage will be in place by the early 1990s.

"The baby boomers are maturing just at the time that consumers of every age are becoming increasingly comfortable with home computers," the Prodigy literature affirms. As the system evolves, apparently Prodigy's role in consumers's lives is also scheduled to change. "At first a mere adjunct to the daily routine, it is starting to become an alternative way to conduct many transactions and a new way to communicate with family, friends and colleagues. Eventually, it will become part of the lifestyles of busy American consumers—the preferred way to manage information, communicate, bank, shop, invest, and make reservations."

Well, we'll see. Meantime, for more information, contact:

> Prodigy Services Company
> 445 Hamilton Avenue
> White Plains, NY 10601
> (914) 993–8848

The Alex System in Canada

On December 5, 1988, Bell Canada launched Alex, a network service named after Alexander Graham Bell. Initially scheduled to be available only in Montreal, plans call for eventual expansion into Toronto, and the rest of Bell Canada's territory. (Bell Canada is the largest telephone operating company in the country with over six million customers in Quebec, Ontario, and surrounding areas.)

Alex is interesting because it combines all of the elements we have discussed so far. One can use either a personal computer or a specially designed ALEXTEL terminal manufactured by Northern Telecom to access the service. The terminal's design was clearly heavily influenced

by the Minitel. It offers eight large function keys labelled "Help,"
"Send," "Next," "Previous," and so on, but it also has a full QWERTY
keyboard and a numeric keypad you can use for dialing. Future models
are expected to allow you to hook up a printer as well.

Like Prodigy, Alex uses NAPLPS graphics. The Canadian government, in fact, put up much of the funding in the late 1970s for the development of the Telidon standard that eventually became NAPLPS.
ALEXTELs can communicate in ASCII as well. At this writing, the
only ongoing fee for using Alex is the monthly rental of an ALEXTEL
(about $8), but even that isn't necessary if you have a personal com-
puter. All subscriber costs are based on usage and are charged to your
telephone bill.

At this writing, Alex is primarily a French-language-based service.
Some features do have bilingual pages that display both French and
English side-by-side, and a few others let you choose one version or the
other. Services include community information, electronic mail, classified ads, national and international news, financial information, consumer tips, games, online shopping, and the other usual suspects. But
users also have access to Bell Canada's white pages and may eventually
gain access to the yellow pages as well, pending certain regulatory rulings. There are also lots of chat services.

Services are classified into five cost and billing categories, including
free services and those ranging in price from about 12 cents to about 45
cents a minute. There is also a category for merchandise and services
you can order and be billed for directly by the vendor. Unfortunately
for consumers, at this writing, it is necessary to dial a separate telphone
number for each tier of service, an inconvenience that is antithetical to
the gateway concept. Clearly, though the Montreal operation is billed as
a full-scale test market, Alex is a system to watch in the future. For
more information:

> Bell Canada
> 700 de La Gauchetiere W.
> Montreal, Quebec H3B 4L1
> (514) 870–4050
> (800) 361–ALEX

CitiNet from Boston to the World

For many years it has been obvious to anyone involved in personal
computer communications that the technology is ideally suited for *local*,
community-based information systems and messages exchanges. Such

systems have been offered in the past, sometimes by an entrepreneural company, sometimes by a public-spirited individual running a BBS. Not until the second half of 1988, however, did any real momentum begin to build, spurred on by the various RBOC plans for gateway services and the general interest created by Minitel's success. It may also be that public awareness is finally catching up with the technology.

In any case, one of the systems that was suddenly propelled to center stage was Boston CitiNet. A service of Applied Videotex Systems (AVS), prior to 1985 Boston CitiNet was known as Yellowdata International to connote the yellow pages information it contained. CitiNet is a free, advertiser-supported service. The only cost is a purely optional $25 per *year* for either an electronic mailbox or access to the chat lines, or $40 per year for both.

In contrast to what you'd expect on a free service of this sort, Citi-Net's offerings are both rich and vast. And distinctly community-oriented. For example, WGBH, Boston's public broadcasting station, puts its daily program listings online, including a separate section called "Series Repeats Schedule" in case you missed the first broadcast. A number of Boston radio stations are online with program listings, listener surveys, request lines, chat, and feedback sections. There's a guide to Boston's many libraries, museums, and historical centers listing upcoming events, lecture schedules, tours, and membership information. At least one commercial movie theater has put its "Now Playing" schedule online.

Professional societies (architects, attorneys, physicians, and others) are also represented, as are many colleges and universities with a combination of instructional information and descriptions of various degree and continuing education programs. There is a large classified advertising feature as well, including a special real-estate section (RealNet) to aid you in searching for an apartment, roommate, or home. The Suffolk County government has even put its registry of deeds online, searchable by seller, buyer, mortgage amount, and other criteria. At least six local elementary and secondary schools also use CitiNet as a bulletin board (password required).

We found the service a pleasure to use, with simple commands and menus and online utility-like GO commands that make it easy for advanced users to zip around the system. We were also pleasantly surprised to discover that, contrary to what we had feared, promotional announcements and ads do *not* appear on your screen. Instead, various sections of the service are supported by companies offering related merchandise or services.

The movie review menu, for example, offers Cineman movie reviews as an option, but it also contains an option giving you the current schedules of at least one movie theater. On an entertainment menu that includes various categories of user-contributed jokes, there is an option offering information on The Comedy Connection, a local Boston comedy and nightclub. The rest of the CitiNet service is organized in a similar way. The advertising is not forced on you, but additional information and even online shopping facilities are available if you want them.

The only thing wrong with CitiNet at this writing is that it is available only in Boston. But that is scheduled to change. The company has already formed AVS Gateway Services, a consulting firm that has contracts with several RBOCs to organize and recruit information and service providers for CitiNet-style systems in cities like Houston, San Francisco, Philadelphia, and others. For more information contact:

> American CitiNet
> World Trade Center, Suite 717
> Boston, MA 02210
> (617) 439–5678

The Cleveland FreeNet

Finally, an interesting development has been taking place at Case Western Reserve University in Cleveland. Under a program initially made possible by grants from AT&T, Ohio Bell, University Hospitals of Cleveland, and the Case School of Medicine, an organization called the Society for Public Access Computing (SoPAC) has begun offering a community computer system that is completely free of charge. In some respects, Cleveland FreeNet, as the system is called, might be thought of as the online equivalent of the public broadcasting system. It is funded on an ongoing basis by contributions from organizations and individuals in and around Cleveland on a purely voluntary basis.

The system offers electronic mail; online computer user groups; special-interest groups covering topics as diverse as air and space, handicapped matters, and culinary arts; online medical and dental information; contact with elected representatives; a "podium" for electronic speeches; and an electronic schoolhouse for teachers, parents, students, and administrators. Other features are being added all the time, governed largely by the interests and desires of FreeNet users.

The software that makes FreeNet possible is owned by the nonprofit Society for Public Access Computing and is available to qualified parties from any other city who want to start a similar system. The cost is a lease payment of $1 a year. For more information contact:

T. M. Grunder, Ed.D
Executive Director
SoPAC
Box 1987
Cleveland, OH 44106

Conclusion

We have always believed that online communication and information services were the greatest thing since Stouffer's frozen foods. For most people, the new worlds and new possibilities that open up when you go online remain the single best reason for buying a personal computer. Unfortunately, the path has never been easy and the rewards waiting at its end don't always measure up to the journey. Yet the *possibilities* are there.

So it isn't surprising after the disasters of several years ago to see videotex redux. Apparently different companies are going to keep trying until somebody gets it right. One would like to be equally optimistic about all of the new systems now coming online. Unfortunately, many companies seem to be so wrapped up in *their* goals and *their* desires that they have forgotten to consult the customer. They have neglected that most fundamental point of all sales successes—"the *you* approach." What do *you* want? How can we serve *your* needs?

We have never read a marketing study in this area, for example, that addressed the simple question of how videotex and online services will fit into the schedules of the average American. Will people come home from work and run immediately to boot up their computers—instead of putting their feet up and perusing the paper or playing with the kids? Will they forego evening television and rented videotapes to go online?

Some people will, of course. And surely some interesting systems and options are now afloat. But it is difficult to see how videotex will ever truly become a mass-market success until it is incorporated into the home-entertainment center. When it is as easy to get stock quotes or do online shopping as it is to click from one channel to another, videotex will have truly arrived. Until then, that faint tune we hear in the distance sounds like nothing so much as someone whistling past a grave-yard.

Part III

—INFORMATION SERVICES—

...12...

Overview: Libraries Like Grains of Sand

T he chapters in this section are set in another part of the forest. Or in another solar system of the electronic universe. Here we enter the realm of pure information—hard-core, industrial-strength information. It's a realm of bibcites, abstracts, and Boolean operators that historically few people who are not degreed librarians or information professionals have entered. Yet it is at the very heart of the much-heralded "Information Age."

Many subscribers to CompuServe, GEnie, and other online utility services are familiar with electronic stock quotes, newswires, and the odd database or two. But from an information perspective, those systems are the baby pond. Real information power can be found only on systems like DIALOG, BRS, NewsNet, and the others we will consider in the chapters that follow.

What kind of power? Well, what would you like to know? You can literally pick any subject, any person, any company or institution, *anything* you want to know about, and within seconds the answer can be scrolling up your screen, regardless of where you are on the face of the earth at the time. The information storehouses you can access with your personal computer are that vast, that comprehensive, and that accessible.

This is not an exaggeration. But there is a catch. To whom much is given, much is expected. The information you want won't pop out of the computer of its own accord. You're going to have to go in and get it, and that will require some work on your part. The amount of information available is so vast that it is difficult to see how it could be otherwise, though some authorities are pinning their hopes on artificial intelligence techniques that may eventually make information retrieval much easier.

In addition, the coverage of many databases is so broad—often embracing hundreds or even thousands of magazines, newspapers, journals, and other publications—that if the keyword or term you are looking for *can* have a number of different meanings in different contexts, you must assume that all of those meanings *will* be represented in the database. The word "hit" can be expected to occur in stories dealing with everything from Broadway to boxing to baseball or, as we'll see in a moment, to online searching. This means that you're going to have to do some thinking before you begin.

The Promise and the Power

With the possible exception of the Dow Jones News/Retrieval Service (DJN/R), the systems we will be discussing in the next seven chapters are quite different from online utilities. You do not have to be an information professional to use them, whether to devastate your competition or simply satisfy your own curiosity, but you do have to be willing to spend a little time and effort learning to use this incredible resource.

This chapter will introduce you to the basic concepts of information-intensive databases. Succeeding chapters will profile the leading online systems through which such databases are available. We will not discuss the finer points of online searching or describe various databases and how you might use them. These and many other hands-on topics are covered in *How to Look It Up Online* by Alfred Glossbrenner (St. Martin's Press, New York), a book for everyone who wants to tap the power of information without first obtaining a degree in library science.

Industry Schematic

The online information industry has two main types of players. There are the database producers, also called "information providers" or "IPs" (pronounced "eye-peas"). And there are the online systems or "vendors" like DIALOG, BRS, VU/TEXT, ORBIT, and the others we'll be considering later. The relationship between the two is often very much that of wholesaler and department store. The IP supplies the database to the vendor, and the vendor makes it available to the public. Often this works well for all three parties—IP, vendor, and customer. The IP is free to concentrate on database development. The vendor handles billing and advertising. And the customer can take advantage of one-stop shopping, using the set of commands to search many databases on the same system and paying one itemized monthly bill.

Electronic Information Basics

What's in a Database?

A database can contain absolutely anything. It could consist of every article in *Time* or *Newsweek* magazine or the most important economic and demographic reports and tables from the Census Bureau or a catalog listing and describing almost every piece of software for Macintosh computers. It could be the Yellow Pages of the nation's phone books, or the full text of a major reference book like *The Encyclopedia of Associations*. Basically, if there's a market for the information (and sometimes, even if there isn't), a database will be created to provide it.

It is crucial to understand the wide-open nature of the field. There are *no* standards. Thus one company can choose to create a database that contains, say, only the cover stories published by *Time* magazine, plus "other selected articles." It may choose to begin its coverage with, say, 1962. A different company might also choose to offer *Time* magazine in its database, but include every article. Its coverage, however, might begin with 1979. Both database producers could say in their promotional literature that they cover *Time* magazine, but as you can see, their coverage is quite different.

We confected the above example to make a point. In reality, competitive pressures virtually rule out the existence of differences in coverage as marked as those in our example. The actual differences are more subtle. But they're there, and as a smart information consumer you should be aware of them.

What Format Does the Information Take?

Because the information in databases can vary so and be so eclectic, it is impossible to classify databases by content other than to refer to their coverage: "This one covers every U.S. doctoral dissertation written since 1861, and that one covers over 300 English and French-language Canadian periodicals."

In terms of information format, however, things are a bit more uniform. There are three major formats you can expect to encounter online: bibliographic, full text, and statistical.

Most of us are familiar with statistical tables, though you may want to look at Figure 12.1 for a classic example of online statistics. Full text, of course, is full text—the complete text of a magazine, newspaper, or other article. All that's missing are any photos, graphs, or other illustrations. And one day they will undoubtedly be available online as well.

Information Services

—————— **Figure 12.1. Cendata (U.S. Census) Online** ——————

Shown below is a small portion of one of the many tables you will find in Cendata, a database prepared by the U.S. Census Bureau. Some statistical databases contain only tabular matter, in which case you must search on the basis of the title of the table. Cendata contains both statistics and paragraphs (not shown here) of text summarizing the data. The information, and much that is not shown, was obtained in just over four minutes at a cost of about $2.80.

11.5.2 - February 3, 1989
TABLE 1: PRICE INDEX AND AVERAGE SALES PRICE OF NEW ONE-FAMILY HOUSES
SOLD - FOURTH QUARTER 1988

PERIOD	Price index (1982= 100.0)	FKI sales price of kinds of houses sold in 1982 (estimated from the price index)		Average sales price of houses actually sold(1)	
		Price (dollars)	Period to period percent change(2)	Price (dollars)	Period to period percent change(3)
ANNUAL DATA					
United States					
1987	116.8	98,000	2.8	127, 200	13.7
1988(p)........................	117.0	98,100	0.2	138,300	8.7
Northeast					
1987	178.3	158,000	13.3	170,900	13.0
1988(p)........................	183.9	163,000	3.1	180,500	5.6
Midwest					
1987	113.4	99,500	4.7	115,500	12.6
1988(p)........................	119.2	104,600	5.1	122,900	6.4
South					
1987	109.6	85,800	0.4	106,600	11.9
1988(p)	108.9	85,300	−0.6	114,400	7.3

PERIOD	Price (dollars)		Period to period percent change(2)	Price (dollars)	Period to period percent change(3)
West					
1987	111 .5	103,200	3.5	134,600	15.9
1988(p)	109.5	101,400	−1.8	156,000	15.9
QUARTERLY DATA					
United States					
1983:					
1st Quarter	101.4	85,100	2.2	86,700	2.5
2nd Quarter	101.7	85,400	0.4	89,100	2.8
3rd Quarter	104.7	87,900	2.9	92,500	3.8
4th Quarter	104.0	87,200	−0.8	90,900	−1.8

(p) Preliminary.   (r) Revised.
- -- Represents zero.

(etc.)

(1) Source of actual sales prices: Current Construction Reports, C25, New One-Family
Houses Sold and For Sale, U.S. Department of Commerce, Bureau of the Census.
(2) Derived from change in price index.
(3) Derived from actual sales price.

Source: Current Construction Reports, Series C27, Price Index of New One-Family Houses
Sold. The C27 report for Quarter 1, 1986 contains a detailed description of the
1982 price index series. C27 reports are available from the Superintendent of
Documents, U.S. Government Printing Office, Washington, D.C. 20402

Annual subscription: $5.00

Questions regarding these data may be directed to Steven Berman, Construction Starts
Branch, telephone (301) 763-7842.

Bibliographic citations, or "bibcites," are another matter. The closest
most of us have ever gotten to a bibcite is having to prepare a list of
them for a high-school or college English paper. Since most electronic
information exists in bibcite form, it is worth taking a moment to understand what you can expect to find online—and how to find it.

Bibcites and Abstracts

Online databases, like those you might create yourself with PFS:File, dBASE III, or some other personal computer database management package, are called "files." Each complete item in the file is called a "record." And each piece of information in the record is called a "field."

The easiest way to keep these terms straight is the classic example of a collection of cancelled personal checks. All the checks together constitute the file. Each individual check is a record. Each piece of information on a check (the date, the payee, the numerical amount, and so on) is a field.

In Figure 12.2, for example, all of the downloaded text constitutes a single *record* in the PTS PROMT (sic) database *file*. The *fields* include the article title, name of the journal, publication date, volume number, issue number, and page numbers. The summary paragraph or "abstract" is also considered a field, as is the collection of keywords and numerical codes at the end of the record.

— **Figure 12.2. File, Record, and Field—Bibcite and Abstract** —

Here is a record from the PTS (Predicasts Terminal System) PROMT (Predicasts Overview of Markets and Technology) database file on DI-ALOG. The article title, the publication, the publication date, and other individual pieces of information constitute the fields. This record can be searched for and retrieved based on the contents of any of its fields, including the contents of the summary paragraphs or abstract. Note: To save space we have edited the record where indicated by elipses.

Tide hasn't turned yet.
Advertising Age November 18, 1985 v. 56 no. 90 p. 43
ISSN: 0001-8899
Availability: Predicasts Article Delivery Service
Article type: Industry Profile   Source type: News
Special feature: Picture; Company; Agency

. . .Liquid Tide, via Saatchi & Saatchi Compton, that positions the brand as providing superior cleaning, water softening and buffering and soil suspension agents. The product was introduced in early-1985 with a $50mil marketing budget. . . .

Lever Bros' Wisk continues to lead the category with an 8.8% market share. The liquid detergent market comprises 30% of the total $3.5bil detergent market. Liquid laundry detergents are more popular in northeastern and North Central US states. New Liquid Bold 3 has been nationally rolled out by P&G and it is positioned as cleaning tough laundry problems plus through-the-wash fabric softening and static control. TV spots use the theme, 'So good, we bottled it.' Grey Advertising handles advertising for both powdered and liquid Bold 3. Colgate-Palmolive . . . with a $13.5mil ad budget. The brand is positioned as a heavy duty cleaner with fabric softener and static control in TV spots, via Foote Cone & Belding. . . .

C-P . . . its reformulated Dynamo 2 . . . $10mil ad campaign, via FC&B. Lever Bros is

increasing ad spending for Wisk will introduce liquid and powder Surf brand detergents. Surf liquid will be supported with a $100mil national ad campaign, via Ogilvy & Mather.
TRADE NAME: Liquid Tide; Wisk; Liquid Bold 3; Dynamo 2; Fab; Surf

AD AGENCY: Saatchi & Saatchi Comptor Grey Advertising; DUNS NO.: 00-698-4876; TICKER: GREY; CUSIP: 397838 Foote Cone & Belding; DUNS NO.: 00-543-7769; TICKER: FCB; CUSIP: 344872 Ogilvy & Mather COMPANY: Procter & Gamble; DUNS NO.: 00-131-6827; TICKER: PG; CUSIP: 742718 Lever Bros Colgate-Palmolive; DUNS NO.: 00-134-4381; TICKER: CL; CUSIP: 194162

COUNTRY: United States (1USA)
PRODUCT: Liquid Household Organic Detergents (2841230); Dry Household Organic Detergents (2841220); TV Advertising (7313200)
EVENT: Marketing Procedures (24); Order & Contracts Received (61); Market Information (60)
ADVERTISING CONCEPT: Campaign Launched (74); Television (21); New Products/Services (57); Positioning (51); Geographic (82); Account Activity (42); Industry Market Data (85)

All records in a bibliographic database contain at least two components: the bibcite and a list of keywords. The bibcite includes the article title, the author's name, and all relevant facts about the source publication. After all, the purpose of a bibliography is to make it easy for someone to locate the books, articles, and other publications it contains.

In Figure 12.2, the bibcite occupies the first six lines of the downloaded text. As you can see, it includes everything you need to know to quickly locate the original article in a library. But it doesn't include any real information.

> **Online Tip:** As explained in *How to Look It Up Online*, many companies are in the "document delivery" or "doc-del" business. For a fee, they will locate, photocopy, and send to you (by fax, Federal Express, or mail) virtually any article you see referenced online. Costs vary but average around $8 to $12 per article. Some firms will even locate and photocopy entire books for you. The reputable services pay an annual fee to the Copyright Clearance Center to cover royalties on photocopied material. Often you can enter your order for an article online. In fact, if you look at Figure 12.2 you will see that Predicasts informs you that the complete article is available from its own article delivery service.

Nor does it contain enough information to make it practical to search for this record. Remember, computers are nothing if not literal-minded. If a word does not exist in a record there is no way the machine can find it, and the bibcite alone doesn't give you much to work with. For this reason, the creators of bibliographic databases almost always add a field of keywords. These words may also be called "indexing terms" or "descriptors."

The people who add these keywords work for the database producer and are called indexer/abstractors. They are professionally trained to read each source article and decide which keywords best describe its contents, the issues, topics, or concepts it covers, and where it fits in the overall scheme of things. The keywords the indexer/abstractor decides on may or may not appear in the source article.

Controlled Vocabularies

How does the indexer/abstractor know which words to choose? The answer is that indexing terms are almost always drawn from a predefined list of words called a "controlled vocabulary." The complete controlled vocabulary used to index a database is called a "thesaurus."

For example, John Wiley & Sons, the producer of the Harvard Business Review Online (HBRO) database, has established a list of 3500 "authorized index terms" that includes everything from "ordnance" to "x-ray apparatus." The words "ammunition" and "x-ray machine," in contrast, are not on the list and are thus not used as keyword descriptors. The only way to determine this fact is to look up "ammunition" in the HBRO thesaurus, where you will be told, "See *ordnance*." Needless to say, if you plan to do much searching of a database that uses a controlled vocabulary, it's essential to have a copy of its thesaurus. Wiley sells the 400-page HBRO thesaurus for about $50.

Including Abstracts—the Other Bibliographic Option

A record consisting of a straight bibliographic citation and a list of key index words can be quite serviceable. Indeed, when the information industry was starting and computer storage costs were high, it usually wasn't economic to offer anything but bibcites and keywords. Then too, communications speeds were four to six times slower than they are now, making it impractical to transmit significant quantities of text. There were few complaints from end-users, however, since most were librarians with easy access to the source material and since online databases represented such a leap forward.

Some commercial databases, like Information Access Company's (IAC) Magazine Index, still offer nothing but bibcites and keywords. (IAC's companion product, Magazine ASAP, offers the full text of many of the articles referenced in Magazine Index.) But it is much more typical these days for the producer to include short summaries or abstracts of the source article as well. They are usually prepared by the same professionals responsible for indexing a database.

The abstract of the *Advertising Age* article in Figure 12.2 gives you a much better idea of whether it would be worthwhile to obtain a copy of the source article. Better still, a good abstract may very well contain exactly the fact, figure, or statistic you're looking for and thus eliminate the need for the source article entirely. As noted, the abstract itself is considered a field in the record, and it is almost always searchable.

How to Find the Information You Want

As a new online searcher it is tempting to believe that because it is more "complete" a full-text database is ipso facto better than one offering bibcites and abstracts. But that is definitely not the case. In fact, much of the time exactly the opposite is true.

A database of abstracts is usually much easier to search. Unless you are looking for a very specific and unique combination of words, searching a full-text database can be treacherous. With so many words, the potential for unexpected (and thus irrelevant) combinations and occurrences of your search terms is enormous. You can easily end up retrieving and paying for articles that have nothing to do with your subject of interest.

Abstracts can also save you both time and money. For example, if you wanted information on the marketing of leading laundry detergents, which would you rather read, a complete 1000-word article or a short, fact-packed abstract of the article like the one shown in Figure 12.2? Which would you rather pay, as much as $7 for the full text or about 60¢ for the bibcite and abstract?

When searching for bibcites and abstracts of interest, the fields of each record are obviously the key to the whole shootin' match. Records are what you are after when you search a database, and fields are the only way you can hit them. In fact, each time a system finds a record containing one of your keywords, it's called a "hit." Finding information is thus a lot like the carnival game where the object is to dump the pretty girl, good-looking guy, or some other clown into the water by hitting a target with a baseball. You know someone's there. You can see him through the protective cage. But you'll never knock him into the pool unless you hit the target.

In the carnival game there is only one target. In a database record there are many. That's important because the more fields a record contains, the more precisely you can focus your search. Needless to say, the number of fields a record contains is up to the database producer.

Imagine a database created from your address book or Rolodex cards.

If there is a field in each record for Phone Number, you could tell the database software to retrieve every record containing the phone number 800–555–1212. That's not terribly useful. After all, how often do you know someone's phone number but not their name?

Suppose we break up the phone number into more precise fields. Suppose we restructure the records so that there is a field for Area Code and one for Phone Number. If you were planning a trip to Los Angeles and wanted to be sure to call all of your friends when you're there, you could easily produce a comprehensive list. Simply tell your database software to retrieve every record in the file in which Area Code = 213.

Now look again at Figure 12.2. As noted, each of the components of the bibcite, as well as the abstract and the attached keywords, are searchable. Just look at what you have to work with: trade names, ad agency, DUNS Number, product, and more, including those numbers in parentheses following the items listed under "Product," "Event," and "Advertising Concept."

Those numbers are a PTS special feature. Predicasts, the database producer, has created a coding system based on the U.S. SIC (Standard Industrial Codes) list. The difference is that Predicasts codes are longer and much more precise. In fact, they are so useful that a number of companies now use Predicasts codes instead of SIC codes for their internal operations. Thus, before you ever sign on to DIALOG, BRS, or VU/TEXT (all of which offer PTS PROMT), you can look up the relevant code(s) in the *PTS Users Manual* to prepare an almost mathematically precise search.

In addition to SIC codes and the codes developed by Predicasts and a similar database called ABI/INFORM, you will also be able to locate information on the basis of codes for Metropolitan Statistical Areas (MSA), International Standard Serial Number (ISSN) for magazines and similar publications, International Standard Book Number (ISBN) for books, and corporate DUNS number (created by Dun & Bradstreet, this is like a Social Security number for a company).

As mentioned, you may also have a controlled vocabulary list to work with. And most important of all, you have your own imagination. Finding information online can indeed be a cookbook-like exercise. But there is no substitute for thought and creativity: Where would the information I seek probably have been published? Which magazine, newspaper, or government report? Which databases cover these target sources? What unique keywords would be most likely to appear in any article focusing on my topic?

Search Language Basics

The search languages and commands database vendors offer to allow you to enter your chosen keywords and codes vary in power. In most cases, however, you will be able to use "truncation," a term most computer owners will recognize as using a "wildcard." Thus if you want to find a record containing the word "publishing," that's what you would search on. But if you also wanted to allow for "publisher" and "publishers," you would search on "publish*" or use whatever other truncation symbol the vendor offered.

Boolean searches are also a standard feature. As users of personal computer database programs know, these involve the operators AND, OR, and NOT. Thus you can prepare a search statement that says, in effect, "PUBLISHING AND (BOOKS OR MAGAZINES) NOT SOFTWARE" to focus on just books or magazines and eliminate any reference to software publishing.

Proximity operators are also fairly standard. If you were to search for GEORGE AND BUSH, you could easily hit records that talked about George Smith and John Bush. That's because you have specified that the names George and Bush must occur somewhere in the same record. To eliminate the problem, you might want to search for GEORGE (W1) BUSH, which translates as "George within one word of Bush." But suppose the text referred to the current President only as "George Herbert Walker Bush." To allow for that possibility, you would probably want to search on GEORGE (W3) BUSH. You would still get "George Bush," but you would also get references to his full name as well.

What Does It Cost?

We've been speaking about search languages and commands in the broadest terms. Other commands are available and those we have illustrated are not intended to be taken as standard. Different systems use different syntaxes. Unfortunately, different systems also follow different pricing policies. So we must speak equally broadly here as well.

In a word, online information is expensive. At least in the absolute sense. You can easily run up a bill of $50 or more and have very little to show for your efforts, particularly if you don't know what you're doing. On the other hand, without in any way wishing to let the vendors and IPs off the hook, there are some mitigating factors, and there are some low-cost alternatives.

A single database like ABI/INFORM from UMI/Data Courier gives you instant access to over 680 U.S. and international magazines, journals, and other periodicals, dating back nearly 20 years, depending on the vendor. (Some vendors offer versions of ABI/INFORM that go back further than others.) Even if a nearby library happened to have every issue of every one of these publications, it would take you days if not weeks to search through them. When you consider that you can accomplish the same search online in about 10 minutes, paying about $1.90 a minute and 68¢ per record displayed doesn't sound so bad.

So it costs you $25. If it's the information you need, it might be able to earn you many times that amount. In fact, even if it isn't the information you need, assuming a competently conducted search, it may still be worth many times the $25 you will pay. After all, sometimes finding that there is *no* information on something can be valuable information in and of itself, as might be the case if you were planning to patent an invention or introduce a new product.

In broad terms, then, three major factors determine what you will pay. First, the specific database. Each one typically carries a different price. Patent databases tend to be the most expensive; databases based on government information tend to be the cheapest. The rest fall somewhere in between.

Second, connect time. On most systems, the moment you "enter" a given database the connect-time meter for that product begins to tick. Prices range from a high of about $300 per hour or $5 per minute for patent databases, to a low of about $30 per hour or 50¢ per minute for a government-produced database. On top of that, you may also be charged for "communications costs"—the price of using a packet-switching network.

Finally, there are display charges. The information industry generally operates on the policy of "The more we display, the more you pay." That means that if you choose to display just the bibcite you will pay one charge, but if you opt for the full record, you will pay more. Other format and price combinations often lie between these extremes. Prices here vary all over the lot from 14¢ per full record to $20 to $120.

One might accuse the information industry of deliberately making it difficult to compare database prices. On DIALOG, for example, a full record from the DISCLOSURE database (SEC filings from over 12,000 companies) costs $20, plus 75¢ per minute in connect time. On Dow Jones, you will be charged $1.75 per minute in connect time, plus $1.25 for every 1000 characters displayed for the identical information.

How in the world is the average person supposed to be able to compare these two prices? Let alone the prices of searching DISCLOSURE on BRS, Nexis, or VU/TEXT? There are only two possible conclusions. Either you aren't meant to be able to compare them—which probably gives the online industry too much credit. Or you as the consumer never entered the thoughts of whoever created these pricing structures. As so often happens in this field, the companies involved took the "me approach" instead of the "you approach" with its inherent concern for the customer.

Low-Cost Alternatives

On the other hand, whoever came up with the ideas for DIALOG's Knowledge Index (KI) and BRS's BRS After Dark systems was really working overtime in your best interests. Designed for students, educators, and anyone else able to postpone their online activities until after business hours, KI and After Dark give you reduced-rate access to many of their parent systems's most popular databases. Thus for an all-inclusive fee of $24 per hour or 40¢ per minute, you can use the Knowledge Index to search ABI/INFORM, Books in Print, .MENU (the International Software Database), several databases from Standard & Poor's, America: History and Life, Magazine Index, Consumer Reports, Marquis Who's Who, the King James Bible, and many other major-league offerings. Equally important, both systems use a simplified search language and give you the option of using menus or operating at command level.

These are the two systems we would recommend for any new user. KI and BRS After Dark offer an excellent, low-risk way to get started in the field of information retrieval. They also give you a lot for your money. After all, their databases are identical to the ones available through their parent systems. However, while their offerings are extensive—ranging from 70 to 125 databases each—they include only a fraction of all that is available.

Sometimes you may not have a choice about where and when you search a particular database. It may be available on only one full-cost system. The complete text of the *New York Times*, for example, can only be found on the NEXIS system (though bibcites are widely available). Similarly, the full text of the *Wall Street Journal* is available only through DJN/R. The same is true of many less well-known databases.

In those situations, the best advice we can give you is to call the vendor's customer service number and make sure that you know exactly what types of charges will be involved for what you want to do and exactly what rates you will pay.

How to Make the Most of Vendors and IPs

Indeed, one of the things you pay for in this part of the forest—and one of the things most newcomers fail to take full advantage of—is customer service. The information industry takes an entirely different approach to customer service than most of us are accustomed to experiencing in the computer and software industry. They take it seriously.

Consequently, you will often find that vendors provide a toll-free number staffed by well-trained people. What's more, not only do the vendors provide customer service, the IPs provide it as well. In some cases, you can simply call customer service, tell the representative what you're looking for, and the individual will tell you exactly what commands to key in. Though it is usually not official policy, often a customer service representative will even test the search strategy while you wait to make sure it will yield the kind of results you seek.

Vendors and IPs are also very good about providing manuals, quick-reference cards, support materials, and in many cases, customer instruction and training. These normally aren't free, but it can be important to know that they are available. All you have to do is ask. Both parties may also send out monthly newsletters and update sheets. Again, it never hurts to ask.

The EasyNet Alternatives

Everyone's information needs are different, of course. If you have no plans to use a vendor's system on a fairly regular basis, there's not much point in learning its commands and otherwise mastering its way of doing things. But what if you need the power of online information for a one-time project or perhaps only on an occasional basis?

If that's your situation, there are at least two alternatives. One is a "gateway" system called EasyNet. The other is to contract with a professional searcher or "information broker." EasyNet is a product of Telebase Systems, and in addition to being directly accessible on its own, it is also accessible as IQUEST on CompuServe or as InfoMaster on Western Union's EasyLink mail system. EasyNet's cachet is twofold. First, as a gateway it gives you access to nearly 20 online systems, and through them, to over 750 of the world's leading databases. You don't have to subscribe to DIALOG, Orbit, or NewsNet, for example. You can search the databases on these systems through EasyNet.

Second, although EasyNet now offers a command option and an option to select your target database, it was originally designed as a menu-driven system. This means that it will take you through a series of menus that will help you define your needs and refine your search strategy. Ultimately, it has the power, based on your input, to pick the appropriate database.

You will still have to type in your own search strategy and keywords, so you will still have to think carefully about what you want to look for. Once you give your "okay," EasyNet will put you on hold for a moment while it connects with the chosen system, translates your search commands into the proper syntax, and conducts a search of the target database. It will then come back to you to tell you how many records match your search criteria and offer to show them to you. The cost for conducting each search is about $8, and the cost of viewing each record the system finds is about $2 apiece. Not cheap, but still cheaper than subscribing to a system you may only use once.

For more information, contact:

> EasyNet
> Telebase Systems, Inc.
> 763 West Lancaster Avenue
> Bryn Mawr, PA 19010
> (215) 526–2800

Hire an Information Broker

Executives, managers, professionals, and everyone else whose success depends on getting the right information at the right time have got to be familiar with the kinds of information available, where it can be found, and how it can be obtained. They also need to at least be aware of the complexities that can be involved and be cognizant of the fact that information is not like yard goods. You can't simply pull a length off a roll, wrap it up, and expect it to satisfy your every need.

At the highest level, information retrieval is an art calling for a great depth of knowledge, a bubbling spring of imagination, and an ability to make creative leaps and connections. Fortunately, for those who are unwilling or unable to do their own online searching, there are "information brokers." The term is not at all descriptive; "professional searcher" or "information professional" would be more to the point. But information broker is how the men and women who practice this art have always been known in the trade.

In the United States today, there are probably fewer than 1000 information brokers. Which in our opinion starkly illustrates the reality of the so-called Information Age: a lot of lip service but very little long green. As talented as they are, few information brokers can make a go of it full time. Most hold day jobs as professional librarians and do their information brokering at night or on the side. The reason is simple: Everyone will willingly accept information for free, but few companies or professionals value it highly enough to be willing to pay for it. As a result, most do without.

That will inevitably change. Smart companies already realize that their competitive edge depends on having the right information ahead of everyone else. And as the companies they beat begin to question why

that it bought the company for $353 million. Knight-Ridder also owns VU/TEXT, one of the leading vendors of local newspaper databases. And while at this writing few visible changes have been made, it seems inevitable that at the very least some kind of linkup will be established between the two. DIALOG users can obtain a VU/TEXT password free of charge, and several VU/TEXT papers have become available on DIALOG itself. Prudently, the information community has taken a wait-and-see approach to the acquisition, but the reaction has generally been positive. After all, no one could ever figure out what a missile manufacturer was doing in the information business in the first place. As an information company itself, Knight-Ridder appears to be a more logical parent.

Getting Started with DIALOG

Whether you think you might be interested in online searching or not, we strongly urge you to phone DIALOG and request a free information packet, database catalog, and publications catalog. The database catalog is about 100 pages long, and it will give you an excellent overview of the hundreds of databases DIALOG places at your disposal.

Each database listing, for example, includes a header telling you the range of coverage (starting year to the present), the number of records in the file, how frequently new records are added, and the name of the database producer. This is followed by 100 to 500 words of description designed to give you some idea of what the database covers. Each entry also tells you the connect-hour charge and the charge for displaying each full record online.

An appendix lists databases by type (bibliographic, full text, numeric, or directory). Another appendix lists each database and the costs for using it. Still another appendix classifies the databases by subject area (Agriculture and Nutrition, Business Information, Patents and Trademarks, Science and Technology, and so on). This particular appendix does double duty, for its primary purpose is to show you the DIALOG OneSearch categories and related databases. With OneSearch, you can simultaneously search all of the databases in, say, the People category, with a single command.

DIALOG Publications and Support

If you're intrigued by what you find in the database catalog—and especially if it all seems so strange and new—your next step should be to consult the DIALOG publications catalog. Here you will find a plethora of videotapes, tutorials, subject field searching guides, classroom instruction programs, and manuals. All of these items are for sale.

DIALOG charges you nothing to open a subscription, but the system manual and other important support materials sell for $90 in the United States and Canada, including shipping. The company offsets this by granting new subscribers $100 in free connect time.

Depending on your level of experience, you may or may not be interested in the other publications, but don't pass over the DIALOG "Database Chapters." These sell for $6 apiece, and they are absolutely invaluable, whether you plan to search a given database on DIALOG or on some other system. Each database chapter runs 25 to 50 pages and concentrates on one particular database, explaining what it covers, how it is put together, and what you'll find in various fields. There are also lots of sample searches and plenty of tips and tricks for using the product to find the information you want. There is absolutely no truth to the rumor that professional searchers have lobbied to have these publications banned because they make online searching so easy that anyone can do it.

DIALOG's customer support is excellent, even legendary. At this writing we know of no one else who offers a 24-hour hotline during the week. And no vendor produces a better newsletter. As noted at the beginning of this chapter, calls from the 50 United States are toll-free and Canadian subscribers may call collect.

If you live elsewhere, your best bet is to phone your nearest DI-ALOG representative (see the list at the end of this chapter). But you are perfectly welcome to phone customer service directly at (415) 858-3810. We are told that this is not uncommon. However, while the customer service staff can usually locate someone fluent in Spanish, Japanese, and French, you should be aware that there is no mechanism in place to serve non-English-speaking callers.

Blue Sheets, Yellow Sheets, and the *Chronolog*

The DIALOG Starter Package sells for $150 and includes your manual (a $50 value), plus an introductory seminar conducted at a nearby large city ($125 value), plus $100 of free connect time. Alternatively, you can simply buy your manual and support materials and sign up for a standard contract. There are no obligations, other than an annual $25 fee to cover your subscription to the *Chronolog*, DIALOG's monthly newsletter/magazine. Corporate or other high-volume users willing to commit to a certain amount of usage can sign up for a discount contract offering substantial savings over the normal connect-time rates.

If you're going to sign up for DIALOG, we have three suggestions. First, in addition to the manual, buy the complete set of DIALOG Blue-sheets ($50). These are one to four-page quick summaries of each database on the system. You'll still want the appropriate database chapters for the databases you plan to search intensively, but much of the time the Bluesheets will give you everything you need.

The Yellowsheets describe each company that has a document delivery contract with DIALOG. Capabilities and prices differ, but in general you are free to specify any Yellowsheet company when ordering an article copy or other document online. The complete Yellowsheet package sells for $15, and depending on your needs, it may or may not be optional for you. But you should definitely purchase the three-inch DIALOG binder ($10). You will want to have your manual, Bluesheets, and possibly your Yellowsheets all in one place, and $10 is a good price for a large, sturdy three-inch, three-ring binder.

Finally, you will definitely need your subscription to *Chronolog*. This newsletter typically contains 20 pages of information designed to alert subscribers to new databases, new commands, price changes, new features, and so on. As you might expect. But it also contains the latest Blue- and Yellowsheets, prepunched for notebook insertion. *Chronolog* is thus part of what might be called the DIALOG living manual.

Online Tip: Though not considered here, DIALOG also offers what it calls the DIALOG Business Connection and the DIALOG Medical Connection. These are menu-driven products that, while they give you access to many of the same databases available on the main system, are exceptionally easy to use. A separate pricing structure applies in each case, and you'll need a separate subscription.

The two "Connection" services current at this writing do have limitations, including a tendency to rely on prepackaged reports ("List of Manufacturers," "Share of Market Data," and so on). But you really can wade right in without reading the manual, and in return for a reduction in search power, they do a good job of insulating you from the main system. If you are involved in either business or medicine, you may want to ask about these services when you call.

The Knowledge Index

The Knowledge Index (KI) is DIALOG's low-cost, after-hours system. The information it offers can also be found on the main DIALOG system, but KI differs from DIALOG in a number of ways. At this writing, KI offers some 80 databases. In addition to those cited in Chapter 12, these include the Harvard Business Review (full text), Peterson's College Database, Magazine Index, Newspaper Index, the Business Software Database, MEDLINE, Magill's Survey of Cinema, and many more.

KI charges a flat rate of $24 an hour (billed to your credit card), regardless of the database you use (except the King James Bible, which is billed at $6 an hour). That price includes telecommunications costs, and there are no display charges. The search language is a simplified version of the language used on DIALOG, but it is quite serviceable. You can use wildcards and you can search on a particular field (AU = Adams, D?), and you can use the basic AND/OR/NOT Boolean operators. You can view your hits in one of three formats (short, medium, and long), and you can order copies of the documents referenced in the bibcites and abstracts you see online. Menus are also available for those who want them.

The KI start-up fee is $35 and it includes your manual (what KI calls its *User's Workbook*) and two free hours on the system. This $48 credit is to be used within 30 days of your first logon. There is no continuing obligation. For a better idea of what KI is like, you might send for the KI demonstration disk containing 54 ABI/INFORM records. The cost is $5.

The KI manual is a three-ring, tabbed notebook, and it includes a four-page descriptive insert for each database. These inserts serve as both Blue Pages and Database Chapters. There are also very good instructions to show you how to use the system. Direct invoicing is available if you prefer. And you can put multiple passwords under a single account for a one-time fee of $25 per password. In return, KI will send you a manual for each password. KI subscribers also receive a quarterly newsletter called the *Knowledge Index News*.

KI is a smoothly running, easy-to-use system that in our opinion is not only ideal for most computer-using adults but also for high-school and college students interested in researching assignments and papers. (The Grolier *Academic American Encyclopedia* is among KI's database lineup.) And best of all, at a flat rate of $24 an hour, the price is right. The system started several years ago with about 25 databases. As you have seen, it now offers triple that number. And in the future it will offer even more.

DIALOG Worldwide

DIALOG has offices in Boston, Chicago, Houston, Los Angeles, New York City, Philadelphia, and Washington, D.C. It also has offices in the other countries listed here.

Argentina, Mexico, Venezuela

Aseores Especializados en
Information y Documentacion,
S.C.,
AEID/DIALOG
2 Cerrada de Romero de Terreros,
49A
03100 Mexico D.F.
Telephone: 543–7207

Australia and New Zealand

Insearch Ltd./DIALOG
P.O. Box K16
Haymarket
Sydney, NSW 20000
Australia
Telephone: (02) 212–2867
Telex: AA27091 (INSRCH)

Brazil

PTI—Publicacoes Tecnucas
Internacionais Ltda.
Rua Peixoto Gomide 209
01409 Sao Paulo SP
Telephone: (55) (11) 257–2157
Telex: 1135844 APTI BR

Canada

Micromedia Ltd./DIALOG
158 Pearl Street
Toronto, Ontario M5H 1L3
Telephone: (800) 387–2689
(416) 593–5211
Telex: 065–24668

Europe

Learned Information
Ltd./DIALOG
Woodside Hinksey Hill
Oxford OX1 5AU
United Kingdom
Telephone: (0865) 730–969
Outside U.K.: (44) 865–7320275
Telex: 837704 (INFORM G)

Dialog Information Services
75, Avenue Parmentier
75011 Paris
France
Telephone: (1) 40.21.24.24

Japan

Kinokuniya Company, Ltd.
P.O. Box 55 Chitose
Tokyo 156
Telephone: (03) 439–0123
Telex: 2322535 (KINO JL)

Masis Center Maruzen Co., Ltd.
P.O. Box 5335
Tokyo International 10031
Telephone: (272) 7211
Telex: 78126630 (MARUZEN J)

Korea

Data Communications Corp. of
Korea (DACOM)
DACOM Building
65-228, 3-GA, Hangang-Ro,
Yongsan-Ku
Seoul, 140-013
Telephone: (02) 796–6105
Telex: DACOM K28311

Scandinavia

Data Arkiv/DIALOG
Esselte Info
Box 1502
171 29 Sonia
Sweden
Telephone: (08) 705–13–00

DataArkiv–Pressklip
Glentevej 65
DK-2400 Copenhagen NV
Denmark
Telephone: (01) 33.52.10

...14...

BRS and BRS After Dark

BRS Information Technologies
1200 Route 7
Latham, NY 12110
(800) 227–5277
(518) 783–7251, collect
TWX: 710-44-4965

CUSTOMER SERVICE
(800) 345–4277
(518) 783–7251, collect
        from Alaska
(Eastern standard time)

Mon.–Fri.: 8:00 A.M.–1:00 A.M.
Sat.: 9:00 A.M.–5:00 P.M.
Sun.: 9:00 A.M.–2:00 P.M.

Hours of Operation
—All hours are given in Eastern standard time—

BRS Search Service

Available

Mon.–Fri.: 6:00 A.M.–4:00 A.M.
Sat.: 6:00 A.M.–2:00 A.M.
Sun.: 9:00 A.M.–4:00 A.M.

Not Available

Mon.–Fri.: 4:00 A.M.–6:00 A.M.
Sat.: 2:00 A.M.–9:00 A.M.
Sun.: 4:00 A.M.–6:00 A.M.

BRS After Dark availability begins at 6:00 P.M. your *local* time during the week and ends at 4:00 A.M. *eastern standard time*. Thus, if you live on the West Coast, nonprime begins at 6:00 P.M. your time and ends for you at 1:00 A.M. All weekend hours are nonprime, but during the weekend only eastern standard time applies.

Access:

Telenet, Tymnet, and BRSnet. On BRS Search Service communications costs are $11 an hour, in addition to database royalties and system connect charges. On After Dark, communications costs are included in the quoted hourly charge. There is no extra charge for 1200-bps access. Direct dial ($3/hour) and In-WATS ($29/hour) access is also available. BRS is also available through the IBM Information Network.

Connect Rate:

Varies with the database on both BRS Search and After Dark, though After Dark's rates are lower.

Capsule Summary

As an organization and database vendor, BRS has a personality that is quite different from DIALOG, its chief competitor. Though it wouldn't be wise to push the analogy too far, in many ways BRS is to DIALOG what Apple is to IBM in personal computers. Both are after the same connect-time dollar and both offer many of the same databases. However, while BRS has actively added databases in recent years, with slightly more than 150 online at this writing, it has a long way to go to equal DIALOG's 355 or more.

There are less definitive contrasts as well. Most vendors are interested in feedback from their subscribers. But BRS has a User Advisory Board which it takes very seriously. Board members are nominated and elected by BRS subscribers. In addition, its business-oriented offerings, while certainly respectable, have long been overshadowed by its offerings for educators and medical professionals.

Corporate mission statements seem to be very much in vogue in this corner of the electronic universe. No one has yet offered to boldly go where no man has gone before, but they do tend to have a majestic sweep. We saw what DIALOG had to say. Here is BRS's corporate mission statement: "To provide superior information products to selected markets without regard to the vehicle of distribution." In the past, BRS Information Technologies has been involved in a multiplicity of projects, not all of them successful.

That may be about to change. In December 1988, England's Robert Maxwell not only acquired the American publishing firm Macmillan, he also acquired BRS Information Technologies. Some years ago, Mr. Maxwell's Pergamon organization bought the SDC ORBIT system, and according to Jim Terragno, ORBIT'S president at the time, "Our objective is ultimately to have one online service." Since only six or seven databases are found on both ORBIT and BRS, such a merger would produce a system with well over 200 offerings. The thinking in the online industry is that such an ORBIT/BRS combine has the potential to give DIALOG a real run for its money.

Some preliminary steps in that direction have already been taken. In April 1989, Robert Maxwell introduced Maxwell Online, and named Jim Terragno as its president. The firm has two operating divisions, ORBIT Search Service and BRS Information Technologies.

Database Highlights

For business users BRS offers databases like ABI/INFORM, the Harvard Business Review Online, Predicasts Annual Report Abstracts, InvestText, PTS PROMT, and the Business Software Database. For educators there are databases like ERIC (Educational Resources Information Center), Ontario Education Resources Information, Exceptional Children Resources, and Resources in Vocational Education. There are chemical and engineering databases as well, including the Kirk-Othmer Encyclopedia of Chemical Technology.

It is in the medical and health-care fields, however, that BRS really comes into its own. Over the years BRS has made a concerted effort to assemble the best collection of medically related databases in the industry. Highlights include:

• The Comprehensive Core Medical Library (CCML)—The complete text of over 70 medical journals, periodicals, and books. Sample journal titles include the *American Journal of Medicine, Annals of Internal Medicine, Lancet, New England Journal of Medicine, Science,* and *Pediatrics.* The book collection contains nearly 25 titles, including *The Merck Manual, MacBryde's Signs and Symptoms, Holland and Brews Manual of Obstretics, Gray's Anatomy,* and the *Cecil Textbook of Medicine.* Each publication can be searched separately, or you can search them all at the same time.

• MEDLINE—The National Library of Medicine's (NLM) database covering the world's biomedical literature. Dates from 1966 forward and includes citations and abstracts from over 3400 medical journals.

• EMBASE—Complements MEDLINE with coverage of over 4000 medical journals worldwide.

• Health Planning and Administration—Produced by NLM and the American Hospital Association, this database includes international coverage of management, financing, organization, personnel, safety, and related subjects.

• Cumulative Index to Nursing and Allied Health Literature—All major English-language nursing and primary journals in 14 allied health fields.

There is much more as well, including at least three databases devoted to coverage of AIDS, three more devoted to cancer, plus Chemical Abstracts, pharmaceuticals and drugs, psychology, veterinary medicine, and many others. These databases are available to all BRS subscribers, but the company has a special option called BRS Colleague for doctors and health-care professionals. BRS Colleague offers menu-driven access to the system, special rates on medically related databases, electronic mail, topical bulletin boards, and more.

Individual BRS Colleague accounts can be opened for a one-time fee of $95. There is a monthly minimum usage fee of $20, but discounts run from three to 15 percent, depending on the number of hours used each month. Group accounts are also available.

BRS Search: Subscriptions and AidPages
Since the situation is so uncertain, it is pointless to spend a great deal of time here detailing current subscription options. We will simply say that under the BRS Open Access Plan, users pay an annual fee of $75. You are then charged connect time, display charges, and communications costs for whatever you do on the system. Costs are comparable to using DIALOG, though they may be slightly lower. BRS also offers an Advance Purchase Plan that involves specified discounts for specified usage commitments. The documentation is adequate, with BRS Aid-Pages filling the same role as DIALOG's Bluesheets. And the search language is quite powerful, though of course, it is quite different from DIALOG's or that of any other system.

BRS After Dark—The Low-Cost Alternative
Regardless of whether BRS is merged into ORBIT or vice versa, it is a virtual certainty that the company will offer some kind of off-hours, low-cost option. DIALOG's Knowledge Index is simply too successful to ignore. At this writing, as it has for many years, BRS offers BRS After Dark. There is an initial fee of $75 and a commitment to spend at least $12 a month on the system. The service gives you access to about 100 of the main system's 150 or so databases. Connect-time charges range from $8 to $81 an hour, while most display charges are about a nickel per record. BRS Search costs, in contrast, are more in the neighborhood of $45 an hour, with display charges averaging around 50¢ per record. You may use After Dark via menus or by commands.

BRS's strength in the area of medical information is no accident. The

system was founded as Bibliographic Retrieval Services in 1977 by
Janet Egeland and Ron Quake, both of whom were employed by the
Biomedical Communication Network of the State University of New
York (SUNY) at Albany. Until its acquisition by Robert Maxwell, BRS
was owned by an arm of Thyssen-Bornemisza, a Dutch industrial con-
glomerate that also owns Predicasts, creator of the PTS PROMT and
other outstanding databases.

Conclusion

The essence of any vendor's system, of course, is the collection of
databases it has assembled for you to search. And since the best way to
learn more about those databases is to send for the vendor's catalog and
price list, that is exactly what you should do with BRS. After all, whatever happens in the future, the databases will continue to exist, and
they will continue to be available on one system or another.

...15...

ORBIT

ORBIT Search Service
Pergamon ORBIT InfoLine, Inc.
8000 Westpark Drive
McLean, VA 22102
(800) 421–7248
(703) 442–0900

CUSTOMER SERVICE
(800) 421–7248
(Eastern standard time)

Mon.–Fri.: 8:00 A.M.–6:30 P.M.

Hours of Operation
—All hours are given in Eastern standard time—

Available

Mon.–Fri.: All day
(except from 9:45 P.M. to
10:15 P.M.)
Sat.: Until 4:00 P.M.
Sun.: Starting at 4:00 P.M.

Not Available

Mon.–Fri.: 9:45 P.M.–10:15 P.M.
Sat.: 4:00 P.M.–Sun. 4:00 P.M.

Access: Telenet and Tymnet or via direct dial

Connect Rate: Varies with the database

Capsule Summary

The ORBIT Search Service, like BRS Information Technologies, is an operating unit of Maxwell Online. ORBIT was created in 1965 by the System Development Corporation (SDC). SDC began as part of the Rand Corporation, and one of its first tasks was to develop an information retrieval system for the Advanced Research Projects Agency (ARPA) of the Department of Defense. Another ARPA project, the ARPANET, was the first system to employ packet-switching technology to connect widely scattered users, most of whom were on university campuses. The ARPA network made headlines in 1988 when a programmer on the East Coast used it to launch a virus attack against systems all over the country. SDC now belongs to UNISYS (Sperry-Burroughs). But in late 1986 ORBIT was acquired by Robert Maxwell's Pergamon Group of Companies and made a part of Pergamon ORBIT InfoLine. In April 1989 it became part of Maxwell Online.

Quantitatively the ORBIT Search Service is the smallest of the Big Three classic bibliographic databases. Qualitatively, the words that best describe it are "exclusive" and "technical." A fair percentage of the 100 or more databases on the system at this writing are available exclusively through ORBIT. The system has more scientific and technical databases than any other kind, followed by engineering and electronics, energy and environment, and numberous industry-specific offerings. A database called SAE, for example, is prepared by the Society of Automotive Engineers. One called COLD covers the literature of Antarctica. APIPAT focuses on petroleum-refining patents from the United States and eight other countries.

Some ORBIT databases are exclusive in another way as well. At least a dozen databases require special permission from the database producer. ORBIT tells you whom to contact to secure permission, but that's about all. You may have to purchase a subscription to the printed publication from which the database is drawn, though if you do you'll probably get a discount when you use the product online.

The system places special emphasis on patents and materials science. For example, a database called INPADOC from the International Patent Documentation Center covers patents published by 55 national and international patent offices. LEGAL STATUS from the same organization offers information about postissue patent changes. World Patents Index from Derwent Publications Limited covers 31 major patent offices, plus Research Disclosure and International Technology Disclosures. CLAIMS from IFI Plenum Data Company offers the most extensive coverage of U.S. patents anywhere.

Those same databases are available on other systems. But at this writing, ORBIT has exclusive rights to JAPIO, the only online source for English-language information about Japanese patent applications not covered by World Patents Index, U.S. Patents (the complete text, plus bibcites, of all U.S. patents issued since December 1970), Computer-PAT (U.S. patents for digital data processing), and LitAlert, the only online source of information about U.S. patents and trademarks whose legal status may change due to actions of U.S. courts. And much more.

> **Online Tip:** Patent and trademark searching can be tricky, and considering the stakes that can be involved, it is not something that should be done by an amateur. Certainly you may want to take a quick look yourself to see if the idea or trademark you are considering belongs to someone else, but before betting the company, hire a professional and have him or her conduct a thorough search.
>
> Many information brokers specialize in patent searches. And often database producers in this area offer such services as well. Pergamon also offers patent and trademark search services, and the company's close proximity to the Patent and Trademark office in Washington, D.C. enables it to quickly furnish copies of the relevant documents.

ORBIT's exclusive offerings in the materials science field include Ceramic Abstracts; Corrosion (effects of over 600 agents on the most widely used metals, plastics, nonmetallics, and rubbers over a temperature range of 40 to 560 degrees Fahrenheit); Forest (wood products industry literature); Metals Data File; Paper, Printing and Packaging Abstracts; Rubber and Plastics Abstracts; and World Surface Coatings Abstracts. There are many other nonexclusive databases with relevant information as well.

Subscriptions and Search Language

ORBIT subscriptions are available free of charge. There is no initial fee or continuing obligation. You will have to buy a main system manual (about $60), however, and you will probably want one or more "database manuals" ($7.50 each), ORBIT's equivalent of DIALOG's database chapters. Connect-time charges average around $100 an hour (patent databases are among the most expensive in the online world), and display charges average around 45¢ to 50¢ per record. Billing is by direct invoice, with a $15 minimum charge per invoice. Given the specialized, industrial focus of many of ORBIT's databases, it seems unlikely that a low-cost consumer-oriented version of the service will ever be offered.

ORBIT is entirely command-driven, and its search language is very powerful. In addition to proximity searching (not available on all databases), truncation, and field searching, and all the other features you would expect in a major system, the language has some unique features.

For example, you can change a command name to some other name more to your liking. Or you can create a synonym for a command so you can use both it and the original. In both cases, your instructions will remain in force for the duration of your session. But you'll have to re-enter them the next time you sign on. There is also a command called TIMEPROMPT that can be toggled on or off. Its purpose is to notify you that the system is indeed working on your search, should your search take abnormally long. At each time interval, you can decide to cancel the search. Or you can ask not to be notified until the search is done.

ORBIT for Non-U.S. Subscribers

In addition to its U.S. office, ORBIT has offices and representatives in at least four other countries:

Europe

Pergamon ORBIT InfoLine, Ltd.
Achilles House
Western Avenue
London W3 OUA
Telephone: (01) 992–3456

Pergamon Press GmbH
Hammerweg 6
D-6242 Kronberg
Federal Republic of Germany
Telephone: 06173–63025

Australia

ORBIT Search Service
P.O. Box 544
Potts Point, NSW 2011
Telephone: (02) 360–2691

Japan

USACO Corporation
13-12 Shinbashi 1-Chome
Minatoku, Tokyo, 105
Telephone: (03) 502–6471

Conclusion

ORBIT clearly isn't for everyone. It offers high-octane information of a specialized nature to what must inevitably be a select group of interested parties. If your business or professional interests involve patents, trademarks, materials science, chemistry, energy and the environment, engineering and electronics, or health and safety, you are probably part of that select group. If so, even if you don't plan to search ORBIT yourself, it may be important for you to know what's available. ORBIT will be happy to send you a database catalog, price sheet, and additional materials explaining the databases and services it offers.

...16...

Dow Jones News/Retrieval

Dow Jones News/Retrieval
P.O. Box 300
Princeton, NJ 08543-0300
(609) 452–1511
(800) 522–3567

CUSTOMER SERVICE
(609) 452–1511

(Eastern standard time)

Mon.–Fri.: 8:00 A.M.–12:00 A.M.
Sat.: 9:00 A.M.–6:00 P.M.

Hours of Operation
—24 hours a day, 365 days a year—
Prime time begins at 6:00 A.M. Eastern standard time. Nonprime time begins at 6:01 P.M. your local time. Weekends and holidays are nonprime as well.

Access:
> Telenet and Tymnet. You may also use ConnNet, for access from any city in Connecticut.

Connect Rate:
> //FYI, the system's newsletter and help section is free; other rates vary from $168/hour to $26.40/hour, depending on the database, the time of day, speed of communications, and subscription plan. Use of 2400 bps incurs an extra charge of 30 cents in prime time and 6 cents in nonprime per Dow Jones "Information Unit" (1000 characters). See the back of this book for a special DJN/R offer.

Capsule Summary

Dow Jones News/Retrieval (DJN/R) is *the* source for current information on financial markets. Lots of systems offer stock and commodity quotes, but no other system covers as many markets and no one else does as much with them. The service is also known for the quality and accuracy of its information. DJN/R personnel constantly watch the quote wire, for example, and they'll phone the exchanges for confirmation should any figures appear out of line.

There is a great deal of other financial information as well, as we'll see in a moment. But there are also some very interesting text searching and retrieval features, plus online stock trading via Fidelty Investor's Express. Plus weather, sports, online shopping via Comp-u-Store, a gateway to the MCI Mail system, book reviews, the Grolier *Academic American Encyclopedia*, and other online utility-like features. Indeed, it is hard to know just how to classify Dow Jones. We have placed it here because in our opinion high-quality, often unique information is the heart of the system. The utility features are a nice extra, but it is difficult to imagine anyone subscribing to DJN/R for those features alone, particularly when most are available at a lower cost on the systems discussed in Part II.

Information Features

News, Weather, and Sports

Accordingly, here we will concentrate solely on information features, starting with Dow Jones News. Dow Jones and Company has its own news service with reporters in almost 100 cities worldwide. Dow Jones was the first private company to be licensed by the FCC to own and operate its own satellite earth stations, which it uses to link its offices and its 17 printing plants. As a result, Dow Jones News stories are usually available to DJN/R customers within 90 seconds of being filed by a reporter. In addition to news from the "broadtape" or ticker on industries, companies, government agencies, international financial markets, the stock market, and the economy, the "DJNEWS" feature includes special stories from the *Wall Street Journal* and *Barrons*.

Searching Dow Jones News is simple, if not terribly precise. You may enter a stock symbol or refer to a list of story codes. The system will then present you with one or more pages of story headlines. Each headline is a menu selection, and to read the story to which it refers, you simply enter your selection.

Next there is the "//BUSINESS" feature, with information from the broadtape, and from the Professional Investor Report, Dow Jones Capital Markets Report, and Associated Press newswires. A feature called "//CMR"—Credit Markets and Financial Futures Report—focuses on the Federal Reserve Board, economic indicators, money markets, financial futures and options, and international credit markets. The Kyodo newswire (Japan) is also available. A feature called "//NEWS" focuses on world and national headline stories as they unfold, whether they have to do with business and investing or not. The Associated Press sports wire is available, as is information from Accu-Weather, the nation's largest private weather-forecasting company.

Securities Quotes and Market Averages

The DJN/R "//CQE" feature offers current quotes from the New York, American, Pacific, and Midwest stock exchanges, plus quotes for companies traded over the counter (NASDQ-OTC). Composite quotes are also available. These are based on reports from the above exchanges, plus the Boston, Cincinnati, and Philadelphia exchanges. In accordance with stock-exchange regulations, there is a 15-minute delay for this feature. Real-time quotes (//RTQ) are also available, but you must sign a separate contract and pay an additional fee of $11 per month.

In its historical quotes database (//HQ), DJNS offers a year's worth of daily volume, high, low, and closing stock prices including common and preferred issues, warrants, and rights. Monthly summaries are available back to 1979; quarterly summaries, to 1978. Commodities and financial futures quotes are available in "//FUTURES." Current quotes are delayed 10 to 30 minutes, depending on the exchange. Historical quotes on more than 80 major commodities and financial futures are also available back to January 1970.

Dow Jones Industrial Averages can be found in "//DJA." This database gives you the daily high, low, close, and trading volume starting with May 24, 1982. You can locate a single day's figures or request all of the averages for a 12-day trading period during the past year. If you want to screen for stocks or other issues on the basis of some criterion, "//TRADELINE" can do the job. This database covers over 120,000 issues (stocks, bonds, mutual funds, and so on) and offers a great deal of historical data.

Most interesting of all is Tradeline's ability to scan for issues meeting a particular specification ("earnings per share greater than or equal to 3," for example). The system will put all matching issues into a set, and you can then screen the set on another specification. You can do this as many times as you wish to progressively narrow the focus. When the resulting set contains a manageable number of issues, you can order the system to print your results in a sorted, customized, columnar report.

Company and Industry Background

A huge amount of analytical and background information is available as well. There is the D&B—Duns Financial Records database with balance sheet and income statement information on over 750,000 companies (most of them privately held). There are SEC 10K and other filings from DISCLOSURE. Corporate Canada, from Info Globe, offers business news and market information on over 2200 Canadian companies. The Corporate Earnings Estimator from Zacks Investment Research is available, as is Media General's Mutual Funds Performance Report, and the main Media General database with its highly detailed numeric coverage of financial and trading data on over 5400 companies. Other databases include Inovest Technical Analysis Reports, Insider Trading Monitor, the MMS International Weekly Market Analysis, Standard & Poor's Online, and InvesText with its hard-to-come-by full-text reports from many of the nation's leading brokerage and investment banking firms (Merrill Lynch, Kidder Peabody, Smith Barney, and nearly 50 others). Fans of the public broadcasting program *Wall Street Week* will find complete transcripts of the last four programs in the feature called "//WSW."

Dow Jones also offers what in the information industry is called "cross-file searching" and an SDI (Selective Dissemination of Information) or current awareness service. It doesn't use these terms, of course. The cross-file searching feature is called "//QUICK." With a single command, //QUICK will search for all information on a specified company in composite quotes, Dow Jones News, Standard & Poor's, the Corporate Earnings Estimator, Media General, DISCLOSURE, Insider Trading Monitor, and InvesText. It will then present you with a menu of your hits. You can pick and choose the items you want to see from the menu, in which case the regular online charges will apply. Or you can opt to view the ALL, in which case there is a flat $39 fee.

The Dow Jones current awareness feature is called "//TRACK." You can create up to 25 search profiles and store them on the system. There is a monthly charge of $5 for profile storage, regardless of the number you create. Each profile can contain up to 25 stock or security issue symbols or Dow Jones news codes for industries, government agencies, and so on. When you have keyed in your selections, the system will ask you to give your profile a name.

Once a profile has been created, you can run it whenever you like. Each time it is run, the system will retrieve the current (15-minute delayed) stock quote for each issue in the profile. It will then automatically go into Dow Jones News and retrieve any current story in which that company's name appears. Story headlines are presented in a menu fashion similar to that used for Dow Jones News, so you can opt to skip a headline or read the story to which it refers.

Text-Searching Features

Dow Jones has long offered subscribers the opportunity to search the full text of the *Wall Street Journal, Barron's,* and the Dow Jones News archive (where stories are stored after remaining for 90 days in the Dow Jones News feature). However, as part of what can only be seen as a major reinvigoration of the entire DJN/R service, the company greatly expanded its offerings in this area in recent years. The overall feature is called "//TEXT" or "//TEXTM." The first is the command-driven implementation and the second offers you menus. Here is what it contains at this writing:

• *The Wall Street Journal*—Every article scheduled for publication back to January 1984. Articles from the current day's issue are available at 6:00 A.M. eastern standard time.

• Dow Jones News—Selected Dow Jones News Service articles and condensed articles from *The Wall Street Journal* and *Barron's* back to June 1979. Articles are available 36 hours after publication each business day.

• *Barron's*—Every article in *Barron's* back to January 1987. Articles from the current week's issue are available the Wednesday after publication.

• *The Washington Post*—Selected articles back to January 1984. Articles are available one day after publication.

• *Business Week*—Every article going back to January 1985. Articles are available one week after the publication date.

• The Business Library—Selected articles from *American Demographics, Consumer Markets Abroad, Forbes, Fortune, Financial World, Money,* and *Inc.* magazines, plus the full text of the PR Newswire and the Japan Economic Newswire. This database is supplied by Information Access Company as a version of that firm's Trade and Industry ASAP product.

• Business Dateline—Selected articles from more than 140 regional and local business publications from the United States and Canada back to January 1985, plus nine daily newspapers and Business Wire. Articles are available four weeks after publication. Supplied by ABI/Data Courier, sample regional publications include "Alberta Business," "Fort Worth Magazine," "Orange County Business Journal," and "The Greater Baton Rouge Business Report."

In the past, one used to dread going into the //TEXT database on DJN/R. Your only option was to use a modified version of the BRS command language (which itself is based on the IBM STAIRS language), and most of the time that meant hauling out a separate manual and spending some time getting up to speed before going online. DJN/R still offers the command option and will supply you with a special manual free of charge. But thanks to the system's menu option (//TEXTM), virtually anyone can now tap these databases. When you key in //TEXTM, here is what you will see:

Dow Jones Text-Search Services
Copyright (C) 1989 Dow Jones & Co., Inc.

PRESS   FOR
1 The Wall Street Journal: Full Text from January 1984
2 Dow Jones News: DJNEWS, WSJ And Barron's from June 1979
3 Barron's: Full Text from January 1987
4 The Washington Post from January 1984
5 Business Week: Full Text from January 1985
6 Business Library: Forbes, Fortune, PR Newswire, Japan Economic Newswire and Four
   Other National Business Publications
7 Business Dateline: Business News from 150 Regional Publications
8 DataTimes: 30 Regional and National Publications

Type ALL (Return) to search simultaneously all files, except DataTimes. NOTE: THERE IS A $.40-PER-MINUTE SURCHARGE WHEN USING THE ALL COMMAND. Press (Return) for details on the contents of each file.

As you can see, from here you can select the database you want to search. Unless you are an experienced online searcher, you probably will not want to opt for the ALL option, since it not only costs more but also holds the potential of burying you with a great deal of irrelevant information unless you are very careful about your search request.

After selecting a database, you will be asked to key in your search phrase. No need to worry about Boolean operators. Just key in the phrase you're looking for. (Note that one cannot use wildcards or "truncation" with this feature.) The system will go away for a second and come back to inform you how many articles meet your criteria. At this point, you can opt to view the articles or add additional search terms to further narrow the set. When you are ready to look at the retrieved information, the system lets you look at just the headline and first page of the article (to decide whether you want to view the whole thing) or look at the entire article right away.

DowQuest and The Connection Machine

At this writing Dow Jones is preparing to introduce an even more powerful text-search feature. Known as DowQuest, the feature relies on the search technique of "relevance feedback" and the raw computer horsepower of a $5-million parallel-processing computer called The Connection Machine manufactured by Thinking Machines. With DowQuest, you key in the five or six best keywords you can think of. The machine conducts its search and presents you with the top 16 stories containing those words, arranged as a weighted list.

At that point, you can review headlines or entire stories or even individual paragraphs within stories. When you see a headline, paragraph, or story that matches what you're looking for, you tag it, which in effect says, "There, that's the kind of thing I had in mind." The Connection Machine assembles the tagged material and uses all of the relevant words within that material to conduct a second search. It then presents you with another weighted 16-item list of stories that match your tagged material. Although there's more to it than this, in essence, DowQuest saves you from having to think of and specify every keyword that might appear in the stories you seek. Parallel-processing technology, which allows thousands of individual central processing units to be focused on the task, makes it all happen quickly. One could do the same thing with an ordinary computer, but it would take forever.

Subscriptions and Documentation

Dow Jones offers three membership plans: standard, Blue Chip, and Corporate. Membership kits are available from Dow Jones by calling (800) 522-3567 (except in New Jersey) or from your local computer retailer. The cost is $29.95 regardless of the plan you choose. Standard and Blue Chip memberships include three free introductory usage hours on the system; Corporate memberships include multiple passwords and ten free hours. All versions include the *Dow Jones News/Retrieval User's Guide*, the main system manual.

Standard members are charged an annual $18 service fee. The service fee for Blue Chip members is $95 per year, but you are entitled to a one third discount on usage during non-prime time hours. The Corporate membership plan involves a one third discount on both prime and non-prime time usage, but the cost is $75 per month for each location on a one-year contract.

The Dow Jones *User's Guide* was designed, written, and produced by McGilvray & Glass, and the edition current at this writing (November 1988) is the best DJN/R manual we have ever seen. The information, commands, and explanations are clearly and thoughtfully presented, and it is exceptionally easy to locate the topics you want. Four quick-reference cards on heavy stock are included at the back of the manual listing the various Dow Jones News, Media General, Tradeline, and other codes needed to tap those services.

The company also sells a variety of software packages specifically designed for use with the service. These include Market Manager PLUS, Market Analyzer, the Dow Jones Spreadsheet Link, and similar titles. Each has a different focus, but all operate on the same principle. Basically, you can tell the package what companies, industries, or topics you are interested in while you are offline. At your signal, the software will then access DJN/R, automatically retrieve the information you seek, and sign off. Once that's done, you can use the package to analyze the retrieved information in a variety of ways.

Dow Jones also operates an active customer support and training program with frequent seminar dates in major cities around the country. Morning sessions typically focus on the system's major news and business offerings. Afternoon sessions concentrate on //TEXT. The cost at this writing is $45 for the first representative from a company or organization and $25 for each additional person. All attendees receive a full free day online. Customized on-site sessions are also available.

Conclusion

The Dow Jones News/Retrieval Service was started in 1974, making it one of the most venerable of all online services. In the early 1980s it made an attempt to court the home-based online utility market, adding features like Grolier's *Academic American Encyclopedia*, Cineman movie reviews, Peterson's College Guides, and Comp-u-Store. Those features are still on the system, but in recent years Dow Jones has increasingly built on its natural strength as the premier source of business and financial information.

Along the way it has greatly improved its system software and user interface. No longer does the system present a page and simply stop, leaving you to wonder if it is merely taking a breather or has finished or what. Today there are "Press (Return) for More" prompts at the end of every page. There are also menus, greatly expanded "help" texts, and a general air of user-friendliness that Dow Jones has heretofore lacked. Most exciting of all to a long-time DJN/R watcher are all the new databases and features that have begun to appear. After several years of quiescence, the system is perking with activity.

It is also, by industry accounts, raking in the cash. At least one industry newsletter ("Interactivity Report," January 1988) noted that in 1987 revenues of Dow Jones Information Services topped $152 million, a 20 percent increase over the previous year, nearly half of which was believed to be due to the Dow Jones News/Retrieval Service. At this writing, the system has close to 300,000 subscribers, and driven at least in part by all the activity in the stock markets in recent years, it is believed to be growing rapidly.

If you manage your own investments, you probably can't afford to be without a subscription to Dow Jones. When you subscribe, we suggest that you spend your first 15 or 20 minutes using "//FYI," the system's free newsletter. In addition to system announcements, this menu-driven feature contains all the information you need on the various features, what they cost, and tutorials on how to use many of them.

...17...

NewsNet

NewsNet, Inc.
945 Haverford Road
Bryn Mawr, PA 19010
(800) 345–1301
(215) 527–8030

CUSTOMER SERVICE
(Eastern standard time)

Mon.–Fri.: 9:00 A.M.–8:00 P.M.

Hours of Operation
—24 hours a day, every day—
Nonprime time runs from 8:00 P.M. to 8:00 A.M. eastern standard time, *not* your local time. Weekends and holidays are billed at nonprime-time rates as well.

Access:
Tymnet and Telenet

Connect Rate:
Basic rate of $60 per hour/$1 a minute for 300 or 1200-bps access. For 2400 bps, the basic rate is $90 an hour/$1.50 a minute. Additional royalty charges apply when reading newsletters online. Costs vary with the newsletter. Key in PRICES online for a complete list.
See the back of this book for a special NewsNet offer.

Capsule Summary

NewsNet is the best kept secret in the online industry. Indeed, if you were in a competitive situation with someone, the *last* thing you'd want to do is let slip over lunch or cocktails the fact that you subscribe to this

218

system. "NewsNet? What's that?" your counterpart would say casually, not wanting to reveal his or her interest. At this point you're already in big trouble. NewsNet is too good to share with anyone but your closest friends and allies, and you'd have to be out of your mind to tell a competitor about it.

There are two reasons why NewsNet deserves such praise, and why it is probably the one online system that virtually all executives, managers, and professionals should subscribe to. The first quality that makes NewsNet so special is the nature of the information its databases contain. Although it has other features, NewsNet is at its heart an electronic vendor of trade, industry, and professional newsletters. These are the types of newsletters whose print editions typically sell for $100 to $500 a year or more for 12 to 24 issues.

Most are produced by seasoned experts or small editorial staffs who have devoted themselves to the intense coverage of a single, relatively narrow field of interest. Typically, newsletters of this sort offer a currency and depth of coverage not found in most trade journals and other industry-specific publications. And, depending on the editor or author, they can provide an insight and perspective available from no other source. In short, reading a good newsletter is like having an expert offer a private consultation concerning matters of great interest to you and your business.

So from the start, NewsNet has top-quality, high-performance information. But the company could easily have screwed it up. It could have created a system so complex, so oriented toward traditional information retrieval, that no one but a trained librarian would ever use it. Instead, NewsNet presents its information via a powerful but natural system that makes it easy for just about anyone to find what he or she wants. Anyone with a modicum of online experience gained elsewhere can use NewsNet almost instinctively. And brand-new online communicators can get to that stage with very little effort.

In essence, all you have to do is pick an industry, specify a date range, and type in a keyword or phrase. The system will go away to look for matches and return shortly to ask if you'd like to see a menu of numbered headlines for the articles it has found. You look at the headlines, note the ones of interest, and key in the corresponding numbers at the prompt. There are other things you can do as well—you might choose to search just one newsletter instead of a group of them, for example—but that's basically all there is to it.

One of the reasons NewsNet works so well and one of the reasons why you can almost always find what you want is that the databases (or newsletters) are so highly focused. That means that if you're searching, say, "Computer Workstations" for references to Sun Microsystems, a leading workstation manufacturer, you can just key in SUN as your search term. If you were searching a database where the coverage was much broader—like one that included *Time, Business Week,* and *Forbes*—a simple keyword like SUN would not be precise enough. You could easily pull up stories dealing with everything from suntan lotion to the French grape crop to the ozone layer, as well as stories about Sun Microsystems.

In addition, if you are familiar with a field, you already know the names, the special terms, and the issues that are involved, and you probably have a pretty good idea of the best date range to search. With NewsNet, you can build on what you already know to find out what you don't.

The system got its start in the spring of 1982 with 17 newsletters. At this writing, nearly 400 newsletters are available, covering over 30 industries and professions. (For representative titles, please see Figure 17.1.) More are being added all the time, often on a daily basis. About 70% of these publications are not available online anywhere else. (NEXIS has about 50 newsletters, some of which are also on NewsNet.) NewsNet is a full-text database, and subscribers have access to most newsletters within *minutes* after their authors have uploaded them to the system.

———— **Figure 17.1. NewsNet: Representative Samples** ————

It is impossible to communicate the breadth and depth of NewsNet's coverage without listing and describing all 400+ newsletters on the system. Here we have done the next best thing. The list that follows includes only some of the newsletters you can search on NewsNet. Taken as a whole it will give you at least a partial indication of the kind of information you can expect to find on the system.

ACCESS REPORTS/FREEDOM
  OF INFORMATION
ADVANCED MILITARY
  COMPUTING
AFRICA NEWS
AIR/WATER POLLUTION
  REPORT
AMERICAN BANKER FULL
  TEXT
AT&T'S PRODUCTS AND
  SERVICES

BIOTECHNOLOGY
  INVESTMENT
  OPPORTUNITIES
CATHOLIC NEWS SERVICE
COMMERCE CLEARING
  HOUSE TAX DAY:
  FEDERAL
CD-ROM DATABASES
COMMON CARRIER WEEK
COMPUTER WORKSTATIONS
CONSUMER CREDIT LETTER

DEFENSE INDUSTRY
REPORT
EAST ASIAN BUSINESS
INTELLIGENCE
EDUCATION OF THE
HANDICAPPED
ENVIRONMENTAL
COMPLIANCE UPDATE
FCC DAILY DIGEST
FIBER OPTICS NEWS
FUSION POWER REPORT
HAZARDOUS MATERIALS
INTELLIGENCE REPORT
INNOVATOR'S DIGEST
ISDN NEWS
JAPAN AUTOMATION
REVIEW
MAINFRAME COMPUTING
MARKETING RESEARCH
REVIEW
MICROCOMPUTERS IN
EDUCATION
MILITARY FIBER OPTICS
NEWS
MILITARY ROBOTICS
NASA SOFTWARE
DIRECTORY
NATIONAL BUREAU OF
STANDARDS BULLETIN
NUCLEAR WASTE NEWS
OFFSHORE GAS REPORT

OUTLOOK ON IBM
PACS & LOBBIES
PUBLIC BROADCASTING
REPORT
REAL ESTATE & VENTURE
FUNDING DIRECTORY
SALES
PROSPECTOR/CANADA
SATELLITE NEWS
SDI MONITOR
SEYBOLD OUTLOOK:
PROFESSIONAL
COMPUTING
SPACE STATION NEWS
STATE CAPITALS: BANKING
POLICIES
TAX NOTES TODAY
TELEVISION DIGEST
TRENDVEST RATINGS
U.S. RAIL NEWS
VIDEODISC MONITOR
VIEWDATA/VIDEOTEX
REPORT
VOCATIONAL TRAINING
NEWS
WALL ST. MONITOR
WORLD FOOD & DRINK
REPORT
XINHUA ENGLISH
LANGUAGE NEWS
SERVICE

Newswires and TRW Credit Reports

In addition to newsletters, the system also offers you access to news-wires that include Reuters, AP Datastream Business News, UPI, and the PR Newswire. There is no embargo on these wires. They are available to you at the same time that editors in the nation's newsrooms receive them. Two full weeks' worth of newswire information, plus the current week to date, is available for online searching at all times.

NewsNet also offers TRW business credit reports. The TRW Business Profiles database—actually a gateway to the main TRW system—provides up-to-date payment histories on nearly eight million businesses on a fee-for-report basis. The cost is $32 per report, plus connect charges. Heretofore the only way to obtain this kind of information was to sign an annual contract with a credit-reporting company, and most contracts start in the $1000 to $2000 range. NewsNet was the first system to offer this service.

Subscriptions, Manuals, and Costs

Initial signup to Newsnet is free. However, there is a $15 per month account maintenance or subscription fee. The minimum subscription period is 30 days. You may also choose to pay all of your monthly fees as an annual lump sum, in which case the cost is $120 (a savings of $60 over the monthly option). Or you can select a six-month subscription for an initial payment of $60 (a savings of $30). (See the special-offer coupon at the back of this book for special savings.)

Usage charges are determined by speed of communications, the particular publications you choose to read, and whether or not you are a subscriber to these publications. The basic connect rate is $60 an hour or $1 per minute for 300 or 1200-bps access. (There is a 50 percent premium for access at 2400 bps.)

The basic connect rate applies when you are searching and viewing retrieved headlines. When you do decide to read a publication, a royalty rate or "read premium" is added to the basic connect rate. These are set by the newsletter publishers themselves. You don't really need to worry about the breakout, since the prices quoted for each newsletter include everything. The good news is that in many cases, if you already subscribe to the printed version of a newsletter, you will be charged a lower read premium or no premium at all. You are then considered a "validated" subscriber to the newsletter, and it may be available to you at NewsNet's basic connect rate.

You can find out what any given newsletter will cost to read or obtain a price list covering every newsletter on the system while online. Rates are quoted for validated and nonvalidated subscribers at 300/1200 bps. If you use 2400 bps, add 50 percent to the quoted rate.

Online Tip: This is a real quickie, but can save you so much money that it is worth highlighting. Your status vis-à-vis validation for a particular newsletter is completely in the hands of that newsletter's publisher. Sometimes, if you ask them politely, certain newsletter publishers will validate you whether or not you subscribe to

> the print version of their product. Use the NewsNet feature that lets you send electronic mail to the newsletter's publisher, or get the publisher's name and address online using NewsNet's INFO command.
>
> You may not meet with success. But since validation can save you hundreds of dollars annually on a newsletter that you read regularly, it is certainly worth a try.

You can sign up for NewsNet by simply calling the toll-free customer service number during regular East Coast business hours. Your ID and password will be issued on the spot. And you have a range of payment options. You can have your charges billed to your MasterCard or VISA. You can opt for CHECKFREE (U.S. subscribers only) billing under which your payments are automatically deducted from your checking account. Or you can choose direct billing. A one-time, nonrefundable $25 application fee applies to this option.

This businesslike approach to the online business is one of the things that makes NewsNet so appealing. Yet another example of this is the Corporate Subscription Plan. Under this plan, one individual within a company can subscribe for $120 a year. For the next two to four individuals who subscribe, the cost is $60 apiece per year. After that, all additional subscriptions are free. Thus the maximum a company would pay would be $120 for the first ID, plus $240 for the next four IDs, for a total of $360 a year. All additional IDs would be free. Corporate Plan subscribers earn discounts of from three to 15 percent, depending on usage volume.

The NewsNet manual is included with your subscription. Filled with examples, tips, and hands-on advice, the new manual was published in 1989. It replaces the pocket guide NewsNet has long used, though such guides are still available for those who want them.

Conclusion

Newsletters are not the stuff of traditional databases and information retrieval systems, and NewsNet is anything but a traditional vendor or online system. (Possibly because of NewsNet's success, in recent years newsletters have begun to show up on traditional systems.) NewsNet is aimed squarely at businesspeople and professionals who need detailed, expert, up-to-the-minute information on their field of interest. That's the kind of information newsletters have always provided, but when it is coupled with the power of a mainframe computer and presented with an easy-to-use interface, the effect is much greater than the sum of the parts.

...18...

VU/TEXT and DataTimes

Local newspapers are the focus of this chapter, and we'd like to begin by asking you to think for just a moment about yours. Nearly everyone lives in an area served by a local paper of some sort, and nearly everyone has an opinion regarding that publication. Your opinion may not be printable. It may be that your local rag screwed up your daughter's wedding announcement, or maybe the editorial page is too far to the left or the right, or too bland for your tastes. On the other hand, you may feel that your local bugle is the greatest paper to come along since *The New York Times*, *The Washington Post*, the *Los Angeles Times*, or the *Chicago Tribune*.

Local newspapers will always suffer by comparison to something else, but think about the kinds of things your paper covers. If there's a large company in your town, you can bet it gets major coverage in the town crier. Expansion plans, layoffs, earnings reports, and other items of local interest. Those pieces of information may be of great significance to people in the area, but they're probably not going to be covered by the nation's major newspapers and almost certainly not by a national magazine.

Now, as a local yokel you may take all of this information for granted. You may merely skim over it on your way to the sports page or the funnies. But suppose you're someone who lives halfway across the country, and suppose you have a very strong business or investment interest in knowing more about that company. Suppose further that the company is privately held and therefore not subject to Securities and Exchange Commission public-disclosure requirements. Do you think maybe you might value rather highly the information the local paper carries? Do you think maybe you might like to do an electronic search of several years' worth of the paper for every reference to the company, its executives, its owners, its prospects and plans? You bet.

It may be that a paper is without honor in its own county, but else-where it is revered as a unique repository of local information that is unavailable from any other source. *The Wall Street Journal* is on Dow Jones, and *The New York Times* is on NEXIS. But if you want local newspapers, you turn to VU/TEXT and DataTimes. Which is what we'll do right now.

VU/TEXT

VU/TEXT Information Services, Inc.
325 Chestnut Street, Suite 1300
Philadelphia, PA 19106
(800) 323–2940
(215) 574–4400

CUSTOMER SERVICE
(800) 258–8080

Pennsylvania residents
call: (215) 574–4421

(Eastern standard time)

Mon.–Fri.: 8:00 A.M.–10:00 P.M.
Sat.–Sun.: 9:00 A.M.–6:00 P.M.

Hours of Operation
24 hours a day, every day. Except that any given database may be down for half an hour each day for reloading. The down time will not take place during regular business hours.

Access:
> Telenet. Free passwords and unified billing are available to sub-scribers to QL Systems, Ltd. of Ottawa, Ontario; PROFILE's (formerly Datasolve) World Reporter; WESTLAW; and OCLC's (Online Library Computer Center) UNISON service.

Connect Rate:
> Varies with the database and your subscription option. The high-est rate is about $120 an hour or $2 per minute; the lowest, about $5 an hour or 8¢ per minute (training and practice databases). The average is somewhere between $105 and $90 an hour. Telecom-munications charges are extra ($9 per hour). No extra charge for 1200 bps, but 2400-bps access is billed at 50% above the stated connect hour rate. There is no nonprime-time discount.

With over 50 regional newspapers online, VU/TEXT has good reason to bill itself as "the world's largest newspaper databank." As noted a moment ago, papers published in cities like Akron, Detroit, Miami, and Wichita are a unique source of information. They are not the place to look for complete transcripts of presidential press conferences. But they are the place to go for frequent and detailed coverage of locally based companies, people, events, trends, and politics.

Thanks to VU/TEXT, you can be sitting in your office thousands of miles away from Richmond or San Jose and by tapping a few keys find out who runs things in those two cities as well as who *really* runs things. If a competitor has built or closed a plant, if you want to know about pollution or quality of life, if you want to get an insight to the local labor situation, a local paper will give you the kind information unavailable from any other source.

VU/TEXT is a Knight-Ridder company, and while it carries most of the Knight-Ridder papers, it has papers from many other publishers besides. The system grew out of an automated clipping file—what newspaper people call the "morgue"—set up by the Philadelphia *Inquirer* and *Daily News*. The software was acquired from QL Systems, Ltd., a company that had previously provided a similar service for the Toronto *Globe and Mail*.

VU/TEXT is thus specifically designed for newspaper search and retrieval. And the emphasis has been on full text from the beginning. The system went up for internal use at the two Philadelphia papers in 1980, and VU/TEXT went commercial in 1982. Since then it has become the leading online service in this area, though DataTimes is coming up fast.

In addition to the local and regional newspapers, there are many other databases on the system. These include the AP newswire, Facts on File, DISCLOSURE, ABI/INFORM, VU/QUOTE (stock and commodity quotes; 20-minute delay), and ECS Marine Credit Reports (financial, credit, and management information on international shipping companies). There is the Transportation News Ticker (ship charter fixtures, cargo, and vessel availability, and so on), the full text of *Fortune*, *Money*, *Time*, *Life*, *People*, and *Sports Illustrated* (back to mid-1986 in most cases), and WARNDEX (Wall Street Transcript).

There is also the entire Business Dateline database with its coverage of more than 150 regional publications in the United States and Canada, plus all of the PROFILE Information (formerly Datasolve) databases (*The Financial Times*, *The Economist*, *The Guardian*, TASS, *New Scientist*, and many more), and QL Search with its coverage of Canadian news sources and more than 80 Canadian databases.

Subscriptions and Manuals

There is no cost for a subscription to VU/TEXT, but you will definitely need the VU/TEXT manual ($35). This contains all the system documentation and "blue sheets" describing each of the system's information offerings. Some of the blue-sheet writeups run to several pages. Most include complete lists of the applicable keywords (indexing terms) used in each database, as well as the names of a given newspaper's "sections" and sample records.

The manual is tabbed, nicely laid out, and well written. There are plenty of examples, and at appropriate points red is used for highlighting or emphasis. It includes a step-by-step tutorial and an extensively annotated command glossary. There is also a Ready Reference Guide to keep by your machine. Again, it is well-laid out and complete.

VU/TEXT offers two main subscription plans. Option I involves a commitment to a minimum of $90 per month in usage. Only the database connect-hour charges apply toward this minimum, however. Telecommunications charges are extra. In return for this commitment, Option I users pay an average of $10 to $15 less for their database connect hours. Option II is the open rate plan. There is no monthly minimum usage requirement. However, database connect-hour prices are $10 to $15 higher, and there is a $10 per month account maintenance fee. All billing under both options is by direct invoice at this writing.

Volume discounts are available on some databases, and they go into effect automatically after five hours of connect time during the month. A discount schedule is available on request. Also, it is easy to see how much you have spent on any given search or during any given session. Simply enter TOT when you want to see your current itemized total charges. All users have the option of entering a name, number, or other project code to identify a research session, and these codes are printed on the monthly bill to make it easy to apportion costs.

The system software is not the best in the world. It has the annoying habit of displaying a page and simply stopping with no prompt or other indication that you are expected to enter a command. But one can get used to anything, and the user workshops VU/TEXT offers in major cities may help. At this writing cities include Boston, Chicago, Detroit, Houston, Fort Lauderdale, New York, Orlando, Philadelphia, Richmond, San Diego, Anchorage, Seattle, and Washington, D.C. The cost is $25 and sessions last approximately three hours. Contact customer service for schedules and details. Subscribers receive the "VU/TEXT Newsline" newsletter. Published about six times a year, it includes the same kind of announcements, search tips, and "war stories" found in most vendor newsletters.

DataTimes

Datatek Corporation
14000 Quail Springs Parkway
Suite 450
Oklahoma City, OK 73134
(800) 642–2525
(405) 751–6400

Access:
Telenet

CUSTOMER SERVICE
(800) 642–2525

(Central time)

Mon.–Fri.: 7:00 A.M.–7:00 P.M.

Connect Rate:
$85 per hour ($1.42 per minute) to $110 per hour ($1.83 per minute). Dow Jones News/Retrieval access, international databases, and the Global Search feature are $165 per hour ($2.75 per minute).

Capsule Summary
DataTimes became available to the public a year after VU/TEXT, and for a long time it operated in its shadow. As the number of newspapers, databases, and other services on the system have grown, so too has DataTimes's reputation. The system is owned by the Oklahoma Publishing Company, which also owns television and radio stations, newspapers, the Opryland Hotel and Theme Park, and, in partnership with Dow Jones, 52 percent of Telerate Systems, a provider of quotes and electronic financial information.

At this writing, DataTimes offers some 30 local newspapers, none of which are available through VU/TEXT. These include the *San Francisco Chronicle*, *Chicago Sun-Times*, *Louisville Courier-Journal*, *New York Newsday*, and the *Dallas Morning News*.

Other offerings include *The Washington Post*, *USA Today*, the Associated Press newswire, *American Banker*, and *Congressional Quarterly Weekly Report*. You can also gateway through to the Dow Jones News/Retrieval service and tap all of its databases and features. For Canadian coverage there is a gateway to Informart Online with its various Canadian newswires, magazines, and newspapers (Toronto, Montreal, Ottowa, Vancouver, Windsor, and so on). A gateway to the Australian Newspaper Network brings you two papers from Brisbane. A gateway to the PROFILE Information (formerly Datasolve) system puts British and European publications in your hands, including the BBC Summary of World Broadcasts (English transcripts of broadcasts from over 120 countries).

Subscriptions and Costs

There is a one-time startup fee of $85, which includes your user manual ($35), a quarterly newsletter, and ongoing training and customer support. Two subscription options are available. Under Option A you commit to a monthly minimum usage of $85 and are charged a connect-time rate of $1.42 per minute ($85 per hour). Under Option B there is no monthly minimum, but there is a monthly account-maintenance fee of $12. Connect time under Option B is billed at $1.83 per minute ($110 per hour). Communications costs are charged separately at about 17 cents a minute. International communications charges vary with the country being accessed.

Connect-time rates apply to all DataTimes databases, unless otherwise noted. Access to Dow Jones, to international databases, and use of DataTimes's Global Search (multifile searching) is charged at $2.75 per minute ($165 per hour). Note: DataTimes is available to Dow Jones subscribers as part of //TEXT.

Conclusion

Local newspapers are a unique resource that have finally begun to come into their own in the online world. But while databases offering bibliographic citations and indexing of newspapers are widely available, the rights to offer the full text are jealously guarded. As noted elsewhere, *The Wall Street Journal* is available only on Dow Jones and *The New York Times*, only on NEXIS. Consequently, even though VU/TEXT and DataTimes offer many of the same nonnewspaper features, each is the sole online source of the local papers it carries.

Anything can happen, of course, but there is no reason to expect this situation to change in the future. Since both systems are owned by powerful information companies, and since between them they cover fewer than 100 of the country's local papers, it is far more likely that both VU/TEXT and DataTimes will compete to add more papers on an exclusive basis. In any event, your best bet is to send for information kits from both companies. Each clearly has a lot to offer.

...19...

NEXIS

Mead Data Central
9393 Springboro Pike
P. O. Box 933
Dayton, OH 45401
(800) 227–4908

CUSTOMER SERVICE
U.S.: (800) 543–6862
Canada: (800) 387–9042
   In Toronto: (416) 591–8740
North America and overseas:
   (513) 859–5398

Available 24 hours a day,
except between 10:00 P.M.
Saturday and 6:00 A.M.
Sunday

Hours of Operation
—All hours are given in Eastern standard time—

Available

Mon.–Fri.: 2:15 A.M.–2:00 A.M.
   Sat.: 2:00 A.M.–10:00 P.M.
   Sun.: 6:00 A.M.–2:00 A.M.

Not Available

Mon.–Fri.: 2:00 A.M.–2:15 A.M.
   Sat.: 10:00 P.M.–Sun. 6:00
   A.M.

Access:
   Telenet, Tymnet, Alaskanet, In-WATS and Mead's own MeadNet.

Connect Rate:
   Basic rate is $33 an hour ($20 per hour in connect time plus $13 per hour for the packet-switching networks). There is no surcharge for

2400 bps, though it may not be available through all network nodes. "File charges" vary with the database and range from $6 to $35 *per search*. A 2¢ per line print charge may also apply.

Capsule Summary

The keyword that best applies to Mead Data Central's (MDC) NEXIS system is *full text*. Although a number of full-text databases have recently come on-stream elsewhere, for years MDC had the full-text franchise virtually to itself. Nearly everything about the system and how you use it stems from the fact that it has been a full-text operation from the beginning.

MDC is a wholly owned subsidiary of the Mead Corporation, a 145-year-old Fortune-200 paper and forest products company based in Dayton, Ohio. What is now MDC got its start as OBAR, a legal research service that began converting the complete record of Ohio case law into machine-readable form in 1968 for the Ohio Bar Association. The Mead Corporation bought the company as part of a planned diversification effort. It soon expanded the offerings and introduced the result as the LEXIS system in 1973. (LEXIS currently competes with a product called Westlaw from West Publishing Company in St. Paul, Minnesota.)

> **Online Tip:** We're going to be focusing exclusively on NEXIS here, but if you're an attorney, you should know about *LEXIS: The Complete User's Guide* by Fred R. Shapiro (St. Martin's Press, 1989). Mr. Shapiro is one of the country's foremost experts on searching the LEXIS system, and his step-by-step, hands-on approach can save your firm literally hundreds of dollars a year.

The date is important because in 1973 there were no personal computers. Pocket calculators sold for what you would pay for a complete computer today. Consequently, to be able to offer LEXIS to lawyers far and wide, Mead began to build and supply dedicated dumb terminals and printers and plug them into its own MeadNet network. Known as UBIQ terminals, the machines had keys bearing labels like "Next Case" and "Next Page" and "Full" (full text) to make it easy to tell the host what to do. The system still operates this way today, whether you are using a personal computer or a dumb terminal.

Six years later, in 1979, Mead introduced NEXIS. NEXIS was originally intended to complement the legal database by offering attorneys access to general news and information. Both products can be accessed on the same host system, and both use the same search software. Both are full-text.

At one time (July 1984), "over 40% of NEXIS use [came] from the legal market," according to Jack W. Simpson, the company's president. But while the percentage of NEXIS users who are in the legal profession is still quite high, in recent years NEXIS has moved to expand its offerings and make them more appealing to businesspeople. It has also completely revamped its pricing structure, and made the system available to personal computer users. Its selling effort, however, remains heavily focused on law firms and corporate accounts.

In the words of a computer salesman we know, "that's goodness" because NEXIS has lots to offer. Perhaps its greatest prize is the full text of *The New York Times*. The final city edition is online in its entirety within 24 hours of publication, and the file dates back to June 1, 1980. That means the Sunday magazine, the book review, the Sunday regional supplements—everything. Nobody else has it.

At this writing nobody else has "The MacNeil/Lehrer NewsHour," either. NEXIS gives you the complete transcripts (typically 50 pages or so per program) from January 1, 1982 on. Transcripts are available within about 21 days of airing. The "Current Digest of the Soviet Press" is available as well, as is the full text of *InfoWorld*, the *Manchester Guardian Weekly*, and the Monitoring Service of The British Broadcasting Corporation (BBC) with its summaries of transmissions from the Soviet Union, Eastern Europe, the Middle East, the Far East, Africa, and Latin America.

There are over 175 full-text magazines, including *Aviation Week & Space Technology*, *Maclean's*, *Time*, *Newsweek*, *Sports Illustrated*, *Fortune*, *Forbes*, *PC Magazine*, *PC Week*, *Playboy*, *Smithsonian*, and *U. S. News & World Report*. There are some 23 wire services, 55 industry newsletters, a clutch of Federal Register and regulation-related files, at least four patent databases, the DISCLOSURE database of corporate SEC filings, and the Trinet corporate information databases. There are also reports from over 30 leading investment banking firms and brokerage houses. Although 15 of these reports and analyses are also available in the InvesText database found on other systems, at least 12 of them are unique to NEXIS. There is much more as well.

Subscriptions and Costs

NEXIS may very well be the easiest to use of all the major-league database vendors, especially for people who have never used an online system before. Part of the reason for this is the system's full-text orientation. Everyone knows what a magazine or a newspaper article looks like, but few are familiar with bibliographic citations and abstracts. And part of the reason is that unlike DIALOG, BRS, and ORBIT, NEXIS was from the beginning designed for what is now called the "end-user" instead of professional researchers and librarians. Once you sign on, you will wish that every system was as easy and natural to use.

Mead has reformed its subscription process. It is no longer the ordeal it once was. But the required $50 per month subscription fee remains a considerable obstacle, particularly for private individuals, consultants, and small companies. On the other hand, you get a lot for your $600 a year. The fee covers all training on an ongoing basis, all manuals (there are several), reference books, and 24-hour customer support. In addition, MDC has set things up so that each account is assigned a single Mead representative. You thus have one person to call for everything. (Search assistance is handled by customer service.)

Mead handles search costs differently than anyone else in the industry. In addition to the connect rate of $33 an hour, you are charged for each search you conduct. This is what MDC calls a "file charge." When you use NEXIS, the first search statement you enter is considered your search. Everything you tack on after that is considered a "modification." The company used to charge for each search modification too, but all modifications are now free.

Thus, if you wanted to search the DISCLOSURE database, the cost would be $15—regardless of the number of companies you specified. You could then view the information for each company at the regular NEXIS connect-time rate of 55 cents a minute ($33 per hour). The individual file charge for *The New York Times*, is $7. The file charge for searching all DISCLOSURE and several other databases in a business "group" is $28. And so on.

You can opt to view online material a page (screen) at a time and write the information to disk. But if you want to "print" it—MDC's term for a neatly formatted, continuously scrolling download—the cost is two cents per line.

You can get a summary of file prices while online, but the system does not provide a DIALOG-style cost estimate at the end of a search. It does, however, summarize the number of searches and modifications you have entered and the total connect time spent for a session. Billing is by direct invoice, itemized by each individual's password.

Online Tip: Here's an interesting idea for those who would like to tap the power of NEXIS but do not need access on a regular basis. Every now and then you might need information on a person or a company, an issue or a problem, or the text of an article you remember reading, for example. To satisfy those needs in 1988 MDC introduced a service called DialSearch.

To use the service, spend a moment thinking about exactly what

Online Tip (cont.)

you want and don't want. Then call the toll-free number and explain your needs to the information specialist on the other end. He or she will ask you some questions to help you focus the query and quote an estimated price. Then hang up and let the Mead search specialist go to work. He or she will conduct the search for you, review the results, and prepare an executive summary to accompany the materials. Then, depending on your needs, the information will be sent to you by mail, by express delivery, or by Fax. You can charge the whole thing to your major credit card.

Mead Data Central estimates that the average DialSearch project costs about $140. For more information, call the following numbers between the hours of 8:00 A.M. and 5:00 P.M. eastern standard time:

(800) 843–6476
(800) 227–8379, ext. 5505, in Ohio

Conclusion

If you're seriously interested in information . . . but why not be honest about it—if you're an information junkie, NEXIS will make your mouth water. If only there weren't that $50 per month fee. Certainly the money goes for a good cause—the plushy feel and personal attention MDC offers are second to none—but some of us can take care of ourselves and would rather spend $600 a year on something else. Still, even though that is the only alternative at this point, MDC has altered its approach in the past and may do so again.

In the meantime, if you subscribe, we strongly suggest popping for an extra $50 and purchasing Mead's own communications software. You can access NEXIS with any comm program (just key in .TTY01 and toggle on your local echo when you first sign on), but the company's "Version 2.1" package makes NEXIS an absolute joy to use. Copies are available for IBM compatibles and Macintosh computers.

Part IV

—COMMUNICATION—

...*20*...

Overview: 50 Ways to Leave Your Message

"From any machine—to any machine—any place in the world." If industries had mottos, that would be the stated goal of the various telex, fax, personal computer, and electronic mail providers and equipment makers that constitute the world's data communications industry. Think about this for just a minute. Your daughter is an exchange student in Japan, and while she's quite comfortable with her personal computer, you can't abide the thing. But you're crazy about your new facsimile machine, which you bought for your business as soon as prices began to fall. One day the fax line rings and, mirabile dictu, what begins coming out of the machine but a letter from your daughter—composed at her personal computer in Yokohama a few minutes ago. You do some checking and discover that for about $300 you can get your daughter a fax board for her PC that would allow her to receive faxes from your machine.

What's more, you don't have to worry about time differences or busy signals, thanks to one of several store-and-forward fax networks that are now available. Just dial a local number with your fax, feed in your message, and hang up. The network will keep dialing your daughter's PC fax board until it gets through.

Now it's your turn to surprise someone. You take a newspaper clipping announcing that the local high school has named its team of "all-time greats," jot a quick note in the margin, and feed the clipping into your fax machine. Moments later your son is amazed to see his name in print—as the facsimile begins to scroll out of his fax machine—in the communications room of a ship several thousand miles at sea.

All of this can be done today, for a cost of about $5 a call. But let's jump some years into the future. By now personal computers have be-

237

come genuinely easy to use and you're willing to accept one on your desktop. One day you read a report citing an inventor who has just received a patent for some process you feel could be crucial to your business. The report didn't give the fellow's address, though it mentioned that he was based in Wyoming. And it quoted him as saying that he was on the road a lot. All over the world, in fact. You want to get in touch with him *fast*—before your competitors do.

Fortunately, there's an easy way. You hit a key telling your desktop computer to dial up your favorite electronic mail system. Then you access its "worldwide directory" feature and key in the inventor's name and "Wyoming." Within seconds, the gentleman's name, home address and phone, office fax number, and the various electronic mail systems he subscribes to are on the screen. Unfortunately, the two of you don't subscribe to any of the same systems. But that's only a small inconvenience. You key in a message on your system and order it forwarded to the inventor on one of his systems. That evening, the phone rings. It's the inventor. He's gotten your message and is calling—from Munich. He was just about to close a deal for the world rights to his invention but wanted to hear your offer first.

From Anywhere, To Anywhere

These are the kinds of systems that have either become available in the last few years or will become available in the not-too-distant future. The world isn't merely on the verge of "from-anywhere-to-anywhere" communications for everyone. It's already here. Thanks to PCs, telephones, fiber-optic cables, satellites, packet-switching networks, affordable facsimile machines, and good old telex equipment. Many more system-to-system interconnections need to be made, and it will be years before a worldwide directory exists. But both goals are being actively pursued. Essentially, all of the components necessary to send and receive messages of the sort described in our examples are in place. And anybody can tap in.

That's what we'll show you how to do in this chapter and in those that immediately follow. Here we'll look at electronic mail in general since, as personal computer users, that is how most readers will be doing most of their communicating. In the next chapter, we'll focus exclusively on MCI Mail and offer some tips on how to make the most of that most popular of systems.

Then we'll look at the PC-to-fax connection, followed by discussion of the venerable worldwide telex network and how PC users can plug in. Most authorities agree that facsimile transmissions will eventually replace the telex network, but as it has for many years in the past, telex is likely to remain the only way to reach millions of people around the globe. Finally, we'll conclude this chapter with a look at computerized conferencing, a communication technique that appears to be coming into its own as more and more managers recognize its productivity-enhancing properties.

Electronic Mail Basics

The advantages of electronic mail, or "e-mail," are so self-evident that if you're a businessperson or professional, the question is not *whether* you should be using it, but how to best implement an e-mail capability. We'll explore these points in a moment, but first, for those who have never been exposed to electronic mail, a very brief introduction may be helpful.

All electronic mail is rooted in a single concept: the ability of computers to store messages just as they store information. It is very simple. When you want to send a letter, you go online with another computer and transmit the message you have prepared. The computer stores that message on its disks or tapes or whatever. At that point your job is over, and you can sign off.

The complementary phase occurs when the person you have sent the letter to goes online with the same computer and, with hope in his or her heart, keys in a command saying in effect "Is there any mail for me?"

The computer responds with the equivalent of a bespectacled postman leaning over an oak countertop and saying, "Why yes, Mr. Jones. I believe I did see something in your box. Would you like me to get it for you now?"

That's it. The only hardware components, other than the telephone system, are your personal computer, the main computer, and your correspondent's machine. Everything in the field of electronic mail involves those three components and the options and possibilities available through each of them. As is so often the case, it is the software that is the key.

The software you run on your machine can be anything from a simple terminal program, to a powerful mail manager package capable of automatically sending your letters to many different systems at whatever time you specify or periodically dialing them up to check for messages. The software on the host computer—the one that runs the electronic mail system—can be a crude, unfriendly program that gives you no help at all. Or it can offer elaborate menus and submenus with online help functions. It can be written to require you to enter a long and complex code when addressing your message, or it may allow you to enter "John Jones," or in some cases, even just "John."

At your command, the host computer may also be able to route your message to one of the 1.7 million telex and TWX machines around the world. Or it may be able to send it to a laser-printing unit in the city nearest your correspondent. Or to a fax machine. Or wherever.

As the recipient of a letter, Mr. Jones may be presented with a different set of options. At the lowest end of the scale, the host computer might be able to deliver your letter only once. In which case Mr. Jones had better toggle on his printer or open his computer's capture buffer to make sure that he has a copy of your letter, since it will not pass that way again. If the host has more sophisticated software, it may let Mr. Jones put your letter into a file to be reviewed later. Or it may ask Mr. Jones if he would like to key in an immediate reply or forward your letter to someone else. There may be many other things Mr. Jones can do as well.

E-Mail Options

Regardless of your situation, the most important question to ask when choosing an electronic mail solution is: With whom do you wish to be able to exchange messages? While some systems are interconnected right now and while more connections will exist in the future, today it is still best to have an account on the same system your correspondent uses.

To approach the same question from a different angle: What do you want to use electronic mail for? If your company already has a local area network (LAN) linking several PCs and if internal messaging is your goal, then some form of electronic mail software package capable of running on the LAN is the obvious solution. If you do not have a LAN but still want to have internal messaging, giving everyone a modem and a mailbox on a commercial system may be the most cost-effective solution. Or it may make more sense to equip a single personal computer with an e-mail package and modem and make it the host.

On the other hand, if you want to be able to contact your best customers, or take advantage of the savings of Electronic Data Interchange software (described later in the chapter), you may have no choice. You may have to subscribe to a particular system. If you're a professional or independent consultant, you have different needs. In the sections below we'll look at each of these situations and offer some ideas and information to point you in the right direction.

Information Sources

Before taking any action, we suggest that you first contact the Electronic Mail Association (EMA) for a free membership directory. The

EMA lists all the leading players among its members and it recently began accepting "user members," companies who either already have an e-mail system or are interested in getting one.

For e-mail users, the first year's membership is $250, and after that the annual fee is $500. Members receive a quarterly newsletter and admission to the two annual member's meetings the EMA holds (there is a small additional cost to cover food and sundries.) For more information, contact:

Electronic Mail Association
1919 Pennsylvania Avenue N.W., Suite 300
Washington, D.C. 20006
(202) 293-7808

Online Tip: If you need product evaluations and other specific information fast, one of the most authoritative newsletters on the subject is "Electronic Mail & Micro Systems" (EMMS) edited by Eric Arnum. Published by International Resource Development, subscriptions are $395 a year (24 issues), but single copies are available for about $25. This newsletter has been published continually for over a decade. It is an excellent source of information about the electronic mail industry and user options. Contact:

EMMS
International Resource Development, Inc.
21 Locust Avenue, Suite 1-C
New Canaan, CT 06840
(203) 966-2525

Corporate Alternatives

If you work for a large company, there is almost certainly someone on staff charged with evaluating personal computer hardware, software, telecommunications services, and the like. Consequently, you'll have to work through that individual or department. The same is true if there is a corporate mainframe and data processing (DP or EDP) department, a management information systems (MIS) department, or LAN manager.

If you run a department or division in a large company yourself or if you are a small businessperson, and you are interested in installing a local area network to link several PCs, printers, and file-servers, it obviously makes sense to talk to whomever will be supplying your LAN gear about electronic mail and messaging packages. Indeed, available e-mail software might be one of your major evaluation criteria when considering LAN suppliers.

Online Tip: One option LAN users may want to consider is the PC-MOS/386 package from The Software Link. This is a multi-user, multitasking operating system that, despite its name, will run on either an 80386 or an 80286 (IBM/AT-compatible) system. Both AT bus and Micro Channel Architecture (MCA) machines are supported. The least expensive version ($595) can handle up to five simultaneous users. The top-of-the-line version ($995) can nominally support up to 25, but the company notes that with today's equipment 16 users is the practical upper limit.

PC-MOS/386 can run virtually all of the network version of the standard applications packages (such as Lotus and dBASE). But it can also run an electronic mail package or bulletin board. Internally the company uses PC Board from Clark Development, but The Software Link and its original MultiLink product have long had a close relationship with the free RBBS-PC bulletin board package (available from Glossbrenner's Choice and many other sources). For more information, contact:

> The Software Link
> 3577 Parkway Lane
> Norcross, GA 30092
> (404) 448–5465

However, if you do not currently have a LAN, it probably does not make good sense to install one solely to gain an e-mail capability. If internal messaging or exchanging information between a headquarters location and salespeople in the field are your goals, there are at least two alternatives. You can either establish a company account on a commercial online system, or you can set up your own microcomputer-based dial-in mail system.

Commercial System Offerings

Let's look at the commercial side first. Here there are two major types of services. There are dedicated mail services like British Telecom's Dialcom, Telenet's Telemail, Tymnet's OnTyme, General Electric's Quick-Comm, Western Union's EasyLink, and similar systems.

And there are the online utilities, many of which offer special corporate account services.

Of course nothing is ever quite clear-cut. There is considerable overlap among the features and categories of services found in these two types of systems. But, while the dedicated mail services may provide access to some databases, bulletin boards, and other utility-like features, and while the utilities may offer telex and facsimile interfaces and hard-copy delivery options, in general, the categories are distinct. For information on dedicated corporate e-mail systems, contact the Electronic Mail Association at the address given earlier in the chapter. For information on the utility services, see the relevant chapters in Part II of this book.

Online Tip: If you'd like to be able to turn the entire electronic mail issue over to someone else and have them take care of absolutely everything, there is a unique company you should know about. It's called Omnet, Inc. Started by Susan Kubany and Robert Heinmiller, Omnet has many years of experience in the e-mail field. The company specializes in handling all the details associated with getting a firm's employees connected with and actively using an electronic mail system. This includes special manuals, customer support, system maintenance, and consulting on an ongoing basis. With Omnet onboard you never have to worry about the one person in your firm who really understands a system quitting or getting sick. Nor do you have to hire someone specifically to manage the e-mail operation as is often the case at large companies. Omnet is always there.

To be sure, the company has something to sell. It offers hookups to Dialcom and Telemail, the two best dedicated e-mail systems in their opinion. There is a maintenance fee of about $15 per mailbox, and there is about a 10 percent markup on connect time. But the company has been in business for many years, so they must be doing something right. Indeed, the firm reports that many of its best customers are those who initially tried to go it alone and can thus appreciate all that Omnet offers.

Omnet has two major divisions—BusinessNet and ScienceNet. The latter has long been used by earth scientists, such as those currently studying the ozone layer in Antarctica. (They communicate by satellite uplink to an Inmarsat bird and downlink to an earth station in Florida.) Omnet has sent and received electronic mail from Mt. Everest as well, and it has helped NASA, the Na-

Online Tip (cont.)

> tional Academy of Sciences, Harvard, Yale, M.I.T., and such lumi-
> naries as William F. Buckley get started with electronic mail. For
> more information, contact:
>
>   Omnet, Inc.
>   137 Tonawanda Street
>   Boston, MA 02124
>   (617) 256–9230

EDI: Electronic Data Interchange

A complete discussion of Electronic Data Interchange (EDI) is
beyond the scope of this book. However, it has a direct relationship to
electronic mail and, with over 80 percent of Fortune-1000 companies
reportedly planning to implement EDI programs, it is clearly a topic
you are going to be hearing much more about in years to come. Accordingly, a brief word of explanation would undoubtedly be helpful.

The goal of EDI is to reduce costs. According to Chuck Townsend,
president of the Birmingham Computer Group, "an estimated 70 percent of data that is inputed in American industry is the result of redun-
dant effort. . . . EDI offers industry the opportunity to bring that data
input down to 30 percent." How? By eliminating much of the paperwork
that flows from most trading relationships.

If you and your customers are part of an EDI network, both of you
can fill out purchase orders, invoices, bills of lading, and other forms
directly on your computer screens. Each screen is called a "transaction
set" under EDI protocols. If your computer and their computer both
operate under those protocols, they can exchange this information electronically. There is no longer any need for a customer to type up a
purchase order and put it in the mail. And there is no need for your data
entry operators to open that envelope and rekey all of the information
into your order processing system.

With many systems, customers can fill out their electronic forms during the day, and at night their computers will transmit the forms—just
like an electronic mail message—to your system. Alternatively, a third
party e-mail system may serve as intermediary, presenting users with
transaction sets to be filled out online. Eventually, companies may be
able to handle their billing and supplier payments the same way through
EDI and EFT (electronic funds transfer).

What makes it all work is the X.11 EDI standard developed by the
American National Standards Institute (ANSI). Naturally a host of

publications and consulting firms now specialize in EDI. Here are a few contacts to get you started should you wish further information:

Birmingham Computer Group
400 W. Maple, Suite 202
Birmingham, MI 48011-1498
(313) 540–0640

INPUT, Inc.
1280 Villa Street
Mountain View, CA 94041
(415) 961–3300

Brooks Associates, Inc.
7510 Lanfair Drive
Louisville, KY 40241
(502) 423–8406

"EDI News"
Phillips Publishing, Inc.
7811 Montrose Road
Potomac, MD 20854
(301) 340–2100
$297 per year; 12 issues, 10 pages
  each.
Available on NewsNet as
  publication TE80.

The Micro-Based Option

If you have a small business or head up a discrete group within a large company, you may well find that the cleanest, simplest, and *cheapest* way to give your people access to electronic mail is to buy a personal computer and set it up as your mail system. The machine will need a hard disk, a modem, and some software, but that's about it. Considering how inexpensive these components are, you can probably get out for under $1000. Your other expense will be equipping everyone in your group with a modem and a communications program, but again, that doesn't have to add up to a lot of money. Connect the host computer to its own phone extension, and you'll be in business.

There will be no long-distance or connect-time charges since most calls will be made in-house. But of course someone who is on the road can call in to pick up and leave messages as well. You might even allow your customers to call, perhaps to place orders or to consult your latest price list by downloading or viewing files stored on the system. As for ease of access, in most cases you will be able to use a script language capability built into the comm programs you give your employees to allow them to tap the system by issuing a single command.

For host software, there are at least two choices. You can run a bulletin board system (BBS) package, or you can run a special e-mail host package. BBS software and options are discussed in a later chapter. For now we can simply say that while some commercial BBS packages are available, most are either public-domain programs or low-cost shareware and most have more features than you can shake a floppy disk at.

For this reason, a pure, dedicated mail-handling package may be the answer. And here the IBM-compatible program that consistently gets good reviews (see *InfoWorld*, February 20, 1989, p. 78 ff., for the most recent one at this writing), is T-Post Remote E-Mail from Coker Electronics. The cost for the host package, T-Post Central, is $229. For an additional $129, you can get T-Post FaxForward, a program that allows a host machine equipped with a fax board to accept mail from PC users and forward it to any facsimile machine. Users can access T-Post Central with any comm program, but for greatest ease of use, Coker recommends its PC T-Post program ($99 each for two or more).

The entire system offers many clever features. It can be run in the background under systems like DesqView or DoubleDOS and be told to continually check for mail. You can send mail "special delivery" in which case T-Post Central immediately calls the recipient's computer and attempts delivery. You can use it as an e-mail bridge or server on a LAN, send mail to distribution lists, up and download files with XMODEM CRC, and much more. But the package's primary goal is to make the sending and receiving of e-mail as effortless and efficient as possible, and this it does superbly. For more information, contact Mark Coker at:

Coker Electronics
1430 Lexington Avenue
San Mateo, CA 94402
(415) 573–5515

Online Tip: CrossPoint is another unique DOS-based or UNIX-based package. Offering both electronic mail and computerized conferencing features, CrossPoint is specifically designed as a executive "power tool" managers can use to coordinate and control complex projects, boost productivity, and chart each point in a decision matrix. The program can be run on a stand-alone machine or on most major LANs (Novell, Banyon, 3-Com, and so on). The main server package sells for $395. Individual user packages are $49.95. A third program, LAN Modem, sells for $395 and allows anyone on a LAN to use any modem on that network. For more information, contact:

Cross Information Company
Canyon Center, Suite 311
1881 9th Street
Boulder, CO 80302-5151
(303) 444–7799

E-Mail for Professionals

If you're a small businessperson, professional, consultant, or someone else whose main e-mail goal is to be able to exchange messages with other individuals, then you'll need an account on a commercial system. At this writing, MCI Mail is unquestionably the system of choice, followed by CompuServe and possibly as a distant third Western Union's EasyLink. Like a telephone network, an electronic mail system's value and usefulness increases with each subscriber it adds, and the more subscribers it has, the more it attracts. Thus, while several individuals may each subscribe to several systems, more than likely they will have a common denominator in MCI, CompuServe, or both. CompuServe is discussed in Chapter 5. MCI Mail is the focus of the following chapter.

What to Look For in an E-Mail System

All other things being equal, an electronic mail system should let you do everything you do right now with paper letters, but do it more quickly and easily—and then some. For example, you should be able to "CC" or "copy in" one or more people, while sending a "blind copy" to others, with just a few keystrokes.

But the system should also let you do mass mailings or broadcast announcements as well. And it should use computer power to make it easy. If you now regularly send paper memos to the same group of people, you should be able to create an electronic mailing list, give it a name, and store it on the system. From then on, routing a copy of an uploaded memo to everyone on the list should be as easy as keying in the name of the file. Keying in something like SEND ASSOC.LST, for example, might be all that is necessary to put a copy of a memo, letter, or report into the electronic mailboxes of ten, twenty, or 200 of your closest associates.

An electronic "address book" feature is a variation on this. With CompuServe's EasyPlex and InfoPlex mail systems, for example, you can save yourself the trouble of keying in an account number like 712345,678 every time you want to send a letter to "Tom" by recording that number and "Tom" in your online address book. From then on, you need only key in "Tom" when you want to send him a letter.

There are many other potential features as well. In fact, in the classic personal computer tradeoff between power and ease of use, some systems may have so many options and features that it can be difficult to figure out how to use them. Don't get distracted. Ask yourself "What do I plan to use electronic mail for and how easily does this particular system let me do it?"

Indeed, one of the best ways to be sure you are making the right choice is to *visualize* yourself using the system. If others will be working with the system, put yourself in their shoes. What steps must be followed to send a letter? Does the system make it easy for you with explanatory prompts and available help functions? What specific things do you typically do with a paper letter today and how does the system handle each of them?

To help prime the pump of your own thinking, we've divided the e-mail process into three headings (sending, receiving, and general considerations) and suggested some questions to ask for each.

Sending Electronic Mail

1. How easily can you upload the letters and memos you have prepared offline with your word processor?

The process should flow smoothly, with the computers (yours and the mainframe) doing all the work. Can you automate the mail sending process with a "batch upload"? Your own comm program will be largely responsible for this function, but it is important to ask how well the host system is likely to work with your comm program's batch option. Ideally, you should be able to blast a file of letters and commands (properly sequenced) into the system and sign off without waiting around for the system to acknowledge each letter.

2. What provisions are there for error-checking?

You will undoubtedly want to be able to send programs, graphics, spreadsheets, and other machine-language files. This can only be done if the host system supports one or more error-checking protocols (XMODEM, YMODEM, Kermit, and so on; see Chapter 3 for more information). Is there a provision for attaching a text note to a machine-language file so that your recipient knows what it contains, or must you send the note as a separate message?

3. What commands are required to copy in one or more recipients? Is there a mass mailing or broadcast option?

The system should make it as easy as possible for you to send the same message to any number of people and to do so on a regular basis if you so choose. So ask about the system's distribution list capabilities and how they work. How many names can be on a given list? And how difficult is it to use this feature? How are blind copies handled?

4. Is there a "verification of receipt" option?

Though not needed for routine correspondence, there will be times when it's important to know whether a correspondent has read your letter yet. Systems that offer a verification option will automatically place a confirmation notice in your mailbox the moment your correspondent downloads (reads) your message. Is there an extra charge for this service?

5. What hard-copy delivery options are available?

Only you can decide whether you need hard-copy delivery options. But if you do, there are two things to consider. First, what options are available? Typical offerings include telex (I and II), Western Union Mailgram, express courier delivery (4-hour or next day), and delivery by U.S. mail.

Second, how easy is it to use these options? Can the same letter be sent a variety of ways to different people with a few keystrokes, or do you have to move to another part of the system and possibly retype or reformat your letter? Also, how do the costs of identical hard-copy options compare on the systems you are considering?

Receiving Mail

6. Will the system present you with a list of all the letters in your mailbox, including the sender's name and a subject line?

Some systems force recipients to read all of the mail in their mailboxes in the order in which the letters were sent. This feature, in contrast, permits a busy manager to read top-priority correspondence at will, saving other letters for another time.

7. Can you send a reply to the sender of a letter the moment you've read it?

Ideally, after a letter has been displayed, the system should permit you to key in an immediate reply and send it with a few keystrokes. The system should remember who sent the letter and handle addressing your reply automatically. Keying in a short, immediate reply is the best way to handle most electronic mail. If you don't do things this way, you will have to print out the letter after you're offline and make a special effort to send a reply. There are certainly times when you'll want to do that, but in most cases a quick reply will do quite nicely.

8. How easily can you forward a letter you've received to someone else?

This option goes hand-in-hand with the instant reply option. Instead of replying, you may want to be able to enter a few keystrokes to route a letter to one of your associates. Or you may want to be able to do *both*. How does the system handle this?

9. Can you file your mail on the system?

Many e-mail systems allow you to place letters in a personal electronic filing cabinet on the system. Although this can be handy in some cases, it generally doesn't make sense to store mail this way. It is almost always cheaper (and more convenient) to download a letter and store it locally on a floppy or hard disk.

A filing option can be very important, however, if you frequently need to send the same letter or message to different people. A letter welcoming new hires to the firm is a good example. Usually, if the body copy of such a letter has been stored as a file on the system, you will be able to send it to a new user by simply entering his or her name and a command like LOAD GREET.TXT.

Obviously this makes much more sense than uploading the identical letter each time you want to welcome a new employee. Be aware though, that storage costs can vary widely. Some systems offer a certain amount of free storage space for each user. Others charge for such space. So be sure to ask.

General Considerations

10. How easy is it for someone to sign on to the system?

What steps must a person follow every time he or she wants to send or receive mail? How long does it normally take? In-house systems usually have the advantage here. But when used with an auto-dial modem, many personal computer communications software packages can make signing on to commercial dial-up services almost as easy.

11. Does the system have a fast response time?

Response time is the time required for the host computer to act on one of your commands. Response time, whether on an in-house system or an outside service, can vary from the instantaneous to the unacceptably long. It all depends on how many other tasks the host is being asked to handle at any given moment.

Vendor-supplied figures on average response time are a good place to start, but nothing compares to hands-on testing. How is an in-house e-mail system affected when the host is running a payroll or other compute-intensive task? How does an outside service respond at ten in the morning or at other peak times during the business day?

Remember: People will be extremely reluctant to use an e-mail system that does not respond instantly most of the time.

12. How will you get people to develop the e-mail *habit*?

The time, money, and productivity-enhancing benefits of electronic mail will never be realized at your firm if people don't use the system. All too frequently, for example, a letter will languish on a system, undelivered, for weeks merely because the recipient forgot to check his or her mailbox. Studies have shown that once people develop the habit, e-mail quickly becomes an indispensable tool. The trick is to plan things carefully to get them to that stage.

Online Tip: One solution to the languishing letter problem is MCI's ALERT service. If you specify this when sending a letter, MCI will telephone your correspondent to notify the individual that a letter is waiting. You must specify the area code and phone number and, at your option, you may specify the time the person is to be called. The cost for this special feature is $1 per message.

AlphaNet Technology Corporation of Toronto has a different idea—the AlphaLink. This is a radio paging receiver mated to a modem that's connected to a computer and to the phone system. When a message arrives in the computer owner's electronic mailbox, the e-mail system transmits a unique signal over radio paging frequencies. The AlphaLink box picks up the page and if it recognizes its unique address, causes the modem to send a signal to a

Online Tip (cont.)

TSR comm program that continually watches the comm port.
When the modem's signal arrives, the program swings into action
to dial the e-mail service and automatically pick up the waiting
message.

   AlphaNet has already started work on a conceptually related
product for fax users. Once installed, this product will allow fax
machine owners to plug into any phone, anywhere, and receive
their messages—even though they maintain only one fax phone
line. Alastair Gordon, chairman of the company, notes that a telex-
related product is in the works as well. For more information, contact:

> AlphaNet Technology Corporation
> 61 Dalewood Road
> Toronto, ON M4P 2N4
> CANADA
> (416) 486–8784

Online Tip: We haven't talked about message security. Most systems have an excellent record on protecting users's privacy,
though we know of at least one case where a leading system vio-
lated those rules. Nonetheless, all e-mail messages can be read by
people other than their intended recipients, so one must assume
that they will be read, even if that isn't actually the case. Consequently, you may want to take steps to protect sensitive correspondence.

   The best way to do this is use a special program to encrypt your
message so that it appears as so much gibberish to an unauthorized reader. Your recipient then uses a copy of the same
program, plus the password or "key" you have previously agreed
upon, to decrypt the file. We know of two IBM-compatible programs that do an exceptionally good job on both ASCII and binary
files. Both use the Bureau of National Standards Data Encryption
Standard (DES) algorithm. One is The Confidant (shareware, $10)
and the other is PC-CODE (public domain). For more information
on these programs see *Alfred Glossbrenner's Master Guide to
FREE Software for IBMs and Compatible Computers,* or use the
order form at the back of this book to order Glossbrenner's Choice
Encryption Disk 1.

X.400, X.500, and Interconnections

In the future, *all* electronic mail systems will be interconnected. That means that one will not only be able to create a message on MCI and send it to a recipient on CompuServe, but you'll be able to create a message on an in-house system or LAN and turn it over to an intelligent processor, which will then send it to your correspondent, regardless of the system he or she subscribes to. As the sender, you won't have to concern yourself with which system the person uses. The intermediary processor will know that, and the message will be sent in a format that all e-mail systems understand. Electronic mail, in short, will become like the telephone.

The CCITT standards that will make this possible are X.400 and X.500. Naturally, these standards are not without controversy, most of it fueled by the "not invented here" syndrome and by vendor concerns about losing control of their customers. A CompuServe official both summed up and exemplified the problem when he said, "I'm not in a hurry to gateway to competitors, because that defeats our advantages. Once everyone is interconnected, electronic mail will become generic . . . and competition will be a pure price battle" (*PC World*, June 1986, p. 268). But a survey of the recent literature in the field clearly points to the widespread adoption of the X.400 e-mail interchange standard in the near future.

Basically, the "X-dot-four hundred" standard involves specifications on the character set that will be used (ASCII or IA5, an international set), how the subject line describing the message content will be handled, and how the "envelope" of an e-mail message will be addressed. The idea is to make sure that the header for every message is uniform. That way any host computer that supports the standard will know exactly where to look for specific routing information. Local area networks, ISDN (Integrated Services Digital Network), and EDI features and applications are also involved, but the address line is the key.

Addresses are also the key to the X.500 standard. This standard projects a future when one caller could look up anyone else's geographic, telephone, and e-mail address listing anywhere in the world from a personal computer. According to the standard, an entry for a particular person will contain information "corresponding to each of the communications methods by which that person can be reached, selected from an open-ended list which includes at least the following: telephone, electronic mail, telex, ISDN, physical delivery (e.g., the postal system) and facsimile. In some cases, such as electronic mail, the entry will have some additional information such as the types of information which the user's equipment can handle."

The X.500 concept grew out of the realization in the telecommunications industry that interconnecting systems via X.400 wouldn't do users much good if there wasn't some kind of directory capability. You can send mail from CompuServe to MCI and vice versa, but you've still got to know your correspondent's address on the target system. With X.500 in place, you would be able to look up anyone's e-mail address as easily as you now phone directory assistance for a phone number.

The catch is, who's going to provide this service? Who's going to create the database and be responsible for maintaining it and keeping it up to date? No one knows at this point. The phone companies are interested, and considering their traditional directory-assistance role and the fact that X.500 entries would include phone numbers, they might be the logical choice. But under the Modified Final Judgement (MFJ) that laid out the lines of demarcation for the AT&T divestiture, they may be prohibited from doing so. Leading e-mail service providers are also interested, but no one is willing to yield to anyone else at this point. In our opinion an industry-supported "supra" service is the most likely long-term solution. Such a service could be modeled on C-Span, the cable television channel that is supported by contributions from the cable television industry to supply coverage of Congress. In any event, the logic behind X.500 is as compelling as that of X.400, so some form of universal directory service is bound to come. But no one can say just when it will arrive.

The DASnet Connection

One of the most interesting solutions to the problem of interconnectivity is DASnet from DA Systems, Inc. DASnet allows a subscriber to one system to send a message to subscribers on over 60 other systems. The company has an account on each of the systems. All users send their mail to that DASnet account. Systems vary in their requirements, but on many you simply use the "TO:" field. On others, the "SUBJ:" field is used. One way or the other, the e-mail address of your correspondent and the name of his or her system will be included in the message.

DASnet's computers automatically poll the various systems at regular intervals throughout the day to pick up messages. Proprietary DASnet software then uses the e-mail address and system information included in each message to route it to your correspondent. DASnet does this by automatically signing on to your correspondent's system and sending him or her your message from the DASnet account.

DASnet capabilities are included as part of the standard membership for many online systems. But if this is not the case on your chosen system, there is an initial DASnet start up fee of $33.50 for U.S. subscribers; $36.50 for non-U.S. subscribers. And there is a monthly subscription charge of $4.50 (U.S.) or $5.75 (non-U.S.). The sender pays the normal charge to send a message on his or her system, plus a per-message and a character count charge to DASnet. DASnet charges vary depending on where the message is going, but typical fees are 10 cents per message and about 25 cents or less per 1,000 characters.

The message recipient pays the normal message reading fees on his or her system. And the person does not have to be a member of DASnet to receive messages. Nor must the person be a member to reply, though if the individual is not a member, then the message sender will be billed for the reply.

You can put your company on DASnet as a site subscription. There is also a telex and fax connection. And more systems are being added all the time. At this writing, however, DASnet connects the following systems and networks, several of which (GeoMail, PeaceNet, etc.) include still other systems:

ABA/net	Meta Network
AT&T Mail	NWI
BITNET	PeaceNet/EcoNet
BIX	PINET
CIGnet	Portal Communications
Connect Professional	PsychNet
Dialcom	SFMT (U.S.S.R.)
EasyLink	Telemail
EIES	Textel
Envoy 100	The WELL
GeoMail	TWICS (Japan)
iNET	UNISON
Internet	UUCP
MCI Mail	

For more information, contact:

DA Systems, Inc.
1503 East Campbell Ave.
Campbell, CA 95008
(408) 559–7434

Computerized Conferencing: Beyond Electronic Mail

Computerized conferencing, or "computer-mediated conferencing" as it is sometimes called, is an extension of electronic mail technology. However, most conferencing enthusiasts would vigorously resist the comparison. They have good reason, because saying that conferencing is just an electronic messaging system is like saying that a Massarati is just an automobile. On the surface it's a true statement, but it leaves out the telling details.

Electronic mail, for example, is a one-to-one form of communication.

Conferencing is a many-to-many medium. The potential can best be illustrated by a real-life example, and the structural differences by an example we have confected.

The year was 1971 and the president had just imposed a wage and price freeze. The freeze created a huge nationwide demand for information, guidelines, rulings, official statements, and policy clarifications. Around the country the federal government's ten Office of Emergency Preparedness (OEP) regional offices were flooded with requests from businesses, labor unions, and administrators. During the first week of the freeze, the New York office alone received over 10,000 calls—an average of nearly five a minute. Clearly, conventional mail and telephone communications clearly weren't up to the job.

What was needed was some form of centralized information exchange that could be accessed by many individuals, regardless of time of day or physical location. A system that Dr. Murray Turoff, professor of computer science at the New Jersey Institute of Technology, had been developing under the aegis of the OEP provided the answer. Known as the Emergency Conferencing System and Reference Index (EMISARI), it allowed officials at the main OEP office in Washington to place policy statements online for regional offices to read at their convenience. Questions could be entered and answered, and both could be displayed for all to read.

Most important of all, groups of people—many of whom could never be brought together in the same place at the same time—could easily use this centralized information exchange to discuss proposals and ideas. At any time of the day or night, discussion group members could use a computer terminal to contact the system. Once online, they could read all of the comments made by all other members and add comments of their own. The system worked well, and versions of it are still used by several government agencies today. EMISARI was the historical beginning of computerized conferencing, and Dr. Turoff is widely acknowledged as the founder of the field.

Online Tip: The seminal work in the field of computer-mediated conferencing is *The Network Nation: Human Communication via Computer* (Addison-Wesley, 1978), by Murry Turoff and Starr Roxanne Hiltz, professor and chairperson of the sociology department at Upsala College. Other important titles include:

Online Communities: A Case Study of the Office of the Future, by Starr Roxanne Hiltz (Ablex, 1984).

Computer-Mediated Communication Systems: Status and Evaluation, by Elaine B. Kerr and Starr Roxanne Hiltz (Academic Press, 1982).

Electronic Communication: Technology and Impacts, by Madeline M. Henderson and Marcia J. MacNaughton (AAAS Selected Symposium 52, Westview Press, 1980).

Since locating a book is often faster if you can search by the author's name instead of wading into multiple subject classifications, it can be helpful to know that Kerr, Hiltz, and Turoff—as well as Peter and Trudy Johnson-Lenz and Jessica Lipnack and Jeffrey Stamps—are among the leaders in the field. Chandler Harrison Stevens and Thomas B. Cross have also published numerous articles on the subject.

Structural Differences

Now let's get into the details with an example designed to illustrate the difference between ordinary e-mail and computerized conferencing. Suppose a fellow named Ed wants to throw a party and invite a group of his friends and business associates. It's a spur of the moment thing, so there's no time to mail out paper invitations. One option would be to send an electronic message to each and every person individually. But that's a nuisance, and besides, this is an informal open house to which you're welcome to bring a friend.

One obvious solution to the invitation problem is to simply post a notice on an online bulletin board system that everyone uses. It could be PC-based BBS, but more than likely it will be a bulletin board offered by an online utility like CompuServe, GEnie, or Delphi. Let's assume that the following notice is posted: "Party at Ed's place Friday night, 8:00, bring a friend." This is, in effect, one (Ed)-to-many communications since anyone can read the notice.

One person who reads it is Susanna. She signs on to the system, looks at all the new postings—which include everything from people offering to sell used computers to solicitations for Amway soap products. She decides to go to Ed's party, but she needs directions. Unfortunately, Ed is going to be out of town for the next few days, so there's no one to phone. Instead, she posts a notice reading: "Help—I need driving directions to Ed's party. Does anybody know: Do you turn left after the Slausson cutoff? Or turn right at the fork in the road?" Like an additional piece of paper being tacked up on a cork bulletin board, this message will be added to the postings.

The next person to sit down at the terminal is Stan. He's been to Ed's place many times and even knows a shortcut that can clip ten minutes off the travel time. So he types "Susanna, Here's how to get to Ed's place . . ." and gives his directions. This, too, will be added to the board and, along with all other messages, be available for everyone to read.

This crude bulletin board system represents the simplest use of a computer's information storage and retrieval abilities for human communication. In fact, that's *all* the computer has done so far. It has accepted information from one of its attached terminals, filed it away, and displayed it on command.

Now let's compress several decades of technological development into just a few paragraphs and expand things radically. We hereby decree that people will now be able use their personal computers to "talk" to the computer hosting the bulletin board, regardless of where they are in the world.

Raoul Karnani in Calcutta, Anthony Polizano in Milan, Monique Musset in Paris; they've all read about Ed's party, and each is planning to catch the next plane out. Each has also put a message in the file notifying Ed—and anyone else who reads the file—that they are on the way.

The Conferencing Solution

Now let's upgrade the software. Let's install a computerized conferencing system and really get things organized. From now on, messages will be filed by category. The number of categories is unlimited—indeed, you can create one of your own on the spot—but no message will be accepted by the system until a category of some sort has been specified.

All messages within a given category will focus on or otherwise be related to the subject of that category—whether the category is "Party at Ed's" or "Corporate Compensation Plans." We'll also give the person who created the category the power to control who has access to it. The category could be open to everyone, or to just a previously prepared list of people, or access could be granted on a per-request basis.

Finally, let's add a subcategory capability. Let's suppose that Ed decides to make this a real wing-ding of an affair. He enlists the help of his friends and various committees are formed (food, entertainment, and parking). The committees are established as subconferences of the main "Party at Ed's" conference. That means that everyone who belongs to the main conference can read and respond to messages entered there. But only committee members also have access to messages stored within their respective subconferences.

In effect, then, computerized conferencing offers the best of electronic mail and bulletin boards with an overlay of message flow control. As a conference organizer, you can control who has access to the messages in your conference. Most conferences in the online world are open and designed to encourage participation, but sometimes confidentiality and privacy are necessary.

Similarly, as a conference user, you can control which messages are presented to you by the conferences you join. If you're a Macintosh user interested in buying a PostScript printer, for example, you might join the main Macintosh conference, the Printer subconference, and the PostScript subsubconference. When you're online, you could then move into the PostScript conference and key in a command to read all the messages that had been added since your last sign-on. You would not have to wade through messages about color image dithering, hyper-everything, and the latest chapter in the Claris saga. Or you might focus on a particular ongoing discussion about downloadable fonts and read each message in the thread to get up to speed on what conference members all over the country have been saying to each other over the past three months. At that point, you might want to add a message of your own to the discussion.

Conferencing Applications

This bird's-eye view will give you a pretty good idea of what computerized conferencing is all about. In essence, it allows many people to key in their individual comments, questions, and suggestions on a particular topic, and it allows many others to read and respond to these messages. In effect, computerized conferencing is like a live conference involving any number of people in the same room interacting, responding, and discussing a topic. The difference is they are doing it with a personal computer and a host system and the discussion is taking place over time. Among other things, that means anyone can plug in and review a complete transcript of what has been said to date. And it means that one can choose to participate when it is convenient to do so instead of having to travel to a given location or wait by the telephone at a given time.

The applications for this technology are legion. With friend Ed and his party we've used a nonbusiness example, but in real life companies as diverse as Exxon, DEC, and Kodak use computerized conferencing to enable far-flung executives to "meet" online and work out policy decisions. The New York Institute of Technology uses a conferencing system to offer full-scale accredited college degree programs online. Western Montana College uses it to link 114 one-room schoolhouses in rural Montana via its Big Sky Telegraph system. And the International Executive Forum (formerly the Western Behavioral Sciences Institute) has long used it to offer training to senior-level executives.

Of the online utilities, the only one offering a true, full-featured computerized conferencing facility is BIX. The entire BIX system is based on CoSy ("cozy"), a conferencing package from the University of Guelph in Ontario.

There are many much smaller systems as well. In addition, there are conferencing software vendors able to offer you everything from a license to run a package on your own mainframe, mini, or micro to a complete turnkey 386-based system, complete with a packet-switching network connection. There are also consultants who specialize in analyzing a company's needs and recommending appropriate conferencing solutions.

You will find that the computerized conferencing business does *not* attract the slick operator and fast-talking sales personnel you may have encountered elsewhere in the micro world. Instead, you will find a lot of very good people who are genuinely interested in helping you solve your communications problems. To plug in, we suggest you contact the Electronic Networking Association, an organization that among other things serves as a trade association and information clearinghouse. Contact:

> Electronic Networking Association
> 2744 Washington Street
> Allentown, PA 18104-4225
> (215) 821-7777

The WELL and UNISON

There are many dedicated conferencing systems but most are, well, dedicated not only to conferencing but also to a particular subject or topic. Consequently, most are not designed for casual use. Nor are they priced for the average online consumer. There are, however, at least two exceptions: The Whole Earth 'Lectronic Link (the WELL) and UNISON. Both offer full-featured conferencing and the opportunity to exchange thoughts with some of the most fascinating people you'll ever meet online. And both are priced right.

The WELL, a service of the Whole Earth Catalog people, costs $8 a month, and regardless of time of day or baud rate charges a mere $3 an hour (5¢ a minute) for connect time. You can dial directly or use the CompuServe network to make your connection. There is an additional $5 per hour charge for using the CompuServe net, bringing the total for most non-California users to $8 an hour (just over 13¢ a minute). Direct billing and credit-card billing are available. For access from Canada, Alaska, or Hawaii, call the WELL's voice line given on page 261.

To sign up immediately, dial your local CompuServe network node. (Call 800–848–8980 for your local number if you don't know it.) Hit a carriage return or two when you are connected. When prompted to enter "Host Name:" key in WELL. Once connected, the system will prompt you through the new user sign-up procedure. If you live in the

San Francisco area, you may dial (415) 332–6106 to log on. For more information, contact:

> The WELL
> 27 Gate Five Road
> Sausalito, CA 94965
> (415) 332–1716 (voice)

Formerly based in Colorado, UNISON is now operated by Patelcomp of Cincinnati. The system offers both the PARTICIPATE and the CoSy conferencing systems and will shortly be introducing a proprietary system of its own as well. The cost is a monthly subscription fee of $6.50, with connect-time charges of $19 an hour (32¢ per minute) during prime time and $12 an hour (20¢ per minute) during nonprime. An 800-number connection is also available for an additional $5 an hour (9¢ per minute). According to Patricia Niehoff, the company's CEO, UNISON is ideal for groups and associations of any kind who need customized network applications. An association of airline pilots, for example, uses UNISON to keep members up to date on legislative and other issues.

UNISON is also for anyone interested in lively public conferences, for real-time conversation, and worldwide electronic mail (via DASnet). As Brock Meeks said in a magazine review, "Unison's demographics range from Baptists to bankers, and a definite sense of community prevails on the system." For more information, contact:

> UNISON
> 700 W. Pete Rose Way
> Cincinnati, OH 45203
> (513) 723–1700
> (800) 334–6122

Conclusion

We have long maintained that the only "computer" skill most people need is merely a modicum mastery of touch typing. *That's* what our children should be learning in computer classes, not how to write a program in BASIC or some other language. A course in Latin would do most people more good, and they'd find themselves "speaking" it just about as often.

Electronic mail and conferencing underscore this point emphatically. If typing is a chore, you will never experience the full power of e-mail and conferencing, for the essence of both is *immediate* interaction. They are not about dictated memos and studiously analyzed reports. They are about the fast exchange of information, without the need for the preliminary chit-chat that precedes the business portion of most telephone calls, without telephone tag, and without the need to make your schedule conform to someone else's or vice versa.

Electronic mail and computerized conferencing are the business productivity tools of the 1990s. In terms of accomplishing more in less time with less effort, their impact on the office will be comparable to that of the electric typewriter. Only this time it won't be just the hired help who's pounding the keyboard.

...21...

Making the Most of MCI Mail

MCI Mail   CUSTOMER SERVICE
Box 1001   (800) 444–6245
11900 M. Street, NW
Washington, D.C. 20036   (202) 833–8484, in Washington, D.C.

                                  (Eastern standard time)

                                  Mon.–Fri.: 9:00 A.M.–8:00 P.M.

Subscription:
> $25 per year for a standard account, $10 per month for the Pre-
> ferred Pricing Option. Basic Service lets you use menus, which can
> be annoying after a while. Advanced Service lets you operate from
> the command line. For more details, see below. See back of this
> book for a special MCI Mail offer.

Access:
> Tymnet access is 25¢ per minute, but access through local MCI
> network nodes and 800 numbers nationwide is free, except for any
> telephone company message unit charges you may incur using the
> local number. Set your system to 7/E/1 or 8/N/1 and enable X-
> ON/X-OFF flow control if that is not your program's default. Your
> system should end each line with a carriage return, but *no* line
> feed. Here are the toll-free modem numbers to dial:

300, 1200 baud		800–234–6245
2400 baud		800–456–6245
Lotus Express and Desktop		
Express up to 2400 baud		800–825–1515

Rates:

	Preferred Pricing Option*		Regular Pricing	
Annual fee:	WAIVED		$25.00	
Advanced service:	NO CHARGE		NO CHARGE	
800 access charge:	NONE		NONE	
Electronic messages:	$.25	up to 7500 characters	$.45	up to 500 characters
	$.25	each additional 7500 characters	$.75	501 to 2500 characters
			$1.00	2501 to 7500 characters
			$1.00	each additional 7500 characters
Domestic fax dispatch	$.25	first page	$.50	first half page
	$.25	each additional page	$.30	each additional half page

Scram Command:

Hit Control-O and then <Enter>. This will freeze the display, generate the ***OUTPUT OFF*** message, and return you to the Command prompt. If it doesn't work the first time, wait a moment and try it again.

Sign-Off Command: EXIT

*Preferred Pricing may include electronic messages up to 7500 characters or domestic Fax Dispatch messages up to one page, or longer. (Each additional increment of 7500 characters/1 page, or any portion thereof, will count as an additional message.) After the first 40 messages each month, messages are billed at regular rates. The $25 annual fee is waived on one mailbox only. Preferred Pricing begins with the calendar month following sign-up.

Capsule Summary

You may use some other system to communicate within your company, but if there's an electronic mail address on your business card, chances are it's for MCI. MCI was the first online system to (1) offer nothing but superb communications options and (2) court individual as well as corporate accounts. As a result, MCI has over the years evolved into what can only be called "the nation's electronic mail system." People may have accounts on many different systems, but *everybody* is on MCI.

In this chapter we'll summarize the system's major features to give you some idea of what you can expect. Then, for those who are already on the system, we'll offer a few tips and tricks designed to help you get even more out of your subscription.

Communications Options

The most basic MCI Mail option is the "Instant Letter." This is a simple electronic mail letter that you initiate by keying in the command CREATE. You will be prompted in turn for the recipient's account number address, the address of anyone who is to receive a courtesy copy, and a subject line. You can then key in your text or upload it as a text file from disk. When you're finished, hit <Enter> and key in a slash (/) in the far left margin. You'll be prompted for a "handling" option but should just hit <Enter> at this point. Finally, you'll receive the "Send?" prompt, at which point you key in "Y" and hit <Enter>.

That's the basic process. But there are additional options and features for each step. For example, you can create a mailing list containing one or more MCI Mail addresses and tell the system to use it by keying in the list's name at the "To:" prompt. If several people in your group want to use the same list, it is possible for one person to create the list and permit others to share it.

Courtesy copies can be sent via any method MCI supports. There's not much to say about the "Subject:" prompt other than that you can either leave it blank or key in up to 70 characters. (As explained in the previous chapter, DASnet subscribers use the subject line to enter their correspondent's address on a different system.) Creating or uploading the message itself is fairly straightforward. The system will accept lines up to 255 characters long. That's good for sending a spreadsheet that has been printed to disk as a text file, but more than likely you'll want to make sure you hit <Enter> after every 80 characters. If your comm program has an "upload throttle" or "pacing" feature, set it for a delay of about one tenth of a second per line. If you experience uploading problems, gradually increase the delay until you're sure no characters are being dropped because you're sending them at a speed greater than the system can handle.

Online Tip: Like most systems, MCI offers an online editor, and like all mainframe editors it is a royal pain to use. If you want to make sure that the system received your message properly, key in READ DRAFT after you have entered the terminating slash (/). If there's a problem, sign off, fix it with your own word processor, and sign back on to re-upload it.

So far we have described a fairly typical e-mail system. What sets MCI Mail apart are the many ways one can send a message. An Instant Letter is the simplest. But one can also specify "paper" printing and delivery. Under this option, your electronic text is shot to the MCI Mail processing center nearest the recipient's land address. (There is an MCI international postal center as well.) The text is then printed with a laser printer and the pages are put into a bright orange envelope and dropped in the mail. If you live in Maine and want to send a hard-copy letter to someone in Los Angeles, it obviously makes sense for the message to cover the first 3000 miles electronically and be deposited at an L.A. post office the same day.

If you're really in a hurry, you can specify "overnight delivery," in which case the letter will be printed and delivered the next day by a courier service. Overnight courier service is available to more than 38,000 U.S. zip code locations and more than 100 countries abroad. Letters can be delivered by regular mail to any location in the world. Your letter must be posted by 11:00 P.M. eastern standard time, Monday through Friday, for guaranteed U.S. delivery by 5:00 P.M. the following day (most letters arrive before noon). Letters posted after 11:01 P.M. on Friday will be delivered the following Tuesday. For international courier service, the posting deadline is 5:30 P.M. For international mail service, the deadline is 8:00 P.M.

Online Tip: You may still encounter the term 4HOUR as a delivery option. This refers to a service under which MCI would guarantee hand delivery within four hours of transmission to certain U.S. locations. The service was discounted for lack of demand, but the term has yet to be expunged from the system or the current manual.

Signatures and Letterheads

Because MCI uses laser printers to generate paper letters, you can store a copy of your signature and your letterhead on the system and specify their use when sending a paper letter. There is a $20 one-time fee for registering a graphic image like a letterhead or signature, but no charge for using it. Letterheads and signatures can be registered at the same time for the same $20 fee. All MCI subscribers can store up to 15 logos, letterheads, or signatures.

If you do not register a letterhead, the system defaults to an MCI Mail letterhead informing the recipient that the letter was electronically transmitted and distributed by MCI Mail. However, you *can* specify BLANK to cause the system to use no letterhead at all. Signatures can only appear at the far left of the letter. MCI also has an array of "holiday" letterheads. These change seasonally (Mother's Day, Valentine's Day, and so on), but "Happy Birthday" is always available.

More Delivery Options

There are additional electronic delivery options as well. You can send a message to a subscriber to (at this writing) CompuServe or the French MISSIVE system. But you must know your correspondent's system address. You can also send a message to any of the 1.8 million telex (I and II) machines in the world. These messages must be formatted to have no more than 69 characters per line and each line must end in a carriage return. (There are other general telex considerations as well, as discussed in the next chapter.) You can also send messages to any facsimile machine in the world, provided you know the machine's phone number.

Storage and Filing

MCI gives each subscriber the equivalent of an office with a desk and filing cabinet. On the DESK are the message you have already read. In the INBOX are messages you haven't read yet. These will be moved to your DESK automatically once you have read them. There is also an area for DRAFTS—messages you have created but not yet sent, plus an OUTBOX for storing text of messages you have sent. There is storage for LISTS (mailing lists), a TRASH area for messages you've marked for deletion, and a GRAPHICS area for storing letterheads, signatures, and other registered graphics. MCI never deletes the contents of your INBOX, but all other correspondence is automatically deleted after five days.

Getting Help

MCI Mail's major weakness is its documentation and online help facility. The manual is nicely produced and it does a fair job of telling you how to use available commands, but it offers few explanations. A great deal of help is available online, but it's not always easy to get at. You begin by keying in HELP. This lists a variety of subtopics. For more information, you must then key in the equivalent of HELP SUB-TOPIC-1. That gives you more information—and more subsubtopics. So you key in the equivalent of HELP SUBTOPIC-1 SUBSUBTOPIC-2. You could start with this last command to get the information you want, but there is no way to know beforehand what words to use. You have to go through the previous iterations.

As a result, at this writing, there is no easy way to get a comprehensive overview of the MCI Mail System. Fortunately, *PC Magazine* columnist Stephen Manes has done something about this in *The Complete MCI Mail Handbook* (Bantam Books, 1988, 498 pages, $22.95). In this excellent book Manes takes you through the ins and outs of MCI Mail with a literate, conversational style you'll find a pleasure to read. And in contrast to the current MCI Mail manual, his book is packed with the kind of hard-to-come-by information you need to really use the power the system places in your hands. No subscriber should be without it.

Tips for Current Subscribers

Advanced and Basic Service

On February 1, 1989, MCI radically changed its subscription policies. Prior to that date, users could opt for Basic or Advanced service. The principal characteristic of Basic service was that subscribers were forced to use MCI Mail menus, while among other things, Advanced users could operate with commands. For Advanced service, customers paid a $10 monthly fee. Under the new policy, all subscribers have Advanced service, with no monthly fee. Basic service is still available for those who want to use menus, but it is no longer the system's default.

The new MCI Mail manual will reflect this change, but until it appears, here are the major features now available to all MCI subscribers:

• String commands together such as SCAN, READ, PRINT, and FOR-WARD with INBOX, OUTBOX, DESK, PENDING, or ALL.

• FORWARD messages to another mailbox.

• Store drafts, and messages read and sent, for five days.

- Use INCLUDE to incorporate or transfer text from one message to another without retyping.

- Use CREATE DOC to suppress the names of recipients included in Instant Letters.

- Store up to 15 logos, letterheads, or signatures.

- Create and maintain mailing lists, including Shared Lists—free of charge.

For more information on Advanced Service features, MCI suggests keying in the following HELP commands:

HELP ADDRESS BOARD
HELP ADDRESS HANDLING
HELP ADDRESS VERIFY
HELP DELETE
HELP FORWARD
HELP HANDLING
HELP HANDLING CHARGE
HELP HANDLING DOC
HELP HANDLING FORM
HELP HANDLING MEMO
HELP HANDLING RECEIPT
HELP HANDLING SIGN
HELP INCLUDE
HELP MOVE
HELP PENDING
HELP SEND
HELP TEXT INCLUDE

Setting Your Personal Profile

If it's been a while since you checked your personal profile on the system, it can pay to do so at your next opportunity. Key in ACCOUNT and respond YES when asked if you'd like to see your current settings. You can set the LINE length of the text MCI Mail sends you to anywhere from 39 to 255 characters (80 is the default). PAGE depth refers to the number of lines the system will display before pausing to prompt you for a command to quit or continue. PAGE can be set anywhere from 8 through 100 lines (24 is the default). (Note: Since you cannot set your page length to zero, you may want to use the PRINT command *instead* of the READ command whenever you want the system to send your text without pausing.) You should also set LF Padding to 0.

The most important setting is probably TERMINAL TYPE. There are three options here: VIDEO, PAPER, and VT100. The VIDEO setting causes the system to pause after displaying each PAGE and prompt you to "Press RETURN for more; type NO to stop." Those prompts are a nuisance while you are receiving mail and afterwards as well, since you will have to remove them if you want to clean up the text before printing. Fortunately, the PAPER setting causes the system to scroll continuously, with no pauses or prompts. (When your terminal type is set to PAPER, the system will not pause after each page, even when you use the READ command.) The VT100 (no hyphen) option isn't documented anywhere. But it works, and you may want to use it if your system or software can emulate a DEC VT-100 terminal.

Online Tip: Here are two time-saving tips. First, you can eliminate a step in the sign-on process by keying in your user ID followed by two slashes followed by your password. Like this:

SJONES//SugarNSpice

The password will not be displayed on the screen after the two slash characters.

Second, most MCI Mail commands can be abbreviated to two letters. Thus, to look at a list of all the items in your outbox, you could enter either SCAN OUTBOX or SC OU. Both upper and lowercase are fine.

Bulletin Boards and Scripts

Though most people don't know about them, MCI Mail also offers "bulletin boards." These are not bulletin boards in the traditional online sense. They're basically collections of files or messages selected by whomever owns the bulletin board on the system. As a user, you cannot automatically post a comment, query, or message, but you can send this material to the board's owner with the request that it be posted.

The boards are intended to allow subscribers to post new product announcements, price changes, inventory updates, newsletters, job openings, and any other business-related item. There is an online directory of boards on the system, though it is far from comprehensive.

Many times you will simply have to know the name of the board you want to view. Still, the directory is a good place to start. Key in HELP BULLETIN BOARD DIRECTORY at the Command prompt. This will generate the current directory.

Among a random sample of boards available at this writing are the Auto Buying Network (30¢ per minute) for information on buying new cars at group rates; American Execulink (30¢ per minute) for "gateway services to international computer networks in Europe, Asia, and South America"; MCI Mail News (free) for news items about the system; Medmal Lawyers (30¢ per minute), offering medical malpractice expert witnesses for malpractice attorneys—"Court appearances welcome!"; and International Access (free) for information on making the MCI Mail connection from abroad.

To look at the contents of any board, key in VIEW at the Command prompt. You will then be prompted for a board name, and after you key it in, you will see "View command:". At this point enter SCAN to produce a numbered list of items and subjects. To read any item key in READ followed by the item number or range of numbers.

In addition to bulletin boards, MCI offers a SCRIPT function. Without getting into great detail, a SCRIPT is essentially a dBASE program file containing dBASE-II-like commands to prompt user interaction. Thus you might create a script to make it easy for a field salesperson to fill in a form listing the orders he or she had written for the day. Or you might use the function to create an employee questionnaire. Or anything else that requires user prompting and uniform responses.

Any subscriber can offer scripts and or set up a bulletin board, though extra charges are involved. Contact customer service for details. Also, be sure to ask about getting a free copy of the special manuals MCI offers for prospective bulletin board owners or script file creators. Also, ask about hiring someone to write your script if you are not a dBASE programmer.

Online Tip: MCI has a free bulletin board containing information on how to set up many leading communications packages, including automatic log-on scripts where applicable. Key in VIEW and when prompted for a bulletin board name, respond with PC GUIDE-LINES. When prompted for a View command, key in SCAN. If you are a Lotus Express user, take a look at the CONNECTION STRINGS to bulletin board instead.

File-Transfer Protocols and "Express" Programs

The one thing you cannot do with ease on MCI Mail is transfer a machine-language file. This is such a glaring omission that it seems sure to be corrected in the near future. In the meantime, you have two options. First, you can use a program called Lotus Express if you're an IBM or compatible user, or Desktop Express if you use a Macintosh. The programs use two protocols to effect their connection and transfer. One is the X.PC protocol to handle the physical link. The other is a proprietary MCI protocol called MEP2 (Message Exchange Protocol–2). Only a program that supports MEP2 can handle a binary file exchange on the system. Both of these "expressly" designed programs work quite well. The problem is that both you and your correspondent must own a copy.

As a last resort, you can convert a binary file into hexadecimal format. Since the hexadecimal numbering system uses the digits from 0 through 9, plus the letters A through F, the resulting file will contain only those characters. For technical reasons, however, the "hex" file will be twice as large as the binary file. Since MCI charges by character count, you may want to use a program like ARC (IBM) or STUFFIT (Macintosh) to compress the binary file before converting it to hex. Both programs are widely available from public-domain and shareware sources.

Hexadecimal conversion is a very old technique, dating to the days when the Apple was new and the CP/M operating system was king. Consequently, there are lots of hex converter programs and you should have no trouble obtaining one from the usual public-domain and shareware sources. (There's one on the Glossbrenner's Choice Comm Pack 3—Communicator's Toolchest. Please see the back of this book for ordering information.)

When converting from hex back into binary form, bring the hex/text file into your word processor and carefully edit out any extraneous text at the beginning and end of the file. If the phrase "Checksum=" and a hex number appears at the end of the file, leave them in. The last hex number in each row of a such a file is usually the sum of the other numbers in the same row. The hex converter program adds these numbers together and compares them with the checksum to verify that there are no errors.

Each of these solutions works, though transmission errors could present a problem in the hex file approach. But in our opinion, both options require either too much money or too much work to be anything but a last resort. The system wasn't designed to transfer binary files, so don't use it for that. If you need to move files around, get a subscription to

CompuServe or one of the other online utilities. It simply doesn't make sense to fiddle around with MCI or with trying to establish a direct person-to-person modem connection.

Conclusion

What MCI Mail *was* designed for, as we have seen, is electronic mail and person-to-person communication. And this it does better than anybody in the business. In our opinion, no one with a personal computer and a modem can afford to be without a subscription.

...22...

Telex

An official at a communications company was recently quoted as saying that "Everyone realizes that telex is not forever." The gentleman was referring to the explosive growth of facsimile machines around the world, but especially in Europe, the United States, and Japan. It seems inevitable that telex machines and the network that connects them—both of which date from the early 1930s—will one day be replaced by electronic mail and fax networks. In the meantime, telex remains the single most efficient way to reach 1.8 million people in the world, and in the far reaches of civilization, it is often the only way.

In this chapter we will quickly bring you up to speed on the telex system and show you how to use your personal computer to send and receive messages from any of these 1.8 million locations. We will start with the telex machine itself, since all of the special requirements and conventions you must observe in this field stem directly from this assemblage of cogs, cams, and gears.

The word "telex" is short for "teleprinter exchange," but the machines are also called teletypewriters (TTYs) or Teletypes. This is the machine that the very early hobbyists often rewired to serve as a computer keyboard. We'll refer to all teleprinting devices as telex machines here, with the understanding that various models differ in their capabilities. The machine was developed by the Siemens-Halske Company in Germany, by Creed and Company in England, and by E. E. Kleinschmidt and the Morkrum Company in the United States during the 1920s and 1930s to overcome the most severe restriction imposed by the telegraph networks that existed at the time: namely, the fact that

274

you had to know Morse or some other code and be pretty handy with a telegraph key to send and receive messages. The telex machine was and is an electric typewriter-like device that has been plugged into the telegraph network. Telex operators still need special training, but the keys and printing mechanism eliminate the need to deal in the "dits and "dahs" of Morse code.

Telex machines are used to send and receive messages in real time, the way two people might use their personal computers to converse with CHAT on The Source or the CB-like facilities of CompuServe, Delphi, GEnie, and other systems. But they are also used to automatically send and receive in unattended mode. Either way, the principal advantage telex offers over the telephone or a more modern form of communication is that it produces a hard copy of what has been said. It can thus eliminate misunderstandings due to a speaker's accent, and it is well suited to communicating price lists, product codes, item numbers, and other information that would be tedious to provide over the phone. Besides, telex is usually much cheaper than a voice telephone connection, assuming you can even reach the person by phone.

The Telex Network

Though the latest models offer CRT screens and computer capabilities, telex was long ago relegated to the backwaters and bayous of communications technology. One of the main reasons it continues to be used by businesses all over the world is not the machines but the network to which they are connected.

Just as every telephone line has its own telephone number, every machine coupled to the telex network has its own address or "telex number." Most have also been assigned a string of characters called an "answerback." Answerbacks vary in length, though they are typically somewhere between 15 and 25 characters long. Most are also descriptive. The Ace Construction Company in New York City, for example, might use an answerback that read "ACECONST-NYC."

Telex machines are designed to automatically transmit their answerbacks whenever the calling machine requests it. This enables the caller to make sure that he or she is talking to the right machine before sending it a message.

That makes sense. But why wouldn't the operator at the receiving machine just type in "Yeah, you got Ace here. What can I do fer ya?" The answer is that there may not be an operator sitting at the receiving machine when the message comes in. In fact, in most telex installations, there is no operator standing by. Telex machines are designed to accept messages automatically, and can thus be thought of as "hard-copy telephone answering machines." This is one of the main features of the telex network, for it means you can send a hard copy message anywhere in the world regardless of business hours or time zones.

All telex machines are equipped with a rotary dial or other dialing mechanism. And since, just as with a computer bulletin board, you can't send a message to a machine if its line is busy, the more expensive models have a one-button redial or auto redial feature. Because many machines on the network communicate with a five-bit "Baudot code," they can only generate 32 different signals. (That is the maximum number of five-unit combinations using on and off bits, and represents two raised to the fifth power.)

Since some of these must be used for control codes like the carriage return and the line feed, the number of printing characters available is even fewer than 32. Machines of this type will handle only uppercase letters, digits, and conventional punctuation marks. All of the machines on the *international* network use this format. This is why you may be asked to limit your messages to these characters when sending telexes and cablegrams from your computer.

Telex I and Telex II (TWX)

There are two main types of telex machines. The model introduced by Western Union after World War II used the five-bit code and operated at 50 bits per seconds (bps) or 66 words per minute. At about the same time, AT&T introduced TWX machines capable of communicating at 110 bps or 100 words per minute. The machines used a seven-bit code that allowed them to generate 128 characters, and they sent characters in 11-bit units (one start bit, seven data bits, one parity bit, and *two* stop bits). Later TWX units (Teletype Model 37) could handle speeds of up to 150 bits per second.

TWX machines are used only in North America. And both in North America and in the rest of the world, they are vastly outnumbered by 50-bps machines. The Teletype Model 33, probably the most widely used machine, is available in versions for both speeds. As you might imagine, telex machines and TWX machines cannot talk to each other directly.

After extended legal action, Western Union bought the TWX network from AT&T in the 1960s. It then linked TWX with its original network in 1965 by setting up a computerized switching and message-forwarding system that automatically converted all letters to uppercase and resolved the other differences between the two types of equipment. The company then renamed the two networks Telex I (the original) and Telex II (TWX).

Enter the Personal Computer

Prior to 1981, Western Union had a virtual monopoly on telex communications within the United States. But that year, Congress passed the Record Carrier Competition Act (RCCA) that in effect said that any communications carrier desiring interconnection with the telex network was to be able to do so on demand. This law and rulings made by the FCC forced Western Union to release its grip on the telex network and permit other firms to solicit customers and connect them to the net. This coincided with the rising use of word-processing equipment and some of the first personal computers in offices across the continent. These companies could see the way things were going, and most were very interested in providing the kind of go-between services that would permit personal computers to send messages to both varieties of telex machines.

Store-and-Forward Systems

Most electronic mail networks these days can send your message to any telex machine on the globe. All of them operate on a store-and-forward basis under which you upload or key in your message, key in the telex address, and sign off. The system then handles any protocol conversions to get the message into the proper shape for its destination network and begins dialing the target machine. Facsimile networks work the same way. In both cases a store-and-forward system insulates you from the frustrations of repeated busy signals. The systems will keep trying until they get through or they will give up after a certain number of attempts. Either way, most e-mail systems will place a confirmation of delivery message in your mailbox or a note indicating that the message could not be delivered for some particular reason.

It is important to point out that the telex/e-mail network operates in both directions. Not only can you send to any machine on the net, you can receive messages from any machine as well. These appear in your electronic mailbox as normal e-mail messages. E-mail systems handle the matter of your personal telex address differently. On Delphi, messages must be sent to Delphi's own telex account, and the first line of each message must contain your Delphi member name or handle on the system. On MCI Mail, your telex number is your account number, without hyphens, preceded by 650. On Western Union's EasyLink, your mailbox number is your telex number.

> **Online Tip:** In Chapter 20 we spoke of DASnet and the X.400 standard and of the day when all e-mail systems will be interlinked. Thanks to the old telex network, however, a linkage among

systems already exists. It's probably not the most cost-effective means of communication, but if you are an MCI Mail subscriber and your friend is on Western Union's EasyLink, you can exchange messages by sending them to your respective telex addresses.

How to Use Telex

Whether your message ends up in someone's electronic mailbox or at a real telex machine, there are some things you need to know to use a telex system effectively from your personal computer. The most important point is the fact that *everything* about the telex system is determined by the 50-bps, 66-word-per-minute telex machine discussed earlier.

For example, there can be no more than 69 characters per line. (The EasyLink limit is 68, but 69 characters is the industry standard.) And, for reasons explained earlier, only uppercase letters and the other characters in the Telex I machine's character set may be used. If you upload in mixed case, some carriers will perform the case conversion automatically before the message is sent free of charge. Some may charge you double the per-character rate if they do the conversion. One way or another, though, your text reaches the telex network in uppercase. That means that all of the messages you receive will be in uppercase as well.

The 50-bps telex machine is also the basis of the telex network's billing system and of the agreements the various carriers have among themselves regarding the apportionment of costs and income. Thus, although you upload your message at 1200 bps, it will be pumped into the network at 50 bps and you will be charged by the "telex minute"—the time required to print out your message on a 50-bps telex machine—or fraction thereof. This is true even if you are sending to an electronic mailbox belonging to someone on another system.

To give you a better idea of what this means, most systems operate on the following equation:

50 bits per second = 400 characters/minute = 66 words/minute

"Words" are estimated at an average of about six characters each, but that's largely irrelevant since characters—including the space character—are what you pay for. If your margins are set for 65 characters per line, 400 characters will equal slightly more than six lines.

Online Tip: How is it that 50 bits per second translates into 400 characters per minute? The answer lies in the total number of bits required to transmit a character via telex. The character units are 7.5 bits long. One unit consists of one start bit, five data bits, and 1.5 stop bits. Thus 50 bits per second equals 3000 bits per minute. Divide that by 7.5 and you get 400 characters per minute.

The only puzzlement is how one can have 1.5 stop bits. Many personal computer communications programs offer you this option as a setting, and you'll understand it in an instant once you know about "bit times." A bit is a given condition of an electrical or communications line. It can be on or off, high voltage or low voltage, one tone or a second tone, or some other pairing of conditions. A "bit time" refers to how long a given condition lasts. Bit times vary, depending on the protocol agreed upon by both machines. When you think about it, this makes a lot of sense. How else would it be possible to transmit 300 bits per second one time and 1200 bits per second at another time if the number of milliseconds each bit occupied did not change?

What's It Like to Send a Telex?

The addressing information you must enter when sending messages of any type on these carriers is also determined by the telex system. For example, here is what you will see and what you must enter when using EasyLink to send an international telex to the Parisian branch of the Ace Construction Company:

```
PTS
/WUW 842323451789(L'ACECONST-PAR)+
GA
IF YOU DON'T HAVE IT HERE BY THURSDAY, I'M OUT OF BUSINESS!
LLLL
```

Only the PTS (Proceed to Select) prompt and the GA (Go Ahead) prompt come from EasyLink. You must enter everything else. The initial string /WUW tells the system that you want to use Western Union Worldwide, WU's international hook up. The 842 is the country code for France. If you were sending to the Ace branch in Tonga, you would have entered 765; for Mozambique, the number would be 946. This is followed immediately by the telex number of your addressee. No spaces, no hyphens, nothing to improve readability or ease of entry. The answerback in parentheses is optional. The plus sign tells EasyLink that you've completed the address, and the four L's signify the end of your message.

The important point here is that regardless of prompting, the same information must be entered on all carriers. The telex system requires country codes, telex numbers, and (optionally) answerbacks. EasyLink makes this simple with its abbreviated addresses feature. You can assign a two-digit number to each address and answerback combination. You may have up to 100 of these entries for your account, and there is no charge for the service. Call customer service for details or contact the automated processing center directly by messaging them at Easy-Link mailbox number 62900500.

How to Locate Telex Numbers

As you can imagine, many companies publish directories of telex numbers. The Cadillac of the field is the *Jaeger-Waldmann International Directory*, and at $187 (including shipping) for all nine volumes. Volumes cover Countries A–F, Countries G–I, and so on, plus "Yellow Pages." There is also a volume organized by answerback so you can look up who a message is from. Most volumes can be purchased separately. You may be able to find a copy of the entire set in the reference section of your library.

> *Jaeger-Waldmann*
> Universal Media
> P.O. Box 45
> Bethpage, NY 11714-0045
> (516) 433–6767
> TLX: 967753 INTL TLX BETH

The Green directories are organized by continent, instead of by country. They too are expensive, ranging from $80 for Africa to $240 for Europe. But like the Jaeger-Waldmann, the Green directories are considered a standard reference.

> *The Green International Directories*
> Teleprint International
> (Customer Service Office)
> P.O. Box 3796
> Chico, CA 95927
> (916) 345–7599

The Western Union directory may be all you need, however, and it is certainly the one with which to start. Over 1900 pages long, it is the size of a major metropolitan phone book. A separate volume called the Western Union Buyer's Guide is also available. This book is over 800 pages long and it is designed to serve as your telex Yellow Pages. If you're an EasyLink subscriber, you can get both Western Union directories for free. Additional copies or copies for nonsubscribers are $30 each, including shipping. Call EasyLink Customer Service for more information at (800) 435-7375, or send your order to:

> *Western Union's Telex Network*
> Western Union Directory Center
> 13022-A Hollenberg Drive
> Bridgeton, MO 63044

Online Tip: As we will see in the next chapter, many companies make special drop-in boards for a computer's internal expansion slots to allow them to talk directly to facsimile machines. A company called American Teleprocessing Corporation (ATC) makes one too, the Proto.Fax ($1595). But in addition to offering fax, this board also interfaces with telex, allowing you to eliminate your telex machine. For telex alone, the company makes the ATC Proto.Call board ($975), which includes a 1200/2400-bps modem and many other features—including a split baud rate detector that lets you download information directly from the Comstar 4 satellite at 9600 bps, while sending over the phone at 1200 bps.

Both boards can operate in the background and automatically receive and store telex messages as they come in. This is the IBM-compatible board most telex carriers recommend for those who want to eliminate a dedicated telex machine. For more information, contact:

> American Teleprocessing Corporation
> 10681 Haddington
> Houston, TX 77043
> (713) 973-1616

Who Offers Telex?

The following list covers many of the leading companies offering telex services to personal computer users. Add to it most of the world's e-mail vendors, and you'll have a very good and very extensive list of possibilities. In our opinion, EasyLink is the system of choice if telex and related types of communication (Mailgrams, telegrams, cablegrams, and so on) are your main focus. However, you will want to contact each company to compare rates and special features:

EasyLink
Western Union Telegraph
  Company
9229 LBJ Freeway
Dallas, TX 75243
(800) 527–5184

FTC Communications (Division of
  McDonnell Douglas/Tymshare)
90 John Street
New York, NY 10038
(800) 221–5428
(212) 669–9741

RCA/MCI International
201 Centennial Avenue
Piscataway, NJ 08854
(800) 526–3969

Graphnet, Inc.
329 Alfred Avenue
Teaneck, NJ 07666
(800) 631–1581
(201) 837–5100

MCI Mail
Box 1001
1900 M Street, N.W.
Washington, D.C. 20036
(800) 424–6677
(202) 833–8484

Dialcom
6120 Executive Boulevard
Rockville, MD 20852
(800) 435–7342
(301) 881–9020

TRT Telecommunications
1331 Pennsylvania Avenue, NW,
  Suite 1100
Washington, D.C. 20004
(800) 368–5670
(202) 879–2200

...23...

Fax

I t has been suggested that the facsimile machine will be the CB radio of the early 1990s. "It's a fad," says a good friend and small businessman. "I'm not getting one. There's no one I need to get a message to *that* fast, and the only people who want to fax things to me are my suppliers. They'd all love to be able to fax me their bills. I say, 'Sorry, just put it in the mail.'"

There's no question that in recent years facsimile machines have taken the world by storm, due mainly to much lower equipment prices. And there are certainly many people who can't make a good business case for the fax machines they've bought. But it seems equally clear that fax is here to stay, and the more people who have a fax capability, the more useful every previously installed fax machine becomes.

Fax offers you all the convenience and global reach of a phone call combined with a hard-copy delivery speed not even Federal Express can match, at least not since that company discontinued its wonderful ZAP Mail service. Besides, it's *easy*. Easy to use and easy to understand. No data bits, parity, and stop bits to worry about. No need to sign on to a remote computer. Just dial the phone and feed in the page you want to send. If anybody should be concerned, it's the electronic mail systems, for by some lights the popularity of fax could put a permanent dent in the e-mail growth curve.

But the electronic mail services have not been idle, and many of them now offer features that can actually enhance anyone's use of fax, and depending on your situation, they can save you hundreds of dollars by eliminating the need to buy a fax machine. We'll look at the e-mail-to-fax option in a moment. And we'll briefly consider the option of installing a fax board in your PC. But first, we'll establish a common frame of reference by briefly reviewing the fax transmission process.

How Facsimile Machines Work

Like a photocopier, a fax machine scans the page you want to send and converts each line into a series of electric pulses. The pulses are fed to a modem, which converts them into a form suitable for telephone transmission and sends them down the line to another modem in another fax machine. The receiving modem converts the incoming signals back into pulses and feeds them to the machine, which uses this information to reproduce your page.

That's the basic process. Now let's add options and features. First, there's the matter of dialing up the distant machine. That machine could be busy, so it would obviously be nice to have an auto-redial feature capable of detecting a busy signal and redialing a number after a brief pause.

That means your fax machine will have to have at least some memory. So why not expand that and give the unit enough memory to store frequently called numbers. And since we're adding chips anyhow, let's add a chip that allows the unit to be programmed to wait until lower long-distance rates go into effect before making its call.

If the same document must be sent to several people, let's make it possible for the machine to do a "broadcast" transmission, calling each number on a list in turn. Obviously the most efficient, and expensive, way to handle broadcast or other multiple transmissions is to let the fax machine scan a document and store it internally. So even more memory chips will be required.

The scanning operation could be flexible as well, offering a high-speed standard resolution and a slower but finer resolution mode. And why should one pay to transmit blank lines? Perhaps the scanning machine could send a single code to indicate a completely blank line. And what about speed? Just how fast can the built-in modem operate anyway?

Finally, there's the matter of output. Most fax machines today use rolls of thermal paper. The paper, like the quality of the received images, is adequate. But it is certainly not the kind of thing you'd turn in as a report. At the very least you will want to photocopy it onto regular bond.

Groups I, II, III, and IV

As we said in Chapter 2, in electronic communications, everything must match. And that requires widely accepted standards. The body responsible for creating fax standards is the same organization responsible for setting computer communications standards, the CCITT. Although the basic fax concept was patented in 1842 by Alexander Bain, modern standards date from 1968 when the CCITT proposed Group I faxes. These antiques communicated at 300 bits per second (bps) and required six minutes to transmit a single A4-size (8½-by-11-inch) page. Group 2 came along in 1976 and doubled the transmission speed. It also added the ability to handle gray scaling (shades) instead of stark black or white.

But it was in 1980 that the Group III standard was introduced, and that is the standard most machines support today. Introduced in 1984, Group IV is completely digital and is not expected to become a major factor until current phone lines are replaced with fiber-optic ISDN (Integrated Services Digital Network) links. As one might imagine, that's likely to take a very long time.

The Group III standard calls for each picture element (pixel) or dot on a page to be assigned a number. The number is transmitted to the receiver, which then prints an image corresponding to that number. (For the technically inclined: Group III fax uses modified Huffman encoding and read encoding to convert scanned lines into digital form.) The CCITT recommendation calls for Group III machines to communicate at 2400 bps, but many manufacturers have boosted that to half-duplex 9600 bps. Such machines usually have an automatic error-detection feature that causes them to fall back first to 7200 bps, then to 4800 bps, and then to 2400 bps if the telephone connection is noisy.

The transmission speed is one of the things that determines how much time is required to transmit a page. Group III gear can require anywhere from 30 to 60 seconds per page. Some Group III units can send a page in as little as 12 seconds, but they accomplish this trick using nonstandard methods that must be supported by the receiving machine as well. As part of the standard, all Group III machines offer two modes of resolution. Standard resolution is 200 dots per inch (dpi) horizontally by 100 dpi vertically. Fine resolution is 200 by 200. (Group IV, the standard used by Federal Express's now defunct ZAP Mail service, offers resolutions as high as 400 by 400 dpi.) The higher the resolution, the greater the amount of information that must be sent, and the longer the time required. Opting for fine resolution typically doubles transmission time.

Finally, fax standards are downwardly compatible. That means that a Group III machine can talk to either a Group I or Group II unit. However, the machines can operate only on the least common denominator. So if you happen to be sending to a Group II machine, your transmission speed will be about three minutes per page, even though your Group III unit could operate faster.

the file to fax mode before it can be transmitted. Can you look at a document on the screen before you send it or print it? If not, you may find that you spend a lot of time printing material that you would ordinarily simply delete, like the "junk fax" letters that seem to be proliferating.

Finally, make sure the board can operate in the background so an incoming fax won't force you to stop whatever you're doing on the system until the transmission is complete. You'll also want to be able to put what you're doing on hold momentarily, tell the board to send a fax, and return to your project to resume work while the transmission is taking place.

Fax Networks

The store-and-forward approach to message delivery discussed in the previous chapter in connection with telex messages is equally useful for facsimile communications. Vendors, particularly those already offering electronic mail, have been quick to respond. Among them, MCI FAX appears to be making the biggest splash. The firm's November 3, 1988 announcement said that MCI was the first U.S. long-distance company to offer a dedicated network for domestic and international fax transmissions. It went on to describe an array of rather interesting features.

MCI FAX can be used only with a fax modem or fax board. It offers fax-to-fax, toll-free fax to allow customers to send you faxes at no cost to them, telex-to-fax to allow messages sent to an MCI telex number to be delivered to your fax, and store-and-forward. Under this last option, MCI keeps trying should the target fax be busy. It also lets you specify the time of delivery to be sure of sending during the cheapest long distance rate periods. Broadcast distribution is also available, either on a one-time basis or via a Broadcast Dispatch feature that lets you store a "mailing list" of fax phone numbers on the system. There are management information reports, remote diagnostics, and security features as well. You can also use a fax machine in someone else's office and charge the transaction to an MCI FAX telephone credit card.

Unlike MCI Mail and other e-mail systems, fax networks like MCI FAX charge by the time required to transmit a message instead of by the number of characters it contains. At this writing, MCI FAX charges you for the first 30 seconds and then rounds up the remaining transmission time in six-second increments. Other systems use larger increments, regardless of the actual time required, so MCI maintains that its system will be cheaper. Charges are equivalent to MCI's regular telephone rates. There are no subscription fees or feature-related fees. All costs are based on usage. For more information, contact:

computer. The only way to send an illustration is to "draw" it using punctuation marks and the standard characters on a keyboard.

There are two main advantages to using an online service. One is the fact that you don't have to buy a fax machine. The other is the fact that fax transmissions sent in this way are usually crisper when they are printed out at your recipient's location. Each time an image is scanned or printed via fax, it loses some resolution. By using an online service to send your text files, you eliminate the initial scanning process and thus improve the resolution of the output.

Online Tip: One of the smaller online services is also one of the most innovative. Xpedite Systems offers a number of very intriguing capabilities, starting with the ability to accept transmissions from fax machines (via a separate fax phone number), convert them to a bit-mapped graphic image file, and transmit them to your PC. Like MCI, EasyLink, and other systems, Xpedite can accept files created on your PC and send them to a fax machine. But Xpedite also lets you put your letterhead on file with the system and opt to use it with your messages.

In addition, Xpedite can accept files formatted by WordStar, Microsoft Word, MultiMate, WordPerfect, and other leading word-processing packages, convert them, and send them to a fax machine with your underlining boldface, and other special print features intact. The system can also translate among word-processor program formats, so you can prepare a file with Word and send it, as an Xpedite electronic mail message, to someone else who uses WordPerfect. The service has many other features as well.

You'll need a PC, a Hayes-compatible telephone modem, and either an Epson or HP LaserJet compatible printer. You'll also need Xpedite's software package. The cost is $49.95, but it includes a $10 credit good for the registration of your letterhead with the system. There are no subscription fees or monthly minimum, though when monthly charges reach $50, users receive a 25 percent discount.

Two costs are involved in using the service. First, the connect-time cost of transmitting your PC file to Xpedite ($7.50 an hour or 12.5¢ per minute). Second, the cost Xpedite incurs in transmitting your document to a fax machine. During prime time this is between 45¢ and 90¢ a minute. During nonprime (7:00 P.M. to 7:00 A.M.) the cost is between 30¢ and 60¢ a minute. Xpedite tells us that it typically transmits a full page in half a minute. The lower

Online Tip (cont.)

per-minute prices reflect the effect of volume discounts. Customer service is available between the hours of 9:00 A.M. and 9:00 P.M., Eastern standard time. For more information, contact:

Xpedite Systems, Inc.
446 Highway 35
Eatontown, NJ 07724
(800) 227–9379
(201) 389–3900

PC Fax: Fax Boards and Fax Modems

The other personal-computer-related option is to purchase a free-standing fax modem or a fax board that can be inserted into one of the expansion slots in your machine. Fax boards look and operate a lot like internal telephone modems. Indeed, at heart they're basically just the modem portion of a Group III fax machine. This means that, unlike your trusty telephone modem, they can talk directly to other fax machines. At this writing, prices range from $400 to $1000.

In addition to being able to talk directly to other fax machines and dedicated fax networks, a fax board gives you the same crisper image advantage discussed above. But it suffers from the same limitation. Unless you spend an equivalent amount on a scanner, you will not be able to send anything not created on your PC. In addition, since fax images are graphics files, they can occupy a lot of storage space. You will certainly need a hard disk in your system, and may want one with a larger capacity than you might ordinarily buy.

Online Tip: Why do graphics files take up so much more space than text files? The answer is that two bytes are required to represent each character in a text file, one byte to symbolize the character and one to designate the various screen attributes of that character (blinking, high-intensity, foreground color, background color, and so on). Those two bytes tell the video hardware everything it needs to know to paint the picture elements (pixels) or dots that make up the character on the screen. Thus while a single character may be displayed as a series of, say, 40 pixels, only two bytes (16 bits) are required, thanks to the video hardware's translation ability. Consequently, a single 25 line by 80 character screen full of text requires $25 \times 80 \times 2 = 4000$ bytes of storage space on disk.

In graphics mode, there is no translation. Each and every pixel on the screen must be specified by from one to eight bits, depending on the kind of graphics card you are using. As a quick example, consider that in its high-resolution graphics mode, the IBM CGA displays 640 × 200 pixels per screen. That's 128,000 pixels at one bit each. Convert to bytes by dividing by eight and you find that 16,000 bytes are required to store a graphics screen of this sort on disk—four times as much space as for a full screen of text.

Fax board manufacturers, naturally enough, compete on features and price. A board may be able to operate in the background, sending and receiving without interfering with your primary computer task. It may be able to accept a wide variety of file types, including not just ASCII text files but files created with popular graphics and paint programs. A regular Hayes-compatible telephone modem on the same board may be offered as well. In the future, if manufacturers can ever agree on a standard, you may be able to use the board to send and receive computer files at 9600 bps in addition to using it for fax communications. (If this option interests you, you should definitely wait until a standard has been announced. The general feeling in the industry is that this will happen relatively soon.)

Finally, since the most advanced fax machines are basically small computers anyway, with their own central processing units and memory chips, pressing your personal computer's greater power and storage space into the service of facsimile communications offers you advanced fax machine capabilities. You can store lots of phone numbers and send a different file to each one, for example. Or you can tell the board to place its calls at many different times.

Capabilities to Look For

As is always the case with computers, software is crucial to the ease with which you can use a fax board. When considering a fax board and software package, ask if the program gives you a phone directory for storing frequently dialed numbers. The ability to tell the board to send at a certain time—like after the phone rates go down in the evening—is also a nice feature.

What kinds of paint program or other graphics files can it handle? And what printers will it work with? Will the board work with a scanner? Does the board have a gray-scale capability so you can print out photos with various shades of gray?

Check for easy-to-use menus, and ask whether the board offers online file conversion allowing you to simply tell the system which file to send. If it doesn't, you will have to go through the extra step of converting the file to fax mode before it can be transmitted. Can you look at a document on the screen before you send it or print it? If not, you may find that you spend a lot of time printing material that you would ordinarily simply delete, like the "junk fax" letters that seem to be proliferating.

Finally, make sure the board can operate in the background so an incoming fax won't force you to stop whatever you're doing on the system until the transmission is complete. You'll also want to be able to put what you're doing on hold momentarily, tell the board to send a fax, and return to your project to resume work while the transmission is taking place.

Fax Networks

The store-and-forward approach to message delivery discussed in the previous chapter in connection with telex messages is equally useful for facsimile communications. Vendors, particularly those already offering electronic mail, have been quick to respond. Among them, MCI FAX appears to be making the biggest splash. The firm's November 3, 1988 announcement said that MCI was the first U.S. long-distance company to offer a dedicated network for domestic and international fax transmissions. It went on to describe an array of rather interesting features.

MCI FAX can be used only with a fax modem or fax board. It offers fax-to-fax, toll-free fax to allow customers to send you faxes at no cost to them, telex-to-fax to allow messages sent to an MCI telex number to be delivered to your fax, and store-and-forward. Under this last option, MCI keeps trying should the target fax be busy. It also lets you specify the time of delivery to be sure of sending during the cheapest long distance rate periods. Broadcast distribution is also available, either on a one-time basis or via a Broadcast Dispatch feature that lets you store a "mailing list" of fax phone numbers on the system. There are management information reports, remote diagnostics, and security features as well. You can also use a fax machine in someone else's office and charge the transaction to an MCI FAX telephone credit card.

Unlike MCI Mail and other e-mail systems, fax networks like MCI FAX charge by the time required to transmit a message instead of by the number of characters it contains. At this writing, MCI FAX charges you for the first 30 seconds and then rounds up the remaining transmission time in six-second increments. Other systems use larger increments, regardless of the actual time required, so MCI maintains that its system will be cheaper. Charges are equivalent to MCI's regular telephone rates. There are no subscription fees or feature-related fees. All costs are based on usage. For more information, contact:

MCI FAX Business Center
P.O. Box 19564
Washington, D.C. 20077
(800) 888-3329

Fax-to-PC: The Final Link

With electronic mail, the telex network, and now facsimile machines and networks, a PC user really can send a message to anywhere from anywhere. The only limitation at this writing is going from a fax to a PC that is not equipped with a fax board. When it becomes possible for a person to use his or her facsimile machine to send you a page via MCI FAX or some other network, a page that you can then download as you would any other file, the circle will be complete.

Actually, the Xpedite service cited earlier can do this on a limited basis right now. But there is still a missing link. Remember that even if it looks like a typewritten letter on your screen, a fax message is still a *graphics* file. That means that you can edit the images in the file with a compatible paint or graphics program, but you can't bring it into your word processor and issue a command to, say, readjust the margins. As far as the computer is concerned the file that looks like a typewritten letter may as well be a rendering of the Mona Lisa. The machine sees it as a bit-mapped picture.

As it happens, however, there is a software solution. At this writing there are at least two leading optical character recognition (OCR) packages that are capable of turning graphic images of text into the real thing. Macintosh users will want to look at Read-It! ($295), from Olduvai Software (305-665-4665). The program offers a feature called EasyLearn that can teach itself new typefaces in about 15 minutes (compared to the two to three hours ordinarily required). IBM and compatible users will want to look at SMaRT STaRT ($495) from Advanced Recognition Technologies (201-487-3440). The program comes prepared to recognize the ten most popular typewriter, printer, and typset typestyles, but it can also be "taught" an unlimited number of additional typestyles. An accuracy rate of over 99 percent is claimed by the company.

Other OCR packages are available as well, and certainly more will be coming on the market, undoubtedly at lower prices. We should add one word of caution, however. Before buying any OCR package, look carefully at the types of files it can read. Fax boards vary in the graphics file formats they can convert received messages into, and obviously one of them must be compatible with your OCR software if that software is to do you any good. Leading file formats include DR HALO, GEM Paint, Microsoft Paint, TIFF, .PCX, and .CUT.

Part V

—APPLICATIONS—

...24...

Electronic Banking

H ow many hours a month do you spend writing checks, stuffing them into envelopes, licking stamps, and updating your checkbook register? How many times have you missed a payment date because all of your credit cards come due on different days of the month? It would be wonderful if we could say, "Well, relax, your problems are solved, thanks to online electronic banking." But we can't. After years of availability, online consumer banking is a mixed bag at best.

Rudimentary home banking programs have been available via CompuServe for several years. But it wasn't until Chemical Bank of New York, one of the nation's major financial institutions, weighed in with its Pronto system in 1983 that serious, fully supported home banking began. Chemical reportedly invested more than $20 million in hardware, software, and development costs. When it weighed out again in January of 1989, the online industry was neither elated nor surprised.

Less than three months later, Chase Manhattan, another big New York bank, drastically altered its Spectrum home banking service, raising the monthly fee and slashing services. Chase eliminated all investment services, including stock quotes, online stock trading, Standard & Poor's, and market information digests. The company reported that less than 10 percent of subscribers used the financial services during any three-month period. Balance inquiry and bill-paying were and are the most popular features. Industry sources report that from its debut in December of 1984 until March of 1989, Spectrum had attracted only about 5000 subscribers.

That's the downside of the home banking picture. On the upside, the Regional Bell Operating Companies (RBOCs) are actively pursuing home banking for the gateway services discussed in Chapter 11. At this writing, at least one bank (Atlanta's Citizens & Southern Bank) is offering home banking services via Prodigy, the videotex system from IBM and Sears. The bank is encouraging participation by making PS/2 Model 25 systems and a special low-interest financing package available to interested customers. Citibank, the nation's largest bank and the operator of one of the most successful home banking services, is actively recruiting former Pronto customers. Bank of America has recently announced enhanced service by giving its HomeBanking and Business Connection customers access to Western Union's EasyLink.

As we said, it's a mixed bag of failures and successes. The one thing that seems certain is that wherever you live, at some time in the not too distant future you will be given the opportunity to sign up for personal computer-based banking. Accordingly, it may be helpful to have some idea of what to look for in a program.

How to Pick a Home Banking Program

Bill-paying is the essence of home banking, and any system must ultimately be judged on how well it handles this function. It may be nice to call up your savings and checking account balances, transfer money between them, or to review the bank's latest rates for certificates of deposit, but you can do all of these things by telephone or at a (usually) nearby cash machine.

The basic outline of the online bill-paying process is relatively simple. You dial a number as you would to go online with any other system. This connects you with your bank's computer and causes that system to prompt you for your name and password. You are then presented with a menu containing a bill-paying option. After you select that option, the system prompts you for which creditors you wish to pay and in what amounts. The system will give you the opportunity to review what you have entered and to change or cancel it if you choose. It will then confirm the transaction, and you will sign off or use some other feature.

That seems logical enough. Indeed, it works exactly as you would expect it to work. But different banks handle things differently, and there are crucial questions to ask regarding each stage of the process. That's what we'll do now, starting with the means of access.

How can you access the bank? The key question is whether using the service is going to cost you any money for connect time. To use the Philadelphia Savings Fund Society's PC-DIRECT service on CompuServe, for example, you must pay regular CompuServe connect rates. Only subscribers in New York, Connecticut, and New Jersey can access Citibank's Direct Access system via a toll-free number. If you live in an area where message units are charged for even local phone calls, you must take that into account as well.

When is service available? To be most useful, a service should be available round the clock and on holidays and weekends. Be sure to ask when does the bank take the system down for maintenance and thus make the service unavailable. Also, check on customer service. Is there a toll-free number? What hours is customer service available?

What does the sign-on process involve? Understandably, everyone is concerned about security. Though it would be rather difficult for someone to sign on and loot your account if he or she were not already on a list of bank-approved payees, one should never say never. The banks have taken two main approaches to this problem. All require one or more levels of passwords. One password may be required to get you onto the system, while a different password may be required to actually write checks, for example.

But some banks go a step further. Citibank, for example, issues customers special software for use with the systems. The disk contains a code that, in conjunction with codes you type in online, gives you access to the system. If your bank uses this approach, be sure to ask how it handles the separate accounts you and your spouse may maintain. In addition, if you use both a desktop and a laptop system, ask what you should do to be able to access your account with both systems.

Which creditors can you pay? This is the most crucial question of all. The ads for many home banking services would lead you to believe that you can handle all of your bill-paying by simply signing onto the system. But if you investigate, you may discover that that isn't true at all. All online banking systems publish lists of merchants, credit-card companies, mortgage-service companies, and others who have agreed to accept electronically transferred payments from those banks. But if your phone or utility company or other creditor isn't on the list, you're out of luck. Or more accurately, you're back at your checkbook again, writing checks and licking envelopes and stamps.

Part of the problem is that the banks like to pay merchants either by electronic funds transfer or by sending them a large check in payment for scores of individual accounts. But the accounting systems used by most merchants simply aren't set up to handle payments of this sort.

What many banks do not seem to realize is that as long as a consumer must haul out the checkbook to write five checks, the marginal increase in time required to write ten checks is not that significant. If the institution offering you home banking services can't handle 95 percent or more of the checks you normally write, you might want to think long and hard before signing up for its program and paying the fees it will charge.

Most banks offer you the opportunity to specify creditors other than those on their approved list, but this often requires a setup and approval process. When the Chemical Bank system was in operation, for example, the bank would contact the merchant to see if he or she would accept Pronto payments. But there was no guarantee. We don't know, but we suspect that this large inconvenience was largely responsible for Pronto's lack of popularity.

At this writing the only bank we know of capable of handling any and all payments, whether they are made to your local dry cleaners or to your landlord or mortgage company, is Citibank, the Proctor & Gamble of financial institutions. Citibank pays some merchants with a single bulk check, but it also has the capability to print out and mail a check to each payee you specify.

How easy is the payment process? Like many online systems, most banks and financial institutions aren't really attuned to the needs of the personal-computer-using public. Consequently, their brochures and promotional literature typically fail to provide any indication whatsoever of how the bill-paying process actually works. Broadly speaking, the bill-paying process is either menu-driven or what can be called command-driven, depending on the bank.

The thing to watch out for is a system that presents you with a list of all its approved merchants and makes you scroll through, ticking off the ones you want to pay. Much better is a system that lets you create your own personalized list of payees. This requires some initial setup the first time through, but once the list is created it will be presented to you each time you enter the bill-paying feature.

You will also want to be able to control the timing of your payments, particularly if yours is an interest-bearing checking or NOW account. You might want to have the bank pay a different group of merchants each day of the month, though if you're going to cut it close to a bill's due date be sure you know when the bank must issue payment to be assured of getting it there in time. Another convenience, particularly if your employer offers a direct deposit paycheck option, is the ability to set up automatic payments of certain regular bills. You might issue instructions, for example, to pay your mortgage or rent on the same day every month. As long as there is money in your account, you never need worry about it again.

What about account updating and reporting? If sample printouts and screens are not supplied with your information package, be sure to ask about the kind of information you can obtain online and what a printout looks like. How frequently is your checking account information updated? Will the system tell you your actual current balance and give you a list of checks you have written that have not yet cleared? Does the bank automatically mail you a statement each month?

What happens when you write a paper check on your account? How can you tell the system that you have done so? And what about cash machine transactions? Where do they fit in? Since different banks deal with these eventualities in so many different ways, we won't attempt to examine them here. But you should definitely ask about these things when considering a home banking program.

How is record-keeping handled? Perhaps most important of all, take the time to step through the bill-paying process in your mind before signing up for a program. Here again the banking industry has generally failed to put itself into the shoes of the customer. Brochures and flyers tend to talk about what a wonderful opportunity the bank is giving you to pay bills by computer with their systems for just $10 (or whatever) a month. But no one addresses such an obvious and crucial concern as "How will I keep my checkbook? Will I be forced to deal with a disorganized sheaf of pages from my computer's printer or what?"

What does it cost? Most banks charge a monthly fee for their home banking services, but the fees vary considerably. At this writing, typical fees are between $8 and $10. Bank of America Business Connection customers pay $50 per month, but this gives them unlimited use of that service. The BofA HomeBanking program is $10 a month.

Typically, you will also be subject to the standard account maintenance fees that have always applied to checking accounts. And of course every bank has its own range of options involving minimum balances of various sorts. Citibank, however, will let you count the money you keep in any other Citibank account (IRA, money market, Keogh, and so on) toward your minimum balance requirement. Other banks may have similar policies.

Other Features

All systems will let you check the balances of your other accounts and transfer money among them. But there are more exotic nonbanking features as well. Citibank, for example, provides its customers with gateway service to the Dow Jones News/Retrieval Service. And as mentioned, Bank of America customers now have access to EasyLink. In both cases customer accounts are debited directly for connect-time charges. You may also be able to access online discount brokerage services on your home banking system.

Conclusion

Probably the prime question for anyone interested in home banking is "How will I get cash when I need it?" Unless you have a very cooperative bank and an exceptionally fine graphics printer, there is no way we know of to obtain cash online. Thanks to the widespread availability of automatic teller cash machines, this shouldn't be much of a problem. Indeed, if you're fortunate enough to have a bank with a really good PC-based banking program, you may never need to visit the bank or write a check ever again. That at least, in our opinion, should be the goal, because increasing flexibility and convenience while reducing the check-writing burden is what online banking is all about.

...25...

Online Stock Trading

There is probably no industry more dependent on computers than the financial industry. There is no way, for example, that the New York Stock Exchange could handle today's heavy trading volumes were it not heavily computerized. And without personal computers, financial planning and portfolio management by everyone from the large financial institutions to the private investor would be much more difficult.

It's not surprising, then, that the financial industry was among the first to make its services available to the public by going online. We've already seen that virtually any stock or security quote, as well as reams of news, analysis, and other financial information, is available to any personal computer user. In this chapter we'll look at how you can take action on that information and possibly save some money at the same time.

Virtually all online stock brokers are discount brokers. That means that in return for leaving out the frills, they offer you trading services at lower commissions than full-service firms. They offer no advice, suggestions, or investment research reports. You don't have to be an expert, but they expect you to generally know what you're doing.

If you're new to the stock market and are at all nervous about making your first trade, this is probably not the place to learn. Find a reputable full-service broker in your town instead. And note that although discount firms are fond of citing "savings of over 75 percent" off Wall Street's posted rates, in reality "you're talking a trade in the range of $50,000," according to an official at one discount firm. Many discount firms estimate that only about 10 percent of their clients do the kind of business that qualifies for such deep discounts. Indeed, where only a

301

relatively small number of shares is involved, you may actually do better at a full-service firm. Discount brokers often charge minimum fees per trade, plus a percentage of the dollar value. Many full-service firms do not impose such minimums.

On the other hand, if you like to make your own decisions, without the static and noise of an eager salesperson, and if you don't mind saving money on commissions, an account with a firm offering online brokerage services may be just the ticket. You will need an account, of course, and you will certainly want to do some comparison shopping regarding commissions and fees. Since even the industry admits that its fees are byzantine in complexity, pick a stock, decide how many shares you'd like to buy or sell, and compare prices based on that single transaction. It's not a foolproof technique for identifying the broker who will give you the best rate on every possible transaction, but if it's a typical trade for you, then you would probably do well picking the lowest-cost alternative.

Means of Access

There are basically three ways to gain access to online trading facilities. You may be able to do so through a home banking service of the sort described in the previous chapter. Or you may be able to dial up a free-standing, dedicated system. These days, however, you'll find that a number of the leading firms in the field are available through an online utility system. CompuServe offers Quick & Reilly and Max Ule. And the Dow Jones News/Retrieval Service has Fidelity Investors Express. Those are the kinds of systems we'll be referring to here. You may want to do your shopping for a discount broker first and, after you have lined up your candidates, ask each if their services are available online.

Online Tip: One free-standing system well worth checking out if you're an active trader is Security Pacific Investments. Security Pacific acquired C. D. Anderson, the company that started it all. In April 1983, C. D. Anderson went live with a system developed by Trade*Plus, Inc. That system is now available through other services as well, and as noted, Anderson has been acquired. Security Pacific claims to offer the lowest cost of all online brokers. There is no start-up fee, and connect time costs either 44¢ a minute in prime time (7:00 A.M. to 6:00 P.M., your local time) or 10¢ a minute in nonprime. There is a monthly minimum connect-time usage requirement of $15, billed to your major credit card. The firm offers a full line of financial products, and the minimum commission is about $36. For more information contact:

Security Pacific Investments
555 Montgomery Street, Suite 700
San Francisco, CA 94111
(800) 822-2222

Online Tip: One of the nation's largest discount brokerage firms, Charles Schwab and Company, also operates a free-standing system. To use it, you'll need to buy The Equalizer, an IBM-compatible package the company sells for $269. (In the past Schwab has had a special deal: $100 off or a free board-mounted 2400 bps Hayes-compatible modem.) There is no charge for signing on and checking your account or placing a trade. However, if you choose real-time stock quotes, the cost is $1.45 a minute while the markets are open. The closing quote database can be accessed for 45¢ a minute after market hours

In addition to online brokerage services, The Equalizer package includes a portfolio manager capable of handling up to 702 portfolios, and the online system offers connections to the Dow Jones News/Retrieval Service and Warner pricing information. The Schwab system does not involve any ongoing charges. There is no annual subscription fee for Dow Jones access, for example. The company's minimum commission at this writing is $39. It's maximum is $49. For information, contact:

Charles Schwab & Company
Department S
101 Montgomery Street
San Francisco, CA 94104
(800) 334-4455

Why Trade Online?

Though online stock trading isn't for everyone, it offers a number of advantages that make it attractive to active investors. The most important advantage is best illustrated by the comment we heard from one online discount firm: "When the bottom dropped out and everything started to head south in October of '87, the guys who weren't online got killed. They couldn't get through to their broker. But our online customers were able to log on and get out fast. No busy signals."

That's an extreme case, to be sure, but it underscores the instant accessibility offered by online brokerage accounts. If the Chairman of the Federal Reserve board announces a change in interest rate policy early Friday evening, or if some development takes place abroad over the weekend, you don't have to wait until Monday morning to call your broker—along with everybody else and his uncles and his cousins and his aunts. You can go online immediately and enter your instructions. They will be executed within seconds of the opening bell. In short, you can enter your buy and sell orders when you want and not be confined by the schedule of the workaday world.

Most online brokerage systems also let you create several stock portfolios containing your investments. Or perhaps they contain those stocks you don't own but are just tracking to test out a theory. No matter. Because most systems interface with a stock quote database, you can always get an instant update on what a given portfolio is worth. No need to laboriously punch *Wall Street Journal* numbers into a pocket calculator.

In addition, when you make a trade, your portfolio will automatically be updated to reflect its new status. Some systems do more than just give you a list of your current holdings when you ask to look at a portfolio. They may be able to produce a report organized by tax lot ID number, for example. Or you may be able to request a report of a portfolio's gains and losses for a given year or to date.

Online Tip: You may find the portfolio-reporting feature on a given system so attractive that you will decide to use it to track all of your investments. If so, make sure you can enter information on stock trades or other investments not made on the system. You may occasionally use a different broker, for example, but want to consolidate your activities with him or her in your online portfolio.

What to Look For in an Online Broker

Services, fees, and extra features vary, of course, and no single broker's system is suitable for everyone. However, one characteristic you will definitely want to look into is how the trades you enter are handled. There is a legal requirement that all trades be reviewed by human eyes before being executed. But there are at least two ways that requirement can be fulfilled. The online brokerage service could actually be little more than an electronic mail system: You transmit your order "message," and the broker either prints it out or looks at it on the screen and uses the information to key in the order just as if it had come in over the phone.

That's still more convenient for you than making a phone call. But there are much faster ways to accomplish the same thing. More sophisticated systems have a direct wire to the trading floor. Your order will come in, be flashed on a screen for human review, and at the press of a key, sent to the floor for execution. Regardless of your investing style, be sure to ask about how fast orders are executed. You may not need top speed, but it is still important to know what's happening at the other end of the line.

You will always receive a printed confirmation of a trade, but you may be able to view confirmation messages online as well. It is also worth checking to make sure that a given brokerage firm offers the investment instruments you want to buy or sell. You can't necessarily assume that all brokers deal in all products. So if you want to buy treasury bills and other forms of government debt, municipal bonds, stock index options, or whatever, make sure that your chosen online broker handles those issues before you open an account.

Finally, be sure to consider all the costs. The biggest expense is the commission you'll pay on each trade, so compare brokers as suggested earlier by asking each for the total fee on the same hypothetical trade. There may also be connect-time costs for accessing the system. Alternatively, connect time may be free, but there might be a monthly subscription fee or minimum usage requirement. And, of course, with the possible exception of the day's closing quotes, any information features you access will almost always involve an extra charge.

Recommendations

If you buy and sell stocks and securities once a month or less and you're interested in choosing an online utility, you will obviously want to pick one that offers online trading. But that feature shouldn't be the determining factor in making your selection. If you're a more active investor, an online trading feature, as well as online financial information, will be much more important. In that case, you'll want to look closely at the relative fees and features of the brokerage firms involved. Here are the addresses of the brokerage firms that can be found on the online utility systems at this writing. You might want to contact each of them to request an information packet describing their services and fees.

Fidelity Investors Express (Dow
   Jones News/Retrieval)
82 Devonshire Street
San Francisco, CA 02109
(800) 225–5531

Ingham, Becker & Co., Inc.
 (CompuServe)
Max Ule Division
202 East 39th Street
New York, NY 10157–9990
(800) 223–6642

Quick & Reilly (CompuServe)
120 Wall Street
New York, NY 10005
(800) 221–5220
(800) 522–8712, in New York

...26...

Online Shopping and Keyboard Commerce

In the 1953 science-fiction classic, *The Space Merchants*, authors C. M. Kornbluth and Frederik Pohl postulated a future society in which absolutely every aspect of daily life has been subsumed by advertising. Posters on subways and buses don't hang passively on the wall waiting for you to notice them—they project electronic images on your retina, regardless of where you are standing. Coffee is no longer drunk only at breakfast and dinner, people drink it throughout the day, even at bedtime. But then they have little choice, thanks to the addictive alkaloid secretly ground into each pound by the manufacturer.

Unfortunately, at times, the electronic universe bears more than a passing resemblance to the world imagined by Messrs. Pohl and Kornbluth. Often it seems that for every company motivated by a desire to provide a superb online service, there are ten others who see the medium primarily as yet another way to sell you things. This is by no means bad, particularly if you're interested in the merchandise they're pushing. But it does lead to a great deal of hyperbole on the part of online retailers about the joys of electronic shopping.

In this chapter we'll look at the two major types of shopping options available online. One is what might be called the comprehensive discount service, as represented by Comp-u-Store. The other is the specialty boutique service, represented by CompuServe's Electronic Mall. Comp-u-Store is available on virtually every online utility system, and it really has no competitors in the comprehensive discount category. The electronic mall concept was invented by CompuServe, and its apparent success has spawned many imitators on other utility systems. Like a real mall, the concept brings many different merchants under the same electronic roof. Unlike a real mall, however, participating stores offer only a small number of selected items for purchase online, although most will be happy to accept your online request for a mail-order catalog.

Pros and Cons of Online Shopping

We will spare you a recounting of the past failures of online shopping services and simply note that the reality of such services consistently fails to live up to its advance billing. Part of the problem is the technology—neither ASCII text nor Prodigy-style NAPLPS graphics can ever substitute for touching, feeling, and trying a product in person. Another part of the problem is that no service has emphasized the concept's inherent strengths sufficiently to outweigh its inherent weaknesses.

The fact is, some ten years into the online electronic revolution, there are still only three good reasons for shopping from your keyboard instead of shopping in person, by catalog, or by phone. The first is the opportunity to use a remote mainframe's power to search through listings of hundreds of similar products for the exact models and brands that meet your specifications. No need to stand in a store laboriously comparing the labels and features of competing brands. Let the computer do the work for you.

In addition, if the database of product listings being searched is reasonably comprehensive, you will be able to quickly scan a list of *all* the makes and models that suit your needs. You are no longer limited to what a nearby store or mail-order catalog happens to carry. And that is the second good reason for shopping online—the opportunity to buy products and specialty items that aren't readily available from conventional sources.

The third reason is the opportunity to save money. An online retailer doesn't need a storefront, with all the rent, heat, light, insurance, taxes, and labor costs that entails. Consequently, the merchant's costs are lower and, theoretically at least, prices should be as well.

Those are the three strengths of the online shopping concept. If every service fully exploited them, we could pass lightly over the negatives. Unfortunately, while Comp-u-Store at least comes close to offering a comprehensive selection at discount prices, most electronic mall-type merchants offer only a few items and save you little, if any, money on prices. In fact, in many cases, in addition to paying the full retail price, plus shipping and handling, you will almost certainly have to pay connect-time charges to someone for the privilege of using an online shopping service of any kind.

Nor, despite industry hype, is online shopping all that convenient. Except in the case of a major appliance, a consumer electronics item, or other big-ticket purchase with potentially big savings, it is difficult to imagine most people routinely booting their computers, firing up their modems, and signing on to an online system solely to go shopping. If you happen to be online anyway and feel like a little impulse buying, that's another story. But this is quite different from making an online shopping service your primary electronic destination.

In addition, while one can easily imagine buying a book, videotape, or some familiar brand-name product online, most products must be touched, felt, and seen before one can make a selection. Would you really want to buy something like a camera without first holding it in your hands, or an exercise bike without personally testing the smoothness of its flywheel? To say nothing of the fact that in America, in-person, shoulder-rubbing shopping, usually at a suburban mall, is one of our major social activities.

Certainly online shopping has its place. And, contrary to what you might expect given everything we have said so far, we have had nothing but good experiences in this area. At the same time, we have never found the merchandise available online to be all that unique, or the discounts so dazzling that the online option leaps immediately to mind whenever the need (or desire) for a product arises. Instead, the first impulse is to leap into the old rustbucket and take a spin out to the local BEST or other discount retailer. It is true that one might pay $10 or $20 more per item compared to some online prices, though that isn't necessarily the case. And you'll have to pay sales tax. But there are no shipping or connect-time charges, and no delays. You get to touch and feel the merchandise in person and walk out with it the same day.

Online shopping can also be a lot of fun. For some reason there is something thrilling about sitting in front of your computer at three in the morning ordering a shipment of smoked salmon, gourmet coffee, or Waterford crystal. Though in the back of your mind you know that there is no reason why the order couldn't wait until regular business hours and no real reason to use your computer since most establishments have toll-free phone numbers.

Comp-u-Store/Shoppers Advantage

Everyone should try online shopping at least once, and in our opinion, Comp-u-Store, or "Shoppers Advantage" as it is now called on Compu-Serve, is the place to start. As noted, Comp-u-Store is available on nearly every online utility system. Comp-u-Store is far from perfect, but it does do more with the inherent advantages of the electronic shopping concept than anyone else.

Comp-u-Store Online is a unit of CUC International, a company formerly known as Comp-u-Card of America. Located in Stamford, Connecticut, CUC is the original shop-at-home service. The company was founded in 1973 to offer its customers computerized price quotes and the opportunity to purchase items at a discount over the phone. That service, called Comp-u-Store, has over 11 million members at this writing, most of whom contact the service by voice phone, not by personal computer.

The firm solicits price quotes on some 250,000 brand-name products from over 1000 manufacturers, wholesalers, and retailers, all of whom have agreed to ship directly to Comp-u-Store subscribers. The information is entered into a computer. Whenever a member requests the price of an item, the computer scans its memory for all available prices and displays the lowest quote on the terminal of the customer service representative handling the call.

Prices typically range from 10 to 40 percent—and occasionally 50 percent—off the manufacturer's suggested retail price. In addition to receiving a price quote, members also have the option of ordering the product at the price given and charging their purchase on a major credit card.

The phone-in service is separate from Comp-u-Store Online, and is still the largest portion of the company's business. But the two work very similarly. The main difference is that the online version replaces the customer service representative's terminal with your own, allowing you to search the database of products and prices whenever you like.

When you access the service through an online utility, a gateway is established to link you directly with CUC's mainframe computers. From that moment on, until you exit back to your utility system, CUC's host computer software is in control. And as with any separate system, this one has its own command and menu structure. There is no cost for using the CUC gateway, other than the normal connect-time charges you pay to your utility service.

Membership, Costs, and Delivery

It is important to emphasize that you do not have to be a member of Comp-u-Store to use the service. Any subscriber to a system offering Comp-u-Store can use the feature to locate products, check prices, and comparison-shop. But if you want to actually order merchandise, you will have to join. The cost is $30 per year, and it brings with it a 50-page user manual, a member code, and an access code. When you gateway through to Comp-u-Store from a utility system you will be asked to enter these codes. (A separate membership is required to use the phone-in service.) Every three months you will also receive a color catalog of selected Comp-u-Store Online merchandise. Special discounts may also be included. At this writing, for example, members receive 20 percent off National's regular daily business rate for car rentals and 10 percent off any promotional rate nationwide. Members who buy or sell a home through an ERA Realty broker receive a discount certificate good for $1000 in merchandise. The membership fee is completely refundable if you are not satisfied with the service. As of November 1988, Comp-u-Store Online had some 60,000 members.

Except for special orders, the normal delivery time for products ordered online is about three weeks, though the company has in the past offered some products for two-week delivery. The service also includes 30-day price protection—if you see a product advertised for less by an authorized dealer, you can send CUC the proof and the company will refund the difference.

Online Tip: How does Comp-u-Store make its money? Three ways: membership fees, commissions on sales, and commissions on the connect time users spend with CompuServe or some other service accessing the Comp-u-Store database. According to Walter A. Forbes, the firm's chief executive officer, the company makes a commission of between two and three percent on sales of the items it offers. Prices for items ordered online are somewhat lower than the same items ordered via the phone-in service since there is virtually no overhead.

Shopping with Comp-u-Store

Now let's take a look at what it's like to use Comp-u-Store. We accessed the service through CompuServe, where as noted, it is called Shoppers Advantage, though the menus and style of operation you find will be the same regardless of your online utility system. Our goal was to see what one could get a particular Sony tabletop CD player for.

Following an initial greeting screen offering more information on the service, the TOP menu appeared:

```
         MAIN DIRECTORY              TOP

              1 All About Us
              2 What's New
              3 Best Buys
              4 Department Store
              5 Shop by Model #
              6 Shop by Product Category
              7 Shop by Product Code
              8 Info/Member Feedback
```

MAIN DIRECTORY   TOP *cont.*

9 Other Services
10 Merchandise of the Month
11 Warehouse Sale

Enter Choice :4

Notice that there are several ways to locate the products you're interested in (items 5 through 7, above). We decided to take the easy way
and go to the department store instead. This feature leads you through
a series of menus designed to help you narrow your focus. You'll end up
at exactly the same spot you would have been taken to had you known
the model number, product category, or product code. Notice the
choices entered below and how they lead eventually to compact disk
players:

DEPARTMENT STORE

1 Bed/Bath
2 Cars/Auto Accessories
3 Computers/Accessories
4 Formal Living/Dining
5 Home Furnishings
6 Home/Office
7 Housewares
8 Leisure
9 Luxury
10 Major Appliances
11 Photo/Optical Equipment
12 Sound Products
13 Tools/Seasonal
14 TV/Video

Enter Choice :12

SOUND PRODUCTS

1 Musical Instruments
2 Tape,CD,Record/Players
3 Receivers,Speakers,Amps
4 Blank Reel-to-Reel Tapes
5 Clock Radios
6 Compact Discs
7 Record Albums
8 Stereo Accessories
9 Stereo Blank Cassettes
10 Stereo Cartridges
11 Stereo Equalizers
12 Stereo Headphones

```
              SOUND PRODUCTS

         13 Stereo Microphones
         14 Stereo Mixers
         15 Stereo Systems
         16 Styli

         Enter choice :2


      TAPE,CD,LP/CASSETTE PLAYERS

         1 Compact Disc Players
         2 Portable Cassette Decks
         3 Portable CD Players
         4 Persona Stereo (Walkman type)
         5 Stereo Cassette Deck
         6 Stereo Reel-to-Reel Decks
         7 Stereo Turntables

         Enter Choice :1
```

   Next, you will be asked for the state to which you will want a product
to be shipped. This is necessary for the price quote, which includes shipping via UPS or comparable carrier. (Note: You can arrange to have
Comp-u-Store ship to any address, making it possible to send perfume,
books and other gifts the way you might use an FTD Florist to send
flowers.) Then you will see lists of manufacturers similar to the following:

```
                 Manufacturer

         1 No preference
         2 AIWA
         3 AKAI
         4 CROWN AUDIO
         5 FISHER
         6 HARMAN KARDON
         7 JVC
         8 KENWOOD
         9 MAGNAVOX
        10 MARANTZ
        11 NEC
        12 ONKYO
        13 PANASONIC
        14 PHILCO
        15 PIONEER
        16 PROTON

        Examples: 2 or 1,2 or 3,5,7
        (you can string up to 10 mfrs)

        Enter choice(s) or
        <CR> for more:
```

Manufacturer

17 QUASAR
18 REVOX
19 SCOTT
20 SHERWOOD
21 SHARP
22 SANSUI
23 SONY
24 SYLVANIA
25 TECHNICS
26 TEAC
27 TOSHIBA

Examples: 2 or 1,2 or 3,5,7
(you can string up to 10 mfrs)

Enter choice(s) :23

Notice that you can specify a single maker, as we did directly above with 23 for SONY. Or you can specify up to ten makers, or enter 1 for "No preference." When you have responded here, the next option is to select models:

MODEL SELECTION

1 List all Models
2 Select by Features
3 Specify Model Number or Title

Enter choice :2

Style?

1 No preference
2 Table
3 Table with remote
4 Table with magazine

Enter choice :4

Under "Model Selection," we chose to select by feature. We already knew we wanted a tabletop model capable of accepting several CDs at once, as opposed to a portable. The "Style?" menu let us specify exactly that. Note that the actual entries on the "Style?" menu will differ with the kind of product you seek. The system next asked us for our upper dollar limit on what we would spend. We chose not to specify a limit. And the system quickly came back with a list of the actual products one could order:

```
Compact disc players          Page 1 of 1
                                        Model   List $   Yours $
                                                ------   ---------
------------------------------------------------------------
Manufacturer: SONY
   1 CDPC26                                      open     259.56


Enter HELP for instructions for
product comparisons

Enter choice(s) or "O" to order :1

Compact disc players (STCD)      SONY (SONY)
Model#: CDPC26
-------------------------------------------------------------------

List Price:         open
Our Price:          259.56
                          Color Surcharge: .00
With Regular Delivery: 259.56 (delivery in 3-4 weeks)

-------------------------------------------------------------------

Colors: Black
-------------------------------------------------------------------
```

COMPACT DISC CHANGER W/ CAROUSEL DESIGN 5-DISC CHANGER (NO CARTRIDGE).
HAS 32 TRACK PROGRAMMING, DELETE SHUFFLE PLAY, TIMER PLAY/SWITCH, 16 STEP
MUSIC CALENDER, DUAL D/A FILTERS, 2 X OVERSAMPLING, 4-FUNCTION
FLUORESCENT DISPLAY AND INCLUDES REMOTE CONTROL.

Enter "O" to Order :

The Comp-u-Store system worked beautifully. As you can see, it was easy to follow the menus to reach the specific product we wanted a quote on. Unfortunately, the results were somewhat disappointing— only one model meeting our specifications. We called CUC to inquire about this since we knew from our real-life shopping that several other Sony models existed. The CUC customer service representative was aware of the fact as well. She told us that Sony CD players were in short supply and that they normally have the full line. That tallied with what local retailers told us, so it shouldn't be held against CUC.

First-Hand Experience

We have ordered a number of items through Comp-u-Store over the years, and have always been very pleased with the service. Shortly after your order is entered, a full-page order confirmation sheet will arrive in the mail. The sheet will list the item, model, quantity, color, estimated delivery date, cost, date of order, type and number of credit card, and the name and address of the vendor who would supply the goods. There are instructions on the back of the page telling you what to do should you have a problem, including how to sign the freight bill (if there is one) should the shipping box appear damaged.

Comp-u-Store, like L. L. Bean, White Flower Farm, Talbots, or any other successful mail-order marketer, clearly has the business down pat. For more information, contact:

> Comp-u-Store Online
> P.O. Box 1016
> Trumbull, CT 06611–1016
> (800) 843–7777
>
> Mon.–Fri.: 9:00 A.M.–11:00 P.M.
> Sat. & Sun.: 9:00 A.M.–6:00 P.M.

CompuServe's Electronic Mall

In 1984, with much fanfare, CompuServe introduced its new Electronic Mall shopping service. The concept was to bring together scores of leading companies and retailers like Sears, American Express, McGraw-Hill Books, Kodak, and Microsoft, under one electronic roof. Of these original Electronic Mall participants, only McGraw-Hill is still on the system at this writing. But many other firms have joined, including Waldenbooks, Penguin Books, John Wiley & Sons, Macmillan's Small Computer Book Club, Bloomingdale's, Crabtree & Evelyn, and Brooks Brothers.

Proprietary software was written to allow these firms to provide price and descriptive information about their products and to allow CompuServe subscribers to easily place an order when they see something they like. Here's how CompuServe explains the process:

> Place an order the easy way! Think of each database as a "store." Each time you enter a merchant's store, a personal order file or "shopping cart" starts rolling. When you choose to buy a product, simply press the letter "O" and that product information is placed in your personal file, as if you had placed the item in a shopping cart. When you leave the merchant database, you "check out" by completing the order form which automatically appears on the screen and reviews the products you've chosen and prompts you for credit card and shipping information. A confirmation number, generated automatically, functions as a receipt. Your order is transferred electronically to the merchant's CompuServe

mailbox, where it is retrieved, confirmed by E-mail and fulfilled the same way a telephone or mail order is.

It's a lot of fun to tool around the Electronic Mall looking at all the product descriptions, knowing that with a few keystrokes you could send the item heading in your direction. But say what they may, it's not shopping. The system isn't designed to give you a comprehensive overview of the various makes and models available. Nor can one easily compare prices. In fact, given the eclectic selection of merchandise, you may not be able to find comparable products in different Mall stores.

Essentially, then, CompuServe's Electronic Mall and its imitators on other utility systems are just variations on direct-mail selling. Think of the promotional flyers you receive from leading retailers. Like electronic mall stores they offer a very limited selection of products. If you like what you see, you check it off on an order form, fill in your credit card information, and mail it back to the merchant. Or you use a toll-free number to order by phone. If the merchant is smart, you will automatically be added to a mailing list and receive the next issue of the firm's main mail-order catalog.

An electronic mall operates in the same way. The only difference is that there are no color photographs and you use electronic mail to place your order. In fact, many merchants appear to be more interested in getting you to send for their free catalog than in moving the specific merchandise they have chosen to offer through their mall stores.

GO-ing MALL

CompuServe is said to have invested heavily in the Electronic Mall and the software that makes it possible. And in truth we found the software easy to use, though, as we'll see in a moment, there was a glitch that after over five years of operation is inexcusable. We signed on to CompuServe and keyed in GO MALL, and here is what appeared:

```
The Electronic Mall       EM-18

__/__/ T H E
__/__/ E L E C T R O N I C
M A L L (R)

1 —Shop by Department
2 —Shop by Merchant
3 Index to Products
4 How to Shop
5 Electronic Mall Feedback
6 SHOPPERS ADVANTAGE Club
7 Mall Headlines & Happenings
8 GET TO KNOW THE MALL

Enter choice!2
```

We knew from reading *Online Today*, CompuServe's monthly member magazine, that Brooks Brothers was now a part of the Electronic Mall. So we decided to "Shop by Merchant" as shown above. This led to the following menu:

```
The Electronic Mall          EM
Select first letter of merchant name:

1   A
2   B - C
3   D - E
4   F - H
5   I - M
6   N - P
7   R - S
8   T - Z

Enter choice!2

The Electronic Mall          EM

1 HOW TO USE THIS GUIDE
2 BALLANTINE BOOKS   [BAL]
    Current bestsellers, gifts and more
    VI/MC                               US/CD
3 BARGAIN HOLIDAYS   [BH]
    Discount Florida accomodations
    AM/CSH                     US/CD/JP/OT
4 BLOOMINGDALE'S   [BL]
    Cosmetics, housewares, gifts
    VI/MC/AM/DI/SC                      US/CD

Enter choice or <CR> for more!

The Electronic Mall          EM

5 BROOKS BROTHERS   [BR]
    Men's and women's apparel
    VI/MC/AM/DI                          US
6 BUICK MAGAZINE   [BU]
    Car information, customer service
    VI/MC                               US/CD
7 BUSINESS INCORPORATING GUIDE   [INC]
    Nationwide incorporating
    NA                                   US

Enter choice or <CR> for more!5
```

We opted for item 5 to be taken to the Brooks Brothers online store. The letters VI/MC/AM/DI stand for Visa, MasterCard, American Express, and Diners Club, the credit cards this merchant accepts. The [BR] next to the merchant's name is its CompuServe page number. One could thus key in GO BR to go directly to the Brooks Brothers store from any feature on the CompuServe system. Here is the Brooks Brothers main menu:

```
Brooks Brothers        BR-4

BROOKS BROTHERS

1 This is Brocks Brothers
2 Ordering Information
3 On-Line Selections
4 * As Featured in April Online Today *
5 Order Our Print Catalog
6 Order from Our Catalog
7 Open An Account With Us

Enter choice 2

Brooks Brothers        BR

ORDERING INFORMATION

1 Our Promise
2 Payment Methods
3 Delivery
4 Sales and Use Tax
5 Shipping and Handling
6 Our Toll-Free Numbers

Enter choice!
```

When you choose "Online Selections" from the main Brooks Brothers menu, you will be asked whether you wish to focus on men's or women's apparel. We chose men's and the following menu appeared:

```
Brooks Brothers        BR-24

CLASSIC BROOKS MEN'S WEAR

1 Warm Weather Clothing
2 Our Famous Dress Shirts
3 Lightweight Sweaters & Knits
4 Colorful Sport Shirts
5 Walk Shorts & Swim Trunks
6 Men's Essentials
7 Hats, Shoes, Etc.
8 Belts And Braces

Enter choice!2
```

Brooks shirts tend to be quite full-cut (read: baggy). Just the thing to go with the, er, portliness that is the major occupational hazard of computer programmers and writers. So we thought we'd take a look at the company's famous dress shirts:

```
Brooks Brothers          BR-39

OUR FAMOUS DRESS SHIRTS

1 THE SHIRT WE MADE FAMOUS
2 DISTINCTIVE BLAZER STRIPES
3 PINPOINT OXFORD PENCIL STRIPES
4 THE PLAIN COLLAR SHIRT
5 SHORT SLEEVES
6 WASH-AND-WEAR BROOKSWEAVE
7 SILK KNIT NECKWEAR

Enter choice!1

1 articles selected
Brooks Brothers



THE SHIRT WE MADE FAMOUS

Brooks Brothers invented the button-down shirt, and introduced it in the early 1900's. Today,
it is recognized as a true American classic. Here is our most popular model, made in our own
workrooms of long staple Pima cotton oxford. In yarn-dyed solids of white, blue, pink, ecru,
yellow or peach. Sizes 14½ to 17½, sleeves 32 to 36.

Price $45   Enter "O" to Order.

      Last page!O

      QUANTITY :1

      CompuServe

      You may order additional items.
      When you are finished, enter
      CHECKOUT to complete your online
      order form.
```

Since we knew that no orders are final until you go through the process of keying in your credit card and address, we opted to "order" the shirt to see what would happen next. The system prompted us for "Quantity:," we keyed in "1," and that was it. Next order, please.

But wait a minute—what about the shirt's size? What about the "yarn-dyed solids of white, blue, pink, ecru, yellow or peach?" Thinking we must have missed something, we went through the process several times. But the system never did ask for our size or preferred color. Since we were on the system very late at night, there was no one to call. Our query would just have to wait until morning. So much for "round the clock, 24-hour shopping convenience."

We did call the next morning, still under the impression that there was something we were doing wrong. It was simply inconceivable that after five years of daily usage and testing the Electronic Mall wouldn't have built-in procedures to catch such a simple error as not prompting for a garment's size and color. But that turned out to be the case. The CompuServe customer service representative did some checking and then called back with the news that the problem would be corrected. "Thank you for bringing it to our attention."

It may be that this is the only such bug in the entire system. If so, it is just bad luck we chanced upon, when researching this chapter. But it is important to point out that we didn't set out to find problems. We did not check several merchants and then decide to highlight this particular instance. The sequence of events took place exactly as described here.

It could happen to anyone. And should something similar happen to you, you might be forgiven for wondering whether online shopping is really ready for prime time. Indeed, you might well conclude that at worst it is a novelty with a very short half-life, and that at best it is just another online feature.

The "Ideal" Online Shopping Service

If you can't do something better, faster, or cheaper *with* a computer than without it, there is little point in using such a machine. In our opinion, the problem with online shopping as it has evolved to date is that it does not exploit the advantages inherent in computers and online systems. For example, computers are dynamite at searching through mountains of data for specific information. So it would be technically possible for a service to offer you a database containing every model of every manufacturer of a particular product. You would no longer be confined to what happened to be on local shelves or available for purchase through the shopping system, as happened to us when we looked for Sony CD players on Comp-u-Store. You would know what *all* of your product options are.

Ideally, you would also be able to hit a key and get the name of your nearest dealer for any product. Hit another key, and the dealer or manufacturer would automatically mail you additional information about a given product. And there would be no need to key in your mailing address for each request. The system would know who you are and automatically transmit your preferred mailing address to the dealer or manufacturer.

None of this calls for state-of-the-art technology. Computers have been doing these kinds of things in other fields for many years. But while Comp-u-Store has come closer than anyone, no company has really focused mainframe computing power on the shopping task. No one has started from scratch and set out to design the ideal online shopping system. Instead, online shopping features are almost always offered as an afterthought. And that, in our opinion, is the main problem, not the fundamental limitations of plain ASCII text. People would gladly put up with those limitations if the services being offered were truly powerful or truly unique. In short, if they really offered a better, faster, cheaper way of doing things.

BCE, OAG, and EAASY SABRE

Though not strictly "shopping" systems, there are three other related online offerings you should know about. All three are comprehensive and computer-scannable. And all three can potentially save you a lot of money. The first is the Boston Computer Exchange (BCE), available on Delphi and CompuServe. Started in 1982 by Alex Randall and his wife Cameron Hall, BCE is the country's leading used computer broker, accounting for nearly 10 percent of the organized secondary market for computers. The company maintains an ever-changing database of equipment wanted and for sale. *PC Week, Computer World,* and other trade publications run the "BoCoEx" weekly index of highs, lows, and closing prices on virtually every make and model of computer derived from this database.

You can search the BCE database yourself via CompuServe or Delphi on the basis of machine manufacturer and asking price. You can then view complete descriptions of any of the items meeting your criteria. If you want to make an offer on an item, BCE will put you in touch with the seller, with whom you negotiate the final price. You then send the money to BCE for deposit in an escrow account, and BCE notifies the seller to ship the equipment. You will then have two days to make sure the equipment is satisfactory. If it is, BCE sends a check to the seller, less its 10 percent commission. BCE also offers its database in printed form. For more information, contact BCE at (617) 542–4414.

The two other features that deserve your attention are the Official Airline Guide—Electronic Edition (now owned by Robert Maxwell, who also owns BRS and ORBIT), and American Airlines Eaasy Sabre. Both are widely available on online systems, and both give you the opportunity to search a comprehensive database of all airline flights offered by all airlines. These systems are based on the same systems used by professional travel agents, so you will have to spend a little time learning how to use them. But it can be time well invested for in addition to putting you in complete control of your own travel arrangements, these systems can turn up flights and fares a busy travel agent might miss. Some users report saving hundreds of dollars this way. You can also book flights and order tickets through both services.

Conclusion

As more and more people go online it is possible that some company somewhere will finally feel it worthwhile to design and offer the "ideal" electronic shopping system. Until that happens, we suggest that you sample the systems currently available. You might even want to make a small purchase or two to see what it's like. But keep your common sense about you. If a system doesn't really offer greater convenience or better prices than are available elsewhere, you may prefer to respond to the "Order?" prompt with "No, just looking, thank you."

...27...

Telecommuting

In an opinion piece in *The Wall Street Journal* (April 4, 1989) management guru Peter Drucker affirms that "The modern big city is the creation of the 19th century's ability to move people." Railroads, streetcars, subways, and automobiles gave people the power to move over great distances to where the work was. "And the elevator added vertical mobility. It was this ability to move people that, more than anything else, made possible large organizations, businesses, hospitals, government agencies, and universities."

"Yet," Mr. Drucker continues, "none of this is necessary any more; indeed, commuting to office work is obsolete. It is now infinitely easier, cheaper, and faster to do what the 19th century could not do: move information, and with it office work to where the people are." Thanks to personal computers, modems, affordable fax machines, and the like.

Using technology to move information instead of people is the essence of "telecommuting," a term and concept put forward nearly 20 years ago by Jack Nilles, an engineer and professor who wanted to curb air pollution in Los Angeles by reducing commuting. Professor Nilles now heads Jala Associates, a Los Angeles-based telecommuting consulting firm.

From the beginning, however, the telecommuting concept has never been broadly and enthusiastically embraced by corporate management. Instead, it has bobbed up and down in the national idea stream, never fully accepted but always somehow there, demanding to be considered. In early 1989 it popped into prominence once again, as part of a sweeping, multipoint proposal to drastically cut air pollution in California. *Business Week* discussed the subject at length as part of an October 10, 1988 cover story, "The Portable Executive." As has been the case for nearly 20 years, studies, reports, and profiles of telecommuting experiments on the part of Fortune-500 companies periodically appear in the press and on television.

In this chapter we'll look at telecommuting, summarize the arguments in its favor and those against, and take a look at where things currently stand and where they are likely to move in the future. We will close with a list of resources you may want to consult for more information.

What Is Telecommuting?

The classic definition of telecommuting calls for some form of computer communication between an employee's home and his or her office. The idea is that if your job normally involves sitting at a terminal or word processor entering data or typing reports, it makes no difference where the terminal is located. As long as the machine can communicate over the telephone, both it and you could be sitting in front of a roaring fire in a cabin in Vermont. When you've finished your quota for the day, you simply dial up your firm's computer and transmit the work to your former office.

Similarly, if you are an executive responsible for collecting and analyzing information, making decisions, issuing reports, and communicating with others, you may be able to perform all of these functions at home. You can transmit your documents to the main office for printing and distribution. And you can confer with fellow managers via electronic mail and computerized conferencing. You can also tap the company's central computer for the information you need to prepare your reports and analyses.

Over the years, however, the definition of telecommuting has broadened considerably. It now includes not only those who transmit their work from home to the office but anyone who uses personal computers and related technology to do work at home that they would normally do at an office. Gil Gordon, a leading telecommuting consultant, estimates that there are only about 20,000 full-time "classic" telecommuters in the country today. At the same time, Jack Nilles found in a 1986 survey of 900 middle managers that some three percent spent more than eight hours a week using a computer at home for company work, while 50 percent spent at least one hour a week. These managers may transmit their work to the office electronically, or they may carry it in themselves in the form of a disk.

Finally, Peter Drucker's point in *The Wall Street Journal* piece cited earlier was not that technology would eliminate centralized work locations, replacing them with a nation of telephonically linked home workers. It was that technology would *move* those locations closer to where most people live. "We already know how office work will be done in the future," Drucker says. "Contrary to what futurists predicted 25 years ago, the trend is not toward individuals working in their homes. People greatly prefer to work where other people are." The trend is toward moving clerical work to suburban offices that are electronically linked to headquarters locations in the cities. Or, to put it another way, toward "corporate telecommuting" where major corporate functions and offices, as opposed to individual employees, are widely distributed and electronically linked.

In truth, no one agrees on what telecommuting is, and certainly no one knows what effect it will have. But a number of things are clear. First, however one defines it, telecommuting is best viewed as part of a much larger phenomenon: the impact of today's technology on how, when, and where people work. Second, telecommuting or technologically facilitated alternative work styles are inevitable. The forces driving the phenomenon are simply too numerous and too powerful to ignore. The required equipment is not only affordable, it's cheap. The number of "knowledge workers"—people who process, analyze, and manipulate information—continues to grow as we move away from an industrial, manufacturing economy toward one based on information and services.

The increased emphasis on quality of life; the country's decaying infrastructure of bridges, roads, trains, and other people-moving facilities; crime and drug problems in the cities where many companies are based; air pollution and the distant but ever-present threat of another 1970s-style oil shortage—all make some form of telecommuting-related change desirable. One should also factor in population trends pointing to growing labor shortages, and the increased bargaining power this gives to those who *are* part of the work force. If desirable alternative work styles exist, in such a seller's market employees will be in a position to insist on being allowed to take advantage of them.

Arguments in Favor

In the best of all possible worlds, telecommuting of some form or another offers many potential benefits to employer and employee alike. No one likes to spend two hours a day—10 hours a week—or more merely getting to and from work. Eliminating the commute thus gives employees more time with family and friends, produces gasoline savings, and reduces the burden on mass transit systems. Some authorities claim that telecommuters give an extra hour to themselves and an extra hour to the company each day by not physically going into work.

Virtually everyone agrees that with more time for themselves and without the stress of fighting their way to work each morning, employees tend to be happier. And hopefully, more productive. A 1988 study by LINK Resources Corporation, for example, reported that when asked how their productivity at home compared to their productivity in the office, 56.5 percent felt they were more productive at home. Slightly more than 19 percent said they were less productive, while the rest felt they were either equally productive in both places or felt that their productivity varied.

There is also the fact that everyone has a different body clock. The nine-to-five work day is derived from the ancient requirement to work when the sun was out because there was no other source of light. But as studies have shown, some people are most productive at night, with their bodies and brains barely up to speed at 9:00 in the morning. Telecommuting could free employees to work when their energy levels are highest.

Some advocates also argue that telecommuting can lead to reduced child-care costs and give women the opportunity to reduce the impact of childbearing on their careers This argument has largely been discredited, though, at least in the case of newborns and very young children. As Kathleen Christensen, author of *Women and Home-Based Work* (Holt & Company, 1986) points out, "You can't do any kind of work that requires concentration and simultaneously watch children." Consequently, Ms. Christensen says, two thirds of mothers who do professional work at home have full-time child care.

Certainly telecommuting can reduce clothing costs for employees, particularly those of the managerial level who must routinely shell out several hundred dollars in order to arrive at work "dressed to play." As a telecommuter you can work in your bathrobe and who's to know? From the employer's standpoint, there is the potential for reduced office expense (rent, heating, electricity, parking spaces, and so on). In the "Telecommuting Newsletter," consultant Gil Gordon notes that employers spend "between $3,000 and $6,000 a year just to put a roof over one employee's head."

Arguments Against Telecommuting

Unquestionably one of the reasons telecommuting has so far failed to gain wide acceptance is simple corporate inertia. Most companies are risk-averse and typically don't take action until there is a clear competitive or economic reason for doing so. Yet inertia is a minor problem compared to active resistance on the part of the managers whose approval is necessary for a telecommuting program to go forward. Many managers maintain that people won't work if there isn't someone there to metaphorically crack the whip.

That is certainly true in some cases, but without wishing to be an apologist for telecommuting, that's too easy an out. It assumes that most people don't like to work, a contention that study after study has disproved. It seems much more likely that the real reason for resisting telecommuting is that most executives don't know how they would manage a workforce scattered all over the countryside. They haven't been trained for it. Indeed, the forms and norms, the systems and the procedures that would make this possible have yet to be created.

Consider the problem of productivity and performance measurement. If your employees are primarily data-entry operators, you can assign each a piecework quota and measure their productivity that way. But how can you measure a telecommuting manager's productivity? If you're an executive accustomed to having instant, on-site access to the managers who work for you, how are you likely to react to having to deal with those managers solely by phone? And while conference calls can be very useful, they can never substitute for impromptu, in-person meetings. Consider too, the potential morale problems if you allow some employees to telecommute while denying this "perk" to others.

For the telecommuter there are drawbacks as well. Most people need regular interaction with other members of a group, and by definition that is one thing telecommuting can never provide. But even if loneliness isn't a problem for you, consider the effect on your career. Most people would agree that one of the keys to career advancement is simply getting noticed. But when you're telecommuting you are out of sight, and possibly out of mind.

There is also more than a little potential for exploitation. In 1986, for example, telecommuters working for California Western States Life Insurance Company sued the firm for denying them vacation, health, and retirement benefits. The company argued that the workers had become independent contractors. The firm eventually settled out of court and dropped its telecommuting program.

Finally, when you work at home, your work is always with you. Even if, as all consultants suggest, you set aside an area or a room dedicated to serving as your office, you can never really get away. As convenient as it is to be able to prepare a report at three in the morning or whenever else you are in top body-clock form, it is also nice to physically leave the office behind for the day and go home. That's something a telecommuter, even a part-time telecommuter, can never do.

Telecommuting Today

The definition of telecommuting is so loose and the field is so fragmented that it is currently impossible to come up with any firm numbers to gauge the phenomenon. The *LINK Resources 1988 Work at Home Survey* reported that some 25 million Americans in 19 million households work at home. The same study found that of these, over two million are corporate employees working at home full-time, while six million are corporate employees working at home one to two days a week. The study doesn't specify whether any of these people are telecommuters. A 1987 report from the Center for Futures Research at the University of Southern California, however, maintains that there are some 600,000 telecommuters nationwide.

About 500 companies, including J.C. Penney, Aetna Life and Casualty, Pacific Bell, U.S. West, Honeywell, and Traveller's Insurance, currently have formal telecommuting programs. But most operate on a very limited basis, involving far fewer than the 1200 employees per program needed to bring the total to 600,000. So where are all the telecommuters? According to Brad Schepp, author of *The One Minute Commute* (Pharos Books, 1989), they're underground. "One of the most significant new developments in this field in recent years," Mr. Schepp says, "is the emergence of the 'guerilla telecommuter.'" These are the men and women who telecommute one to two days a week without being part of a formal program. Rather than fight the corporate battles necessary to get a program established, they simply make a private arrangement with their bosses and begin quietly to telecommute. Often, according to Mr. Schepp, a company's top managers aren't even aware that such informal telecommuting programs exist within the firm. And no one is anxious to tell them since doing so would require the establishment of an official policy and unwind spools of red tape.

The telecommuting initiatives of some employees have a parallel in the personal computer world. It wasn't too many years ago that managers who were fed up with the chronic delays in getting anything out of the data processing department took it upon themselves to buy their own personal computers. Hiding the cost in personal expense reports and departmental budgets was infinitely easier than seeking formal authorizations, most of which were typically denied.

By the time corporate DP managers realized that they were losing control over their company's data processing activities, it was too late. The only alternative was to bow to the wishes of the workforce and establish formal programs to equip employees with personal computers. It may be that telecommuting will follow the same grassroots path. Indeed it may have to, for no company will embrace telecommuting unless it is in its best interests to do so, and retaining valued employees and keeping them happy is at least as powerful a motivation as economic or competitive considerations.

Where to Get More Information

Whether you're someone who would like to begin telecommuting or an executive interested in establishing a program for your company, you don't have to operate in the dark. There are a number of books, consultants, and networks you can tap for guidance. Listed below are just a few of the resources available:

Associations and Networks

Paul and Sarah Edwards
Association of Electronic
 Cottagers (AEC)
677 Canyon Crest Drive
Sierra Madre, CA 91024
(818) 355–0800

The Work-at-Home Special
 Interest Group (SIG)
Paul and Sarah Edwards, SysOps
on CompuServe (Key in GO
 WORK)

Telecommuting Consultants

Ms. Lis Fleming
P.O. Box 1738
Davis, CA 95616–1738

Mr. Gil Gordon, President
Gil Gordon Associates
10 Donner Court
Monmouth Junction, NJ 08852
(201) 329–2266

Mr. Jack Nilles
Jala Associates
971 Stonehill Lane
Bel Air, CA 90049
(213) 476–3703

Ms. Joanne Pratt
c/o Shoptalk
Home–Office Computing
730 Broadway
New York, NY 10003

Newsletters, Books, and Magazines

"Telecommuting Review: The
 Gordon Report"
TeleSpan Publishing Corporation
50 West Palm Street
Altadena, CA 91001
(818) 797–5482

*The Telecommuter's Handbook:
How to work for a salary without
 ever leaving the house*
Brad Schepp
Pharos Books, March, 1990

*Telecommuting: How to Make it
 Work for Your Company*
Gil Gordon and Marcia M. Kelly
Prentice-Hall, 1986

*Telecommuting: The Future
 Technology of Work*
Thomas B. Cross and Marjorie
 Raizman
Dow-Jones-Irwin, 1988

The Electronic Cottage Handbook
Lis Fleming
P.O. Box 1738
Davis, CA 95616–1738

The Telecommunications–
Transportation Tradeoff:
Options for Tomorrow
Jack M. Nilles, et al.
John Wiley & Sons, 1976

Women Working at Home: The
Homebased Business Guide and
Directory
Marion Behr and Wendy Lazar
287 pages; $12.95, plus $1.25
shipping and handling
WWH Press
P.O. Box 237
Norwood, NJ 07648

Working from Home
Paul and Sarah Edwards
J.P. Tarcher, dist. by Houghton
Mifflin, 1984

Worksteads: Living & Working in
the Same Place
Jeremy Joan Hewes
Doubleday/Dolphin, 1981

Home–Office Computing
Magazine
Scholastic, Inc.
730 Broadway
New York, NY 10003
(12 issues: $19.97)
(212) 505-3580

...28...

Education Online:
Bachelor's, Master's,
Doctoral Degrees, and More

Education can be defined in many ways, but central to all defini-
tions is the exchange of information. When you think about it, a
teacher is basically someone who by dint of study, experience,
and contemplation has attained a high degree of understanding and
knowledge about a particular subject. And a student is someone who is
interested in extending his or her knowledge. Education is thus fundamentally the transfer of information from the teacher to the student.

Obviously, education is also much more than this. A good teacher is
never content to merely feed a student chunks of information. If that
were all there was to education, there would be no need for lectures,
tutorials, term papers, and discussions. Good teachers are also interested in helping their students develop their own critcial faculties. But
here again, whether as a one-on-one discussion or as comments on a
student's paper or exam, the essence of the activity is information exchange.

The point here is this—ivy covered walls, "cattle drive" mixers, eating hall food fights, and football games in the fall are certainly important
elements of the American college experience, but they are not essential
to earning a degree. Nor for that matter, is your presence on campus,
provided there is a way to exchange information with the same professors you would encounter in a lecture hall or tutorial.

Information exchange, of course, is also the essence of personal computer communications. So it will probably not surprise you to learn that
you can take courses online. What will surprise you, however, is the
wide range of courses now available and the many opportunities that
exist to earn bachelor's, master's, and doctoral degrees from fully ac-

credited colleges and universities, all while sitting in your home in front of a personal computer.

In this chapter we'll describe how a typical program works, look at the major advantages and disadvantages of online education, and give you addresses and contact points for obtaining more information on many of the leading online educational programs.

The Electronic University Network

The most extensive of all online higher education programs at this writing is offered by the Electronic University Network (EUN). As information supplied by EUN states, "The Electronic University Network is a federation of colleges, universities, and businesses that use telecommunications to bring college courses and degrees, and business and industrial training, to corporate employees and other adults who want to study away from the college campus."

Among the nearly 20 colleges and universities affiliated with the network at this writing are the universities of Illinois, Iowa, California, Maryland, San Francisco, and Tennessee, plus Ohio University, Penn State, Washington State, Oklahoma State, Memphis State, and the State University of New York, plus California State Polytechnic, De-Anza College, John F. Kennedy University, Thomas A. Edison State College, and Regents College of the University of the State of New York.

Some 37 Fortune-500 companies are affiliated with EUN as corporate members. Member companies include EUN in their tuition reimbursement programs, provide employees with information on course and degree opportunities, and work with EUN to provide on-site services, sample materials, and demonstration software. Corporate members at this writing include Bank of America, AT&T, Citicorp, Federal Express, Honeywell, Litton Industries, Owens-Corning Fiberglass, Pratt & Whitney, Wells Fargo, and Weyerhaeuser.

The role of the Electronic University Network is to supply the software and the host system that makes it possible for member institutions to offer their courses online. EUN handles administrative chores and corporate contact as well. It is the colleges and universities who determine course content.

Courses are available in writing, literature, mathematics, history, natural sciences, psychology, and many other subjects. But the major emphasis is on business-related courses, including accounting, finance, marketing, computers and data processing, management, and statistics and quantitative methods. This emphasis makes sense, because the vast majority of EUN students are working adults seeking career advancement. In all, EUN currently offers over 150 courses.

There are a number of ways to use EUN and similar online offerings. You might take courses as part of a continuing education program, without working toward a degree. Or you might combine EUN-earned credits with those earned at your local college. By planning and coordinating your courses you may be able to earn your degree from that college more quickly. In any case, most online programs require you to be enrolled in an accredited degree program offered by some college or university if you want to earn credit, and it is that college that actually awards the credit.

Through EUN you can enroll in a number of external degree programs (degrees awarded by colleges without requiring attendance at classes on campus). Thomas A. Edison State College, established by the New Jersey Board of Higher Education in 1972, offers Bachelor of Science degrees in business administration, Associate in Arts degrees in liberal arts, and Associate in Science degrees in management. You can also earn accredited certificates in specific fields, including accounting, finance, marketing, and operations management. Alternatively, you can enroll in Regents College of the University of the State of New York through EUN. Regents College offers Bachelor's and Associate Degrees in business and in the liberal arts.

At the graduate level, you can enroll in John F. Kennedy University through EUN. Established in 1964, John F. Kennedy University offers a fully accredited Master of Business Administration external degree program. The university is located near San Francisco, and attendence at several week-long on-campus seminars during the program is required.

Most courses offered through EUN conclude with a term paper, final project, exam, or a combination of these. For credit in many courses you will take CLEP (College Level Examination Program) exams sponsored by The College Board and administered by Educational Testing Service (ETS). You have either one year to complete a course or the amount of time allowed by the sponsoring institution, whichever is less.

How Does It Work?

The materials used in each EUN course are chosen and organized by the instructor. But while the content varies, there are three main categories of material for each course. The *Electronic University Network Course Manual* is a ring binder containing all nonbook study materials. It includes sections on planning and organizing your work, the *Course TeleGuide* with instructions and introductions to each lesson, information about the sponsoring college, and information on preparing for the exam. The second component is the core textbook, almost always one of the established "standard" texts in the field. Third is a study guide and supplementary printed materials designed by the instructor to accompany the text. Some courses have a fourth component—special course-related software and video or audio tapes.

Students also receive the Electronic University Network's "instructional delivery" software. The package is called Protege and consists of a menu-driven communications program, text editor, electronic mail program, and course-specific learning templates. (You get a separate disk for each course.) Versions are available for IBMs and compatibles, the Apple II line, and Commodore 64s and compatibles.

We looked at the IBM version of Protege and can report that it really is easy to use. From the time you key in PROTEGE, you need to know nothing more about how to use a computer than how to type at a keyboard. Sending a message to your instructor or downloading his or her assignments and comments is as easy as pressing a function key. There is no need to worry about setting comm program parameters, electronic mail addresses, or uploading a file. Protege takes care of everything.

Each time you complete a lesson, you transmit it to your instructor for feedback and comment. (Protege will not allow you to send a lesson unless it is complete.) The instructor downloads your material from an electronic mailbox using a program called Mentor. He or she then has 48 hours to upload a reply. A tracking program on the EUN system monitors upload and download dates and times to make sure that instructors reply promptly. Note, however, that as a student you can take as long as you need to prepare a lesson, provided you complete the course within the alloted time (one year or less).

Online Education Pros and Cons

That's the kind of scheduling flexibility that makes online education so attractive to busy adults, a group that accounts for 42 percent of those taking college courses electronically, according to *Business Week* (May 9, 1988). Not only can you learn at your own pace, taking all the time you need with a lesson, you can also learn on your own schedule. If your job requires that you be out of town for a week, or if work or child-care demands are particularly heavy, you can put your college work aside momentarily and pick it up again when things settle down. For most working adults, physically attending scheduled classes in the evening is a major problem, particularly if the community college or other institution is several miles away. For them, the ancient and increasingly obsolete requirement that students and professor physically assemble at a given location at a set time makes continuing education virtually impossible.

Many adults who do manage to take on-campus courses report that being in a classroom situation dominated by 18-year-olds is not always a pleasant experience. And, of course, some people tend to be innately shy about asking questions or making comments in class. The online alternative suffers from none of these disadvantages. It is almost always based on a one-to-one relationship with an instructor. And as a result, advocates point out, students usually get much more personal attention than in a typical college setting.

On the downside, online students do not benefit from the same human interaction with fellow students and professors that often takes place on campus. There isn't the same opportunity to learn from the questions posed by others in a class or test your ideas by arguing freely with others. Some online education systems do offer computerized conferencing for class discussions, but good as these systems are, it isn't the same. Nor will an online "lecture" ever have the impact of a bravura performance by an outstanding professor. And of course there are some subjects that can't be taught online, at least not with today's technology. A lab course, after all, requires a lab.

Yet as we said at the beginning of this chapter, the essence of education is the transfer of information. And advocates would argue that the personalized attention each student receives from professors from fully accredited colleges through online courses more than offsets what one must give up by not attending class in person.

Finally, in addition to offering busy, working adults the chance to further their education, often with the help of their company's tuition assistance plan, the online alternative is perfect for those with physical handicaps that would make attending school in person extremely difficult. It can also make college educations available to those in prisons. And, given the worldwide telecommunications links that now exist, international and Third-World students can earn degrees from U.S.-based colleges and universities, while U.S. students can take courses and degrees offered by institutions abroad. All without ever leaving home.

For More Information . . .

Although we used the Electronic University Network as our example, it is important to point out that while its special software makes the system particularly easy to use and while it offers the greatest range of courses, there are many other fine programs. More than likely, you'll make your choice based on the areas of study and degree programs offered. (Nova University, for example, offers not only master's but doctoral programs in subjects likely to be of greatest interest to computer analysts, professional librarians, and school teachers.)

You'll want to contact all of the institutions listed below for free information about their programs. And you may want to periodically check in at the Education Forum on CompuServe (GO EDFORUM) to ask if any new institutions have come online.

Electronic University Network
385 Eighth Street
San Francisco, CA 94103
(800) 225-3276
(415) 552-6000

You can also dial your local Tymnet node and key in INFORMATION at the first and second prompts that will appear. The resulting menu contains a selection that will give you extensive free online information about the Electronic University Network.

Connected Education,
92 Van Cortland Park South,
  No. 6F
Bronx, NY 10463
(212) 548-0435
MCI Mail: Connected Education
CompuServe: 72517,3107
Source: AAH298

American Open University
New York Institute of Technology
211 Carleton Avenue
Central Islip, NY 11722
(800) 222-6948
(516) 348-3000

Nova University
Center for Computer and
  Information Sciences
3301 College Avenue
Ft. Lauderdale, FL 33314
(800) 541-6682, ext. 7047
(305) 475-7047

NRI School of Electronics
McGraw-Hill Continuing
  Education Center
3939 Wisconson Avenue, N.W.
Washington, D.C. 20016
(202) 244-1600

...29...

Bulletin Board Systems

Sometimes you'll hear the general-interest press—and others who never let the fact that they don't know what they're talking about stand in their way—refer to CompuServe, GEnie, and other commercial systems as "bulletin boards." That's a mistake one would ordinarily be inclined to let pass, were it not that it does an injustice to both kinds of systems. CompuServe and its competitors are far more than message-exchange systems, and real bulletin boards are anything but the products of large, bland corporations. In fact, as we'll see in this chapter, individuality is the very essence of a bulletin board system or "BBS."

BBSs, The Concept

A real computer bulletin board system consists of the same components everyone uses to go online: a computer, a modem, and a telephone connection. The difference is in the software. Bulletin board software can be thought of as a specialized form of communications program. Instead of allowing the computer owner to dial out, BBS programs are designed to allow other users to dial in. They can thus turn any personal computer into a "host" system. The person who owns, sets up, and runs a bulletin board is called its system operator or "sysop" (pronounced "sis-op").

The sysop is also responsible for the board's personality. Indeed, most sysops view their boards as their own unique creations, and they are forever tinkering with them the way some people tinker with souped-up stock cars. Thus, even if you are an experienced user, you never know what you'll find when you sign on. For example, at your option, some boards are capable of putting on quite a show, complete with pseudo-animated graphics, music, and other surprises.

Other boards are more sedate, channeling their originality into the selection of files they offer for download or the lively discussions and message exchanges they host. They sysop can focus a board on any topic he or she finds interesting. Most give their boards a name and publicize its existence throughout the BBS community. Once the word gets out, they have merely to sit back and wait for people with the same interests to call. The makes and models of the host system and the caller's computer are irrelevant since any communicating machine can talk to any other.

It is hard to know how many BBSs are in operation today, though reliable estimates place the number in the neighborhood of 14,000. And that's just in the United States. There are BBSs, or "mailboxes" as they are sometimes called abroad, in many other countries as well. The number and variety of topics covered is breathtaking. For example, here are the names and primary focus of just a few of the boards in operation today:

- Big Sky Telegraph—Educational plans and services to rural Montana schools.

- Catholic Information Network—Early texts and writings of the Roman Catholic Church.

- Dallas Law SIG BBS—Lawyers' forum on legal issues related to telecommunications.

- Hay Locator—Database of hay and straw suppliers and buyers.

- Greenpeace Environet—Ecological, disarmament, and related issues.

- Micro Message Service—*USA Today*, Newsbytes, and Boxoffice magazines.

- National Genealogical BBS—Family history and genealogical research.

- The Second Ring—Online computer magazine index operated by the San Jose Public Library.

- Colorado West BBS—Ham and packet radio.

- The Cyber-Zone—Science fiction.

- The Droid—Online tradewars and baseball games.

- Gay Community—Message exchange and downloads for the gay community.

- Midrash—Messianic Judaism, religion, and philosophy.

- The Silver Streak—Science, engineering, and Turbo Pascal.

- White Runes of Tinuviel—Tolkein subjects and Dungeons and Dragons.

Most sysops operate their boards as a hobby, but even so, running an active board can be a lot of work. There are questions to answer, messages to respond to, programs to test for viruses, and files to clean out. Consequently, some sysops offer download-only systems with virtually no messaging capabilities. These systems can serve as "publishers" of news, information, and selected topic-specific articles, but most act as distribution points for public-domain (PD) and shareware software. The number of megabytes of PD software a system has to offer is a mark of distinction in the BBS community, with some boards boasting 75 to 100 megabytes or more. Here the make and model of your machine will make a difference, for while Macintosh users can talk to and download programs from an IBM-compatible system, or vice versa, that system will almost certainly offer only IBM-compatible programs.

How to Plug In: Getting Lists of Good Numbers
This is only a brief sketch of the kinds of things you'll find once you enter the BBS world. And more than likely making your initial sojourn will cost you little or nothing. Some bulletin boards do charge token membership fees and issue passwords like a commercial system, but the vast majority are free to all callers. Your only expense will be any long-distance charges you incur in dialing up the board you want to try. We'll have more to say on that subject in a moment. For now we will simply note that unless you live in a very small town on the plains or in some remote location, you will almost certainly be able to find a board located within your local calling area.

The key thing is to find a list of good numbers, by which we mean numbers that are still connected to operational boards. The attrition rate among new sysops is high. Many novices publish their board numbers only to find that they really don't want to make the required commitment. As noted, operating a good board can take a lot of time and energy. In addition to routine computer housekeeping, a conscientious sysop will review all uploaded files to make sure no one has put a copyrighted program on the board. Most also review each day's messages for stolen credit card numbers and other dicey information.

And of course there is the time spent tuning, tweeking, and tinkering with the hardware and software. Add to this the fact that every sysop is a target of opportunity for all the addlepated computer punks who get their jollies by trying to wreck every board they call, and it's no wonder BBSs come and go with such frequency.

> **Online Tip:** A sysop's legal liability for the information people post on his or her board is not clear. (Is your local supermarket liable because someone tapes a list of stolen MasterCard numbers to its community news cork board? Is the U. S. Park Service liable because someone staples the same list to one of its trees?) But since more than one innocent sysop has had his system confiscated by police because of something someone uploaded to his board, many tend to be more than duly diligent about preventing questionable information from slipping by.
>
> If these topics are of more than passing interest, you might want to get the following book: *SYSLAW: The Sysop's Legal Manual* by Jonathan D. Wallace, Esq. and Rees W. Morrison, Esq. (LLM Press, 1988, $21).

The ephemerality of bulletin boards is a fact of online life, however, and it simply means that you must pay particular attention to the freshness of the BBS phone lists you use. Because of this, books and magazines are not usually very good sources. The lead time between the submission of the last bit of copy and the publication date can be three months to a year, and inevitably many of the numbers will be out of service by the time the book or magazine hits the stands. However, there is at least one exception, the FOG/*Computer Shopper* list.

The FOG/*Computer Shopper* List
Computer Shopper is a tabloid-sized magazine that regularly runs to 520 pages or more. It makes a valiant attempt at providing editorial content and articles, but people really buy it for the ads. Whether you're interested in a tiny clock crystal or a full-blown system, you can find it advertised, often at a deep discount, in *Computer Shopper*.

For our purposes here, the most important feature is the 15 to 20-

page BBS directory found in each issue. The list is compiled and maintained by FOG, a leading user group based in Daly City, California. The initials used to stand for First Osborne Group, but with over 17,000 members and over 140 affiliated chapters worldwide, FOG has long been a leading group for users of all CP/M and MS-DOS computers. The group is assisted in its efforts by members of the Public Remote Access Computer Standards Association (PRACSA).

The *Compute Shopper*/FOG list is unique for a number of reasons. It is organized by state, with numbers for Canadian provinces included at the end of the list. Each BBS receives a short write-up including its city, available baud rates, operating hours, the sysop's name, and two or three sentences describing the board and what it offers. This is much more information than most BBS lists provide.

The information comes from the sysops themselves, but all of the numbers are initially verified by FOG and PRACSA members. If a number "is found to be inaccurate, it will be immediately deleted from the listing." Furthermore, "if an update report is not received every three months, the listing will also be deleted. All SysOps are responsible for forwarding accurate information to [FOG]."

You may be able to find *Computer Shopper* on your favorite newsstand, and it has recently begun to appear in the magazine racks of major bookstores. Published monthly, subscriptions are $29.97 a year. For more information, contact:

> Subscription Department
> *Computer Shopper*
> 5211 S. Washington Avenue
> Titusville, FL 32781
> (407) 269–3211
>
> Delphi: CSHOPPER
> MCI: CSM

The FOG RT on GEnie

FOG also operates a RoundTable on GEnie. You can access the FOG RT by keying in FOG at the main GEnie menu prompt. The RT will always have the most up-to-date FOG BBS list for you to download. The file to look for will have a name similar to REMSYS11.ARC, where the numbers represent the month of the year. The file is typically about 120K long, and it contains three lines per board with all the vital statistics and necessary information. To locate the current file, search the library on the keyword COMPUTER SHOPPER or BBS.

Online Tip: If you're a sysop who would like to be listed, send the information detailed above to:

> FOG
> Remote System Listing
> P.O. Box 3474
> Daly City, CA 94015-0474
>
> Voice: (415) 755-2000
> (Weekdays: 10:00 A.M.–6:00 P.M., Pacific time)
> Modem: (415) 755-8315

You will also find it worthwhile to look into PRACSA. This is an association of sysops formed to "educate users and the general public in the use of remote computer systems while providing guidelines and assistance for those wishing to operate such systems in an efficient and law-abiding manner." Many of the nation's top system operators belong and will be happy to advise you in getting your system up and running. The dues are $10 a year, prorated to December 31 at 85¢ a month.

There are a number of ways to get more information. The PRACSA-preferred way is to dial up the main PRACSA board at (415) 948–2513. However, you can also contact sysop Irv Hoff via CompuServe at 76701,117 or call his voice line at (415) 948–2166. PRACSA president David McCord can be reached (voice) at (415) 948–3820 during regular business hours. Finally, you can obtain membership information and an application by contacting the address shown below (enclosing a self-addressed address label and a first-class stamp would be appreciated):

> PRACSA
> P.O. Box 1204
> San Jose, CA 95108

Lists Online: The Electronic Alternative

The main point in favor of a conscientiously prepared printed BBS list is the amount of information it provides. As noted, the *Computer Shopper*/FOG list gives you four or five descriptive sentences for each entry, so you'll have some idea of what to expect when you connect with a given board. The main disadvantage of all printed lists, aside from the problem of currency, is simply that they are printed: The numbers are on the page instead of in your computer where they belong.

Since you have a modem, however, there's an easy solution. One of the best places to look for bulletin board numbers is on other bulletin boards. Virtually every board will have at least one list of numbers in its file area. However, the richest, most varied phone number collections can be found in the SIG libraries of the online utility systems profiled in Part II of this book. Use the system to search a SIG data library for lists by specifying one of these two keywords: BBS or LIST.

For example, on April 11, 1989 we signed on to CompuServe, keyed in GO IBMCOM to get the IBM Communications SIG, and then keyed in DL0 to get to Data Library 0—New Uploads. When we entered S/DES/KEY:LIST to scan the database on the keyword LIST and display the matching files and their descriptions, the following were among the files that appeared:

[72677,3305]
USBBS.ARC/binary   01-Apr-89 43774   Accesses: 78

   Keywords: BBS LIST DARWIN NATIONWIDE USBBS

   April '89 edition of the Darwin USBBS list, a nationwide list of DOS BBS systems. Edited by Meade Frierson. Please rename to USBBS59.ARC (or ZIP or LZH or whatever).

[76004,1552]
WCLIST.ARC/binary   28-Mar-89 29509   Accesses: 39

   Keywords: PHONE NUMBERS BBS LIST MUSTANG SOFTWARE WILDCAT PUBLIC

   3-28-89. This is a list of public <WILDCAT!> bulletin boards. Over 900+ in all, located in every state in the country, and overseas. If you're looking for BBS's to call and need some data phone numbers then this file is for you.

You could also select CompuServe's BROWSE option from the data library menu and simply specify LIST or BBS as your keyword when prompted to do so. You will probably want to search separately on both words to be sure of finding all relevant files. In addition, note that the description for USBBS.ARC refers to "DOS BBS systems." That doesn't necessarily mean that they focus solely on IBM and compatible topics (they don't), but if you want to find Apple, Macintosh, or Commodore-specific systems, your best bet is to conduct a similar search of the appropriate machine-specific CompuServe SIG. Finally, we've used CompuServe as our example, but most of the online utility systems also have SIG libraries containing BBS phone lists.

Online Tip: Some BBS phone lists purport to be comprehensive, others focus on boards dealing with a particular subject or located within a certain area code. The list names can be "creative," to say the least. So creative that puzzling out the filenames used for BBS listings can drive you crazy at times. But since there's nothing you can do about it, you might as well learn how to figure them out. This is a particularly good skill to develop if you plan to look for your lists on other BBSs, since most systems do not permit the lengthy descriptive paragraphs found on CompuServe, GEnie, and other commercial systems. After a while, you'll be able to guess what a BBS listings file contains without downloading it or looking at the description. In fact, you can start with this list of BBS phone number files downloaded from a favorite board:

Filename	File Size	Date
ADULTBBS.ARC	2,816	05-31-89
BBS215.TXT	13,696	02-08-87
GOVTBBS.ARC	3,584	01-26-88
HAWAII.ARC	1,920	05-31-86
MEDBBS.JO˙	3,072	01-16-86

How to Cut Long-Distance Costs

The best way to "work the boards" is to take advantage of your communications software's dialing directory or phone list. If you're a novice user, start by keying in five or six nearby numbers from a list of BBS systems. Take extra care to get the numbers right or you'll end up with an irate voice on the other end of your line instead of the familiar modem tone. Most programs will record your numbers on disk and let you dial each one in turn by entering a single key selection from the dialing directory menu. Many programs will also let you specify a list of dialing directory entries for them to dial in turn. If the first number is busy, they automatically dial the second one, and so on until they get a connection. This is an important feature, since most boards have only one incoming phone line and the best ones tend to be busy much of the time.

If you really get into bulletin boarding you will want to search boards and online utility libraries for any public-domain programs capable of *automatically* converting a file of BBS numbers into a dialing directory for your comm program. There is no guarantee that such a program exists for your communications software, but some user may very well have written exactly the program you need. If you're lucky enough to find one, you may never have to key in another BBS number by hand. ProComm users will find such a program on the Glossbrenner's Choice Disk Comm Pack 2—ProComm Utilities. But it will be useful only if you have an IBM or compatible and ProComm. (The full ProComm communications package, version 2.4.3, is on Glossbrenner's Choice Comm Pack 1.) See the back of this book for ordering information. For more details on the program, as well as hands-on instructions for locating and downloading free programs from BBSs, see *Alfred Glossbrenner's Master Guide to FREE Software for IBMs and Compatible Computers.*

One can cope with busy signals and with getting numbers into a program, but what do you do if you find yourself transferring $100 to $300 a month to Ma Bell or your chosen long-distance carrier? Be warned: Working the boards can be addictive and phone bills of that level are not uncommon among dedicated BBSers.

One alternative is to do your calling late at night when the phone rates are at their lowest. A better solution may be to take advantage of one of the services specifically designed for BBS users. One service is PC Pursuit (PCP) offered by Telenet, and the other, much newer service is Starlink, offered by a firm with close relations with Tymnet.

Both systems use the same general technique to save you money. Briefly, you call your local Telenet or Tymnet node to start the connection. Unless you live in an area where telephone message units are a factor, this costs you nothing. Once you're connected to your local node, you can use the packet-switching network to zero in on a distant city. If you were in New York, for example, you might tell your local node to connect you to one of the network's nodes in Seattle. When that connection has been made, you can issue a command to dial *out* of the Seattle node to connect with a local Seattle bulletin board. This, too, is a local call that does not incur long-distance charges. When you're finished in Seattle, you might repeat the process to connect with a node in Tampa to sample a board located in Florida. And so on.

There are a few catches, of course. First, not all cities may be available through the program. At this writing, Telenet's PC Pursuit offers connections to some 34 metro areas; Starlink offers 150 cities. Second, while both services are available round the clock, the really big savings are available only after regular weekday business hours. For PC Pursuit this is between 6:00 P.M. and 7:00 A.M.; for Starlink, between 7:00 P.M. and 6:00 A.M. With both services, nonprime-time rates are in effect all day during the weekends and on national holidays.

Both services charge a one-time sign-up fee of $25. PC Pursuit then charges you $30 per month. In return, you can make up to 30 hours of data calls during nonbusiness hours, weekends, and holidays. If you use more than 30 hours, you will be charged between $4.50 and $7.50 per hour.

Starlink charges a monthly service fee of $10 and $1.50 per hour if you are in the continental United States. Charges for Canadian users and residents of Alaska and Hawaii are higher and, unlike continental rates, involve both an hourly charge and a charge for each thousand characters.

PC Pursuit used to offer unlimited nonprime-time access and a lower monthly fee. When it raised prices in May 1989, the move was widely booed in the BBS community. The system may deserve such disaprobation—some users report long delays in making connections and other frustrations—but if you're going to spend 30 hours a month, PCP is still cheaper ($30 per month to Starlink's $55). On the other hand, Starlink does give you access to many more cities. The system is so new at this writing that we cannot report on the general quality of service.

Both systems offer a free online sign-up procedure. Set your system to 1200 bps and dial (800) 835-3001 or (703) 689-2987 to log on to "In Pursuit of . . . ," Telenet's PCP bulletin board. While online you can get more information about PC Pursuit and register for the service. Alternatively, you can call a voice line at 800-TELENET to request an information packet and application blank.

For information and instant sign-up for Starlink, dial the Starlink modem line at (804) 495-4670. Starlink is a service of Galaxy Information Network, P.O. Box 9455, Virginia Beach, VA 23452. We asked for an information packet, but were told that to keep costs down, all information is provided online.

Keeping Up to Date

The only way to really plug into the bulletin board world is to regularly work the boards. But there are a number of ways to keep up to date if that is not possible. As you can imagine, BBSers don't spend all of their time on BBS systems. Many of them use the online utilities as a convenient common meeting ground and file exchange. Print publications are another possibility, and one that we especially like is Jack Rickard's *Boardwatch Magazine*. This is a professionally published, full-size magazine that normally runs 15 to 20 pages. Each issue contains hardware and software tips, profiles of interesting boards, announcements of new electronic services, plus an extensive, current list of board numbers. We would not recommend it for a complete computer novice, but if you've had a little experience you may find that it's just the ticket. The cost is $28 a year (12 issues) or $3.95 per copy. Contact:

Mr. Jack Rickard
Boardwatch Magazine
5970 South Vivian Street
Littleton, CO 80127
(303) 973-6038

Conclusion

Bulletin board systems, like the electronic universe as a whole, offer you information, adventure, and a sense of community. Dialing up a board is an ideal and virtually cost-free way to enter that universe. And it's easy, particularly if you follow our advice and put several board numbers in a dialing queue so your comm program can cycle through them seeking a connection. Once you've plugged in, you'll discover store-and-forward mail systems like FidoNet that can pass your locally uploaded message across the country or even around the world at little or no cost to you. You'll encounter oceans of public-domain and shareware software.

And you'll find that the BBS community is so diverse, that it can answer virtually any question on any topic. It's simply a matter of locating a board frequented by the kind of experts you seek. After a while, you yourself will probably start to visit the same boards again and again. You may even become a regular and find yourself using your "home" board's phone number as your main electronic mail address. Or you may decide that working the boards is not your cup of tea. Either way, you owe it to yourself to experience the bulletin board phenomenon first-hand to find out. And with the tools provided in this chapter you should be able to easily do just that.

...30...

International Access

There are undoubtedly some exceptions, but generally you can access any of the online systems discussed in this book from virtually every country on earth. Most systems have a "dial-up" number that connects directly with the host computer. Several have In-WATS (Incoming Wide Area Telephone Service) 800 numbers for their U.S. customers. Some, like DIALOG, even make it possible to connect with through the Telex I and II (TWX) networks.

More than likely, though, the least expensive way to contact a North-American-based system from abroad will be through a packet-switching network. Whether you live outside the United States or are an American planning to be traveling abroad, the process of connecting with U.S.-based packet-switchers requires a bit of explanation.

In the United States, anyone can buy a modem, subscribe to a system, and access that system by dialing a Tymnet, Telenet, or other public data network (PDN) number. These networks operate only within U.S. borders, and the cost of using them is usually passed on to the customer as part of the bill issued by the database vendor.

Other countries have domestic PDNs as well, and they too operate only within their national borders. Connections between two countries are handled by yet another class of network known as international record carriers or IRCs. The major IRCs include ITT, RCA, TRT, FTC (owned by McDonnell Douglas, the same company that owns Tymnet), Telenet's international division, and WUI (Western Union International, a subsidiary of MCI Corporation).

Thus, someone in Paris who wished to log on to DIALOG in Palo Alto, California, would connect with TRANSPAC, the French public data network. TRANSPAC would connect with one of the international record-carrier networks, and the IRC would connect with one of the U.S. packet-switchers, which would then connect with the DIALOG computers. (For hard-core techies only: The IRCs follow the CCITT X.75 network-to-network protocol, while the U.S.-based networks use the CCITT X.25 network-to-host protocol to make their connections.) In order to do this, the caller must have an account with both TRANSPAC and DIALOG.

The Crucial Role of the PTTs

In almost every country other than the United States, the telephone and public data networks are owned and controlled by the national government through agencies known generically as PTT (Postal, Telephone, and Telegraph) authorities. Thus, if you live outside the United States, you must contact your local PTT office to set up an account that will let you use your nation's data network. Usually it's a relatively simple matter of providing a billing address and possibly paying a small fee.

Once your account has been established, the PTT will issue you a Network User Identifier number or NUI. This is the account number you will enter each time you connect with your country's PDN. You will also need to establish an account with the online system you want to access. The U.S.-based system will bill you for usage and for U.S. telecommunications costs. Your national PTT will bill you for the use of its network and for international communications costs.

The policies of the PTTs vary widely regarding data communications. In some countries, if you want to use a modem you must pay a one-time licensing fee to the PTT. In other countries there is an annual or a monthly fee associated with the NUI account. In still other countries, you must lease the modem directly from the PTT.

The charges levied by the PTTs for the domestic portion of the linkup also vary. There may be hourly connect charges, and there may be "traffic charges" measured in "kilocharacters" or "kilopackets." Some PTTs also levy a tax on communications costs as well. IRC charges are set by international tariff agreements.

U.S. Citizens Traveling Abroad

If you are going abroad and you want to be able to access an online system or your office computer in the United States, it is best to plan ahead. Policies and procedures are not as simple abroad as they are in this country. Fortunately, both Tymnet and Telenet have international specialists on staff who can help you make your preparations. You can contact them at the following addresses:

International Sales Office—Suite
 200
TYMNET
2080 Chainbridge Road
Vienna, VA 22180
(800) 368–3180
(703) 356–6993

International Services
Telenet Communications
 Corporation
12490 Sunrise Valley Drive
Reston, VA 22096
(703) 689–6300

Undoubtedly the simplest procedure is to bring your U.S. modem with you and make your connection by dialing the vendor's direct or In-WATS phone number from wherever you happen to be abroad. This is also the most expensive option, and you should definitely make sure that the procedure is legal in the country you will be visiting. If you will be taking a modem with you, it is also advisable to bring a receipt or other document proving that you bought the modem in the United States for your own use and do not intend to resell it inside the country. Non-U.S. customs officials have been known to confiscate modems that lack such documentation.

Regardless of where you are, if you are calling a U.S. data network or online system directly you will be able to use your U.S. "Bell standard" 300/1200-baud modem. But you should be aware that while U.S. and Canadian modems and networks follow the Bell standard, the rest of the world uses modems and networks that conform to standards set by the CCITT, the Consultative Committee on International Telephone and Telegraph communications, an arm of the United Nations.

If you are going to be connecting through another country's PDN, you will need a CCITT-compatible modem. A CCITT V.21 modem, for example, communicates at 300 bits per second (bps). A CCITT V.22 modem communicates at 1200 bps. CCITT V.22 *bis* is the standard for 2400 bits per second. As discussed earlier in this book, virtually all 2400-bps modems follow the V.22 *bis* standard. So you won't have a compatiblity problem at that speed. However, since the quality of phone systems varies widely throughout the world, you may find that the error rate is unacceptably high at 2400 bps. You may thus still want a modem capable of the lower CCITT compatible speeds. (Many top-of-the-line U.S. modems now offer both Bell and CCITT compatiblity.) Your best bet, of course, is to check with any friends or fellow employees living in your destination country.

Getting an NUI Account

In addition to the modem, you will need an NUI account number to gain access to the local PDN. Here again, policies vary with the country. In some cases a billing address within the country is sufficient. In others you will need to establish a bank account in the country as well. PTT approval for your network user ID can take anywhere from a few days to several weeks.

In some countries special agreements have been signed to expedite this process. For example, Tymnet has established NUI exchange programs with about half a dozen countries, including the United Kingdom and Japan. Designed for the user who must go abroad on a moment's notice, this program allows Tymnet to issue you an NUI and bill you directly for the costs you incur using a non-U.S. data network. Some online systems have also established communications networks or made arrangements with such networks abroad.

The X.121 Address

In addition to an NUI and a CCITT modem, callers from abroad must know the proper "X.121" address of the system they want to connect with. Like all "X" and "V" designations, this is a CCITT-recommended standard. In this case, the standard specifies a 14-digit number that you might think of as an international ZIP code for online systems. The number is also referred to as an "NUA" for "network user address." As defined by the CCITT, the first four digits are the "data network identification code" or DNIC ("dee-nick"). Since most countries have only one data network, there is usually only one DNIC per country. But in the United States, where there are many privately owned networks, each of the major PDNs has been assigned its own DNIC. Telenet's DNIC is 3110, Tymnet's is 3106, and so on. This is necessary so that a call coming in from abroad can be routed to Telenet, Tymnet, or whatever other carrier the caller specifies once it arrives on U.S. shores.

The significance of the remaining ten digits can vary with the network. But for U.S. networks, the next three digits are usually the telephone area code of the host system. For example, since DIALOG is in Palo Alto, its area code is 415; NewsNet is in Philadelphia and its area code is 215. The next five digits are the actual network address of the host. In international communications, if the address does not occupy five digits, zeros are used to bring the total up to five. The final two digits are optional, but when they are used they refer to the port address on the host.

You should always check with the online system you wish to access to get the proper X.121 address, since they do sometimes change. However, as an example, if you were to sign on to DIALOG using Telenet in the United States, you would enter the telephone area code and DIALOG's network address: 41520. (On Tymnet you would enter "Dialog," and the network would translate this into the numerical address.) If you were to sign on to the same system from abroad via Telenet, you would enter Telenet's DNIC first to specify that system (3110), followed by the telephone area code (415), followed by three zeros to round out the network address to five digits, followed by the address itself (20), followed by, in this case, a two-digit port address (04). The grand total would look like this: 31104150002004.

Which IRC? Which U.S. Carrier?

Does it make a difference which international record carrier transports your call to the United States or which U.S. carrier you specify with the DNIC? Understandably, both Tymnet and Telenet answer this question differently. According to Tymnet, five of the six major international record carriers use Tymnet-supplied equipment. And as mentioned earlier, FTC Communications is owned by Tymnet's parent, McDonnell Douglas (as is TRT). It is suggested that this can make for a smoother interconnect between the IRC and the U.S.-based Tymnet network.

Telenet's answer is based on its status as an international record carrier with some 22 direct connections between foreign countries and the United States. Where those direct connections exist, a higher quality of service may be possible because fewer "hops" or network interconnections are involved. If a British caller selects Telenet as the IRC on a call, the call goes from the British network to London, where it is connected to Telenet's IRC facilities. From there it goes up to the InfoSat satellite and back down to the Telenet gateway facility in Reston, Virginia, and from there into the U.S. Telenet network. In contrast, if a different IRC is used, the call arrives at that company's U.S. gateway and must be connected to Telenet's gateway before going on into the Telenet network.

You must always select a U.S. carrier you want to use by specifying the DNIC portion of the X.121 address. But you may or may not be able to select the IRC to be used as well. The PDNs in some countries offer you a "Carrier Select" option each time you sign on. In other countries, or in the absence of your specification, the IRC will be selected by a random rotary system designed to apportion the business equally among the various IRCs. However, although it isn't widely known, in some cases you can ask the PTT to code the NUI it issues so that a particular IRC will automatically be used to transport all of your calls. Usually this involves adding a digit or two to the NUI number.

Free Online PTT Information

We strongly advise phoning Tymnet or Telenet at the numbers given earlier for the latest information. However, both systems do maintain free online systems containing rate information, the contact-person and address of a country's PTT authority, and more. To gain access to these systems, dial and connect with Tymnet or Telenet as you normally would. Then follow the steps outlined below.

For Tymnet, simply key in the word INFORMATION when you see the "please log in:" prompt. That will log you into the Tymnet Information Service and cause a menu to be displayed on your screen. At this writing, item 4 on the menu will select "INTERNATIONAL ACCESS INFORMATION."

For Telent key in MAIL immediately after the Telenet "at sign" (@) prompt. (No spaces.) Respond to the "User name?" prompt with INTL/ASSOCIATES. Then respond to the "Password?" prompt with INTL. (This will not show up on your screen as you key it in.) That will log you into the Telenet International Information System and generate a menu with nine selections pertaining to international access.

Online Tip: At the risk of confusing the issue, you should know that in some cases you can also use the telex network to make contact with a packet-switcher like Telenet. ITT's InfoTex, RCA's Data-Link, and WUI's Telelink, for example, have the ability to convert telex Baudot code into ASCII and back again and smooth out the speed differences between the 50-baud communications rate of a telex machine and the much higher speeds of a packet-switching network. For technical reasons, 50 baud on a telex machine equals 400 characters a minute. In other words, telex is S-L-O-W. But you can do it.

You can even use the telex-to-Telenet connection to access the Telenet International Information System described above. The only difference is that instead of keying in MAIL, key in 202141. (You may also use 202142.) Then proceed as above.

Conclusion

Since book publishers generally frown on sending authors on globe-trotting tours to sample the world's data communications connections, we are not in a position to test and verify everything discussed here. However, these points are obviously of more than passing interest to anyone who plans to do any communicating from abroad. The key thing is to be aware that the rest of the world handles computer communications quite differently than we do in the United States, and one should thus not take anything for granted. If there is even a possibility that you and your laptop will have to go abroad on a moment's notice at some time in the future, don't wait until the last minute to get your ducks in a row. Contact Telenet and Tymnet at the numbers provided here. Perhaps most important of all, try to find someone at your company who's been there and ask his or her advice.

...*31*...

Online from Anywhere:
Celluar Modems, Packet Radio,
Remote Software, and More

I magine that you're sitting on a bicycle seat absorbing the quiet beauty of the Grand Tetons in northwestern Wyoming. You're so moved by what you see that you want to record it, so you reach into your pack, pull out your computer, and begin typing an entry in your journal. Nothing remarkable in that. Everyone seems to be keeping a journal these days, and anyone with a battery-powered laptop could do the same thing.

But then you decide to transmit your latest entry to some friends on GEnie. Right now. You're out in the middle of nowhere. It's one of the prettiest pieces of nowhere you've ever seen, but still, there isn't an electrical outlet or telephone for miles around. You go to the pack again, but this time you pull out a modem-like box called a TNC (terminal node controller), a Solarex SX-10 sun-powered battery, and your multimode 2-meter Yaesu transceiver. Less than a minute later you've got everything cabled together. And a minute after that, you're signing on to the system, thanks to your packet radio equipment and a network of repeating stations that bridge the 1400 miles or so separating you and GEnie's host computers in Ohio.

Now *that's* amazing. Particularly when you consider that the radio equipment required can cost as little as $400. (Top-of-the-line systems cost between $600 and $700.) Yet a man named Steven K. Roberts has routinely done exactly that sort of thing for many years, and as he points out in his book, *Computing Across America: The Bicycle Odyssey of a High-Tech Nomad*, anyone can go and do likewise. Mr. Roberts's book is available for $9.95 in paperback and $15.95 in hard cover, including shipping and handling, from Learned Information, 143 Old Marlton Pike, Medford, NJ 08055 (phone 609–654–6266; Visa and MasterCard accepted). If you're a GEnie subscriber you can read current and past articles by Mr. Roberts (uploaded from the road) in the system's "Personal Computer News" section (GEnie page 518, at this writing).

Like modems, TCNs sport an RS-232 serial port and can be connected to any make or model of computer. Special packet radio programs are available (many of them are shareware or public domain), but a regular communications program will do for software. And just as the packet-switching telephone networks use the X.25 protocol, radio packet-switching uses the AX.25 protocol. This means that messages and files are automatically chopped up into 128-byte chunks, stamped with routing information, and sent on their way. A checksum is also calculated and sent with the packet as part of the protocol's built-in error correction. Packets are never considered delivered until an acknowledgment is returned from the receiving station, so the data you get is always 100 percent correct. The worst that a noisy connection can do is slow things down, forcing each packet to be resent several times until an error-free one gets through.

Packet radio uses a relatively short-wavelength VHF signal that doesn't carry all that far. So to go for distance, you've got to link together a series of repeater stations arrayed in the general direction of your destination. Each packet radio station is also capable of receiving and rebroadcasting packets. Because signals are processed digitally, amateur radio operators (hams) call them "digipeaters." Since each station has its own address or call sign, if you've got a map of the digipeaters leading to your target system, you can string together their addresses in sequence and rely on each station to forward your message packets to the next station on the list. It's rather like an enormous chain letter.

At this writing, the practical limit on a connection is about eight digipeaters, though you can add more if you're willing to put up with additional delays. Yet eight is often enough since, depending on their locations, eight stations span thousands of miles. The permanent, "high-profile" (good antenna placement and transmission power) stations are well known and frequently used for city-to-city communications. Those are the kinds of locations you'll find on a digipeater map. But since every TNC can serve as a repeater, any station that's on the air at the time you make your connection can be used. In fact, most TNC boxes can be toggled into beacon mode, allowing them to announce their availability for message forwarding.

The packet radio world is very similar to the online world we've discussed at length in this book. There are PBBSs (Packet Bulletin Board Systems) offering electronic mail, news bulletins, and files for downloading. Some PBBSs also offer store-and-forward message systems. And some multitasking PBBS setups have the ability to accept incoming radio transmissions and patch them through to a conventional modem and phone line. This is how one would connect to GEnie or some other online system via packet radio.

Most packet radio takes place on high-frequency bands at 1200 bits per second. But packet radio can also be used with shortwave radio to girdle the globe. No digipeaters are required here, but speeds are limited to 300 baud. On other bands, speeds of up to 56 kilobits per second are possible. The one thing you absolutely cannot do on any amateur radio band is use the hookup for commercial purposes.

In addition to your computer, setting up a system requires an FM amateur transciever, a TNC, and enough space to put up a small (about four-feet high) antenna. The other sine qua non is an amateur radio license. Ham operators must be licenced by the Federal Communications Commission. There are currently five classes of licenses, and all of them, even the Novice level, permit packet radio operations. Earning a license requires taking a written exam on radio theory, rules and regulations, and operating principles. It also requires a test on Morse code (the test is on receiving, but you're supposed to know how to both send and receive). In the future, however, pending the adoption of certain policy changes, you may be able to obtain a sixth class of license without learning Morse code.

For more information, guidance, and general help, you'll want to check into the amateur radio SIG on CompuServe (GO HAMNET). This SIG maintains a data library dedicated to packet radio and others dedicated to amateur satellites, regulatory affairs, license exams, and many other topics. To view issues of "Gateway: The ARRL Packet Radio Newsletter," search DL1—News and Newsletters on the keyword GATEWAY.

The ARRL or American Radio Relay League is your best point of contact for packet radio and other information. Membership is $25 per year, and you don't have to be a licensed operator to join. In fact, ARRL encourages "associate" members who are either simply interested in the field or interested in eventually qualifying for a license. You can reach them at:

American Radio Relay League
225 Main Street
Newington, CT 06111
(203) 666–1541

Online, On the Road

Though the sight of some young Master of the Universe tooling down the road in his BMW, one hand resting lightly on the wheel while the other presses a car phone in his ear, is enough to strike fear into the heart of any defensive driver, there can be no doubt that car phones have been a boon to salespeople, account reps, service representatives, and anyone else who must spend a lot of time on the road. There's no longer any need to search for a phone booth along the way, hoping the phone it contains is still in working order. Now you can dial as you drive (or sit in traffic) without ever leaving your car, thanks to "cellular phone" technology.

As you probably know, in the past, mobile telephones relied on a single centrally located radio station in each city. Since only a limited number of channels were available, the number of people who could have mobile phones were severely restricted. Cellular phone systems, in contrast, rely on what might be loosely called a network of short-range radio stations, each of which is linked to the conventional phone system. As you drive down a road approaching the broadcast limits of one station, your call and connection are handed off to the next station whose cell you are entering. Sophisticated computers and software are required to make it all possible, but the result has been that virtually anyone can now have a mobile telephone.

But what about computer communications and modems? As long as you park your car in one spot, there is no technical reason why you can't use its phone with your laptop computer and modem to go online with the world. Once you begin to move, however, all kinds of problems can crop up. Data transmission is much less error-tolerant than voice. The 200 to 700-millisecond signal loss that occurs when a call is handed off from one cell to another can play havoc with conventional computer communications, to say nothing of potential static and radio frequency noise.

Fortunately, there's a solution. The solution is well patented, so at this writing, it is available from only one company, Spectrum Cellular Corporation of Dallas. Spectrum's core technology is its Spectrum Cellular Adverse Environment Protocol, which it calls SPCL. SPCL uses forward error correction, error detection and retransmission, and variable packet sizes (depending on the quality of the connection) to produce error-free cellular data communication.

The SPCL protocol software is hardwired into the celluar modems Spectrum sells under its own brand and manufactures for sale by others. Many of the Bell Operating Companies sell Spectrum units, for example. Two components are required. The Bridge is the modem you take with you in your car. The Span is the modem you connect to your base station. The units can communicate at either 300 or 1200 bits per second. The Span can be used as a standard Hayes-compatible modem as well, and one Bridge can be used to talk to another Bridge in a different car for mobile-to-mobile communications. Both units are equipped with auto-answer and auto-dial features. Each lists for about $600.

Spectrum also sells a variety of hardware packages that range from a single mobile phone to a Toshiba, Zenith, Epson, or other computer, a printer, a mobile phone, and the Spectrum Bridge in a single 24 × 17 × 8.5-inch case. There is also a product called GoFax 88 that consists of a portable Group-III fax machine and an acoustic coupler. And there is SpanNet, a base-station device that uses two phone lines, a built-in Spectrum Span unit, and an external conventional modem to let you contact any telephone-accessible online system or mainframe from your mobile location. For more information on Spectrum products, contact:

> Spectrum Cellular Corporation
> 2710 Stemmons Freeway
> 800 North Tower
> Dallas, TX 75207
> (800) 233–2119
> (214) 630–9825

Remote Software

Whether you establish your connection with a remote system via packet radio or cellular or conventional phone lines, once you're connected, it is the software running on the remote system that determines what you can and cannot do. At the very least, the remote system must be running bulletin-board-style host software enabling it to answer the phone and connect you to the system.

If your needs are limited to uploading and downloading files and leaving messages for co-workers, a bulletin board program will almost certainly fill all of your needs. However, if you want to operate the remote machine as if you were sitting in front of its keyboard and do things like run Lotus 1-2-3 from its hard disk, you'll need special remote access software.

Users of IBM-compatible systems have long been able to effect a limited kind of remote access with the DOS CTTY command. This command can be used to redirect the PC's attention such that it accepts and "displays" all data through one of the communications ports. With an auto-answer modem and a series of previously prepared batch files, you can arrange to call into your system and run it from a distant keyboard. But CTTY is too complicated for a novice to use and, as the "TTY" in its name implies, it is limited to teletype-style, one line-at-a-time communications (it has no full-screen or graphics capabilities.)

Dedicated remote software is much easier to use, though it is not intended for brand-new users. In fact, remote software is probably most popular among those who must support novice users. If you have ever tried to talk a new user through a problem over the phone, you know the true meaning of patience. You are probably also familiar with the itching feeling in your fingers—if you could only get to the user's keyboard and temporarily take him or her out of the loop, you could probably solve the problem in about two seconds.

That is exactly what remote software lets you do. You can take over the person's machine by telephone without having to take to the road to go there yourself. Needless to say, service people, corporate microcomputer managers, and support staffs love remote software. And, if you're a business person, you may too. If you leave your office PC on, loaded with remote software, you'll be able to access its files and run its programs wherever you happen to be at the time.

The leading IBM-compatible remote packages include Close-Up, Carbon Copy, pcANYWHERE, and REMOTE. For more information, contact:

Close-Up
Norton-Lambert
P.O. Box 4085
Santa Barbara, CA 93140
(805) 964-6767

Carbon Copy
Microcom
1400 A Providence Highway
Norwood, MA 02062
(617) 762-9310

pcANYWHERE
Dynamic Microprocessor
  Associates
545 Fifth Avenue
New York, NY 10017
(212) 687-7115

REMOTE
Microstuff
1000 Holcomb Woods Parkway
Roswell, GA 30076
(404) 998-3998

Online Tip: Generally it does a computer no harm to be left on for hours or days at a time. The really stressful moments for most machines take place when you turn them on and power suddenly begins to flow like water through a broken dam. The only other thing to be concerned with is deterioration of your monitor's phos-

Online Tip (cont.)

phors caused by displaying the same image all the time. So you
may want to shut the monitor off or use a public-domain program
capable of blanking the screen after a set period of inactivity.

Alternatively, there are at least two ways to turn your computer on from a remote telephone. One is to use a module manufactured as part of the BSR System X-10 line of power-control
equipment. System X-10 modules are typically sold to turn lights
and appliances on and off at set times or from a central control unit
that sends signals through your house wiring. But a Telephone
Responder module is also available. For information, contact:

BSR (USA) Inc.   BSR (Canada) Ltd.
185A Legrand Avenue   P.O. Box 7003, Station B
Northvale, NJ 07647   26 Clairville Drive
                                      Rexdale, Ontario M9V 4B3

The other alternative is the Turn-On, from S. L. Waber (formerly Dynatech, Inc.). This unit serves as both a single-switch,
surge-suppressed power strip and as a remote switch. Basically,
when you call your computer's phone line, the Turn-On senses the
ring and feeds power to all outlets. When you hang up, the Turn-
On shuts everything off. The list price is $395. For more informa-
tion, contact:

S. L. Waber, Inc.
5800 Butler Lane
Scotts Valley, CA 95066
(800) 638–9098
(408) 438–5007

How to Hot-Wire a Hotel Phone

Few things are more frustrating than to be in a hotel room with your
portable laptop computer and modem all set to upload the day's sales
figures to your corporate system, only to find that there is no way to
unplug the phone to gain access to the RJ-11 jack your direct-connect
modem requires. One alternative is to buy an "acoustic coupler" from
Radio Shack or your local computer store. This is a modem that sends
and receives sound signals through the mouth and earpiece of a telephone handset. Acoustic couplers are rarely used anymore, so you may
find that it is a special-order item. In any case, be warned that most
acoustic couplers are designed to work with fairly standard handsets. If

the hotel has "styled" phones it may be difficult to impossible to fit the coupler's send-and-receive cups to the unit.

Another alternative is to assemble a traveling kit of inexpensive components specifically designed to help you overcome hotel phone problems. You may want to include a modular "Y" connector plug that lets you plug two telephone cords into the same phone jack, and a telephone extension cord and in-line coupler to let you place your computer wherever you want in the room. You will also want an electrical extension cord for the same reason. You'll need a screwdriver and a small pocket knife as well.

The key component is a special phone cable with a regular RJ-11 plug on one end and loose wires ending in alligator clips on the other. Sometimes you can find such cables ready-made at Radio Shack and similar stores. If not, you can almost always find a line cord with a modular plug on one end and loose colored wires terminating in spade lugs on the other. Get two insulated alligator clips and attach them to the red and green wires. (You can ignore the yellow and black leads.) The modular plug is for your direct-connect modem. The colored leads are for gaining access to the phone system.

There are at least five points of telephone access in most hotel rooms: the mouthpiece, the transformer block inside the phone set, the wall jack, the phone wire junction box usually found along the baseboard, or the phone cable itself. Obviously your first step is to make absolutely sure no RJ-11 jacks are available. (Be sure to check for wall-mounted phones, many of which can be removed by sliding them upward on the wall. Most will have an RJ-11 jack behind them.)

In the absence of available jacks, start with the mouthpiece. Unscrew its cap, gently knock out the carbon microphone unit, and attach your cable clips to the two contacts you will then see. It doesn't matter which clip goes where. If you can't get the mouthpiece off, remove the phone set housing and place the handset back on the hook. Then locate the transformer block with its maze of multicolored wires. Attach your red and green clips to the red and green transformer wires.

If this isn't possible, see if you can find a telephone junction box along the baseboard of the room. Remove the wall plate and attach your red and green leads to the red and green wires there. If all else fails, there is one last option, and that is to *gently* scrape enough insulation off the phone cable to expose the red and green wires within and make your connection there. If you decide to do this, make your entry at two different points so the bare spots on the two wires can't touch each other after you're finished. With a bit of luck, you may discover that someone else has previously done the same thing and you can use his or her contact points.

When dialing out through one of these hookups, leave the handset on the hook (unless you are connected through the mouthpiece) and proceed just as if you had a conventional connection. If that doesn't work, dial your number manually, key in ATD to tell your Hayes-compatible modem to seize the line, and then replace the handset in its cradle and continue.

Conclusion

As computer communications becomes more widespread, going online on the road will inevitably become more convenient. Traveling businesspeople, among others, will demand it. Some business-class hotels are already prepared to rent or loan you a personal computer. One can easily foresee a day when breakfast tables at such hotels are equipped with a phone jack, in addition to a flower and a complimentary copy of *USA Today*.

A few years ago, who would have thought airlines would be able to offer in-flight telephone service? Yet today most planes have several portable phones onboard for their passengers to use. The voice quality leaves something to be desired, but as we've seen with cellular phones, there are ways to accomplish error-free data communications in such an environment. Consequently, in the next edition of this book it seems entirely likely that we'll be discussing not only "online on the road" but also "online in the air."

...Appendix A...

Resources

Database Directories

Directory of Online Databases
Cuadra/Elsevier
P.O. Box 872
Madison Square Station
New York, NY 10159

There are a number of excellent database directories on the market, but the "Cuadra Directory," as it is known, is considered by many to be definitive. Single copies are $75. A one-year subscription brings you a complete directory issue (about 600 pages) every six months and two quarterly update supplements. The cost is $175.

The directory is indexed by name, subject, database producer, online service/gateway, telecommunications network, vendor, and geographic location. It is available for electronic searching through numerous online services and as part of Microsoft's BOOKSHELF CD-ROM product.

Datapro Directory of On-Line Services
Datapro Research Corporation
1805 Underwood Boulevard
Delran, NJ 08075
(609) 764-0100
(800) 257-9406

This publication from McGraw-Hill's Datapro subsidiary is the most exhaustive and complete directory of databases, producers, and online services available. It is supplied in two three-inch three-ring binders, and it is updated monthly. The cost for an initial one-year subscription is $511. Renewals are $461. Subscriptions include unrestricted telephone consulting via Datapro's toll-free number.

Newsletters and Magazines

Online and *Database*
Online, Inc.
11 Tannery Lane
Weston, CT 06883
(203) 227-8466

Online: $85/year; 6 issues.
Database: $85/year; 6 issues.

Online and *Database* are the information industry's scholarly journals. Consequently, most articles are written by and for professional researchers, information brokers, and librarians. Both are excellent sources of tricks and tips for getting the most out of specific databases or online systems.

The differences between these two publications have never been clear. There is no duplication of articles or coverage. Your best bet is probably to see if a nearby library has a copy you can review before you subscribe.

Database Searcher
Meckler Corporation
11 Ferry Lane
Westport, CT 06880
(203) 226-6967

Cost: $79/year; 12 issues

This is a newsy, hands-on publication for professional searchers. Spiced with insider gossip, practical tips, and pungent editorial commentary, it bears the unmistakable imprint of its editor, Barbara Quint. Ms. Quint is a national treasure. She knows more about the ins and outs of databases and searching than most people could learn in a lifetime. Not everyone agrees with her views, but everyone finds them interesting. If you're a professional searcher or hope to become one, you will find this magazine worth every cent.

"VIEWTEXT"
Phillips Publishing, Inc.
7811 Montrose Road
Potomac, MD 20854

Cost: $397/year; 12 issues; 12 pages.

Phillips publishes over a dozen other newsletters focusing on various aspects of personal computers and telecommunications. "VIEWTEXT" is a very meaty publication devoted to interactive telecommunications topics ranging from videotex and teletext (television-based) to interactive cable. This newsletter includes coverage and analysis of the latest events, market trends, government regulations, and interviews with experts in the field. Available on NewsNet.

"Worldwide Videotex Update"
Worldwide Videotex
P.O. Box 138
Babson Park Branch
Boston, MA 02157

Cost: $125/year; 12 issues; 8 pages.

This publication reports news and information on videotex/teletext projects, services, and products around the world. It emphaisizes news that can be of value for formulating marketing strategies, particularly the activities of potential customers and emerging markets. Available on NewsNet.

Information Today and *Link-Up*
Learned Information, Inc.
143 Old Marlton Pike
Medford, NJ 08055
(609) 654-6266

Information Today: $29.50/year.
Link-Up: $24/year.

Information Today is the information industry's leading trade journal. Although it includes some of the same kind of hands-on articles found in *Online* and *Database* greater emphasis is given to interviews with industry figures, short database and product profiles, and stories developed from press releases and news items.

Link-Up is the publication we would most highly recommend for non-information professionals. Written from the consumer's perspective, it offers news, tips, hardware and software reviews, and features likely to be of greatest interest to the end-user.

...Appendix B...

The ASCII Code Set

ASCII is a seven-bit code. However, because each ASCII character is usually sent with an eighth or parity bit, it is sometimes referred to as an eight-bit code.

Many of the codes from 0 through 37 are used for synchronous communications and for communicating with teletype-like devices. They have special meanings in those situations, but those meanings are largely irrelevant to personal computer users.

With the exception of an <ESCAPE> key, there are no specific keys for the codes 0 through 31 on most machines. These codes can be sent, however, using the <CONTROL> key (or your machine's equivalent) and a letter key.

		Control Character Keystrokes
0	NUL (Blank or Null)	
1	SOH (Start of Header)	<CONTROL> <A>
2	STX (Start of Text)	<CONTROL> <B>
3	ETX (End of Text)	<CONTROL> <C>
4	EOT (End of Transmission)	<CONTROL> <D>
5	ENQ (Enquiry)	<CONTROL> <E>
6	ACK (Acknowledge—Positive)	<CONTROL> <F>
7	BEL (Bell)	<CONTROL> <G>
8	BS (Backspace)	<CONTROL> <H>
9	HT (Horizontal Tabulation)	<CONTROL> <I>
10	LF (Line Feed)	<CONTROL> <J>
11	VT (Vertical Tabulation)	<CONTROL> <K>
12	FF (Form Feed)	<CONTROL> <L>

13 CR (Carriage Return or   \<CONTROL> \<M>
    ENTER)
14 SO (Shift Out)   \<CONTROL> \<N>
15 SI (Shift In)   \<CONTROL> \<O>
16 DLE (Data Link Escape)   \<CONTROL> \<P>
17 DC1 (Device Control 1)   \<CONTROL> \<Q>(X–ON)
18 DC2 (Device Control 2)   \<CONTROL> \<R>
19 DC3 (Device Control 3)   \<CONTROL> \<S>(X–OFF)
20 DC4 (Device Control 4)   \<CONTROL> \<T>
21 NAK (Negative Acknowledge)   \<CONTROL> \<U>
22 SYN (Synchronization)   \<CONTROL> \<V>
23 ETB (End of Text Block)   \<CONTROL> \<W>
24 CAN (Cancel)   \<CONTROL> \<X>
25 EM (End of Medium)   \<CONTROL> \<Y>
26 SUB (Substitute)   \<CONTROL> \<Z>
27 ESC (Escape)
28 FS (File Separator)
29 GS (Group Separator)
30 RS (Record Separator)
31 US (Unit Separator)
32 SP (Blank Space)   \<SPACEBAR>
33 Exclamation Point— !
34 Quotation Mark— "
35 Pound Sign— #
36 Dollar Sign— $
37 Percent Sign— %
38 Ampersand— &
39 Apostrophe—'
40 Left Parenthesis— (
41 Right Parenthesis—)
42 Asterisk— *
43 Plus Sign— +
44 Comma— ,
45 Hyphen— -
46 Period— .
47 Slash— /
48 Zero— 0
49 One— 1
50 Two— 2
51 Three— 3
52 Four— 4
53 Five— 5
54 Six— 6

55 Seven— 7
56 Eight— 8
57 Nine— 9
58 Colon— :
59 Semicolon— ;
60 Less than— <
61 Equals— =
62 Greater Than— >
63 Question Mark— ?
64 At Sign— @
65 A
66 B
67 C
68 D
69 E
70 F
71 G
72 H
73 I
74 J
75 K
76 L
77 M
78 N
79 O
80 P
81 Q
82 R
83 S
84 T
85 U
86 V
87 W
88 X
89 Y
90 Z
91 Left Bracket— [
92 Reverse Slant— \
93 Right Bracket—]
94 Circumflex Accent— ^
95 Underline—_
96 Opening Single Quote— '
97 a

 98 b
 99 c
100 d
101 e
102 f
103 g
104 h
105 i
106 j
107 k
108 l
109 m
110 n
111 o
112 p
113 q
114 r
115 s
116 t
117 u
118 v
119 w
120 x
121 y
122 z
123 Left Brace— {
124 Vertical Brace— |
125 Right Brace— }
126 Tilde Mark— ˜
127 DEL (Delete or Rubout)

This is the end of the standard ASCII Code Set. The so-called "high codes" begin at 128 and continue through 255. These are nonstandard and their meanings vary with the software or the computer.

...Special Online Service Discount Offers...

CompuServe

CompuServe subscribers who purchase this book are eligible for a $12.50 usage credit. Take advantage of this offer to explore Compu-Serve's electronic universe and free software treasure rooms by completing the coupon below, and mailing it to the address shown.

Instructions
1. Complete the Bonus Coupon and mail to:

> CompuServe
> Consumer Billing Department
> P.O. Box 20212
> Columbus, OH 43220

2. One coupon redemption per user ID number.
3. Coupon is not transferable.
4. No photocopies will be accepted.
5. This $12.50 usage credit offer expires December 31, 1990.

Alfred Glossbrenner's *The Complete Handbook of Personal Computer Communications* (Third Edition)

BONUS COUPON OFFER
$12.50 USAGE CREDIT

USER ID NUMBER: _____

NAME: _____

ADDRESS: _____

CITY: _____ STATE: _____ ZIP: _____

SIGNATURE: _____ DATE: _____

GEnie

We have arranged a special FREE GEnie subscription offer for readers of this book.

When you call to subscribe, key in the number given below at the U# = prompt. This will entitle you to subscribe for free. GEnie has lots of online help available, so you may or may not need a copy of the manual. If you do, the cost is $12.95, plus $2 shipping and handling, for a total of $14.95. Here is the number to key in:

XTX99670,GLOSS

Please see Chapter 6 for the numbers to dial and sign-up instructions.

Delphi

Through a special offer to readers of Mr. Glossbrenner's latest book, Delphi has arranged for you to join at a special price. Join using the instructions below and your lifetime membership is only $29.95 (regularly $49.95).

To join Delphi:

1. Dial (800) 365-4636 with any terminal or PC and modem. (Once you join, a Member Services Representative will give you a local number to call in your area.)
2. At the Username prompt, type JOINDELPHI
3. At the Password prompt enter GLOSSBRENNER1

The lifetime membership includes a copy of Simon & Schuster's *Delphi: The Official Guide* by Michael Banks (512 pages; Brady Books, 1987), a $19.95 value, and an initial credit toward one hour of online time (worth $7.20).

For more information, call Delphi Member Services at (800) 544-4005, or at (617) 491-3393 from within Massachusetts or from outside the U.S.

Delphi is a service of General Videotex Corporation of Cambridge, Massachusetts.

BIX

By special arrangement with BIX, readers of this book can sign up for a one-year subscription at a rate of $25 per quarter instead of the standard $39 per quarter. You will be billed quarterly and can cancel at any time. BIX guarantees that everyone who takes advantage of this offer will receive at least four quarters (one year) at $25 each. That represents a savings of $56 over the standard one-year subscription ($100 instead of the standard $156).

You can subscribe immediately by calling your local Tymnet node. [Phone Tymnet's Customer Service at (800) 336–0149 for your nearest node number.] When your local node answers, key in an A. You will then see the "please log in:" prompt. Key in BIX, and when BIX prompts you for "Name?" key in this code word:

UG.BKGLOSS

Then simply follow the instructions that will appear. Be sure to have your Visa, American Express, or MasterCard card ready. (BIX subscriptions are also available via company purchase order. Call customer service at (800) 227–2993 for details.) Since you will be asked to select the name you wish to use on the system at that time, it might be a good idea to think about it beforehand since all user names are permanent.

People/Link

There is an initial one-time charge of $24.95 This normally does not include any free connect time. But by special arrangement with American People/Link, readers of this book will receive $25 worth of evening, nonprime connect time. That's approximately five free hours. To subscribe by modem, call (800) 826–8855. When you are connected you will see a menu asking where you heard about People/Link. Respond by either keying in GLO or by entering the menu item related to this book. Have your Visa or MasterCard number ready in both cases. Regardless of how you subscribe, People/Link will send your user ID to you by paper mail. When you receive it, you can begin using your subscription.

NewsNet

NewsNet will give you your choice of three discount packages:

Package 1—A one-year subscription for $120. This is a savings of $60 over the monthly rate, and it includes $60 of free time, for a total savings of $120.

Package 2—A six-month subscription for $75. This is a savings of $15 over the monthly rate, and it includes $60 of free time, for a total savings of $75.

Package 3—A new subscriber bonus of $30 in free time for a month-by-
month subscription.

All free connect time must be used within the first 30 days of sign-up.
Costs incurred beyond the terms of this offer will be billed at the regular prevailing rate.

Please clip this coupon along the dotted line. Circle the number of the
package of interest, fill in the blanks, and mail to NewsNet at the address given below. Only original coupons will be honored. No facsimiles
or copies accepted.

To receive your ID and password without delay, call (800) 345–1301.
In Pennsylvania, (800) 537–0808. Outside the United States, (215)
527–8030. You can then begin using NewsNet immediately and still receive your chosen discount.

Please send me your SUBSCRIPTION INFORMATION PACKAGE
containing introductory offers for free online time. I am interested in
(please check one: Package 1—One-year/$120 savings; Package 2—Six-
month/$75 savings; Package 3—New month-by-month subscriber/$30 in
free time.

Name: _____ Title: _____

Company: _____ Business Phone: _____

Address: _____

City: _____ State: _____ Zip: _____

        NewsNet, Inc.
        945 Haverford Road
        Bryn Mawr, PA 19010

Dow Jones News/Retrieval

As a purchaser of this book, you are entitled to a free password and one hour of connect time when you become a member of Dow Jones News/Retrieval. The free connect time must be used within 30 days of receipt of your password, and the normal $18 annual service fee still applies. This offer includes your comprehensive *User's Guide*, a subscription to *Downline Magazine*, and special promotions made available periodically throughout the year.

To get your free password, call Doris Runyon at (609) 520-4649 or mail in this coupon.

Yes! I want to be a Dow Jones News/Retrieval subscriber. I would like to be billed for subsequent usage:

_____ Directly from News/Retrieval   _____ American Express Card

Card No. _____   Exp. Date _____

Signature (required): _____

Name: _____   Title: _____

Company: _____

Address: _____

City: _____ State: _____ Zip: _____

Daytime Phone Number: _____

Computer Make & Model: _____

Mail to: Dow Jones News/Retrieval
Dept. DR
P.O. Box 300
Princeton, NJ 08543-0300   CHP

MCI Mail

Here's a special offer direct from MCI Mail® worth $25.

Send in the coupon on the following page and we'll automatically register you for MCI Mail's Preferred Pricing Option (sm)—plus we'll waive the $25 registration fee.

What's the Preferred Pricing Option?

As a Preferred Pricing Option subscriber, you can send up to 40 electronic messages or domestic faxes for just $10 per month.* That's as little as 25¢ apiece, the same price as mailing a letter.

Send in the coupon today and begin using your PC to send faxes, E-mail, telexes, even postal and courier-delivered letters. Call (800) 444–6245 for full pricing information. In Washington, D.C., call (202) 833–8484.

*This offer is valid on new MCI Mail registrations only. Preferred Pricing may include electronic messages up to 7500 characters or domestic Fax Dispatch (sm) messages up to one page. (You can send longer transmissions, with each additional increment of 7,500 characters/1 page, or any portion thereof, counting as an additional message.) After the first 40 messages each month, messages are billed at regular rates. Note: Limit of one MCI Mail Preferred Pricing Option per customer/company. Preferred Pricing begins with the calendar month following sign-up.

MCI Mail Coupon

Yes! Sign me up for MCI Mail's Preferred Pricing Option today and waive the $25 registration fee.

Full name: _____ Title: _____

Company name: _____

Street Address: _____

City: _____ State: _____ Zip: _____

Daytime phone: _____ Mother's maiden name: _____

Equipment type: _____

Type of MCI Mail account: _____ Business _____ Personal

Credit card: _____ American Express _____ Mastercard _____ Visa

Credit card account number: _____

Exp. Date: _____

Signature (required): _____

Return completed form to:

MCI Mail
PC Communications Handbook
1718 M Street, NW, Suite 299
Washington, D.C. 20036

Only original coupons honored. No facsimile or other copies accepted. Offer expires November 30, 1990.

Glossbrenner's Choice
Free Software

ORDER FORM
Glossbrenner's Choice Disks

Name: _____

Address: _____

_____

City: _____ State: _____ ZIP: _____

Phone (in case we need to call regarding your order): (____) _____

[Please PRINT clearly.]

Number of disks   Totals

_____ 5.25-inch floppies × $5 = _____

_____ 3.5-inch diskettes × $6 = _____

Shipping and handling: $2.00

TOTAL Enclosed: _____

INSTRUCTIONS:

1. Either photocopy the order form or use a separate sheet of paper and include the same information.
2. Clearly *print* your address information above.
3. Check off the disks you want on the list below, or use quick names like CORE 1, COMM 7, TYPING 1, etc. on a separate paper.
4. Total the checkmarks and multiply by $5 for 5.25-inch floppies, or by $6 for 3.5-inch diskettes. Add $2 per order for shipping and handling.
5. Make check payable to FireCrystal Communications and mail to:

> Glossbrenner's Choice
> FireCrystal Communications
> 699 River Road
> Yardley, PA 19067

NOTE: Price includes taxes, postage, shipping, and handling only. If you like and regularly use a shareware program, please be sure to send its author the requested registration fee. Prices are subject to change without notice.

All orders must be *pre-paid* with U.S. funds drawn on a U.S. bank. U.S. dollar-denominated Canadian Postal Money Orders and U.S. dollar-denominated checks drawn on a bank with a U.S.-based clearing branch are fine.

These programs are for IBM, MS-DOS, and compatible users only. For more information on these disks and the programs they contain, please see *Alfred Glossbrenner's Master Guide to Free Software for IBMs and Compatible Computers* (St. Martin's Press, New York).

FANSI Console

—— Core Collection Disk 1 (CORE 1)—FANSI Program/CED/LIST
—— Core Collection Disk 2 (CORE 2)—FANSI Documentation/PC-DeskTeam/PC-Window

FANSI Console is the program that offers one-button scroll recall to page or scroll back through text that has disappeared from the screen. Once you try it, you won't want to go online without it. LIST is Vern Buerg's famous file display program. Use it not only to scroll through text files, but to remove garbage characters, clip out text and write it to a separate file, or instantly find any word in a file.

Word Processing, Typing, and Encryption

—— PC-Write Disk 1 (PCW 1)—Program Disk (1 of 3)
—— PC-Write Disk 2 (PCW 2)—Utilities Desk (2 of 3)
—— PC-Write Disk 3 (PCW 3)—Reference Disk (3 of 3)
—— Typing Disk 1 (TYPING 1)—PC-FASTYPE
—— Encryption Disk 1 (ENCRYPTION 1)—PC-CODE3/4 and The Confidant

These are programs you will use to prepare electronic mail before you go online and edit material you download after you sign off. PC-WRITE is a full-powered word processor without parallel. PC-FASTYPE is the best typing tutorial program going. And the two programs on EN-CRYPTION 1 will so scramble your transmissions that no one but the intended recipient will be able to decode them.

Communications

—— CommPack 1 (COMM 1)—ProComm 2.4.3
—— CommPack 2 (COMM 2)—ProComm Utilities
—— CommPack 3 (COMM 3)—The Communicator's Toolchest
—— CommPack 4 (COMM 4)— ProComm PLUS Test Drive

ProComm is consistently rated among the top communications programs in the IBM-compatible world. COMM 1 is all you need, though you may find COMM 2 helpful as it contains various utilities distributed by ProComm's authors.

COMM 3 contains what we feel are the most important utility programs for an online communicator. Both PKARC and PKZIP file compression/extraction packages are included, for example, as is OZBEXT, a program that allows virtually any communications program to support the CompuServe Quick-B protocol. There is also a program for those rare situations when you need a "hex converter."

COMM 4 is ProComm PLUS, a commercial communications program distributed by its authors in fully functional "test drive" form. This simply means "without an on-disk manual." Manuals are supplied when you purchase the product. "PLUS" is a fine program, but we still like Pro-Comm 2.4.3 better.

Specialized Communications Programs

—— CommPack 5 (COMM 5) — GEnie Utilities/PC-VCO/ZOO.EXE
—— CommPack 6 (COMM 6) — The CompuServe AutoSIG (ATO) Program

—— CommPack 7 (COMM 7) — TAPCIS — Automated CompuServe Access
—— CommPack 8 (COMM 8) — ALADDIN —Automated GEnie Access
—— CommPack 9 (COMM 9) — GIF and RLE Graphics Decoders and Display Programs
—— Hercules/CGA Emulators (HERC/CGA)

For more information on these programs, please see Chapter 5 (CompuServe) and Chapter 6 (GEnie). Bob Berry's CompuShow graphics display program on COMM 9 is particularly remarkable. You will need a CGA, EGA, MCGA, VGA, or Hercules monochrome graphics adaptor to display GIF and RLE graphics files. The disk HERC/CGA contains the best emulator programs, though they may not be necessary for your equipment.

Bulletin Board System

—— Minihost (MINI)—Minihost Personal BBS Package
—— RBBS-1—RBBS-PC Program Disk
—— RBBS-2—RBBS-PC Documentation
—— RBBS-3—Required text files, external protocol drivers, and miscellaneous utilities
—— RBBS-4—BASIC Source Code
—— RBBS-5—Assembler Subroutines
—— Wildcat Disk 1 (WILD 1)—Wildcat BBS Package (1 of 2)
—— Wildcat Disk 2 (WILD 2)—Wildcat BBS Package (2 of 2)

Chapter 29 discussed how to *access* bulletin board systems. The programs on these disks are for those wishing to *operate* a BBS. For new users we recommend Don Mankin's Minihost. Simple to set up and use, Minihost is designed for consultants, small-business people, attorneys, and others who need remote access to their own systems. It is ideal for small offices and work groups and for anyone wishing to tap an office or home computer from a distant location. RBBS-PC and Wildcat are full-blown BBS packages for anyone aspiring to become a sysop with a board open to the public.

Index

...ABOUT THE AUTHOR...

Alfred Glossbrenner has been called "the Isaac Asimov of personal computing," a sobriquet that, while flattering, probably shouldn't be taken too seriously considering the disparity in the two writers' output: fourteen books of Glossbrenner's to the Good Doctor's hundreds (and still counting). Nevertheless, it is Mr. Glossbrenner's intent to build a foundation for the understanding of all things computer and to, in some small way, help bridge the gap between "the two cultures" of science and the humanities first identified by C. P. Snow in 1959.

Few images are more repellent than an eternity of human subservience to inhuman machines. Yet few scenarios are so easy to avoid, for nothing about computer hardware, online databases, telecommunications, or software (free or otherwise) is difficult to understand—once it has been explained properly. From there it is but a short step to making the machines work for *you* as you begin to sample the incredible power they place in your hands.

Mr. Glossbrenner preaches the gospel of computer power through computer understanding from a variety of pulpits, including articles and columns in leading computer magazines, lectures, books, and consulting projects for associations, Fortune-500 firms, and small businesses. Mr. Glossbrenner lives with his wife (and his computers) in a 1790s farmhouse on the Delaware River in Bucks County, Pennsylvania.

Your suggestions and ideas are always welcome, particularly in regard to topics you would like to see covered or covered in greater detail, possibly in a newsletter or in future editions of this book. Although it is impossible to guarantee a reply, as always, we will make every attempt to respond to all letters. The author can be reached electronically at

70065,745 on CompuServe or AGLOSSBRENNER on MCI Mail. Land mail should be sent to:

Alfred Glossbrenner
FireCrystal Communications
699 River Road
Yardley, PA 19067

Other bestsellers from Alfred Glossbrenner . . .

ALFRED GLOSSBRENNER'S MASTER
GUIDE TO FREE SOFTWARE FOR IBMS
AND COMPATIBLE COMPUTERS
544 pages, Appendices, Index
$18.95 Paperback
• A Selection of the Macmillan Small Computer
  Book Club
• A Selection of the Library of Computer and
  Information Sciences

"Exhaustive and detailed . . . . Anybody with an appropriate machine
and a desire to save money can profit from [it]."
                              —L. R. Shannon in *The New York
                              Times*

"So clear and witty that even a computer novice can understand and
enjoy the book."
                              —*Trenton Times*

"Your door to the world of pubic-domain software and shareware."
                              —*Home Office Computing*

HOW TO LOOK IT UP ONLINE
496 pages, Appendices, Index.
$14.95 Paperback
• A Selection of the Macmillan Small Computer
  Book Club
• A Selection of the Library of Computer and
  Information Sciences

"A valuable handbook for professional information seekers or amateurs
desiring to increase their knowledge of the vast online world."
                    —*Booklist*

"Bravo!"

                    —*ScholarNotes*

"Alfred Glossbrenner has done it again."
                    —*Online Today*

"As Karl Malden might say: 'Don't go online without it.'"
                    —*Louisville Courier-Journa*"

"Readers familiar with Glossbrenner's erudite style will welcome his
newest addition . . . The wealth of material is insightful . . . Great
reading from cover to cover."
                    —*Computer Book Review*

To order these books, please use the coupon below.

ST. MARTIN'S PRESS, INC.   CASH SALES DEPARTMENT
175 FIFTH AVE., NEW YORK NY 10010

Please send me: _____ copy(ies) of ALFRED GLOSSBRENNER'S
                        MASTER GUIDE TO FREE SOFTWARE
                        FOR IBMS AND COMPATIBLE COMPUT-
                        ERS @ $18.95 each*
               _____ copy(ies) of HOW TO LOOK IT UP ONLINE
                        by Alfred Glossbrenner @ $14.95 each*
               _____ copy(ies) of THE COMPLETE HANDBOOK
                        OF PERSONAL COMPUTER COMMUNI-
                        CATIONS (All-New Third Edition) @ $18.95
                        each*
*Plus $1.50 postage and handling for the first book and 50¢ per copy for
each additional book. I enclose a check or money order for $_____.

_____   Return Coupon with check to:
Name (please print)   St. Martin's Press
                                       Cash Sales Department
                                       175 Fifth Avenue
_____   New York NY 10010
Address

_____
City   State   Zip